AGENDA FOR A
SUSTAINABLE AMERICA

Copyright © 2009
Environmental Law Institute
2000 L Street NW, Washington, DC 20036

Published January 2009.

Printed in the United States of America
ISBN 978-1-58576-133-3

For Tess, Becky, and all who will inherit this world

Table of Contents

I. Introduction

II. Six Areas of Greater Progress

III. Consumption, Population, and Poverty

IV. Conservation and Management of Natural Resources

PREFACE

More than 15 years have passed since the United Nations Conference on Environment and Development, or Earth Summit, took place in Rio de Janeiro in 1992. Over 110 heads of state participated, a greater number than had attended any prior international conference. For the first time, the nations of the world endorsed sustainable development. These nations also adopted a plan of action, called Agenda 21, to achieve it, and a set of principles (the Rio Declaration) to guide the effort.

In simple and direct terms, the world's leaders described the challenge we face: "Humanity stands at a defining moment in history. We are confronted with a perpetuation of disparities between and within nations, a worsening of poverty, hunger, ill health and illiteracy, and the continuing deterioration of the ecosystems on which we depend for our well-being." They then described the opportunity that sustainable development provides, asserting that it "will lead to the fulfillment of basic needs, improved living standards for all, better protected and managed ecosystems and a safer, more prosperous future."

Each nation made a commitment at the Earth Summit: to work to achieve sustainable development within its own borders and as part of its international activities. One of those countries, under the leadership of President George H.W. Bush, was the United States.

This book is the third review in an ongoing project to evaluate U.S. efforts for sustainable development and make recommendations for future actions. The reviews have occurred on or after the fifth, tenth, and fifteenth anniversaries of the Earth Summit. These anniversaries are worth marking because the Earth Summit was not just another international meeting; it put sustainability—one of the 20th century's most important ideas—on the world's stage.

The first review, conducted with the help of my students in a seminar at Widener University School of Law, was published as an article by the *Environmental Law Reporter*.[1] Much to my surprise, given the intense attention that the Earth Summit had received, it was the only assessment by anyone outside of government on the U.S. performance during those five years.

The second review, *Stumbling Toward Sustainability*, was published by the Environmental Law Institute just before the World Summit on Sustainable Development in Johannesburg in 2002.[2] It contains chapters written by more than three dozen experts. Each chapter focused on a particular topic, evaluated U.S. progress in the decade following the Earth Summit, and made recommendations for the next five to ten years.

Agenda for a Sustainable America follows the 15-year anniversary of the Earth Summit. It has the same essential structure as *Stumbling Toward Sustainability*, but it focuses on the period since 2002. Like the previous book, it also makes recommendations for the next five to ten years. The contributors to this volume have considerable knowledge and experience as well as a range of perspectives. They are from universities, nongovernmental organizations, and the private sector. They also represent a range of disciplines. Their willingness to contribute to this volume indicates the importance of the subject.

This book has both critical and constructive components. It is intended to provide a critical appraisal of U.S. activities, indentifying both progress and shortcomings. It is also intended to be constructive, primarily by making recommendations. The broader aim of the book is to help build an analytical and policy foundation for sustainable development in the United States, not only for specific issues and problems but also as a conceptual framework for achieving prosperity and human well-being.

Agenda for a Sustainable America was written before the current economic downturn, yet the severe financial problems the world faces make this book's recommendations more urgent than ever. When we make decisions for sustainability, we make decisions that improve our economic situation, create jobs, improve our infrastructure, enhance environmental quality, and increase our security. In other words, decisions for sustainability give us more value for the investments we make than if we are seeking only economic growth. That makes sense in any situation, but is of particular importance during difficult economic times.

Agenda was also written before the recent presidential election. New administrations provide an opportunity to revisit premises and start afresh. Much of this book could be useful in that effort because many chapters focus on the role of the executive branch in achieving sustainability. Of course, the book is not just about the federal government or about governance at any level. It is also for all of us in our various roles—as citizens, family members, employees, volunteers, teachers, and students, and as members and leaders of many organizations.

A great many people have inspired and supported this project over the years. The Environmental Law Institute continues to be the publisher; its support has made this effort possible. For this volume, Don Brown, Marian Chertow, Scott Schang, and Marianne Tyrrell have been particularly helpful. Peter Whitten proved to be an exceptionally able and wise editor. Paula Heider, Kim Peterson, and Jessica Snyder afforded secretarial and administrative support. Diane Goltz and Ed Sonnenberg helped locate difficult sources. Allison Miles provided useful research assistance. Becky Dernbach proved to be an exceptionally good proofreader. As always, my wife, Kathy Yorkievitz, has been a constant source of support and useful advice. Finally, the contributing authors to this book are its greatest strength, and they have my deepest gratitude.

ENDNOTES

1. John Dernbach & the Widener University Law School Seminar on Law and Sustainability, *U.S. Adherence to Its Agenda 21 Commitments: A Five-Year Review*, 27 ENVTL. L. REP. (Envtl. L. Inst.) 10504 (Oct. 1997).
2. STUMBLING TOWARD SUSTAINABILITY (John C. Dernbach ed. 2002).

EDITOR AND CONTRIBUTING AUTHOR

John C. Dernbach

John C. Dernbach is a Distinguished Professor of Law at Widener University in Harrisburg, Pennsylvania. He has written widely on sustainable development, climate change, and environmental law. He edited *Stumbling Toward Sustainability* (Environmental Law Institute 2002), which assessed U.S. sustainable development efforts in the first decade after the Earth Summit and made recommendations for the next 5 to 10 years. Before taking his teaching position at Widener, he worked in a variety of positions at the Pennsylvania Department of Environmental Protection. He is a council member for the ABA Section on Environment, Energy, and Resources, and former chair of the ABA Committee on Climate Change, Sustainable Development, and Ecosystems.

CONTRIBUTING AUTHORS

Nathaniel Aden is a senior research associate with the China Energy Group of the Lawrence Berkeley National Laboratory, where he specializes in energy policy analysis, industrial energy efficiency, and energy-related carbon emissions mitigation. He has published articles on the environmental implications of energy policy in China, including the unexpected growth of energy-related carbon emissions since 2002.

Robert Adler is the associate dean for academic affairs and James I. Farr Chair in Law at the University of Utah, S.J. Quinney College of Law. Prior to entering academia, he practiced environmental law for 15 years. His most recent books are *Restoring Colorado River Ecosystems: A Troubled Sense of Immensity* (Island Press 2007) and *Environmental Law: A Conceptual and Pragmatic Approach* (Aspen 2007, with David Driesen).

Sabina Ahmed is a program coordinator at the World Resources Institute.

Gary D. Bass is the founder and executive director of OMB Watch, which addresses government accountability and citizen participation. Dr. Bass is also an affiliated professor at Georgetown University's Public Policy Institute, where he teaches about advocacy and social change. He serves on numerous nonprofit boards and advisory committees, and has received numerous awards, including being listed as part of the *NonProfit Times* Power and Influence Top 50 for the past 10 years, being inducted in 2006 into the National Freedom of Information Hall of Fame, and being selected as one of the 2007 Federal 100, which goes to those who had the greatest impact on the government information systems community. In 1989, Dr. Bass started RTK NET (www.rtknet.org), a searchable website providing information about toxic chemicals released into our communities.

Donald A. Brown is an associate professor in the Environmental Ethics, Science, and Law Program in the Program on Science, Technology, and Society at The Pennsylvania State University. Before holding this position, Mr. Brown held a number of senior positions in law and policy for the Pennsylvania and New Jersey environmental protection programs and the U.S. Environmental Protection Agency. Mr. Brown is also director of the Pennsylvania Environmental Research Consortium, an organization comprised of 56 Pennsylvania universities and the Pennsylvania Departments of Environmental Protection and Conservation and Natural Resources that works on environmental and sustainable development issues. During the Clinton Administration, Mr. Brown was Program Manager for United Nations Organizations at EPA's Office of International Environmental Policy. In this position, he represented the EPA in U.S. delegations to the United Nations negotiating climate change, biodiversity, and sustainable development issues. Mr. Brown's latest book is *American Heat: Ethical Problems With the United States' Response to Global Warming*.

Carl Bruch is a senior attorney at the Environmental Law Institute, where he also codirects ELI's international programs. He has written extensively on public participation, compliance and enforcement, and environmental governance.

Wynn Calder is director of the Association of University Leaders for a Sustainable Future (ULSF) and principal of Sustainable Schools, LLC. ULSF conducts research on sustainability in higher education and serves as secretariat for signatories of the Talloires Declaration (1990). Sustainable Schools consults with colleges, universities, and K-12 schools to build environmental sustainability into strategic planning, teaching, and institutional practice. Mr. Calder has spoken widely on sustainable operations and sustainability in the curriculum, consults on strategies to green campuses, and conducts campus sustainability assessments. He is review editor for the *Journal of Education for Sustainable Development*, news editor for the *International Journal of Sustainability in Higher Education*, and he has written extensively on the topic of education for sustainability. He is a cofounder of the U.S. Partnership for Education for Sustainable Development. Mr. Calder serves on the senior council of the Association for the Advancement of Sustainability in Higher Education and on the advisory council of the Cloud Institute for Sustainability Education.

Federico Cheever is director of the Environmental and Natural Resources Law Program and professor of law at the University of Denver Sturm College of Law. Professor Cheever is also chair of the Sustainability Council for the University of Denver. He began teaching at the University of Denver College of Law in 1993, specializing in environmental law, wildlife law, public land law, land conservation transactions, and property. Professor Cheever writes extensively about the Endangered Species Act, federal public land law, and land conservation transactions. He coauthored a natural resources casebook, *Natural Resources Law: A Place-Based Book of Problems and Cases*, with Christine Klein and Bret Birdsong (2005). Over the years, Professor Cheever has represented environmental groups in cases under the Endangered Species Act, the National Forest Management Act, the National Environmental Policy Act, the Wilderness Act, and a number of other environmental laws.

Marian R. Chertow is the director of the Industrial Environmental Management Program at the Yale School of Forestry and Environmental Studies. Her publications include a book on environmental policy and numerous articles on the subject. Professor Chertow's teaching and research focus on waste management, industrial ecology, environmental technology innovation, and business/environment issues. She also serves as director of Environmental Reform: the Next Generation Project at the Yale Center for Environmental Law and Policy, leading a three-year effort to shape the future of environmental policy. Prior to Yale, she spent 10 years in environmental business and in state and local government.

Jaimie P. Cloud is the founder and president of the Cloud Institute for Sustainability Education in New York City. The Cloud Institute is dedicated to the vital role of education in creating awareness, fostering commitment, and guiding actions toward a healthy, secure, and sustainable future. Ms. Cloud has written several book chapters and articles, teaches extensively, and writes and facilitates the development of numerous instructional units and programs that are designed to teach core courses across the disciplines through the lens of sustainability. She is a member of the Advisory Committee of The Buckminster Fuller Institute, the International Advisory Committee for the Tbilisi+30 Conference, the cochair of the Commission on Education for Sustainability of the North American Association for Environmental Education, and a member of the advisory committee of Greenopolis and the Sustainability Education Planning Committee for the National Association of Independent Schools.

Robin Kundis Craig is the Attorneys' Title Insurance Fund Professor of Law at the Florida State University College of Law. She is nationally recognized for her work on the Clean Water Act, the connection of fresh water regulation to ocean water quality, marine biodiversity and marine protected areas, property rights in fresh water, and science and water resource protection. As a result of her research on the Clean Water Act, including her book *The Clean Water Act and the Constitution* (Environmental Law Institute 2004; 2d ed. 2008), in 2005, the National Research Council of the National Academy of Sciences appointed her to a two-year committee to assess the effects of the Act's regulation of the Mississippi River, then appointed her in 2008 to a follow-up committee to assess the potential for a basinwide nutrient TMDL to improve the hypoxic zone in the Gulf of Mexico.

Julian Dautremont-Smith is the associate director of the Association for the Advancement of Sustainability in Higher Education (AASHE), where he coordinates AASHE work to advance the American College and University Presidents Climate Commitment and development of the Sustainability Tracking, Assessment, and Rating System (STARS) for colleges and universities. While an undergraduate at Lewis & Clark College, he spearheaded a successful and nationally recognized effort to bring the college into compliance with the emissions targets of the Kyoto Protocol on climate change. In the year between graduating from Lewis & Clark and joining AASHE staff, he cofounded a business to produce biodiesel while studying sustainable development in Barbados on a J. William Fulbright scholarship.

David Driesen is University Professor at Syracuse University, one of 13 people to hold this title in the university's history. He specializes in international and domestic environmental law. Professor Driesen's writing includes two books, *Environmental Law: A Conceptual and Pragmatic Approach* (Aspen 2007, with Robert Adler) and *The Economic Dynamics of Environmental Law* (MIT Press 2003), and numerous articles in journals, most of which address the law and economics of environmental law. Before entering academe, he served as an attorney in the Natural Resources Defense Council's air and energy program.

Anne Ehrlich is the policy coordinator for the Center for Conservation Biology at Stanford University. She has carried out research and coauthored many technical articles in population biology and has written extensively on population control, environmental protection, and the environmental consequences of nuclear war. Ms. Ehrlich served as one of seven outside consultants to the White House Council on Environmental Quality's *Global 2000 Report*, and has served on the boards of directors of The Sierra Club, Friends of the Earth, The Ploughshares Fund, and the Pacific Institute for Studies in Development, Environment, and Security, among others. She is a member of the American Academy of Arts and Sciences and has been awarded several prizes for environmental achievement. Her most recent book is *The Dominant Animal; Human Evolution and the Environment* (2008), coauthored with Paul Ehrlich.

Joel B. Eisen is a professor at the University of Richmond School of Law, where he teaches environmental law, energy law, and property. He also teaches a course on environmental law and policy to undergraduate students in the University of Richmond's Environmental Studies Program. Professor Eisen has published extensively in law periodicals and general periodicals. He is a coauthor of *Energy, Economics and the Environment*, the 2006 edition of which has been adopted in over 40 energy law and policy courses. In spring 2009, Professor Eisen will be a Fulbright professor of law at the China University of Political Science and Law in Beijing.

Kirsten Engel is a professor of law at the James E. Rogers College of Law at the University of Arizona, having joined the faculty in 2005 with a broad background in environmental law and policy that spans academia and public-sector practice. Professor Engel is widely published on environmental federalism and state and local responses to global climate change. She recently served as a member of Arizona Governor Janet Napolitano's Climate Change Advisory Group, and has held visiting professorships at Harvard Law School and Vanderbilt School of Law. Between leaving her faculty post at Tulane

Law School and joining the law faculty of the University of Arizona, Ms. Engel served as senior counsel for the Public Protection Bureau and acting chief of the Environmental Protection Division of the Massachusetts Office of the Attorney General. Prior to entering teaching, Ms. Engel worked as a staff attorney for the Sierra Club Legal Defense Fund and at the U.S. Environmental Protection Agency.

Carmela Federico is a sustainability education consultant who has worked at The Cloud Institute for Sustainability Education, the Children's Environmental Literacy Foundation, and the New Jersey Higher Education Partnership for Sustainability.

Ira Robert Feldman is president and senior counsel of Greentrack Strategies, a multidisciplinary practice focusing on strategic environmental management, regulatory innovation, and sustainability policy. He originated the greentrack (or dual track/alternate path) approach to environmental regulation and management; championed the implementation of a new generation of environmental management tools; created voluntary environmental excellence initiatives; and advanced the state of the art in environmental auditing and disclosure. He has been a leading proponent for the use of voluntary standards as an adjunct to mandatory regulation. His current research and writing focus on environmental performance metrics, environmental management systems, stakeholder engagement, ecosystem services, and climate change adaptation. He teaches at the University of Pennsylvania's Masters of Environmental Studies Program. He is also an adjunct professor at American University's Washington College of Law.

Jonathan Barry Forman is the Alfred P. Murrah Professor of Law at the University of Oklahoma. Professor Forman is also vice chair of the board of trustees of the Oklahoma Public Employees Retirement System (OPERS), and is active in the American Bar Association, the Association of American Law Professors, and the National Academy of Social Insurance. Professor Forman has also lectured around the world, testified before Congress, and served on numerous federal and state advisory committees. He has more than 250 publications including *Making America Work* (Urban Institute Press 2006). In addition to his many scholarly publications, Professor Forman has published articles and op-eds in numerous newspapers and magazines. Prior to entering academia, he served in all three branches of the federal government, most recently as tax counsel to the late Senator Daniel Patrick Moynihan of New York.

Roy Gardner is a professor of law and the director of the Institute for Biodiversity Law and Policy at Stetson University College of Law. He teaches and does research on environmental and international law and has published extensively on these topics. Prior to teaching at Stetson, he worked for the Department of Defense, where he participated in negotiating international agreements with Russia, Ukraine, Kazakhstan, and Belarus to facilitate the dismantling of the former Soviet Union's nuclear weapons. He has received Stetson University's Homer and Dolly Hand Award for Excellence in Faculty Scholarship and a National Wetlands Award for education and outreach.

Lynn Goldman is a pediatrician and professor of environmental health sciences at John Hopkins Bloomberg School of Public Health, where she specializes in environmental risks to children. Prior to joining Hopkins, she was the chief of the Division of Environmental and Occupational Disease Control at the California Department of Health Services, and the assistant administrator of the Office of Prevention, Pesticides, and Toxic Substances at the U.S. Environmental Protection Agency. She is a member of the Environmental Defense Fund's board of trustees.

Tom Graedel is a professor of industrial ecology, professor of chemical engineering, professor of geology and geophysics, and director of the Center for Industrial Ecology at Yale School of Forestry and Environmental Studies. The author of four textbooks on industrial ecology, he centers his research on developing and enhancing industrial ecology, the organizing framework for the study of the interactions of the modern technological society with the environment. Professor Graedel's current interests include studies of the flows of materials within the industrial ecosystem and the development of analytical tools to assess the environmental characteristics of products, processes, the service industry, and urban infrastructures. He is a member of the U.S. National Academy of Engineering.

Dieter T. Hessel is a Presbyterian minister specializing in social ethics who resides in Cape Elizabeth, Maine, where he directs the ecumenical Program on Ecology, Justice, and Faith, and is an adjunct professor at Bangor Theological Seminary. From 1965 to 1990, he was the social education coordinator and social policy director of the Presbyterian Church (USA). His recent books include *Earth Habitat: Eco-Injustice and the Church's Response* (Fortress, 2001); *Christianity and Ecology: Seeking the Well-Being of Earth and Humans* (Harvard, 2000); *Theology for Earth Community: A Field Guide* (Orbis, 1996).

Frances Irwin is a policy analyst and writer on issues ranging from public access to information and participation, environmental governance, and environmental policy reform to chemicals and materials policy and people and ecosystems. She has worked with state, national, and international civil society groups including the Vermont Natural Resources Council, The Conservation Foundation, and the World Wildlife Fund. As a fellow at the World Resources Institute, she most recently coauthored an action agenda and a guide for decisionmakers and coedited a volume of papers on governance of ecosystem services.

Amit Kapur is a consultant with PE Americas, where he specializes in the emerging field of industrial ecology. His work focuses on life-cycle assessment, material flow analysis, and dynamic modeling of stocks and flows. Prior to joining PE Americas, Dr. Kapur was a research fellow at the Center for Sustainable Systems, University of Michigan. His postdoctoral research focused on sustainable concrete infrastructure materials and systems. He developed a dynamic stock and flow model to analyze the contemporary and historical flows of cement in the United States. Using different lifetime distributions, the model estimated the overall in-use stock of cement in infrastructure in the United States.

Kevin Kennedy is a professor of law at Michigan State University College of Law. Before joining the Michigan State faculty, he practiced law in Hawaii for four years, and then served as a law clerk at the U.S. Court of International Trade in New York. After his clerkship he was a trial attorney for the U.S. Department of Justice, where he represented the Department of Commerce and U.S. Customs in international trade litigation. In addition to nearly 60 law review articles and book chapters on international law and international trade regulation, Professor Kennedy is the author of a monograph, *Competition Law and the World Trade Organization*, and the coauthor of a treatise, *World Trade Law*.

Mark D. Levine leads the China Energy Group at Lawrence Berkeley National Laboratory (LBNL), a group he created in 1988. From 1996 to 2006, Dr. Levine was director of the Environmental Division at a division of 400 people working on energy efficiency policy analysis and R&D. Dr. Levine is a board member of five leading nonprofits in the United States and is a member of the Energy Advisory Board of Dow Chemical Company, the board of directors of CalCEF, an energy VC firm, and the advisory board of the Asian Pacific Energy Research Centre in Tokyo. In 1999, he was elected a fellow of the California Council on Science and Technology. In 2008, he was selected as the recipient of the Obayashi Prize for his contributions to sustainable urban development. In addition to authoring numerous technical publications, he has led or co-led teams for the Intergovernmental Panel on Climate Change and major energy scenario studies of the United States, China, and the world.

Ezequiel Lugo is a staff attorney to the Hon. Douglas A. Wallace at the Florida Second District Court of Appeal. He has published articles on insect conservation, international law, and ecosystem services.

Marc Miller is a professor of law at the University of Arizona James E. Rogers College of Law. He writes and teaches on biodiversity and sustainability, and on criminal justice. His current work explores the internal administration of executive branch agencies. He is the coeditor of The Edge, a new series of books on environmental science, law, and policy. The Edge is a joint project of the University of Arizona Institute for the Study of Planet Earth, the Rogers College of Law, the Biosphere 2 Institute, and the University of Arizona Press.

Joel A. Mintz is a professor of law at Nova Southeastern University Law Center and a member scholar of The Center for Progressive Reform. His scholarly interests include environmental enforcement, hazardous waste regulation, and state and local government finance. Professor Mintz is the author or coauthor of six books and numerous articles, book chapters, book reviews, essays, and op-ed pieces. Before entering legal education, he was an attorney and chief attorney with the U.S. Environmental Protection Agency. He is a recipient of his university's President's Faculty Scholarship Award, and EPA's Special Service Award and the EPA Bronze Medal for Commendable Service.

Smita Nakhooda is a senior associate in the Institutions and Governance Program of the World Resources Institute . She is a member of WRI's International Financial Flows and the Environment Project, which works to align public and private investment with environmentally sustainable development and poverty reduction. Her work has focused on the role of the Multilateral Development Banks in global efforts to address climate change. She also leads the Electricity Governance Initiative, an effort to bring civil society, policymakers, regulators, and sector actors together to assess policy and regulation of the electricity sector using a common framework to define good governance.

Trip Pollard is a senior attorney with the Southern Environmental Law Center (SELC). He is the director of SELC's Land and Community Program, which uses public education, policy reform, and legal advocacy to promote smarter growth and sustainable transportation. Mr. Pollard is involved in shaping policies and decisions throughout the Southeast. He also has written dozens of reports and articles on transportation, land use, energy, and environmental issues. He has lectured widely, and he has served on numerous governmental commissions, advisory bodies, and the boards of many organizations.

K.W. James Rochow is President of the Trust For Lead Poisoning Prevention and an environmental law and policy consultant headquartered in Washington, D.C. He has helped orchestrate the global phaseout of leaded gasoline and initiate integrated approaches to toxics pollution and environmental health. Most recently, Rochow has worked on natural resource sector reform and failed state reconstruction in West Africa for the World Bank, UNDP, and the Government of Liberia. He has also taught international environmental law and policy at numerous universities in the United States and abroad, most recently at the University of Pennsylvania Law School.

Patricia E. Salkin is the Raymond and Ella Smith Distinguished Professor of Law, associate dean, and director of the Government Law Center at Albany Law School. She teaches courses in land use law, housing law and policy, New York's administrative law, and current legal issues in government and government ethics. She is also on the adjunct faculty at the University at Albany's Department of Geography and Planning, where she teaches courses in planning law and planning ethics. Dean Salkin is a past chair of the ABA's State & Local Government Law Section. She is the vice chair of the Municipal Law Section of the New York State Bar Association and a founding member and chair of the State Bar's Standing Committee on Attorneys in Public Service. She serves as chair of the Amicus Curiae Committee for the American Planning Association, and chaired a task force on eminent domain for the State Bar. Professor Salkin is an appointed member of EPA's National Environmental Justice Advisory Council.

Jim Salzman holds joint appointments at Duke University as the Samuel Fox Mordecai Professor of Law and as the Nicholas Institute Professor of Environmental Policy. In more than fifty articles and five books, his scholarship has addressed topics spanning trade and environment conflicts, the history of drinking water, environmental protection in the service economy, wetlands mitigation banking, and the legal and institutional issues in creating markets for ecosystem services. Elected a Fellow of the Royal Geographical Society, he has delivered lectures on environmental law and policy on every continent except Antarctica, and has been a visiting professor at Yale, Harvard, and Stanford, as well as at Macquarie (Australia), Lund (Sweden), and Tel Aviv (Israel) Universities.

Ward Scott is a recent graduate of the University of Denver College of Law. He holds a B.A. in environmental studies from Denison University.

Frances Seymour is the Director General of the Center for International Forestry Research (CIFOR), with headquarters in Bogor, Indonesia. CIFOR's purpose is to advance human well-being, environmental conservation, and equity by conducting research to inform policies and practices that affect forests in developing countries. During her first year at CIFOR, Ms. Seymour led the development of a new strategy for the organization. She is a coauthor of *Do Trees Grow on Money?*, a CIFOR report released at the UNFCCC climate conference in Bali in December 2007. Prior to joining CIFOR in August 2006, Ms. Seymour founded and directed the Institutions and Governance Program at the World Resources Institute (WRI) in Washington, D.C. At WRI, she guided the launch of The Access Initiative, a global civil society coalition promoting citizen involvement in environment-related decisions. She previously served as Director of Development Assistance Policy at World Wildlife Fund for three years. From 1987 to 1992, Ms. Seymour worked in Indonesia with the Ford Foundation, where her grant making focused on community forestry and human rights. She has served on numerous boards and advisory committees, and is a member of the Council on Foreign Relations.

Dan Tarlock is a Distinguished Professor of Law at the Chicago-Kent College of Law and honorary professor of law at the UNESCO Centre for Water Law, Policy, and Science at the University of Dundee, Scotland. He teaches land use, property, energy and natural resource law, and international environmental law. He has published a treatise about water rights and resources, coauthored four textbooks on related subjects, and recently coauthored, with Holly Doremus, *Water War in the Klamath Basin: Macho Law, Combat Biology, and Dirty Politics*. His current research focuses on the legal aspects of domestic and international aquatic biodiversity protection and drought management. Professor Tarlock is currently one of three U.S. special legal advisors to NAFTA, and is a frequent consultant to local, state, federal, and international agencies. He was the chair of a National Academy of Sciences/National Research Council committee to study water management in the western United States, and was the principal drafter of the Western Water Policy Advisory Review Commission report.

Jonathan Weiss is senior environmental counsel at the national consulting firm of ManTech SRS Technologies, where he advises clients on a broad range of emerging sustainability issues. He is also an adjunct law professor at The George Washington University, where he has taught sustainable regional growth for the past decade. He served in the Clinton Administration, first at the U.S. Environmental Protection Agency and then as an aide to Vice President Al Gore. As an adviser to the vice president on sustainable community development, he helped develop and implement policy and coordinate the efforts of more than a dozen federal agencies.

Andrew Zabel currently practices law in Seattle, Washington. His practice focuses on environmental issues for tribal, municipal, and corporate clients.

I. Introduction

CHAPTER 1

Sustainable Development and the United States

John C. Dernbach

This book is about the meaning of an essential and challenging idea for the United States: sustainability.

Sustainable development is among the most important ideas to come out of the 20th century—and it may be, in the long run, the most important. Sustainable development deserves that label because it provides a framework for humans to live and prosper in harmony with nature rather than, as we have for centuries, at nature's expense. Everything we care about—a growing economy, human well-being, and security—is compromised, undermined, or lessened by environmental degradation. Conversely, a cleaner environment contributes to a greater quality of life, a growing economy, and more security.

The United States, as we know, has the world's biggest economy (in spite of the impending recession), the world's most powerful military, impressive scientific and technological capability, a system of higher education that draws students from every continent, and considerable (if recently diminished) moral and political influence.

This book evaluates recent U.S. actions from a sustainable development perspective and, of greater importance, provides a roadmap or agenda for sustainability for the next 5 to 10 years. While most of us have at least a vague idea that the United States (along with the rest of the world) is not on a sustainable course, we do not have a particularly clear idea of what to do. This book's 41 contributing authors provide a detailed and comprehensive answer to the big question: What does sustainable development mean for the United States?

We live in times of growing danger and growing opportunity. The world's population is likely to increase by about three billion in the next half century,[1] and the world's economy is projected to increase to four to five times its present size in the same period.[2] Yet with today's population and today's economy, the overall condition of Earth's ecosystems, on which human life and well-being depend, is worsening. In addition, the 2.6 billion people (40 percent of the world's population) who now live on less than two dollars per day[3] should have an opportunity to improve their lives. The sooner we act to put the United States on a more sustainable course, the more likely we are to be able to ensure a better quality of life for those who follow us. The longer we wait, the fewer choices we will have, and the greater dangers we will face. Time is not a renewable resource.

Sustainability draws on a long (albeit too sparse) history of humans living harmoniously with the rest of creation in specific places or contexts. Some indigenous peoples have lived for millennia without damaging their surrounding environment. More recently, many modern societies have been successful in protecting parts of the environment, or reducing or eliminating particular ecological threats, for the benefit of future generationNations Conference on Environment and Development, commonly known as the Earth Summit, in 1992 in Rio de Janeiro, the nations of the world had never committed themselves to *systematically* pursuing sustainable development in all places and contexts. The audacity of the project—a set of principles known as the Rio Declaration[4] coupled with a global plan of action called Agenda 21[5]—is exemplified by the commitment made by virtually every nation to implement these principles and this action plan. These commitments have given global visibility to the idea of sustainable development.

As Agenda 21 made clear, sustainable development needs to be realized in the particular economic, natural, and other settings of each specific country.[6] And the United States will move toward sustainability, or not, only if it is more beneficial to us than conventional development. We will not do it because we agreed to do it at an international conference, or because it is the right thing to do, or because we care about the environment, although these motivations are important. We will move toward sustainability only if—and then because—it makes both us and our descendants better off.

This book starts with a simple but powerful premise: *Sustainable development would make the United States more livable, healthy, secure, and prosperous.* Policies that promote sustainability would reduce risks to our national security, improve our economic efficiency and productivity, enhance our health and communities, create jobs, improve the lives of the poorest among us, and foster greater human well-being in other countries. And it would achieve these things while protecting and restoring the environment for our generation and for generations that follow.

The Rio agreements also made clear that developed countries must lead the effort to achieve sustainability; they have the most resources, the most sophisticated technologies, the greatest know-how—and also the greatest responsibility for causing many of the environmental problems that sustainable development addresses. While all countries have a role to play, developed countries have the greatest responsibility. And among the developed countries, the dominant nation—in economic, military, educational, scientific, and technological terms—is the United States.

This country thus has a major role to play. Our nation's global energy, ecological, and economic footprint is so large that it is difficult to imagine how the world can achieve sustainability unless the United States also does. We can lead or follow, but we are too big to get out of the way. What we do within our own borders, moreover, can influence other countries, both positively and negatively. We can create models of sustainability that are so attractive that other countries will want to emulate or improve on them. Or, by appearing fearful or indifferent in spite of our wealth and power, we can dissuade less wealthy and powerful countries from doing what they also need to do.

For better and for worse, the success or failure of the United States in moving toward sustainability will influence and perhaps determine whether the rest of the world succeeds in the project of sustainable development. The ancient Greek mathematician Archimedes famously said, "If I had a lever big enough, I could move the world." The United States could be that lever for sustainable development. This book is going to press as the United States is in its sixth year of the war in Iraq, which has undermined America's standing in the eyes of many. In addition, our status as the "one great superpower" is likely to change with the growth of Chinese and Indian economic and political power and the continuing integration of Europe. Because of America's global footprint and its history of international leadership on other issues, however, the United States could—and should—take a leadership role on sustainable development.

Understanding Sustainable Development

Although there are many definitions of sustainable development, the most important is the one that has been approved by the world's nations, including the United States, at several summit meetings. This definition first requires an historical understanding of "development," the word that "sustainable" modifies.

The United States led an effort at the end of World War II to create an international system based on economic development, human rights, and peace and security, all grounded on good governance and the rule of law.[7] We worked to establish the United Nations, certain in our conviction that an effective international organization was needed to ensure peace and security. We conceived and provided most of the funding for the Marshall Plan, which played a key role in the reconstruction of Europe. We helped found the major institutions and treaties that ensure the stability of the global economy: the International Monetary Fund, the General Agreement on Tariffs and Trade, and the World Bank. We helped draft the Universal Declaration of Human Rights, adopted by the U.N. General Assembly in 1948, which provides the foundation for major human rights treaties. Taken together, these things—peace and security, economic development, and human rights—constitute development as the term is internationally understood. Development is intended to promote human opportunity, quality of life, and freedom. And development has done just that: The global economy has grown, creating greater wealth for more people; there has been no third world war; people are living longer in many nations; and people are better educated. These achievements, of course, are not simply of interest to specialists. They capture what we mean by progress.

But these international agreements and this framework did not address the environment and natural resources, and tacitly accepted the then-prevailing view that environmental degradation is not serious or can be managed. This kind of blindness to environmental problems existed because we either did not look for them or did not treat seriously what we saw. When we do look, we now see that environmental conditions around the world are deteriorating. Conventional development has come with a price, and it is a price we can no longer afford to pay.

Sustainable development adds environmental protection and restoration to the post-World War II international system's goals of economic development, peace and security, and human rights. Environmental degradation is no longer the price of progress; environmental protection and restoration is part of what progress means. But sustainable development also recognizes that the historical goals of development—the quality of human life, opportunity, and freedom—should continue to be our ultimate objectives. Sustainable development is ecologically sustainable human development. Because of several global conferences, it is now the internationally approved framework for maintaining and improving the human condition.

In 1983, the U.N. General Assembly created the World Commission on Environment and Development (known as the Brundtland Commission) to address growing concerns "about the accelerating deterioration of the human environment and natural resources and the consequences of that deterioration for economic and social development."[8] The Commission's 1987 report, *Our Common Future*, provides what is still the best known definition of sustainable development: "Development that meets the needs of the present without compromising the ability of future generations to meet their own needs."[9] The Commission concluded that sustainable development would provide a way for the world to address environmental degradation and poverty, and that the two problems are inextricably linked. Poverty contributes to environmental degradation, and environmental degradation contributes to poverty. *Our Common Future* also provides two additional clues to the meaning of sustainable development. First, unsustainable development occurs when there is increasing poverty and environmental degradation. Second, we will know that we are on the road to sustainability when poverty diminishes and environmental conditions improve.

American experience provided much of the intellectual foundation for this report. The conservation movement in the United States in the early 20th century showed that the productivity of U.S. agriculture, for example, depended on soil conservation, and that the continued availability of municipal water supplies required protection of the watersheds from which the water flowed. Sustainable development applies conservation to a broader range of issues.[10]

The 1992 Earth Summit was convened in Rio de Janeiro in response to *Our Common Future*. At the Earth Summit, where the United States and other countries approved the Rio Declaration and Agenda 21, each nation agreed to work toward sustainable development within its own borders and as part of its international activities. Agenda 21 is divided into four sections covering social and economic issues, conservation and management of natural resources, the role of major groups, and the means of implementation. Each of its 40 chapters includes recommended actions for governments and civil society on subjects as diverse as poverty, production and consumption patterns, deforestation, waste management, and the role of business and industry.

Of the 27 principles in the Rio Declaration adopted at the Earth Summit, the key action principle is integrated decisionmaking. Conventional development decisions by governments and private actors—for transportation projects or economic development, for example—must be based on environmental considerations and result in environmental protection.[11] Other Rio principles include reduction of unsustainable production and consumption patterns, appropriate population policies,[12] the precautionary approach (i.e., that the lack of complete scientific certainty on environmental matters should not be used as an excuse for delaying action),[13] common but differentiated responsibilities (i.e., all countries are responsible for sustainable development but developed countries have a greater responsibility because of their impact and capabilities),[14] intergenerational equity,[15] and public participation and access to justice.[16]

Finally, countries also agreed at Rio that there ought to be periodic reviews of progress toward sustainable development. Agreements without follow-up and evaluation, they reasoned, mean nothing at all. Toward that end, they created the Commission on Sustainable Development,[17] which meets annually to review progress on specified topics.

The international commitment to Agenda 21 and the Rio Declaration was reaffirmed at the 2002 World Summit on Sustainable Development in Johannesburg.[18] And the Johannesburg Plan of Implementation moved the sustainable development agenda forward in two important ways. First, it gave greater attention to poverty, describing poverty eradication "as the greatest global challenge facing the world today and an indispensable requirement for sustainable development."[19] Less than two years earlier, the U.N. General Assembly had adopted the Millennium Development Goals (MDGs). Although the MDGs addressed security, environment, and human rights, they are perhaps most influential for their ambitious poverty-reduction agenda, including halving by 2015 the fraction of the world's population that lives on less than one dollar per day.[20] At the Johannesburg summit, nations explicitly reaffirmed the world's commitment to the MDGs.[21]

Second, the Johannesburg Plan of Implementation also relied more on partnerships for implementation than did Agenda 21. The premise is that national and international goals should not and cannot be achieved by governments alone but by governments acting together with nongovernmental organizations and the private sector.[22]

In truth, the goals of environmental protection and poverty reduction coexist in uneasy tension. Developed countries bring the environmental protection agenda to the table because of problems such as climate change, to which their own high level of development has disproportionately contributed. Countries such as China and India have been more concerned about economic development because of their lower development levels and much greater poverty. Yet the world's finite ability to absorb environmental degradation and the obvious needs of the word's poor make both environmental protection and poverty reduction necessary. For that reason, most governmental and nongovernmental entities involved in sustainable development are working for both environmental protection and poverty reduction.

Of course, there continue to be questions about the meaning of sustainable development.[23] The Rio Declaration, Agenda 21, and the Johannesburg Plan of Implementation provided a set of internationally endorsed principles and actions that help define the meaning of sustainable development for specific contexts. While some continue to search for a single and more precise definition, that search is probably misguided. Sustainable development may not be open to a more specific meaning any more than concepts like freedom or democracy.[24] We all have a general idea of what freedom and democracy mean; each embraces a set of core principles, and we can surely identify obvious examples of unsustainable development or the absence of democracy. The challenge in any given situation, however, is to determine what is necessary to achieve sustainable development. Disputes about the sustainability of a particular project or activity are inevitable, but a more precise rendering of the term is not likely to help resolve them.[25] We will define and further sustainable development, in other words, by the actions we take and by what we learn from those actions.

The security dimensions of sustainability also raise questions, particularly for those who see sustainability as having just three substantive components—environment, economy, and equity (or social). Yet peace and security are part of the Earth Summit agreements. The Rio Declaration states: "Warfare is inherently destructive of sustainable development."[26] It also states: "Peace, development and environmental protection are interdependent and indivisible."[27] These conclusions are deeply rooted in both common sense and human experience;

most activities are difficult or impossible in the absence of peace and security. At the same time, under the Rio texts, security does not trump sustainability's other dimensions. For many domestic issues, in fact, where decisions may have little or no effect on security, it is fine to limit a discussion to sustainability's economic, social, and environmental dimensions. But even here, as we were tragically reminded on 9/11, peace and security provide a foundation.

Is sustainable development a destination, or is it a journey? The destination is a society in which the ordinary effects of human activity protect and restore the environment and minimize or eliminate poverty. That is plainly not the world we have today, and in that sense sustainable development is a destination. The journey toward a sustainable society should not be confused with the destination itself, any more than a traveler from the United States to Europe should confuse the plane ride with the continent. Yet we are not likely to get to this destination in a generation, or even in our lifetimes; it may take until mid-century before we can say we have even made a transition to sustainability.[28] Most if not all of our time and energy, in other words, will be devoted to the journey, away from activities that are less sustainable toward those that are more sustainable. While it is appropriate to focus our efforts on the journey, we should not confuse it with the destination.

The destination versus journey question is not just about the choice of a metaphor; it goes to the heart of what sustainable development means. In a world where most of our activities have some negative environmental impact, actions that merely reduce our negative impact are better—and could be labeled as steps toward sustainability—but they are probably not sustainable. In fact, the idea of sustainable development emerged as a reaction to continuing environmental degradation. In a sustainable society, by contrast, an ordinary effect of human behavior will be to protect and restore the environment.

Finally, sustainable development raises profound questions about our ethical or religious duties toward other humans. When projects and activities pollute the air or otherwise hurt the environment, they almost always harm other people sooner or later. Similarly, when we make serious progress toward a sustainable society, we will make ourselves and future generations better off.

Plan and Purpose of the Book

This book assesses U.S. efforts on sustainable development since the 2002 Johannesburg Summit.[29] The period after 2002 nearly coincides with the time since the September 11, 2001, terrorist attacks, and it includes most of the George W. Bush presidency. The assessment is needed to understand where we are and where we are heading.

This book also offers recommendations for the next 5 to 10 years, when a new president will be in office. The recommendations are needed to help us understand what we need to do in the near future to make progress toward sustainability. The journey toward sustainability will likely take a much longer time than the next 5 to 10 years, but implementation of these near-term recommendations would put us well on our way. The book focuses on law and policy because law and policy provide much of the structure for our society and the decisions we make. Changing laws and policies is an obvious and important way to move toward sustainability.

Although the book addresses the international activities of the United States, it is primarily focused on domestic actions. For the United States, international leadership on sustainable development is less about what we tell other countries than what we do at home. The United States could also have a profound effect on other countries by creating attractive and compelling models of sustainability.

The contributors to this book bring extraordinary expertise in their particular fields. Their chapters cover a wide range of topics, focusing mostly on the environmental dimension of sustainability (as opposed to, for example, economic and social sustainability or its national security aspects).

Each chapter describes what sustainable development means and does not mean for that particular topic, describes and assesses sustainable development efforts in the United States since 2002, and makes specific recommendations for the next 5 to 10 years. The contributing authors explicitly or implicitly use Agenda 21, the Rio Declaration, and other internationally agreed texts to determine the meaning of sustainability for their topics. Readers may or may not agree with each of the recommended actions, but the proposals provide a platform for a constructive dialogue on how to proceed.

Section I includes two chapters that summarize the findings and recommendations contained in this book—a report card on U.S. progress since 2002 and an overview of the book's recommendations, or agenda, for a sustainable America. Section II focuses on six areas where the most progress has been made since 2002: local governance, brownfields redevelopment, business and industry, colleges and universities, kindergarten through 12th-grade education, and religious organizations. These are not the only areas where progress has been made, and the choice of which areas to include is a judgment call. In fact, the authors in each of these chapters identify major efforts that are still needed. The point of this section is not only to show that there is some good news, but to stimulate questions about why we are making more progress in these areas, and what can be learned from these areas that could be applied elsewhere. The rest of the book is organized by topic.

The theologian Thomas Berry has said that ecologically sustainable human development is the "Great Work" in front of us—our challenge and opportunity to make a significant contribution to the human venture.[30] The challenges of sustainable development are different from other challenges we have faced, and are perhaps more difficult as a result. Yet they also provide considerable opportunities—not only economic opportunities but also opportunities for greater international cooperation and for a society that more consciously and effectively protects the interests and well-being of present and future generations.

The decisions we make about sustainable development are defining decisions for the United States. They are decisions about who we are, what we want, what we value, and how we want to be remembered.

With this book, the question is no longer whether there is a way for the United States to achieve sustainability.[31] The question instead is whether we are willing to summon what is best about us—our ingenuity, creativity, determination, capacity for hard work, cooperative spirit, sense of fairness, and compassion for those who follow us—to do the great work of achieving a sustainable America. The roadmap contained in this book provides a point of departure for the rest of the journey.

ENDNOTES

1. U.S. Census Bureau, International Data Base, Total Midyear Population for the World: 1950-2050, *available at* www.census.gov/ipc/www/idb/worldpop.html (projecting 2050 population of 9.5 billion).

2. NAT'L RESEARCH COUNCIL: OUR COMMON JOURNEY: A TRANSITION TOWARD SUSTAINABILITY 70 (1999)

3. U.N. DEVELOPMENT PROGRAMME, HUMAN DEVELOPMENT REPORT 2007/2008, at 25 (2007).

4. U.N. Conference on Environment and Development (UNCED), Rio Declaration on Environment and Development, U.N. Doc. A/CONF.151/5/Rev.1, 31 I.L.M. 874 (1992) [hereinafter Rio Declaration].

5. UNCED, Agenda 21, U.N. Doc. A/CONF.151.26 (1992) [hereinafter Agenda 21].

6. *Id.* at ¶ 1.6.

7. GREG BEHRMAN, THE MOST NOBLE ADVENTURE: THE MARSHALL PLAN AND THE TIME WHEN AMERICA HELPED SAVE EUROPE (2007); ELIZABETH BORGWARDT, A NEW DEAL FOR THE WORLD: AMERICA'S VISION FOR HUMAN RIGHTS (2005); STEPHEN C. SCHLESINGER, ACT OF CREATION: THE FOUNDING OF THE UNITED NATIONS (2003).

8. G.A. Res. 41/187, pmbl., U.N. Doc. A/RES/41/187 (Dec. 11, 1987).

9. WORLD COMM'N ON ENV'T & DEV., OUR COMMON FUTURE 43 (1987).

10. INT'L UNION FOR CONSERVATION OF NATURE & NATURAL RES., THE WORLD CONSERVATION STRATEGY: LIVING RESOURCE CONSERVATION FOR SUSTAINABLE DEVELOPMENT (1980).

11. Rio Declaration, *supra* note 4, at princ. 4 ("In order to achieve sustainable development, environmental protection shall constitute an integral part of the development process and cannot be considered in isolation from it."); John C. Dernbach, *Achieving Sustainable Development: The Centrality and Multiple Facets of Integrated Decisionmaking*, 10 IND. J. GLOBAL LEG. STUD. 247 (2003).

12. Rio Declaration, *supra* note 4, at princ. 8.

13. *Id.* at princ. 15.

14. *Id.* at princ. 7.

15. *Id.* at princs. 3 & 21.

16. *Id.* at princ. 10.

17. Agenda 21, *supra* note 5, at ¶¶ 38.11 & 38.13.

18. World Summit on Sustainable Development (WSSD), Plan of Implementation (2002), *available at* www.un.org/esa/sustdev/documents/WSSD_POI_PD/English/WSSD_PlanImpl.pdf.

19. *Id.* at ¶ 7.

20. G.A. Res. 55/2, U.N. Doc. No. A/RES/55/2 (2000), *available at* www.un.org/millennium/declaration/ares552e.pdf.

21. WSSD Plan of Implementation, *supra* note 18, at ¶ 1.

22. *Id.* at ¶ 3.

23. *See, e.g.,* David G. Victor, *Recovering Sustainable Development,* FOREIGN AFF., Jan./Feb. 2006, at 91.

24. Michael Jacobs, *Sustainable Development as a Contested Concept, in* FAIRNESS AND FUTURITY: ESSAYS ON ENVIRONMENTAL SUSTAINABILITY AND SOCIAL JUSTICE 21, 25 (Andrew Dobson ed., 1999).

25. *Id.* at 25-26.

26. Rio Declaration, *supra* note 4, at princ. 24.

27. *Id.* at princ. 25

28. OUR COMMON JOURNEY, *supra* note 2, at 7.

29. This book is a successor to STUMBLING TOWARD SUSTAINABILITY (John C. Dernbach ed. 2002), a much larger volume published just before the Johannesburg Summit. STUMBLING TOWARD SUSTAINABILITY assessed United States efforts in the 10 years after the 1992 Earth Summit and, like this volume, made recommendations for the next 5 to 10 years. Both are efforts by and for Americans to understand what sustainable development can and should mean in an American context. These two volumes represent the only nongovernmental effort to assess U.S. sustainable development efforts in a continuous and comprehensive manner.

30. THOMAS BERRY, THE GREAT WORK: OUR WAY INTO THE FUTURE 2 (1999). "The Great Work now, as we move into a new millennium, is to carry out the transition from a period of human devastation of the Earth to a period when humans would be present to the planet in a mutually beneficial manner." *Id.* "What is needed is a sustainable way of life." *Id.* at 114.

31. And its predecessor, STUMBLING TOWARD SUSTAINABILITY, *supra* note 29.

CHAPTER 2

Progress Toward Sustainability: A Report Card

The Contributing Authors

America is approaching a tipping point on sustainability. We are recognizing that environmental problems *also* limit economic opportunity, job creation, and social well-being, and even compromise our national security. While there continue to be holdouts who view greenhouse gas emissions, loss of biodiversity, toxic chemicals, sprawl, and other environmental problems as "merely environmental," their number and influence is shrinking. It is also increasingly evident that we can build a more robust economy, improve national security, and create good new jobs by protecting and restoring the environment. We are near the point where it will be impossible to take action of consequence—whether it be in economic policy, education, foreign relations, environment, or even the war on terrorism—without this broader and deeper perspective on sustainability.

All of that said, the United States is not on the verge of actually becoming sustainable. Far from it. Since 2002, we have most often moved in the wrong direction—toward greater consumption of energy, materials, land, and other resources, and more negative environmental impacts, with damaging social, economic, and security consequences. But we are at least reaching a point where decisionmakers understand issues within a sustainability framework, and understand why that perspective is both attractive and necessary.

The pace, scope, and intensity of sustainable development activity has increased in the United States since 2002. At that time, in "virtually every area of American life, a few people and organizations [were] exercising leadership for sustainability."[1] The number of such people and organizations, in both public and private sectors, has greatly increased since that time. Their activities are increasing in confidence and sophistication, they are achieving positive and attractive results, and these results are encouraging others to imitate and improve on what they have accomplished. They are also asking better questions, and providing better answers, on what it means to be truly sustainable.

The prominence of climate change and the visibility of its effects on all issues and sectors have also grown since 2002. Climate change has become a major driver in recent sustainability efforts by corporations, religious organizations, colleges and universities, and local and state governments. And it is increasingly clear that climate change will affect all other natural resources—including freshwater, oceans and estuaries, and biodiversity—in ways that are likely to adversely affect human quality of life. Climate change, in other words, is becoming the public face of unsustainable development. It is increasingly seen as a dominant—if not *the* dominant—sustainable development issue.

This chapter is an overview, based on the contributions of the book's 41 authors, of what we have achieved or not achieved since 2002. While it is framed as a report card, it is in narrative form, and does not contain "grades." Virtually all of the chapters report some positive developments, even if their overall conclusions are negative. We leave it to the reader to decide who or what deserves an "A" or an "F," or something in between.

On some topics, there was enough positive news to warrant special treatment. These six chapters are contained in Section II of the book. These may not be the only topics that warrant such treatment, but they are identified separately to emphasize that some areas have shown more progress than others. We would be much further along the journey to sustainability if all areas of American life had made as much recent progress. The stories in Section II provide clues about how to move ahead as well as reason to be optimistic.

Six Areas of Significant Progress

The United States has made significant progress since 2002 in at least six areas: local governance, brownfields redevelopment, business and industry, higher education, kindergarten through 12th-grade education, and religious organizations.

Local governments have made tremendous strides toward sustainability in recent years, amid broader recognition that a good environment can enhance quality of life and bolster local economic competitiveness. Mayors in particular have attracted increasing notice in launching and supporting many path-breaking green measures. The Mayors Climate Protection Agreement has now been endorsed by more than 850 mayors from all 50 states, the District of Columbia, and Puerto Rico. Yet fragmented regional governance, sprawling (and often inequitable) land use patterns, and the lack of consistent federal and state support continue to pose formidable challenges to local efforts to address critical sustainability issues.

A hallmark of sustainable land use development is remediation and reuse of brownfields, which are properties contaminated by prior industrial activity. Over the past two decades, states have fostered brownfields redevelopment through voluntary cleanup programs. These programs received a boost in 2002 when the federal Superfund statute was amended to protect developers from certain liabilities if they conduct voluntary cleanups. Still, a parcel-by-parcel approach continues to dominate brownfields law and policy, rather than an overall vision for the community.

Sustainable business practices in the United States went from being just a "movement" to the mainstream of the market in 2007. American business has accepted the fact that climate change is real and has potentially dire consequences. It is also increasingly clear to business that pursuing the triple bottom line—economy, society, and environment—provides many profitable opportunities. A growing number of American and European businesses have entered into multi-stakeholder partnerships to improve public health or environmental quality, or to reduce poverty. Others are issuing voluntary public reports on their social and environmental impacts and accomplishments, and many have adopted voluntary standards for labor conditions, environmental practices, and human rights. Corporations making sustainability efforts are also increasingly attractive to investors.

Sustainability in kindergarten through 12th-grade education has made remarkable progress since 2002, although the overall effort is still fragmentary and incomplete. State educational standards increasingly support education for sustainability. More and more schools and educational institutions are embracing sustainability paradigms; providing students with sustainability-enhancing knowledge, attitudes, and skills; and assessing progress toward sustainability. On the other hand, the recent heightened focus on testing in traditional subjects makes it difficult for sustainability's newer, interdisciplinary approach to gain a foothold.

Colleges and universities across the United States are increasingly practicing sustainability across the entire range of their activities. Despite the continuing drive to specialize within traditional academic disciplines, courses that incorporate sustainability concepts are being developed in a variety of disciplines. Sustainability-oriented research is increasingly funded in the sciences, and initiatives are also under way to bring the social sciences and humanities into the research dimension. Initiatives to make campus operations more sustainable are now standard practice, and some universities and colleges are actively promoting sustainable development in their surrounding communities and beyond.

A growing number of Americans of every religious faith affirm a global and ecumenical ethic of a just and sustainable earth community. Some congregations now have committees or action groups, as well as special moments of ritual life, that affirm the spiritual and ethical importance of "caring for creation." More faith communities in the United States intend to reduce their ecological footprint and protect the commons by eating locally grown organic food (including humanely treated food animals), purchasing imported products that are "fair-traded," using appropriate technology, and conserving energy while reducing waste. The question now is how seriously religious communities and ethicists in the United States will act to grapple with climate change and other eco-social threats.

Consumption, Population, and Poverty

The United States continues to consume a disproportionate share of the world's energy and natural resources, has a rapidly growing population, and faces significant problems of poverty and social and economic inequity.

The United States leads the world in the overall use of natural resources and, in most cases, in per capita use of resources, including fossil fuels and other natural resources and materials. The consumption of construction materials accounts for the largest share of the material footprint of the United States, due largely to the rapid growth of the housing sector. At the same time, manufacturing and construction systems have been slowly shifting toward green products and clean technologies.

Over the 20th century, the United States developed a superlatively wealthy society on the basis of cheap and abundant fossil fuel energy. Since 2002, America has shown mixed progress in transitioning to a more sustainable energy system. On the positive side, the energy and carbon intensity of the country's gross domestic product (GDP) continued to show favorable long-term trends of decline, and energy end-use efficiency also continued to improve. However, increased fossil fuel consumption (and the resultant growing greenhouse gas emissions), stagnant efficiency standards (until late 2007, when Congress strengthened some standards), and expanding corn-based ethanol production have been factors moving the energy system in a less sustainable direction.

Population growth in the United States raises particular environmental concerns because of the high level of Americans' per capita consumption. Between 1990 and 2000, the nation's population increased more than over any 10-year period in U.S. history, and the first decade of the 21st century may well surpass the 1990s. Yet since 2002, there have been no major changes to U.S. policies that might have demographic effects, such as immigration regulations, restrictions on abortions, the tax code, and foreign aid policies.

Deepening economic inequality and high levels of poverty are major problems for the United States economy, for our democratic institutions, and for our environment. A less equitable distribution of economic resources works against sustainable consumption and production; those with low and moderate incomes usually cannot afford the initial up-front investment for more energy-efficient automobiles and homes.

Conservation and Management of Natural Resources

The overall structure of our environmental and natural resources laws has changed relatively little, with a few modest forward steps and perhaps a greater number of backward steps, despite continuing challenges that are made harder by climate change.

Although U.S. residents enjoy enviable access to ample supplies of safe freshwater, pollution continues to pose risks to human health, aquatic ecosystems remain significantly impaired throughout the country and face increasing risks due to urbanization and other development, and water supplies will be strained as population continues to grow and as global warming affects the amount and distribution of water supplies. Federal programs to protect and manage freshwater resources continue to operate under a legal regime that has existed for several decades. The most recent promising initiatives have occurred at the state, local, or private levels.

America's ocean policy continues to be fragmented. Despite the recommendations of two independent commissions, the George W.

Bush Administration has resisted an ecosystem-based approach. Recent legislative proposals and President Bush's designation of a large coral reef ecosystem off Hawaii as a marine national monument provide some reason for hope.

The greatest amount of air pollution comes from burning fossil fuels. From 2002 to 2006, atmospheric concentrations of ground-level ozone, carbon monoxide, fine and coarse particulates, lead, sulfur dioxide, and nitrogen dioxide all declined to a modest degree. Yet regulatory efforts by the U.S. Environmental Protection Agency (EPA) during the period are a mix of forward and backward steps, and the United States has still not met the Clean Air Act's health-based requirements concerning the scope and timing of reductions for urban air pollution.

Despite the government's commitments in the United Nations Framework Convention on Climate Change to "aim" to stabilize greenhouse gas emissions at 1990 levels and to exercise leadership in reducing greenhouse gas emissions, in 2006, U.S. emissions were significantly above 1990 levels. In 2001, President Bush repudiated the Kyoto Protocol, which would have required the United States to reduce its greenhouse gas emissions by 7 percent from 1990 levels by 2008 to 2012. To some degree, energy legislation adopted in 2005 and 2007—mandating greater efficiency in appliances, lighting, and motor vehicles, among other things—will reduce future emissions. In addition, public support for stronger action has increased in response to growing scientific evidence.

Biodiversity conservation remains an illusive goal in the United States. Although no standard, systematic assessment of the state of biodiversity exists in the United States, the clear message from a variety of sources is that we are squandering our rich heritage of species and ecosystem diversity through continuing habitat destruction. Conservation remains a formal domestic and policy objective, but the 1992 Biodiversity Convention remains unratified. The Bush Administration has compromised the country's public and private biodiversity by its general hostility to environmental protection and mandatory greenhouse gas reduction, and by its successful efforts to open large tracts of public lands, much of them important wildlife habitats, to energy exploration and production. One bright spot is growing attention to marine biodiversity. Another is acceleration in the private acquisition of large amounts of undeveloped land and the dedication of this land to uses that are generally consistent with biodiversity conservation.

Efforts toward sustainable forestry are also a mixed story. Three forces are moving private forest management toward more sustainable practices: state and federal forestry laws; the continued increase of land conservation transactions on private forest land; and the growth in forest product certification, which allows retailers to label forest products as grown in a sustainable manner. In the past few years a significant amount of state forest land has been certified by the Forest Stewardship Council (an international entity) and the Sustainable Forestry Initiative (created by the American Forest and Paper Association, but now legally independent), or both. On the other hand, in 2005, the U.S. Forest Service authorized large-scale exceptions to a 2001 regulation that generally prohibited road construction and timber harvesting in roadless areas of national forests. As this book went to press, the fate of the "roadless rule" remained tied up in the courts.

Waste and Toxic Chemicals

Americans continue to generate large amounts of waste and toxic chemicals, although some efforts to reduce the amount or toxicity of waste and chemicals are promising.

Efforts to manage toxic chemicals and pesticides since 2002 are a mix of forward and backward steps. For pesticides, the United States has made progress toward sustainability in terms of exercising appropriate caution, assuring intergenerational equity, and taking more hazardous pesticides and specific pesticide uses out of commerce. On the other hand, the Toxic Substances Control Act, which is now more than 30 years old, has not been amended despite a growing view that the statute should require more information about chemicals and do more to reduce risks. In addition, the Bush Administration has opted to use only voluntary approaches for managing risks of nanomaterials, and to ignore their unique properties and possible implications for health and the environment.

American laws concerning hazardous waste have made little progress toward sustainability since 2002. EPA initiated a voluntary waste minimization program for 31 toxic, persistent, and bioaccumulative chemicals. Yet the amount of hazardous waste generated actually increased between 2004 and 2005, and U.S. laws still do not mandate decreases in the generation of industrial hazardous wastes. Implementation of the Superfund Act has been handicapped since 1995 by the absence of special taxes to support cleanups; reliance on general fund revenues has meant a significant decline in cleanups. In addition, the United States has still not ratified the Basel Convention on the Control of Transboundary Movements of Hazardous Wastes.

The most obvious and tangible result of consumption in the United States is the amount and variety of trash we generate. American patterns of consumption have intensified: larger homes, more possessions, and increasing levels of construction and demolition wastes. Landfills continue to receive most of the waste generated. Recycling and composting continue to make some gains, but with dramatic variations in the states. Pay-as-you-throw programs, in which disposal fees are based on the amount of waste generated, now reach one-quarter of the country's population, and studies indicate they can reduce residential waste generation.

Land Use and Transportation

Land use and transportation patterns continue to be unsustainable overall, in spite of increasing smart-growth initiatives in some states and changes in our federal transportation and energy laws. Transportation and land use patterns are a primary cause of almost every environmental problem facing the United States.

Despite some recent initiatives, the years since 2002 have seen reduced activity at the state level to promote sustainable land use within the context of smart growth. The Supreme Court's 2005 decision in *Kelo v. City of New London*, which held that economic development is a valid constitutional purpose when a government condemns private property, helped provoke a backlash against land use controls, even though this issue is unrelated to smart growth.

Passenger and freight highway travel have increased rapidly, rising far faster than population or economic growth. In 2005, Congress adopted the most recent renewal of the federal surface transportation law with funding formulas that unfortunately reward unsustainable transportation patterns. On the other hand, the law continues a framework first established in 1991 that recognizes that transportation should promote energy conservation, environmental protection, and other goals in addition to mobility. In December 2007, Congress increased fuel economy standards for passenger vehicles to at least 35 miles per gallon by 2020. Even if fully implemented, this would still be significantly below the standards of a number of European and Asian nations. Rising fuel prices have spurred public demand for change and have begun to alter travel behavior.

International Trade, Finance, and Development Assistance

The United States has put environmental provisions in bilateral or multilateral trade agreements, increased its official development assistance, and supported a public/private partnership that effectively promoted the phasing out of leaded gasoline in sub-Saharan Africa. Sustainable development has not, however, been systematically incorporated into the major programs for international assistance and trade, nor is the clean-fuels partnership designed to address the many other sources of lead exposure additional to leaded gasoline.

Fostering sustainable development is an expressed goal of the World Trade Organization's Doha Round of negotiations. But there has been no serious discussion about the interface of trade, environment, and sustainable development since the negotiations were initiated in 2001. If the Doha Round fails, U.S. bilateral and regional free trade agreements will have to carry more of the trade/sustainable development load. The Bush Administration has concluded bilateral and regional free trade agreements with 13 countries that contain environmental provisions modeled on the 1994 North American Free Trade Agreement with Mexico, Canada, and the United States, which ensures that investments within their borders are carried out in an environmentally protective manner.

Between 2001 and 2005 the United States significantly increased its official development assistance (ODA) to developing countries, and is now the largest net donor among developed countries, although the country still ranks low among Organisation for Economic Co-operation and Development (OECD) (i.e., developed) countries in official development assistance as a percentage of gross national income. Much of the increase in U.S. international assistance is related to the Iraq War, and its effectiveness in accomplishing strategic and sustainable development objectives is in doubt.

Private financial investments in developing countries now dwarf ODA. Export credit agencies (ECAs) and multilateral financial institutions have considerable potential to influence the environmental character of private financial flows to developing countries. In 2003, the ECAs of OECD countries (including the United States) began to require that all projects comply with the environmental standards of the host country or the standards of the World Bank Group, which are typically higher than those of host countries. Although the Group of Eight (G8) top industrialized countries asked the World Bank to take a leadership role in helping its clients address climate change, the United States has undermined the Bank's efforts to prioritize climate change in its operations.

The United States has played a constructive role in at least one international partnership that emerged from the World Summit on Sustainable Development in 2002. At the Johannesburg Summit, which encouraged the use of public-private partnerships for sustainability, EPA and the United Nations Environment Program initiated the Partnership for Clean Fuels and Vehicles, a loose affiliation of international organizations, businesses, and trade groups with the goal of accelerating the global phaseout of leaded gasoline. The partnership has been particularly successful in persuading governments to phase out leaded gasoline in sub-Saharan Africa, although many other lead exposure problems remain.

State and Federal Governance

States have been more active on climate change than on sustainable development in general. The federal government has imposed increasing restrictions on access to information and public participation. More generally, the federal government has done little to foster sustainability in the United States.

The record on statewide sustainable development efforts is largely disappointing. Only 10 states have readily visible and explicit statewide sustainability efforts, and most of these efforts are limited to reducing the energy and environmental impacts of state government operations. On the positive side, in the absence of strong federal leadership on climate policy, states have been filling the void with programs to conserve energy, create greenhouse gas emissions registries, promote renewable energy, and limit greenhouse gas emissions from vehicles and power plants.

Since 2002, the federal government has quietly shifted policies and practices to ones based on the public's "need to know," increasingly leaving the government in charge of determining who needs to know and what they need to know, and undermining the informed discussion required for sustainability. While the threat of terrorism is real, the Bush

Administration's invocation of terrorism and national security often appears to overreach. On the other hand, the ongoing technological revolution in information, coupled with broadening access to the Internet and other telecommunications technologies, has provided new and widely used tools for informing and mobilizing the public.

The federal government has done relatively little to foster sustainable development since 2002. The United States has no overall national strategy for sustainable development, and is a long way away from employing the strategic analysis and decisionmaking required for sustainable development. The federal government has moved toward environmental indicators, but not sustainable development indicators (which would include social, economic, and even security measures). But there has been no comprehensive effort to address the variety of sustainability threats we face, including climate change, perhaps the most urgent and obvious of all sustainability issues.

ENDNOTE

1. John C. Dernbach, *Synthesis*, *in* STUMBLING TOWARD SUSTAINABILITY 1, 2 (John C. Dernbach ed., 2002).

CHAPTER 3

Agenda for a Sustainable America

The Contributing Authors

How do we get to a sustainable America? The report card contained in Chapter 2 showed that we have made more progress in recent years in some areas than in others. Yet in every single area of American life and activity, we have a long way to go.

The contributing authors of this book together provide more than a hundred recommendations for the next decade. These recommendations encompass 10 basic themes, and they provide a basic map of the direction we need to go. They are:

1. The United States should systematically reduce its ecological footprint.

2. The United States government must adopt, as soon as possible, greenhouse gas emission reduction programs that will reduce U.S. emissions to our fair share of safe global emissions.

3. The United States should create more employment opportunities in environmental protection and restoration, and make it easier for unskilled and low-income persons to enter and remain in the workforce.

4. Sustainable development should be an organizing principle for all levels of government.

5. Nongovernmental actors should play a major role in achieving sustainability.

6. Individuals, families, and consumers should have more sustainable options in the decisions they make.

7. Sustainable development should become a central part of public and formal education.

8. The United States should strengthen its environmental and natural resources laws.

9. The United States needs to play an international leadership role on behalf of sustainable development.

10. The United States needs to improve the information and data available to the public to make decisions for sustainability.

As these recommendations suggest, sustainable development requires actions by governments at all levels but cannot be achieved by government alone. All segments of American society—individuals, nongovernmental organizations, businesses, the scientific and technological community, educational institutions, religious organizations, and families—need to play an active and constructive role. The agenda contained in this book is intended to guide or inform that effort.

The recommendations concerning government, moreover, are not about more government or less government but rather better governance. Governments at all levels make better and less costly decisions when they incorporate environmental considerations and goals in advance, rather than try to patch things up afterwards. Many of these recommendations, too, would have the government reduce environmentally damaging subsidies and ensure that individuals and businesses can make more sustainable choices.

These recommendations also indicate that the task is achievable. For a wide range of activities, the contributing authors have identified steps that we can take in the next 5 to 10 years to move toward sustainability in the United States. *These are not long-range, pie-in-the-sky recommendations; these are steps we can take right now.*

And this agenda will make us better off than we would otherwise be. It will save us money, improve our security, improve the quality of life in our communities, make us healthier, create new jobs that pay well, and foster the development of new scientific and technological developments. The journey to sustainability will not be easy, but continuing our present course puts our security, economy, well-being, and environment at great risk.

The rest of this chapter sets out in greater detail the 10 recommendations that constitute a roadmap for the next 5 to 10 years of the journey toward a sustainable America.

1. The United States should systematically reduce its ecological footprint.

- Practice energy efficiency: Substantially tighter efficiency standards are needed for many appliances as well as automobiles, light-duty vehicles, and heavy-duty vehicles. In addition, research, development, and large-scale demonstration of energy-efficient commercial buildings is needed to prepare the way for net zero-energy commercial buildings.

- Conserve materials: Manufacturers and consumers should "reduce, reuse, recycle, and remanufacture" to supplement and preserve virgin supplies of nonrenewable resources. Consumer products should be made largely with recycled and nontoxic materials, should be readily recyclable themselves, and should employ the more abundant of the nonrenewable resources, such as iron and aluminum.

- Design to reduce environmental impacts: Manufacturers and producers should reduce the amount of material required in each product, use renewable materials for construction (such as insulation and roofing), and design to limit energy and water use as well as toxicity.

- Phase out fossil fuels: A movement toward phasing out oil and coal would not only catalyze the development of lower- or zero-emission vehicles but also lessen dangers from air pollution and greenhouse gas emissions, as well as oil drilling, oil spills, petroleum refinery emissions, and leaking underground storage tanks. It would also improve national security by lessening our dependence on foreign oil and produce enormous health and environmental benefits.

2. The United States government must adopt, as soon as possible, greenhouse gas emission reduction programs that will reduce U.S. emissions to our fair share of safe global emissions.

- The United States needs to adopt both emissions caps for various sectors and a mix of financial incentives and regulatory requirements that will achieve the reductions needed to return to 1990 emissions levels within the next few years. Implementation of energy-production- and consumption-based carbon taxation or a cap-and-trade system for carbon emissions would move the entire U.S. energy system in a more sustainable direction. A carbon tax, or a cap-and-trade or fossil fuel phaseout program that raises energy prices, should be coupled with rebates paid out in the form of refundable tax credits to protect low-income families and reduce the burden on middle-income taxpayers.

- The United States should take leadership in achieving an international consensus on the levels of atmospheric concentrations of greenhouse gases that constitute a dangerous interference with the climate system. The goal of the U.N. Framework Convention on Climate Change is to stabilize atmospheric concentrations at safe levels. Definition of safe atmospheric levels would enable all nations to understand what their individual obligations would be.

3. *The United States should create more employment opportunities in environmental protection and restoration, and make it easier for unskilled and low-income persons to enter and remain in the workforce.*

- Connect waste management and pollution control to job creation. Not only has interest in recycling and composting created many jobs, but as resources become more constrained, we can expect new opportunities in key environmental industry sectors such as resource recovery for parts of the country that are ready with both investment and training for job growth.

- Replace the current welfare system with a comprehensive tax-and-transfer system. The goal is to "cash out" as many welfare programs as possible and use those funds to help pay for refundable tax credits. These refundable tax credits would simplify the current system by replacing personal exemptions, standard deductions, and the many other child and family benefits in the current income tax system.

4. *Sustainable development should be an organizing principle for all levels of government.*

- State and local governments should exercise leadership on land use for sustainability. Land use planning and decisionmaking needs to be integrated with climate change. The stakes are not only regionwide and statewide; they are national in scope, particularly in regard to climate change.

- States should increase their use of areawide brownfields initiatives and integrate brownfields remediation and reuse with their existing economic development programs by addressing multiple brownfield sites in the same community.

- The federal government and state governments should systematically provide incentives for comprehensive sustainability policies for local and regional governments on a range of issues, including climate change, transportation, housing, education, energy efficiency, infrastructure reinvestment, immigration, environment, land use, pollution prevention, and regional coordination.

- States need to move toward a system that better promotes regional governance and shares taxes within a region.

Through strong smart-growth laws, integrated statewide planning, and more sensible funding, the states can influence growth, encourage regional cooperation and supportive local zoning, and help end the revenue penalty suffered by low-income jurisdictions.

- Municipalities should engage in open, integrated planning that takes into account environmental, economic, and equity considerations, including climate change. They should also implement local zoning that fosters mixed-use, smart-growth development and uses the natural environment to buffer communities from natural disasters.

- State and federal policymakers should protect and enhance the role of states as laboratories for sustainability reforms. After articulating the specific goals and assumptions behind sustainable development policies, states should share data about the success or failure of their efforts. The federal government should preserve state policy innovation by avoiding federal preemption of state climate initiatives except where a direct conflict with federal law exists.

- States should develop comprehensive goals for a sustainable society and specific indicators of progress. This approach would integrate all of the societal goals of sustainability, viewing it as the means for human societal development and understanding the impact of that development on the natural environment.

- The United States should employ an ongoing and systematic sustainable development strategy. The federal government needs to conduct an ongoing analysis of actual or potential threats (including environmental threats) to its interests, prioritize them accordingly, and develop strategies for addressing them. The federal government needs to reinvigorate its commitment to support strong and independent scientific evaluation of potential environmental threats to better inform such policy development.

- The federal government should develop a set of sustainable development indicators that cover the environmental, social, economic, and security aspects of national life. These indicators would help us better understand where we are, what we need to do next, and how the various aspects of our national life are related.

5. Nongovernmental actors should play a major role in achieving sustainability.

- Business leaders should develop multi-stakeholder partnerships within the framework of specific commitments made by the United States under international law. The partnerships concept embraced at the World Summit on Sustainable Development was based on the premise that such partnerships would support international agreements, not replace them. Greater public reporting on partnerships would provide a means of assessing successes and failures, as well as more external accountability.

- Business leaders should embrace voluntary reporting on their social and environmental effects or face mandatory reporting. Mandatory reporting requirements could be avoided by establishing an external verification mechanism for voluntary reports.

- Faith communities should teach the vision and values of eco-justice ethics informed by insights from natural sciences and rooted in the sacred texts of religion. The scriptural portrayal of the fifth and sixth days of creation (Genesis 1:20-31), for example, which Jews and Christians have traditionally viewed as a mandate from God for human domination of nature, actually underscores human interdependence with, and stewardship responsibility for, the vast community of diverse life.

- Faith communities should continue to emphasize that simpler living and energy-saving, earth-community-building initiatives are expected of all who claim to care for creation. Because the deepening environmental crisis is cultural as well as ecological, one of the religious communities' most significant contributions is to inspire reverence, gratitude, repentance, and self-discipline—to the benefit of earth community.

- The federal government should provide better public access to information on such topics as climate change, ecosystem services, and the newer environmental and health risks arising from nanotechnology and endocrine disruptors. In order to protect our shared resources, or commons, and better engage in a national conversation over sustainable development, the public must have better and more accessible information.

- The federal government should adopt and implement a new generation of access principles. Federal agencies should operate under the assumption that they have an affirmative responsibility to disseminate information, which means they would need to justify any action to withhold information.

- Individuals, nongovernmental organizations, corporations, and others need to move toward sustainable development in their communities, their work, and their lives. Too much effort is needed on too many fronts for government to do it alone.

6. Individuals, families, and consumers should have more sustainable options in the decisions they make.

- Public and private partners involved in forestry on both public and private land should work together to promote forest certification for wood products as a preference in consumer decisions. Forest certification has proved influential in encouraging sustainable forest management on both private and state forest land in both the United States and other countries.

- Far more effort, including funding, needs to be devoted to providing attractive, reliable, affordable alternatives to driving—including freight rail, light rail, high-speed rail, bus rapid transit, bicycling, and walking.

- Cleaner and more efficient vehicles should be encouraged or required through a variety of incentives and regulations, including even more stringent fuel-efficiency standards, tax incentives for manufacturers and purchasers of high-efficiency and alternative-fuel vehicles, government fleet purchases of efficient vehicles, and research and development grants.

7. Sustainable development should become a central part of public and formal education.

- States and school districts should provide standards and capacity building for education for sustainability at the kindergarten through 12th-grade (K-12) level. More explicit support for sustainability in influential and state-mandated content and performance standards would produce widespread improvement in education for sustainability. Diverse public and private entities need to advocate for and support this effort.

- Parents, universities, business, and government should model sustainability, involve schools in their own efforts to progress toward sustainability, and advocate for education for sustainability in our school systems. Nothing will help K-12 education for sustainability more than growth in societal demand for educational programs that equip students to create a more sustainable world and an increased funding stream to equip schools to meet this demand.

- Universities and colleges should increase and expand support for sustainability in each of the core areas of university life, including curriculum (to ensure that all students achieve basic sustainability literacy), research (to provide the knowledge needed to accelerate the movement toward sustainability), operations ("greening the campus"), outreach and service (in their communities), student life (making sustainability an integral part of campus culture), and institutional mission (integrating sustainability with strategic planning).

- External stakeholders of colleges and universities, including nonprofit organizations, businesses, and governments, should support and encourage sustainability in higher education.

- The federal government needs to embark on a pervasive educational campaign at all levels of society, including increased investments in marine science research, so that Americans will understand why their marine resources are important and how their individual choices can contribute to a sustainable ocean in the future. A similar campaign should be conducted to enhance public understanding of how human societies are dependent on ecosystem services.

8. The United States should strengthen its environmental and natural resources laws.

- We must invest in water resources. Although U.S. water supply and sanitation systems remain among the best in the world, many systems are aging and require significant repairs or upgrades, and growth will require substantial investments to maintain public health and other benefits. To avoid past mistakes, however, future investments should focus on more sustainable uses of land and water.

- We must control pollution runoff. Runoff is now the leading source of water pollution in the United States. A mandatory system of enforceable, best-practice standards for sources of runoff pollution would close the biggest gap in U.S. water pollution programs.

- Ocean waters must be managed on an integrated ecosystem basis. The United States needs to improve the coordination of its regulation of ocean activities and resources, preferably through a comprehensive national oceans policy that will govern all ocean activities across regulatory jurisdictions. This policy should be founded on sustainable use and a stewardship ethic, and should mandate ecosystem-based management of marine resources.

- The regulatory system for air pollution, among other things, should be redesigned to encourage advanced technology. An environmental competition statute would authorize polluters who clean up to collect the costs of that cleanup, plus a premium, from competitors with higher pollution levels. Such a policy would stimulate a race to improve environmental quality by improving technology.

- State and federal land management agencies in the United States should affirmatively subscribe to the Montreal Process criteria as goals for sustainable forest management. These criteria include biodiversity, forest ecosystem health and productivity, maintenance of soil and water resources as well as contribution to the global carbon cycle, and maintenance and enhancement of social and economic forest benefits. Adoption of a uniform policy based on the Montreal Process criteria would both further sustainable forest management and facilitate cooperation among state and federal land management agencies.

- Congress should amend the Toxic Substances Control Act to ensure more sustainable development, production, and use of chemicals. Needed reforms include mandating stronger management of chemical risks, promoting green chemistry, enhancing the right-to-know for chemical users and the public, and incorporating scientific advances in toxicity testing and exposure assessment.

- Congress should develop a regulatory framework for the assessment and management of risks related to nanotechnology. The current EPA voluntary approach falls well short of this goal.

- Congress should amend our hazardous waste laws to require industrial facilities to decrease their generation of hazardous wastes by certain deadlines. This amendment should be designed to allow industrial plant managers sufficient time to design and implement operational changes tailored to the specific circumstances of their own facilities.

- Congress should amend the Superfund statute to remove the liability exemption for lending institutions that have the capacity to influence hazardous waste management practices at borrower facilities in which they hold a security interest. Congress should also reinstate Superfund's taxes on certain industries to replenish its trust fund and facilitate more cleanups.

- To better integrate environmental objectives with social, economic, and security objectives, the United States needs to make greater use of legal and policy tools that send appropriate economic and price signals. The United States should also reduce or eliminate environmentally damaging subsidies.

9. The United States needs to play an international leadership role on behalf of sustainable development.

- The United States should deepen its commitment to international agreements. Collectively, these agreements add up to a common understanding that population stability, environmental integrity, prudent resource use, and equity considerations must all be inextricably linked in any design for a sustainable human future.

- The United States should take a leadership role in bringing the Doha Round of trade negotiations to a successful conclusion. Agricultural subsidies, particularly by the United States and the European Union, have historically encouraged overproduction of field crops such as corn, cotton, wheat, and soybeans, which in turn has put pressure on natural resources, including water and arable land. A substantial reduction in farm subsidies would foster sustainable development in the agriculture sector.

- The United States should make sustainable development a priority in multilateral and bilateral trade agreements.

Agreements should contain provisions for financing sustainable development as well as appropriate incentives. Agreements should also include provisions for benchmarking progress on sustainability, including economic growth and poverty reduction.

- The United States should continue to increase its official development assistance (ODA) to the extent that it is effective in achieving sustainable development goals.

- The United States should seek to ensure that export credit agencies (ECAs) adopt robust minimum standards and do not finance projects that have damaging environmental and social impacts. The ECAs need to support projects and exports that make a significant contribution to sustainable development.

- The United States should play a stronger role pressuring multilateral development banks and other global financial institutions to facilitate private-sector finance for sustainable development. The World Bank Group, in appropriate partnership with others, could provide leadership on this set of issues, and the United States is a majority shareholder in the Bank. The challenge is to make environmental protection central to long-term poverty reduction.

- The United States should support and help disseminate an updated international action plan for lead poisoning prevention. Dispersed lead continues to cross national boundaries in the form of industrial emissions and discharges, waste streams, consumer products, and cultural practices. Its impacts are overwhelmingly felt in poor and minority communities.

- The United States should help international, regional, and issue networks to incorporate best practices for lead poisoning prevention and to link to community-based programs, international initiatives, and to each other. The United States should also help to create community-based pilot projects to achieve coordinated international solutions based on the action plan for prevention.

- The United States should ratify the Convention on Biological Diversity. Ratification would establish biodiversity conservation as an overarching legal objective in the United States and stimulate the development of a comprehensive national biodiversity conservation strategy.

- As part of an international leadership effort to better manage waste and toxic chemicals, the United States should also ratify the Stockholm Convention on Persistent Organic Pollutants, the Rotterdam Convention on Prior Informed Consent, and the Basel Convention on the Control of Transboundary Movements of Hazardous Wastes.

10. The United States needs to improve the information and data available to the public to make decisions for sustainability.

- The U.S. government should analyze its environmental resource base and develop policies to ensure that its population does not exceed the carrying capacity of environmental resources, including the ability to draw on foreign resources.

- Congress should authorize a national commission on biodiversity conservation. The commission should (1) synthesize the existing science of biodiversity conservation to develop biodiversity measurements and conservation indices so that the status of biodiversity can be tracked and the efficacy of programs evaluated; (2) survey the existing legal mandates of the major federal land management and regulatory agencies to determine how well they promote biodiversity conservation and whether revisions to those mandates are necessary; and (3) assess the role of private land acquisition in biodiversity conservation.

- A national report card should be issued on smart growth. The public needs a score card to indicate, among other things, the actual number of acres of land preserved through various smart-growth strategies, the number of affordable housing units created through smart growth and environmental justice initiatives, and the number of road trips reduced as a result of implementing smart-growth principles. Continued progress in smart growth requires measurable benchmarks.

- States should develop measures to assess progress toward sustainability for brownfields redevelopment, and implement evaluation methods to determine whether the environmental risks to public health and welfare have truly been lessened or eliminated, and whether the original problems have a tendency to recur. States should also assess whether the promised economic benefits of brownfields development are being realized.

- Interested federal, state, and local officials need to standardize their accounting methods to account for municipal solid waste, construction and demolition waste, and non-hazardous industrial waste. The absence of standardized accounting makes it difficult to know how we are doing and what we need to do.
- The United States should urge the Organisation for Economic Co-operation and Development (OECD), which defines and monitors official development assistance, to incorporate sustainable development into its definition of ODA.
- The United States needs to consider the possibility that more significant changes in governance are needed to put the country on a sustainable course. We are faced with a variety of challenges—climate change, the budget deficit, health care, and Social Security—that often seem politically intractable. A major obstacle, though certainly not the only one, is the challenge that two-, four-, and six-year election cycles pose to solving problems that will take decades to solve. The president and Congress should consider establishing a National Commission for a Sustainable America to evaluate and make recommendations on changes in national governance, including both Congress and the Executive Branch, that may be needed to address these issues.

* * * * *

At the conclusion of *Hot, Flat, and Crowded: Why We Need a Green Revolution—and How It Can Renew America*, Thomas Friedman writes: "We need to redefine green and rediscover America and in so doing rediscover ourselves and what it means to be Americans. We are all Pilgrims again. We are all sailing on the *Mayflower* anew. We have not been to this shore before."

We have no experience with modern industrial societies that are sustainable, so we cannot be entirely clear about the exact destination. But the general direction is clear enough, and we have a roadmap for the next 5 to 10 years of the journey. We know what we need to do, and we also know why. As Americans, we are called to face this challenge and to seize this opportunity.

II. Six Areas of Greater Progress

Chapter 4

Local Governance and Sustainability: Major Progress, Significant Challenges

Jonathan D. Weiss

Localities in the United States have made tremendous strides toward sustainability in recent years. Mayors in particular have attracted increasing notice in responding to climate change and in implementing a number of groundbreaking green measures. This rising profile of local leadership on issues of sustainability, perhaps best epitomized by Mayor Richard Daley of Chicago, and the strong progress of other local sustainability efforts is indeed a positive trend. At the same time, this trend can often obscure the difficult challenges that remain for local sustainability—namely, our sprawling land use patterns; fragmented regional governance and cooperation; and the limits of what is possible without active support from federal and state governments.

This chapter first discusses recent progress toward sustainability made by mayors and other local entities. It then explores the challenges that remain to the advancement of such local efforts. Finally, the chapter recommends changes in law and policy to address these challenges. Ultimately, such changes are needed at all levels of governance in order to bring about an integrated approach to local sustainability. Local governments cannot do it alone.

Local Progress Toward Sustainability

To discuss local progress toward sustainability, this chapter adopts what are popularly called the "three Es" of sustainable development—environment, economics, and (social) equity. This framework reflects the goal of sustainable development, adopted at the United Nations Rio Earth Summit in 1992, as "development that is economically efficient, socially equitable, and responsible and environmentally sound."[1] A key for localities is to strive to bring together all three of these components, particularly environmental considerations, as part of an integrated decisionmaking process. Pursuing local sustainability can take many forms. Agenda 21, the action plan to implement the principles of the Rio Declaration, cited among other things the need for sustainable use of land, sustainable energy and transportation systems, and improved human resource development. And it encouraged localities to develop their own sustainability strategies.[2]

Achieving sustainability at the local level—the places where people live—is critical to influencing sustainability in general. Our growing interest in making local areas and the built environment more sustainable is evidenced by the vocabulary that has emerged since the 1990s. New terms like "sustainable communities/cities/regions," "livable communities/cities/regions," "smart growth," "new urbanism," "transit-oriented development," "green buildings/housing/neighborhoods/cities," and "brownfields" are now in common usage. And there is today a broader recognition that a good environment can enhance quality of life and bolster local economic competitiveness.[3]

Since 2003, several new comparative indices and rankings have been developed to measure the progress cities have made toward sustainability. SustainLane, an Internet and media company, began compiling city sustainability rankings in 2005 and 2006, measuring performance in 15 areas of sustainability, from public transit use to green buildings to housing affordability.[4] In 2007, SustainLane published the data in *How Green Is Your City?*[5]—the first systematic report card ranking the sustainability of the 50 largest U.S. cities. SustainLane captured and described a broad array of local initiatives among these cities, with many localities creating new environmental or sustainability offices or hiring sustainability coordinators.[6]

Such initiatives are taking place around the country, in cities large and small. In 2007, Fayetteville, Arkansas (population 67,158) hired its first sustainability coordinator and has proclaimed its ambition to "become the center of the sustainability movement."[7] *Newsweek* summed up the trend: "[A] remarkable patchwork of [local sustainability] programs is emerging. . . . In the process, city officials are discovering that these measures save money, reduce demands on overstretched utilities, and make cities more pleasant places to live and work."[8] While not all localities are integrating the three Es of sustainability in the same way, and not all use the term "sustainability," it is striking how many localities are innovating along these lines.

Climate Change and Mayoral Leadership

If there has been a single issue that has galvanized local interest in sustainability, it has been climate change. New climate change inventories and initiatives for carbon emission reduction were common to all of the top-ranking cities in the SustainLane city rankings.[9] And, as noted, U.S. mayors, both Democrats and Republicans, are seizing a leadership role.

While some cities have been involved in climate change as far back as 1993 through the work of the International Council for Local Environmental Initiatives (ICLEI), the turning point came in early 2005 as the Kyoto Protocol went into effect without the participation of the United States. At that time, Seattle Mayor Greg Nickels called on other mayors to reduce greenhouse gas emissions by 7 percent—the same cut that would have been required of the nation under Kyoto. What emerged was the Mayors Climate Protection Agreement, officially endorsed by the U.S. Conference of Mayors in June 2005. The agreement pledges that as part of reducing greenhouse gas emissions by 7 percent, the mayors will take such actions as reducing sprawl, promoting transportation alternatives, supporting green buildings, and cutting city power use.[10] To date, more than 900 mayors from all 50 states, the District of Columbia, and Puerto Rico have accepted the Kyoto Protocol by pledging to the U.S. Mayors Climate Protection Agreement.[11]

A key spur for local action was the perception among mayors that the federal government was dithering on climate change and energy conservation. As Mayor Nickels put it, "City by city across America mayors are taking action. Isn't it time our federal government joined the fray? Our grandchildren would appreciate it."[12]

In 1993, ICLEI had the foresight to launch the Cities for Climate Protection campaign to help local governments reduce greenhouse gases. However, ICLEI worked mainly with smaller, notably liberal cities such as Santa Monica, California.[13] As an organization, it also remained too wedded in its general work to the cumbersome language adopted at the 1992 Rio Earth Summit, calling for implementation of local Agenda 21s. ICLEI called its efforts "Community 21," a reference few communities understood and that ICLEI was never able to popularize. But since 2005, the U.S. Conference of Mayors has worked hand in hand with ICLEI, raising the profile of the latter organization. ICLEI now even uses the helpful explanatory tagline of "ICLEI—Local Governments for Sustainability" to describe itself.

Leadership in Chicago and New York City

Arguably, the highest-profile cities now tackling sustainability are Chicago and New York, thanks in no small part to their respective mayors. Since Mayor Richard Daley took office in 1989, he has burnished his reputation as the "green mayor" through a broad array of initiatives, focusing on urban greening, energy efficiency, and enlisting private-sector engagement.[14] The city has created rooftop gardens on top of city hall and other government buildings, more than 100 miles of bicycle paths, and stunning new parks. It has planted half a million trees while encouraging brownfields redevelopment and green affordable housing. And it is in the process of retrofitting 15 million square feet of public buildings with efficient equipment for heating and cooling, lighting, and ventilation. When the retrofitting project is complete, energy savings for the city are estimated to be $6 million annually, with annual savings estimated at 30,000 tons of CO_2, 84 tons of nitrous oxide, and 128 tons of sulfur dioxide. Chicago has set a goal of drawing 20 percent of its energy from renewable resources by 2010.[15]

To Mayor Daley, improving the environment helps promote the city, retain and draw residents, and strengthen Chicago's economic competitiveness. While the mayor has received some criticism for not doing more to empower community-led groups, he is successfully institutionalizing his efforts and forging innovative partnerships, such as a public-private partnership to build the first shopping center in the Midwest for environmentally focused stores and services. Says Chicago Alderman May Ann Smith: "We're creating places people want to be, not places people want to flee."[16] Viewing sustainability in a broad context, the mayor has also made improving the Chicago public schools a top priority and continues to work with neighboring jurisdictions on promoting metropolitan cooperation. The New York Times summed up Chicago's progress:

> Chicago has become a global model for how a metropolis can pursue environmental goals to achieve economic success. During the last decade, the city's performance has been off the charts, local boosters say. Chicago attracted more than 100,000 new residents, added tens of thousands of downtown jobs, prompted a high-rise housing boom, reduced poverty rates, built thousands of

affordable homes, spurred a $9 billion-a-year visitor and conven-
tion industry, and transformed itself into one of the most beautiful
cities in America.[17]

More recently, Mayor Michael Bloomberg has grabbed headlines
for his bold efforts in New York. In September 2006 he created the
city's first-ever Office of Long-Term Planning and Sustainability.[18]
Then in April 2007 he announced PlaNYC—an aggressive strategy to
improve NYC's sustainability by the year 2030. The approach includes, among other things, a commitment to reducing the city's carbon emissions by 30 percent over two decades, improving existing infrastructure, ensuring that all residents live within 10 minutes of a
park, creating homes for a million more residents, and adopting traf-
fic-congestion pricing based upon a system currently used in Singapore and London.[19] As with Mayor Daley, Mayor Bloomberg is also
experimenting with sustainable policy reforms in a host of other areas,
including school reform, affordable housing, and anti-poverty measures. Though his congestion pricing proposal was notably scuttled by
the state legislature, Bloomberg has generally received kudos for his
sustainability efforts and has maintained strong popularity.[20]

Other Local and Regional Efforts

While giving attention to these high-profile, mayoral efforts, we
must also remember that their efforts build on the pioneering work of
nonprofit groups and others in their communities, as well as the pioneering work of a number of other communities. Such other communities long established in their sustainability planning include Santa
Monica, California; Portland, Oregon; Chattanooga, Tennessee; and
Austin, Texas, to name just a few.[21] Counties are also undertaking a
host of innovative measures. The National Association of Counties
(NACo) maintains a Center for Sustainable Communities, which recognizes counties involved in creative partnerships through its Sustainable Communities Awards Program. Recent winners have included
Arlington County, Virginia (for its transit-oriented, mixed-use development); Woodbury County, Iowa (for its sustainable local food systems program); and King County, Washington (for its parks and public
transportation project).[22] Sarasota County, Florida, is developing a
holistic, performance-based approach with a number of programs and
practices that aim to integrate environmental, economic, and social
concerns—from preserving open space to building affordable hous-

ing to reforming zoning laws and permitting in order to promote mixed-use, green development.[23]

Meanwhile, some collaborative regional efforts are moving forward. Envision Utah, a non-profit public/private partnership of over 150 government, business, civic, religious, media, community, and environmental leaders, is a model of a consensus-building approach to smart growth planning. The partnership formed in 1997 to develop a growth strategy for the Greater Wasatch Area, a 100-mile-long corridor along the Great Salt Lake and the Wasatch Mountain range. Its first major project was to develop the Quality Growth Strategy for the region out of a planning process that featured intensive public engagement in scenario planning. Envision Utah assists local municipalities in implementing the strategy through demonstration pilots and a toolbox of resources. This planning effort has led to some public and municipal attitudinal and policy changes supporting smarter growth, along with greater emphasis on public transportation.[24] Inspired by Envision Utah, the Urban Land Institute has promoted several regional visioning projects across the country through its multi-stakeholder Reality Check planning exercises.[25]

Nonprofit groups are also increasing linkages with each other to promote local sustainability efforts and issues. The U.S. Green Building Council, the Natural Resources Defense Council (NRDC), and the Congress for New Urbanism developed in 2007 a new Leadership in Energy and Environmental Design for Neighborhood Development (LEED-ND) program. The program, which is designed to certify environmentally friendly developments, builds on the highly successful LEED building standards created in 2000. Drawing on LEED standards, green affordable housing has also taken off in recent years. The Enterprise Foundation and NRDC are teaming up to undertake a $550 million Green Communities Initiative to build "environmentally friendly affordable homes across the country."[26]

Challenges to Local Sustainability

Sprawl and the Dearth of Regional Planning

For all the progress being in made in cities like Chicago and the increasing examples of energy-efficient and new urbanist development, continued sprawl in the outer, largely auto-dependent suburbs has carried on. A 2007 research team led by Gerrit Knaap of the University of Maryland studied development patterns in five areas (Maricopa

County, Arizona; Orange County, Florida; Minneapolis-St. Paul, Minnesota; Montgomery County, Maryland; and Portland, Oregon) and concluded:

> For advocates of "smart growth," the good news is that single family lot sizes are falling and neighborhoods are becoming more internally accessible. For the same advocates, the bad news, however, is more extensive: houses are becoming larger, neighborhoods are becoming more isolated, land uses remain separated, and pedestrian accessibility to commercial uses is falling. If these trends continue, it is likely that housing will remain unaffordable and traffic congestion will only get worse.[27]

If there has been a silver lining to the ongoing economic recession and the spike in oil prices during the first half of 2008, it is that they have fueled the signs of a new countertrend. As the *New York Times* reported in June 2008, "Suddenly, the economics of suburban life are under assault as skyrocketing energy prices inflate the costs of reaching, heating, and cooling homes on the distant edges of metropolitan areas."[28] Living closer to cities in smaller spaces has become more desirable, as evidenced by real estate values, and there has been a bump-up in public transportation usage.[29] At the same time, more and more people are beginning to see the link between climate change and the way in which cities grow.[30]

However, it remains to be seen how far this countertrend can go. There remain real obstacles to turning back the clock on sprawl and overcoming the governance barriers that have been erected. The political, economic, environmental, and social geography of metropolitan areas has changed tremendously in the past few decades. As areas have sprawled outward, the number of jurisdictions has increased, with the issues that localities face now often transcending limited jurisdictional boundaries. Poor land use patterns in one municipality lead to a number of externalities that affect residents in other municipalities, such as increased traffic, air pollution, water pollution, water consumption, and the destruction of wetlands.

The issues of social equity across metropolitan areas are particularly thorny, including widening income divisions across regions and increased discrepancies among local tax bases. Such problems are most acute for lower-income residents clustered in older or isolated neighborhoods, where residents often lack access to affordable housing and good public schools. Other challenges include the growing imbalance (the so-called spatial mismatch) between where jobs are located and where the people who need those jobs live; the lack of adequate public transportation; and the precipitous drop in the number of middle-class families in urban areas like New York City. In addition, as communities absorb more and more immigrants and become more multicultural—itself a positive trend—we are left with the challenge of effectively incorporating the needs and circumstances of these new residents into planning strategies and decisions.

All of these issues cry out for stronger regional planning and governance. However, while there has been much talk in this area and examples of progress like Envision Utah, not enough has been done. Even Envision Utah, which deserves to be applauded, has not yet led to any major state laws or regional governance structures in the Greater Wasatch Area.[31]

As a sign of the difficulty of regional cooperation, the U.S. Conference of Mayors no longer teams with NACo as part of the Joint Center on Sustainable Communities; losing the mayors' participation, "Joint" was dropped from the name of the Center, which now serves only counties. The Joint Center had once earned praise for promoting cross-boundary partnerships and integrated decisionmaking.[32]

Lack of Consistent Federal and State Support

Clearly, one of the reasons for the rise in the national stature of mayors on sustainability has been the vacuum of federal leadership on sustainability initiatives. But if the local initiatives that mayors have led are to be truly institutionalized and brought to scale, the federal government, and often state governments as well, need to do more to provide leadership on sustainability and support for localities in pushing for sustainability and regional governance. What takes place at the local level is influenced by policies and practices at higher levels of governance. Moreover, for localities to make truly lasting progress on climate change in particular, strong national and international leadership is needed.

Climate change itself is the ultimate externality. Even if a vulnerable coastal city is committed to reducing greenhouse gases and even if it works with its suburbs so that together they reduce greenhouse gases and grow in a smarter way, all of its efforts will be for naught amid dramatic rising sea levels if there is not a broader policy that deals with the problem on a regional and national scale. Local sustainability and national sustainability must be mutually reinforcing.

The new Barack Obama Administration alone cannot solve our local sustainability challenges, but it offers hope that stronger partnerships, incentives, and coordination may become available to help support and reinforce local efforts.

Recommendations

To promote local sustainability, a number of key steps can be taken at the federal, state, regional, and municipal levels. Localities act within the context of constitutional and statutory authority set by higher levels of government, and they need supportive policies and laws—the "rules and tools"—from these higher levels of government in order to truly thrive. Given the current economic and budget realities facing our nation and communities across the country, it is critical that these steps be placed in the context of how they can help strengthen national and local competitiveness.

1. National Level: We need federal incentives for smart sustainability policies in a cross-section of areas, including climate change, transportation, housing, education, energy efficiency, infrastructure reinvestment, immigration, environment, land use, and regional coordination.

The U.S. Congress and the Obama Administration should enlist specific conditional funding mechanisms that provide incentives for municipalities to cooperate and grow intelligently and expand the power of metropolitan planning organizations (MPOs), which are designed in part to assist in federal transportation funding decisions as applied to metropolitan regions. One important law that the federal government must enforce is the Clean Air Act[33] requirement for local compliance on air standards and the requirement that federal highway funding be cut in the case of noncompliance. Lawmakers should also replicate the regional transportation framework in other areas that require regional planning, such as water resources and access to affordable housing. Further, to the extent that gas prices drop back to pre-2008 levels, Congress should increase the gasoline tax (while not unduly burdening low-income citizens or rural communities) and steer these funds toward local job-creating sustainability projects, automotive energy-efficiency research, and public transportation. This would help discourage our persistent over-reliance on automobiles while encouraging the recent positive countertrends in housing location preference, alternative energy development, and transportation behavior.

2. State and Regional Level: States need to move toward systems that better promote regional governance and smart growth, and help reduce harmful regional inequities.

Current state laws frequently promote the autonomy of individual municipalities to the detriment of sustainability efforts at the local level. Moreover, they often compel such municipalities to rely on local property taxes to support public schools and other municipal functions. Such a system creates competition and inequities across municipalities in a region, and it serves to fuel urban sprawl by making tax-poor, older, usually urban neighborhoods less attractive to families. Such older municipalities are thus often left without the sufficient revenue and financial base necessary to adopt new sustainability measures and support quality schools. Through strong smart-growth laws, integrated statewide planning, and more sensible funding, the states can also influence growth, encourage regional cooperation and supportive local zoning, and help reduce the revenue penalty suffered by low-income jurisdictions.

3. Municipal Level: Mayors and communities must not only live up to the Mayors Climate Protection Agreement; they must take advantage of the new consciousness about climate change by linking that consciousness to other sustainability areas.

Municipalities need to engage further in open, integrated planning that takes into account environmental, economic and equity considerations, and must adopt and implement supportive local zoning and measures that can foster mixed-use, smart-growth development. As discussed, such actions would greatly benefit from cooperation with other jurisdictions, though it is recognized that strong federal and state incentives may be required in order to do so. But as we have learned from many of the local successes, much can be accomplished within a single municipality, and lessons can be passed on between municipalities. An increasing number of governments, for instance, are moving to (and some even beyond) standards set by Salt Lake City by requiring LEED approval for all of its own buildings, plus any commercial or residential building that receives city funding. Municipalities can also make a further dramatic difference through better placement of these facilities, in order to promote smart growth.

Conclusion

Localities have come a long way in taking sustainability into their own hands. American local leaders once visited their counterparts abroad to learn about best practices. While they should still do so, now more and more leaders from abroad are coming to the United States to learn about our innovations and progress. Our mayors are becoming international stars. Our eco-architects are in demand globally. But we cannot forget how much work needs to be done to truly grow our communities in robust, sustainable, and inclusive ways. It is a long-term process that involves changing the rules of the game and enforcing those new rules, transcending governmental boundaries at all levels, and including citizens in the process. To become truly sustainable, localities cannot go it alone.

ENDNOTES

1. This definition was adopted in 1992 by the Rio Declaration on Environment and Development and Agenda 21 of the U.N. Conference on Environment and Development.

2. U.N. Conference on Environment and Development (UNCED), Agenda 21, U.N. Doc. A/CONF.151.26 (1992).

3. *See* MATTHEW KAHN, GREEN CITIES: URBAN GROWTH AND THE ENVIRONMENT (2006).

4. Warren Karlenzig, *What Makes Today's Green City, in* GROWING GREENER CITIES (Eugenie Birch & Susan Wachter eds., 2008). The increased use of such measurements is also making it easier for communities to adopt indicators to help track their progress toward sustainability.

5. WARREN KARLENZIG, HOW GREEN IS YOUR CITY? THE SUSTAINLANE U.S. CITY RANKINGS (2007).

6. Karlenzig, *supra* notes 4 and 5.

7. Ylan Mui, *Green Valley in Wal-Mart's Back Yard*, WASH. POST, Sept. 7, 2007; *New Sustainability Coordinator Gets to Work*, City of Fayetteville Newsletter, June 2007, at 2.

8. Ann Underwood, *Mayors Take the Lead*, NEWSWEEK, Apr. 16, 2007, at 69.

9. Karlenzig, *supra* note 4.

10. U.S. Conference of Mayors, U.S. Mayors Climate Protection Agreement, *at* http://usmayors.org/climateprotection/documents/mcpAgreement.pdf.

11. U.S. Conference of Mayors, Mayors Climate Protection Center, List of Participating Mayors, *at* http://usmayors.org/climateprotection/list.asp (last visited July 1, 2008).

12. *600 Mayors in All 50 States and Puerto Rico Take Action to Reduce Global Warming*, FORBES, July 13, 2007, *at* www.forbes.com/prnewswire/feeds/prnewswire/2007/07/13/prnewswire200707131211PR_NEWS_B_NET_DC_DCF034.html.

13. Jonathan Weiss, *Local Governance, in* STUMBLING TOWARD SUSTAINABILITY (John C. Dernbach ed., 2002).

14. Keith Schneider, *To Revitalize a City, Try Spreading Some Mulch*, N.Y. TIMES, May 17, 2006.

15. City of Chicago, Conserve Chicago Together, website *at* http://egov.cityofchicago.Org/city/webportal/portalEntityHomeAction.do?entityName=Conserve+Chicago+Together&entityNameEnumValue=144 (last visited July 1, 2008).

16. Neal Peirce, *Sustainable Cities*, PROSPECT, Jan./Feb.2007.

17. Schneider, *supra* note 14.

18. Press Release, New York City Office of the Mayor, Mayor Bloomberg Announces Creation of Office of Long-Term Planning and Sustainability (Sept. 21, 2006), *available at* www.nyc.gov/html/om/html/2006b/pr335-06.html.

19. *See generally* PlaNYC 2030, *at* www.nyc.gov/planyc (last visited July 1, 2008).

20. David Chen & Dalia Sussman, *Bloomberg's Popularity Survives Darkening Mood of City, Poll Finds*, N.Y. TIMES, June 17, 2008.

21. *See* KENT E. PORTNEY, TAKING SUSTAINABLE CITIES SERIOUSLY (2003); THE SUSTAINABLE URBAN DEVELOPMENT READER (Steven M. Wheeler & Timothy Beatley eds., 2004).

22. The National Association of Counties, Sustainable Communities Awards Program, *available at* www.naco.org/Template.cfm?Section=Technical_Assistance&template=/ContentManagement/ContentDisplay.cfm&ContentID=24011 (last visited July 1, 2008).

23. Sarasota County Government On-line: Sustainability, www.scgov.net/sustainability/ (last visited July 1, 2008).

24. Envision Utah, *at* www.envisionutah.org (last visited July 1, 2008).

25. Urban Land Institute, *at* www.uli.org/Content/NavigationMenu/MyCommunity/RegionalVisioningandCooperation/RealityCheck/Reality_Check.htm (last visited July 1, 2008).

26. Press Release, Natural Resources Defense Council, Enterprise and NRDC Launch $550 Million Initiative for Healthy, Environmentally Friendly Affordable Housing (Sept. 28, 2004), *available at* www.nrdc.org/media/pressreleases/040928.asp; *see* Green Communities Initiative, *at* www.greencommunities online.org/index.asp (last visited July 1, 2008).

27. GERRIT-JAN KNAAP ET AL., NAT'L CTR. FOR SMART GROWTH RESEARCH & EDUC., MEASURING PATTERNS OF URBAN DEVELOPMENT: NEW INTELLIGENCE FOR THE WAR ON SPRAWL (2007).

28. Peter S. Goodman. *Fuel Prices Shift Math for Life in Far Suburbs*, N.Y. TIMES, June 25, 2008.

29. *Id*; *see also* Clifford Kraus, *Gas Prices Send Surge of Riders to Mass Transit*, N.Y. TIMES, May 10, 2008.

30. REID EWING ET AL., GROWING COOLER (2007).

31. *See* Envision Utah, *supra* note 24.

32. Weiss, *supra* note 13.

33. 42 U.S.C. §§7401-7671q, ELR STAT. CAA §§101-618.

Chapter 5

Brownfields Development: From Individual Sites to Smart Growth

Joel B. Eisen

In the late 1980s, communities across America faced a number of obstacles to successful urban redevelopment. One obstacle, though hardly the only one,[1] was "the fear and uncertainty associated with potential environmental contamination [that] was seriously undermining efforts to keep urban areas vital."[2] This fear of environmental contamination focused on abandoned or underused urban sites that were not already the target of federal environmental attention and enforcement, such as those highly contaminated sites found on the National Priorities List. These sites differ widely in their prior uses, including former steel mills and other industrial properties, gas stations and other commercial tracts, and even residential properties.

Collectively, these have come to be known as "brownfields." Federal law today defines a brownfield site as "real property, the expansion, redevelopment, or reuse of which may be complicated by the presence or potential presence of a hazardous substance, pollutant, or contaminant."[3] The term differentiates these sites from "greenfields," which are suburban and exurban locations that developers have been thought to prefer for new construction.

Remediation and reuse of brownfields is a hallmark of sustainable land use because the societal and economic benefits of remediating and rehabilitating an underused urban parcel are often greater than those of comparable development taking place at greenfields locations.[4] These benefits are mentioned frequently in the large (and growing) body of brownfields literature, where brownfields redevelopment is seen as especially desirable because it meshes with the goals of the smart growth movement. However, not all brownfields redevelopment activity is "smart," for development of individual sites continues to be parcel-specific and state brownfields programs do not fully integrate well-known benchmarks of sustainable development. These benchmarks, to which this chapter's recommendations are linked, include:

- Effective public involvement in brownfields remediation
  and reuse decisions;
- Integrated decisionmaking procedures in state voluntary
  cleanup programs (VCPs); and
- Measurable outcomes for sustainability embodied in program designs.

The Brownfields Challenge

The extent of the brownfields problem remains significant, as indicated in a 2004 report by the National Association of Local Government Environmental Professionals (NALGEP) and the Northeast-
Midwest Institute (NEMW). The report states: "Virtually every community in America is plagued by idle properties that lay abandoned for
years due to fear of environmental contamination, unknown cleanup
costs, and potential legal liability issues. It is estimated that there
could be as many as 1 million of these so-called "brownfield" properties nationwide."[5]

However, the past two decades have seen the birth of what could be
called the brownfields industry.[6] Extensive redevelopment activities
are taking place at formerly abandoned or underused sites,[7] spurred by
two major legal developments: (1) the emergence in virtually every
state of voluntary cleanup programs (VCPs) and other brownfields
programs and initiatives; and (2) federal protection for brownfields
developers through a 2002 amendment to the Comprehensive Environmental Response, Compensation, and Liability Act (CERCLA, or
"Superfund law").[8] The 2002 law provides protection against subsequent liability for cleanup of a brownfield site for a developer that
conducts a cleanup in a state VCP, so long as it meets the requirements
of the 2006 rule of the U.S. Environmental Protection Agency (EPA)
to make "all appropriate inquiries" (AAI) before acquiring ownership
of brownfields sites.[9] The AAI rule establishes specific requirements
for conducting due diligence into the previous ownership, uses, and
environmental conditions of a site for the purposes of qualifying for liability protections available to landowners under CERCLA.

Current brownfields redevelopment initiatives go far beyond attention to liability protection, however, involving full-fledged programs
at the state and federal levels. The EPA's Office of Brownfields
Cleanup and Redevelopment administers its Brownfields Program to
"empower states, communities and other stakeholders in economic

redevelopment to work together in a timely manner to prevent, assess, safely clean up and sustainably reuse brownfields."[10] To that end, EPA offers grants for activities such as assessment of site contamination and cleanup, as well as loans, training, and education programs.[11] Several other federal agencies also offer funding and other resources for brownfields projects.[12] Section 211 of the 2002 federal brownfields law added the new section 104(k) of CERCLA, establishing a federal grant and loan system for brownfield site characterization and assessment and brownfield remediation.[13] Up to $200 million per year was authorized for brownfields assessment and cleanup under this program.[14] It has been reported, however, that these programs have not been fully funded and that more public funding is necessary for successful brownfields remediation and reuse.[15]

State programs for the remediation and reuse of brownfields have matured rapidly since their inception in the late 1980s, with 49 states now featuring such programs and many (including such pioneering states as Minnesota and Pennsylvania) having over a decade of experience in processing sites through their programs. By 2002 it could be said that "[a] decade of experience with state and federal brownfields programs has yielded broadly perceived successes."[16] In cities across the nation, brownfields have been converted to industrial, commercial, residential, and recreational uses. Examples abound in cities such as Houston,[17] Chicago,[18] and Trenton,[19] to name a few.

Brownfields and Smart Growth

In the past several years, there has been a much greater link between the smart growth movement and brownfields remediation and reuse. Smart growth refers to the myriad "creative strategies to develop in ways that preserve natural lands and critical environmental areas, protect water and air quality, and reuse already-developed land," which stand in opposition to the existing patterns of development that result in suburban and exurban sprawl.[20] EPA's Smart Growth in Brownfield Communities initiative asserts that "[b]rownfield redevelopment is an essential component of smart growth, as both seek to return abandoned and underutilized sites to their fullest potential as community and economic assets."[21] As another report puts it, the two movements—brownfields redevelopment and smart growth—developed from different roots but have similar goals: "Redevelopment of existing buildings and land, including contaminated brownfield sites, has been pursued since the early 1990s, and is a separate activity from the smart growth initiatives. However, both share the same goals of providing economic growth, creating jobs, and creating a healthy environment."[22]

Because urban sites are often good candidates for infill development that can preclude the need to build at a greenfields location (and thereby avoid the perpetuation of suburban and exurban sprawl), "[r]euse of urban space . . . is seen almost reflexively as smart growth."[23] But one should be careful to avoid viewing all brownfields revitalization as consistent with smart growth, because most brownfield sites are developed on a parcel-by-parcel basis, under the control of site developers—not as part of a plan for sustainability. Under these conditions, "there is no guarantee that the growth it promises to provide is 'smart.'"[24]

Brownfields and Sustainable Development

Three conditions must be satisfied for brownfields remediation and reuse programs to achieve sustainable development:

(1) *Effective public involvement in brownfields remediation and reuse decisions.* As Agenda 21 of the U.N. Conference on Environment and Development notes, "citizens must be involved in major environmental decisions and receive timely and coherent information to enable them to take part in relevant decisions." To accomplish this in the brownfields revitalization context, an effective public participation system is needed to provide for input by the affected community throughout the process, from project selection to remediation and completion of the project." One report argues, "Involve Citizens From the Start—Community involvement and consensus is one of the most important ingredients for a successful brownfield project."[25] At the federal level, EPA's Sustainable Brownfields Model Framework calls for brownfields revitalization to take place as a "conscious, intended collaboration between private sector organizations, public agencies, and the community as a whole."[26] State VCPs rarely require such collaboration, however, and only those developers savvy enough to form partnerships with affected communities typically seek local input.

(2) *Integrated decisionmaking procedures in state VCPs.* Agenda 21 calls for "the progressive integration of social, economic, and environmental issues" in governmental decisionmaking.[27] In any brownfields remediation and reuse project, there are many important points where consideration of a broad range of factors is necessary.

First, at the stage where the merits of a proposed revitalization project are being assessed, the project should fit within an overall plan of development for the affected community. One report observes, "Communities will succeed in brownfields revitalization when they consider these properties as community and economic opportunities that happen to have an environmental challenge, and connect brownfields initiatives to their broader community vision and revitalization priorities."[28] Second, once a project has been selected and remediation is taking place, the state should exercise vigorous oversight to ensure that the cleanup is sufficient.

In practice, much of the decisionmaking related to brownfields redevelopment takes place at the state and local levels. The states bear responsibility for administering cleanups in VCPs, and developers rely on state releases from liability after the 2002 federal law limited the EPA's ability to reopen a cleanup conducted in a VCP.[29] Of course, local governments are involved because they exercise their traditional control powers over land use decisions.

Unfortunately, most state and local approaches to brownfields redevelopment continue to fall short of the ideal of integrated decisionmaking. The parcel-by-parcel approach continues to dominate in state VCPs, and states do not typically require brownfields developers to show that their proposed reuse of the property bears any relationship to an overall vision for the community, nor do states evaluate this after remediation work has been done and the new uses of the sites are in place. Project selection continues to be left to developers, and states have largely delegated administration of the cleanup phase to developers themselves (or, in an increasing trend, to independent contractors licensed by the states).

(3) *Measurable outcomes for sustainability.* To date, there has been little "systematic, careful documentation of actual practice at a wide range of [brownfield] sites."[30] Because a large number of projects have been processed through state brownfields programs and VCPs, more should and indeed could be done to assess whether brownfields remediation and reuse has truly been beneficial to the affected community.[31] States should assess the success of their brownfields programs using concrete metrics that reflect the broad scope of their urban redevelopment goals, which requires them to go far beyond observing simply whether a project has created jobs or increased the local tax base.

If brownfields revitalization is indeed to be considered as part of smart growth strategies, it is necessary that program effectiveness be evaluated in an appropriate context. One commentator calls the relative lack of data on whether brownfields reuse is providing the claimed benefits a "lost opportunity . . . to empirically test different approaches to real property remediation."[32] In-depth analysis might suggest in a given state (or for a given type of project) that voluntary cleanup programs have spurred economic redevelopment appropriate for a community. Or it might not, and for this reason, "state regulators may be consequently reluctant to perform this searching analysis."[33]

Thus, while much progress has been made toward sustainable reuse of brownfields, considerable work still needs to be done.

Recommendations

Three conditions for sustainability were listed in the chapter's introduction:
- Effective public involvement in brownfields remediation and reuse decisions;
- Integrated decisionmaking procedures in state voluntary cleanup programs (VCPs); and
- Measurable outcomes for sustainability embodied in program designs.

The following four recommendations are designed to meet those requirements.

1. Increase the use of areawide brownfields initiatives. States should do more to integrate brownfields remediation and reuse with their existing programs for promoting economic development. One promising way in which this is taking place—in states such as New Jersey and New York—is the establishment of areawide brownfields initiatives, in which state regulators attempt to address multiple brownfields in the same community.[34] A prominent feature of these initiatives is early and extensive involvement by citizen steering committees. These programs can provide for more enhanced public participation and a wider focus on community redevelopment than the narrow, parcel-by-parcel approach. This recommendation would enhance public participation as well as integrated decisionmaking by coordinating remediation and economic development.

In New Jersey's Brownfields Development Area (BDA) initiative, for example, the state's Department of Environmental Protection

(DEP) "works with selected communities affected by multiple brownfields to design and implement remediation and reuse plans for these properties simultaneously."[35] A recent article by a former assistant commissioner of DEP responsible for developing the initiative notes that "the BDA Initiative guarantees local involvement" because by law it gives "the reuse preferences of the steering committee substantial persuasive force."[36] He also notes that the initiative has the potential to address contamination that has migrated across multiple sites, rather than just that which is present at an individual site.[37]

A recent report by the Lincoln Institute of Land Policy observes that "[i]n contrast to site-specific remediation, the areawide approach of the [New Jersey] BDA provides a framework that addresses the larger physical, political and social contexts of an affected community."[38] The broader approach makes it a much more potent vehicle for achieving sustainable development than the parcel-specific approach. Similar initiatives should be considered by more states.

2. Develop measures to assess progress toward sustainability. It is difficult to get a handle on the overall impact that brownfields projects have on communities because doing so requires, "among other things, accounting for the wide variety in state program features, the numbers of cases handled, and the types and numbers of results. It also requires looking longitudinally at a statistically significant sample of sites to see whether environmental problems develop or persist after a period of years."[39] For true sustainable development, however, this sort of long-term analysis is exactly what is required.

In particular, states should develop evaluation methods that address two distinct sets of issues. First is whether the environmental risks to public health and welfare have truly been lessened or eliminated, or whether the original problems would recur in the future, after sites have presumably been remediated in state VCPs. Many states allow sites into their brownfields programs that are more contaminated than one might expect given the model of a brownfield site as one that is lightly contaminated and not currently the target of state or federal environmental enforcement.[40] Thus, it should not be assumed that the problem has simply vanished, but instead state environmental regulators should have safeguards in place for long-term monitoring of brownfield sites that have been processed through their programs.

Second, the states should conduct "a more thorough analysis of whether brownfields developers . . . are consistently providing prom-

ised economic benefits in return for involvement with and remediation of their sites."[41] Such an analysis requires more than simple
repetition of developers' promises that jobs and tax revenues will flow
from particular projects. One broad effort to assess whether a goal of
"returning formerly contaminated sites to long-term, sustainable, and
productive use" is being met was a multi-program, multi-factor analysis by EPA's Region 3 conducted in 2006.[42] Regional EPA staff, working with a number of stakeholders, sought to develop quantifiable data
on land uses occurring on cleanup sites to establish baseline information" that would go beyond anecdotal data to assess "[t]ypes of uses
and reuses occurring," the "[r]elationship between the cleanup status
of sites and reuse," "[l]ocal economic, social, or ecological benefits
from reuse on cleanup sites," and "[c]hallenges in collecting this kind
of information prior to developing and promoting broader national
measures for land revitalization goals."[43] Analytical rigor on this
model should become more widespread in brownfields programs.

   3. Promote "green building" practices in site reuse. Development
at an infill site often involves a complete overhaul of existing infrastructure, so it is an ideal time to employ the increasing array of building design and construction techniques that enhance environmental
performance of new buildings. EPA notes on its sustainability website
that "[g]reen or sustainable building is the practice of creating healthier and more resource-efficient models of construction, renovation,
operation, maintenance, and demolition."[44] "Green" buildings incorporate energy and environmentally desirable techniques, from energy
conservation to the use of healthy building materials and waste reduction strategies. This recommendation, of course, directly addresses a
project's environmental performance.

   The NALGEP/NEMW report states that sustainable brownfield reuse involves "[p]romot[ing] environmentally responsible reuse via
green building, low impact development practices, smart growth
strategies, preservation of parks and open space, transit-oriented development, and pollution prevention."[45] One outstanding example of
how this can work in practice is the Chicago Center for Green Technology, a brownfield redevelopment in Chicago whose building quali-
fied for the U.S. Green Building Council's Leadership in Energy and
Environmental Development (LEED) platinum rating, the culmina-
tion of a rigorous evaluation of green building and design techniques
used in the Center's construction.[46] EPA has several initiatives that
link green buildings and brownfields revitalization. Its Green Build-

ings on Brownfields Initiative has sponsored a number of pilot projects, and its ER3 Initiative helps developers identify techniques such as those used at the Chicago site.[47] As EPA notes, "[b]y incorporating sustainable practices and principles into their projects, developers of contaminated sites can minimize the impact of the project on the environment without sacrificing profitability."[48] More brownfields developers should take advantage of these opportunities.

4. Develop "second generation" policies to improve performance of state VCPs.

The NALGEP/NEMW report states:

> Despite the tremendous progress of state voluntary cleanup programs, there are opportunities to improve state brownfields programs by: (1) providing sufficient staff to ensure timely approvals for voluntary cleanups; (2) increasing funding for site assessment, cleanup, and predevelopment costs; (3) better leveraging funding from state underground storage tank programs with other sources of brownfields funding, to promote the cleanup and reuse of sites contaminated with petroleum; and (4) obtaining greater involvement in brownfields projects from state economic development, transportation, infrastructure, land use and housing agencies.[49]

A recent article on the performance of New Jersey's large and active VCP reported a number of shortcomings, including a slow pace of cleanups and suboptimal oversight of contaminated sites.[50] In part, as the report above notes, this stems from funding and staffing levels that are inadequate to process sites efficiently through the program.[51] A worrisome development in New Jersey is the resistance by state regulators to assuming even minor increases in their oversight responsibilities, as shown in their recent VCP regulations.[52] If states such as New Jersey are to exercise vigorous oversight over brownfields developers, they must take a more active role in ensuring that cleanups are done properly and in a timely way. This recommendation directly addresses all three conditions for sustainability.

The states are missing another opportunity to improve their brownfields programs because at present these programs tend to operate independently of their counterpart agencies in state governments.[53] This does not allow for the sort of searching analysis of long-term project benefits that should be a central feature of brownfields policies. A specific instance in which state economic development and environmental regulators could cooperate would be an ongoing determination of whether the sites that have been processed through brownfields programs and VCPs match those that fit state and local development criteria.[54]

Conclusion

Simply stating that brownfields remediation constitutes sustainable development or is consistent with smart growth principles may not make sense in the context of a given project or as part of an urban development strategy for an entire community. Unfortunately, state regulators continue to follow a developer-centered approach that puts control of site decisions in the hands of developers and is loath to undo the advantages conferred on developers for coming voluntarily to the states. This is a major trend that should be reversed, with a second generation of brownfields policies adopting the recommendations set forth above,[55] if the programs are to attain the goals of sustainable development.

ENDNOTES

1. KRIS WERNSTEDT ET AL., RESOURCES FOR THE FUTURE, THE BROWNFIELDS PHENOMENON: MUCH ADO ABOUT SOMETHING OR THE TIMING OF THE SHREWD? 4 (Nov. 2004) [hereinafter BROWNFIELDS PHENOMENON] (mentioning such factors as "the expectations and behavior of public and private parties involved in the development, environmental, and financial risks; the importance of subsidies; and the investment climate of host communities" as important in brownfields revitalization decisions), *available at* www.rff.org/Documents/RFF-DP-04-46.pdf.

2. NAT'L ASS'N OF LOCAL GOV'T PROFESSIONALS & NORTHEAST-MIDWEST INST., UNLOCKING BROWNFIELDS: KEYS TO COMMUNITY REVITALIZATION 3 (2004) [hereinafter UNLOCKING BROWNFIELDS].

3. 42 U.S.C. §9601(39)(A) (2002).

4. *See generally* UNLOCKING BROWNFIELDS, *supra* note 2, at 2.

5. UNLOCKING BROWNFIELDS, *supra* note 2, at 3; *see generally* U.S. CONFERENCE OF MAYORS, RECYCLING AMERICA'S LAND: A NATIONAL REPORT ON BROWNFIELDS REDEVELOPMENT (2006), *available at* http://usmayors.org/74thAnnualMeeting/brownfieldsreport_060506.pdf (last visited Apr. 26, 2007) (discussing brownfields challenges).

6. Joel B. Eisen, *Brownfields at 20: A Critical Reevaluation*, 34 FORDHAM URB. L.J. 101, 101 (2007) [hereinafter Eisen, *Brownfields at 20*].

7. *See generally id.*

8. *See* Small Business Liability Relief and Brownfields Revitalization Act of 2002, 42 U.S.C. §§9604-9605, 9607, 9622, 9628 (2002). EPA provides a snapshot of each state's VCP and brownfields programs in U.S. EPA, STATE BROWNFIELDS AND VOLUNTARY RESPONSE PROGRAMS: AN UPDATE FROM THE STATES, *available at* epa.gov/brownfields/pubs/st_res_prog_report.htm (last visited Apr. 26, 2007).

9. *See* Standards and Practices for All Appropriate Inquiries, 40 C.F.R. §312 (2005). EPA's All Appropriate Inquiries page is located at www.epa.gov/brownfields/regneg.htm.

10. U.S. EPA, BROWNFIELDS FEDERAL PROGRAMS GUIDE 27 (2005).

11. *See generally* U.S. EPA, Office of Brownfields Cleanup and Redevelopment website, www.epa.gov/brownfields/ (last visited Apr. 19, 2007).

12. *See generally id.*

13. 42 U.S.C. §9604(k).

14. *Id.*

15. UNLOCKING BROWNFIELDS, *supra* note 2, at 7.

16. Joel B. Eisen, *Brownfields Development*, *in* STUMBLING TOWARD SUSTAINABILITY 465 (John C. Dernbach, ed. 2002) [hereinafter Eisen, *STS 2002 Brownfields Chapter*]

17. UNLOCKING BROWNFIELDS, *supra* note 2, at 2.

18. *See* consultants' 2005 report prepared for the City of Chicago Department of Environment discussing the Chicago Center for Green Technology built on a former brownfield site, *available at* http://www.epa.gov/

smartgrowth/pdf/Chicago%20SG%20Brownfields%20Project%20Final.
pdf (last visited Apr. 26, 2007).

19. Eisen, *Brownfields at 20, supra* note 6, at 111.

20. *See generally* U.S. EPA's Smart Growth website, www.epa.gov/smart
    growth/about_sg.htm (last visited June 1, 2007); Smart Growth Online,
    www.smartgrowth.org/ (last visited June 1, 2007).

21. *See* U.S. EPA's Smart Growth website, Smart Growth in Brownfield
    Communities Web page, *available at* http://www.epa.gov/piedpage/
    brownfields.htm (last visited Mar. 31, 2007).

22. *See, e.g.*, CHICAGO DEP'T OF ENV'T, *supra* note 18, at 2.

23. Eisen, *Brownfields at 20, supra* note 6, at 129. For an international perspec-
    tive, see J.W. Dorsey, *Brownfields and Greenfields: The Intersection of
    Sustainable Development and Environmental Stewardship*, 5 ENVTL.
    PRACTICE 69-76 (2003), abstract *available at* http://journals.cambridge.
    org/action/displayAbstract?fromPage=online&aid=332495# (last visited
    Apr. 26, 2007).

24. *Id.*

25. UNLOCKING BROWNFIELDS, *supra* note 2, at 6.

26. Eisen, *STS 2002 Brownfields Chapter, supra* note 16, at 464 (quoting U.S.
    EPA, SUSTAINABLE BROWNFIELDS MODEL FRAMEWORK 3 (1999)).

27. Eisen, *STS 2002 Brownfields Chapter, supra* note 16, at 462.

28. UNLOCKING BROWNFIELDS, *supra* note 2, at 6.

29. Small Business Liability Relief and Brownfields Revitalization Act of
    2002, 42 U.S.C. §9601(41) (2002).

30. BROWNFIELDS PHENOMENON, *supra* note 1, at 1.

31. Eisen, *Brownfields at 20, supra* note 6, at 102.

32. *Id.* at 102 n.7 (quoting David A. Dana, *State Brownfields Programs as Lab-
    oratories of Democracy?*, 14 N.Y.U. ENVTL. L.J. 86, 86 (2005)); *see also*
    BROWNFIELDS PHENOMENON, *supra* note 1, at 4 (noting that "[t]he empiri-
    cal literature on brownfields—a topic that cuts across many disciplines and
    scales and is open to a wide range of methodological approaches—remains
    undeveloped relative to its potential").

33. Eisen, *Brownfields at 20, supra* note 6, at 131.

34. For descriptions of New York's program, see NY-Brownfields.com,
    www.ny-brownfields.com/index.htm (last visited Apr. 26, 2007); SUS-
    TAINABLE LONG ISLAND, BROWNFIELDS TO GREENFIELD$: A MANUAL
    ON BROWNFIELDS REDEVELOPMENT, *available at* www.sustainableli.org/
    documents/BrownfieldstoGreenfields-Final.pdf (last visited Apr. 26,
    2007).

35. N.J. Dep't of Envtl. Prot., Brief Synopsis of NJDEP's Brownfields De-
    velopment Area Initiative, *available at* http://www.state.nj.us/dep/srp/
    brownfields/bda/bda_synopsis.htm (last visited Mar. 31, 2007).

36. Eisen, *Brownfields at 20, supra* note 6, at 132-33 (quoting D. Evan van
    Hook et al., *The Challenge of Brownfield Clusters: Implementing a Multi-
    Site Approach for Brownfield Remediation and Reuse*, 12 N.Y.U. ENVTL.
    L.J. 111 (2003)).

37. Eisen, *Brownfields at 20*, *supra* note 6, at 133.

38. KRIS WERNSTEDT & JENNIFER HANSON, LINCOLN INST. OF LAND POL'Y, AREAWIDE BROWNFIELD REGENERATION THROUGH BUSINESS-BASED LAND TRUSTS AND PROGRESSIVE FINANCE 7 (2006), *available at* www.lincolninst.edu/pubs/dl/1096_Wernstedt_complete_web.pdf (last visited Apr. 26, 2007).

39. Eisen, *Brownfields at 20*, *supra* note 5, at 102.

40. *Id.* at 115.

41. *Id.* at 131.

42. U.S. EPA, REGION 3, HAZARDOUS WASTE CLEANUP SITES LAND USE & REUSE ASSESSMENT (2006) [hereinafter ER3 INITIATIVE], *available at* www.epa.gov/region03/revitalization/R3_land_use_final/full_report.pdf (last visited Apr. 26, 2007).

43. *Id.*

44. *See* U.S. EPA, Green Buildings Web page, http://www.epa.gov/opptintr/greenbuilding (last visited Apr. 26, 2007).

45. UNLOCKING BROWNFIELDS, *supra* note 2, at 10. *See generally* U.S. EPA, SUSTAINABLE REUSE OF BROWNFIELDS: RESOURCES FOR COMMUNITIES, *available at* http://www.epa.gov/brownfields/policy/BF_Sustain_Trifold.pdf (last visited Apr. 26, 2007) (discussing "green" building practices).

46. UNLOCKING BROWNFIELDS, *supra* note 2, at 110.

47. U.S. EPA, Environmentally Responsible Redevelopment and Reuse (ER3), http://www.epa.gov/compliance/cleanup/redevelop/er3/ (last visited Apr. 26, 2007); U.S. EPA, Green Buildings on Brownfields Initiative, *available at* http://www.epa.gov/swerosps/bf/policy/initiatives_eo.htm#gb (last visited Apr. 26, 2007).

48. ER3 INITIATIVE, *supra* note 42.

49. UNLOCKING BROWNFIELDS, *supra* note 2, at 9-10.

50. *See generally* Eisen, *Brownfields at 20*, *supra* note 6.

51. *Id.*

52. *Id.*

53. UNLOCKING BROWNFIELDS, *supra* note 2, at 8-9.

54. *See, e.g.*, N.J. Dep't of Comm. Aff, Office of Smart Growth, Maps and GIS Data, www.state.nj.us/dca/osg/resources/maps.shtml (last visited Mar. 31, 2007) (collection of GIS data showing how sites fit within state smart growth plans).

55. Eisen, *Brownfields at 20*, *supra* note 6, at 134.

Chapter 6

Business and Industry: Transitioning to Sustainability

Ira Robert Feldman

A stubborn resistance to sustainability thinking persisted in the U.S. private sector throughout the 1990s. As the World Summit on Sustainable Development (WSSD) approached in 2002, William Thomas noted that the extent to which businesses would translate sustainability concepts into practical measures and execute them was unclear.[1] "[S]ome leading American companies are among those pioneers working on the sustainability frontier. But the journey is in its early stages and the U.S. business community is by and large still formulating a case for, and a plan of action concerning, sustainable development."[2]

While businesses were visible at WSSD, particularly in championing partnerships through Business Action for Sustainable Development (BASD),[3] that initiative did not immediately affect the course of business activities in the United States. Instead, it appeared that government might act first, as early in the George W. Bush Administration certain key appointees at the U.S. Environmental Protection Agency (EPA) and the Council on Environmental Quality (CEQ) were known to favor sustainability-oriented policy and regulatory structures.[4] While several leading companies—notably DuPont, IBM, Interface, and Genencor[5]—were already implementing their sustainability visions, and several states had embraced sustainability through executive orders, progress in the United States for much of the first half of the decade remained episodic at best. A promising opportunity to embrace sustainability had been missed post-WSSD, and, as informed by the history of Love Canal and OPEC oil shortages, many feared that it would take a crisis to catalyze change.

Thus, although General Electric, Wal-Mart, and Goldman Sachs announced pathbreaking environmental policies in 2005, the more recent accelerated pace of change caught many by surprise. Indeed, we may look back at 2007 as the year that represented a tipping point for sustainable business practices in the United States: "[t]he greening of business has gone from movement to market as companies understand there [are] opportunities for improving the bottom line and creating new business value."[6] For what many have termed "sustainable business practices" or "triple bottom line" thinking, and others have addressed under the rubric of "corporate social responsibility" (CSR), and, more recently, what the financial sectors have termed "Environment, Social and Governance" (ESG) standards, there has been a game-changing convergence, not yet fully appreciated due to the breadth and divergence of the spheres and disciplines involved.

Although no single cause fully explains the shift we are seeing, acceptance of the real threat posed by climate change has had the greatest impact on the mindset of U.S. business. Understanding that "business as usual" is an untenable long-term strategy in the face of overwhelming scientific evidence, some businesses are responding to climate change by identifying the opportunities it presents, perhaps "one of the greatest investment, business and job creation opportunities of this generation . . . from carbon trading to renewable and cleaner energy generation and energy efficiency."[7] Another indication of a change in approach by business leaders was the formation in 2007 of a coalition that took the lead in urging President Bush to support a cap-and-trade system.[8] It remains to be seen, however, whether climate change will come to be understood and addressed by business and industry as the quintessential sustainability issue of our time.

This chapter provides the context for the ongoing transition to sustainability by business and industry in the United States. It identifies four key trends—multi-stakeholder partnerships, voluntary reporting, private regulation, and the role of the financial sector—that are significant for business in the transition to sustainability. The chapter also provides three brief illustrative case studies, dealing with Wal-Mart's sustainability program, General Electric's Ecomagination initiative, and Coca Cola's Global Water Stewardship program. It concludes with a set of recommendations for businesses seeking to gain advantage from the key challenges ahead.

What Does Sustainability Mean for Business? Why Is It Important in the United States?

While a transition to sustainability is already in progress, albeit at an early stage in the U.S. market, the business community is still far from consensus on the meaning of sustainability and corporate social responsibility (terms now often used interchangeably). There is clearly increasing momentum for both among the leading companies in the United States, albeit with different variations and formulations. There are signs of a broader acceptance and deeper entrenchment of sustainable business practices,[9] with sustainability reporting on the rise and the launch of several sectorwide sustainability initiatives in the United States in 2007.[10]

A survey[11] in 2006 polled the predominantly North American member companies of the Global Environmental Management Initiative (GEMI) and Business for Social Responsibility (BSR), two business associations that emphasize the importance of sustainability for business success. A number of companies noted that sustainability is increasing in business importance in such areas as product design, procurement, and collaboration with external stakeholders. Respondents noted increasing alignment between CSR efforts and business strategy, including 68 percent who believed that sustainability was "tied to company's business success" and 94 percent who were highly confident that CSR's impact on business strategy would increase.

Several recent books by U.S.-based practitioners, scholars, and other thought leaders have presented sophisticated articulations of the business case for sustainability and examples of recent experience from leading companies.[12] Further indication of progress is provided by reports and studies intended for use by the business community such as those issued by U.S.-based GEMI and BSR, and, with a more international perspective, from the World Business Council for Sustainable Development (WBCSD) and the Prince of Wales' Business and Environment Program.[13] Especially influential in the U.S. market are the conferences and sustainability-related activities led by The Conference Board[14] and the World Environment Center (WEC).[15] In the climate change arena, leading businesses have participated in the Business Environmental Leadership Council (BELC) of the Pew Center for Global Climate Change.[16]

On the negative side of the ledger, influential voices from many quarters still deride or dismiss sustainability and CSR on a dishearteningly regular basis. In a *Foreign Affairs* article David Victor argues that sustainability has lost its original meaning and scoffs at the "cocktail party version" of sustainable development that "gleams with promises of harmony and globalism."[17] Sustainability is mocked as "the interconnection of everything," "wooly thinking," and "a compass [that] . . . swings in all directions,"[18] and Victor asserts that it will have practical relevance only if it can accommodate local preferences and capabilities. The notion of CSR is regularly confused with corporate philanthropy, especially in *The Economist*,[19] or when viewed as a threat to the Milton Friedman "shareholders first" orthodoxy. Others assert that "non-strategic" CSR is "partly to blame for meaningless voluntary codes that define the private regulatory sphere . . . [,] business behavior that is at direct odds with short- and (reasonably) long-term profit maximization."[20]

For many organizations, it is still the norm to address areas such as environmental management, governance, human rights, and labor—all relevant to sustainable business practices or CSR—as separate issues stovepiped under different departments, rather than managing them as a cross-functional or synergistic sustainability bundle. Particularly for experienced environmental professionals in the United States, weaned on regulatory compliance for a generation, sustainability can be a difficult concept to grasp. Environmental sustainability can be seen as "the evolution of industry practices such as pollution prevention, environmental stewardship, and design for environment, that aim to reduce pollution costs through process improvements."[21] Thus, for many organizations, sustainability is limited to the environmental dimension, rather than the more robust triple bottom line conception of sustainability. Unfortunately, the implementation of an environmental management system, or participation in one or more voluntary programs, is often conflated with sustainability. Such strategic environmental management efforts may indeed be laudable attempts to move "beyond compliance," but should not be equated with sustainability.[22]

The drivers for sustainability are more complex than simple avoidance of government regulation. According to Jennifer Howard-Grenville, "drivers for change on the issue are coming from a broader set of social interests, not simply from the traditional regulatory and economic drivers that have strongly influenced environmental or labor practices in the past."[23] Sustainability creates opportunities for companies to gain competitive advantage by addressing changing stakeholder expectations with new technologies, products and services. According to Deloitte LLP, a consulting and financial services firm, companies require "fundamental business model innovations" to gain from sustainability opportunities, including "innovating products and services with a broader life-cycle view" and "leveraging non-traditional collaborations."[24]

But is it possible even to define the "sustainable" or "responsible" company? In a recent speech, Achim Steiner, head of the U.N. Environment Programme, listed these hallmarks of sustainable business practice:

- Redefine company vision, policies and strategies to include the triple bottom line of sustainable development;
- Develop sustainability targets and indicators (economic, environmental, social);
- Establish a sustainable production and consumption program with clear performance objectives that take the organization beyond compliance in the long-term;
- Work with suppliers to improve environmental performance, extending responsibility up the product chain and down the supply chain;
- Adopt voluntary charters, codes of conduct or practice internally as well as through sectoral and international initiatives to confirm acceptable behavior and performance;
- Measure, track, and communicate progress in incorporating sustainability principles into business practices, including reporting against indicators as found in the Global Reporting Initiative (GRI) Guidelines.[25]

Some would claim that these indicia are merely superficial add-ons, and hardly represent the transformational changes needed to move business to the sustainability level. That may be so, but it is genuine progress when the leading edge recognizes these actions as appropriate initial steps in a longer transition to sustainability.

Progress Toward Sustainability Since Johannesburg: Four Trends

To further illustrate progress in the U.S. market, since 2002 and going forward, this section describes four significant trends affecting sustainable business practices: multi-stakeholder partnerships, voluntary reporting, private regulation, and financial sector engagement.

Multi-Stakeholder Partnerships

In 2002, as the WSSD approached, William Thomas noted the importance of partnerships: "For most companies, the journey toward sustainability will also require changes in the nature of relationships with governments, communities, and environmental groups . . . [,] including the use of partnerships and alliances. . . ."[26] More recently, Wal-Mart has learned that "[p]roductive partnerships can include supply and value chain partners, non-government organizations and academics with requisite expertise as well as government policy makers and scientists. Such partnerships can provide insight as well as key resources to deliver sustainable value solutions."[27]

The introduction of multi-stakeholder "type II partnerships"[28] at the WSSD in 2002, a departure from government-only outcomes, provided businesses and corporations with new impetus to operationalize sustainability and advance the goals of Rio's Agenda 21. At the 11th meeting of the U.N. Commission on Sustainable Development (CSD) held in 2003, reporting guidelines for these partnerships were established. As of February 24, 2006, "[a] total of 319 partnerships had been registered with the Commission secretariat," of which "61 partnerships [had] reported updates on their activities."[29] However, "while reporting was encouraged, it is still voluntary."[30]

More generally, collaboration through partnerships enables corporations to tailor "strategic, goal-oriented action plans" to each "company's characteristics and core competencies," thereby enabling "innovative applications of these competencies" that fit the company's sustainability goals.[31] Corporate collaborative partnerships present opportunities for corporations to address their impacts and foster mutual gain relationships with local communities through "new relationship[s] between private capital and the public interest."[32]

One such partnership is reporting "real, tangible development benefits to the local communities including increased access to resources, such as health, education, water and sanitation; poverty mitigation; and the development of human capital and community empowerment."[33] Elsewhere, the very real benefits to partnering corporations include "the securing of an informal social 'license to operate'; the reduction of dependency of the local communities; the sharing of costs; the winning of new contracts based on past performance; and the improvement of existing performance (financial or otherwise)."[34]

The widened perspective that partnerships provide can help bring legitimacy, verification, and accountability to a corporation's sustainability initiatives. But these characteristics can be weakened by partnerships' nature as voluntary, decentralized, and self-regulating,[35] attributable in part from weak transparency mechanisms, stemming from "unclear guidelines and a lack of mandatory reporting requirements."[36] Therefore, the United Nations risks conferring legitimacy without accountability for WSSD partnerships.[37]

Finally, "[t]he performance of these collaborative initiatives depends on how well they make decisions and on their legitimacy to key stakeholders," says Simon Zadek, of AccountAbility, which "in turn depends on their governance and accountability structures, processes and norms."[38] Ideally, businesses and corporations would support such collaborative cooperation when they are invested in the partnership, implement outcomes and decisions, and face reputational risk.[39]

Voluntary Reporting

Voluntary sustainability reporting, also styled as "CSR" or "citizenship" reports, allows businesses to evaluate their social and environmental consequences and communicate information to the public for review and scrutiny. The reports, especially those based on the Global Reporting Initiative (GRI), which released its revised G3 guideline in 2006, are proving a popular option for enhanced transparency and accountability. According to the Social Investment Research Analysts Network (SIRAN) and KLD Research & Analytics, 49 of the 100 U.S. companies in the S&P 100 Index now disclose information beyond the financial, including environmental, social, and governance issues. Moreover, 38 companies in the S&P 100 Index are using the GRI's Sustainability Reporting Guidelines.[40]

Sustainability reporting may be, for now, "the tail wagging the dog" of corporate sustainability because this is often the only sustainability-oriented effort in place at many organizations. This is not necessarily a criticism. Preparing a sustainability report can be a useful entry point—if it leads to the development of metrics to be used in decision making and in managing identified risks.[41] With or without a public report, the GRI reporting framework can be a useful tool for driving organizational performance through internal reporting.

Private Regulation

Many American and European businesses have adopted voluntary standards for labor conditions, environmental practices, and human rights; these are often institutionalized in corporate and industry codes, multi-stakeholder initiatives, and private standard-setting bodies, often with reporting and monitoring requirements.[42] Private regulation, or "civil regulation" as it is described by David Vogel, attempts to fill the governance gap between the law and the market. It represents a dimension of what political scientists have characterized as the global privatization of regulation through increased reliance on market-based strategies and nongovernmental regulatory mechanisms.[43]

In one defined subset of private regulation, which Benjamin Cashore labels as "non-state, market driven" (NSMD) governance systems, "rulemaking clout does not come from traditional Westphalian state-centered sovereign authority, but rather from companies along the market's supply chain, who make their own individual evaluations as to whether to comply to the rules . . . of these private governance systems."[44] Thus, these programs appear to work because they generate potential compliance incentives (or disincentives) along supply chains, through price premiums, market access, or the prevention of negative boycott campaigns.[45]

The forest sector arguably presents the foremost example of an international NSMD governance system, with the emergence of the Forest Stewardship Council (FSC) and its competitors addressing standards for and certification of sustainable forestry.[46] Indeed, the FSC program is using private-sector certification programs to force sustainable forest management standards upward. "FSC competitors, like the Sustainable Forestry Initiative championed by the AF&PA [American Forest & Paper Association] in the United States, initially took a different NSMD stance, in which business interests strongly shape rule making, while other non-governmental and governmental organizations act in advisory capacities."[47] At present, the FSC and its competitors coexist, but it is too soon to tell whether the result will be the "privatizing up" of sustainable forestry standards or a watering down of the FSC model.[48]

Similar certification programs are expanding to address some critically important issues, including fisheries depletion, food production, mining, inhumane working conditions (such as apparel industry sweatshop practices), human rights abuses, and sustainable tourism.[49] As these governance systems emerge in such sectors as food, coffee, tourism, and fisheries,[50] "[t]heir potential impact is far from trivial—if completely successful, current efforts alone would govern 20 percent of products traded globally."[51]

Financial Sector

The growing acceptance of sustainability by the financial sector has become a major driver since 2002. Socially Responsible Investment (SRI) was a well-established but niche market in 2002. By the close of 2007, however, sustainability policies reached the Wall Street mainstream,[52] with such a leading player as Goldman Sachs articulating sustainability-based, sector-specific methodologies to outperform the market.[53]

Many actors on Wall Street now recognize that opportunity always accompanies risk. Independent rating agencies such as Innovest and KLD have developed risk profiles of multinational corporations based on the carbon content of their products (among other factors), causing a slow movement of public and private investments from bad to good environmental corporate actors.[54] Reinsurers, with Swiss Re taking the lead, have seen that climate change is real, with inevitable, dramatic impacts upon their business model.[55]

The leveraged buyout in 2007 of TXU, the largest power utility in Texas, also sheds light on the evolving role of the capital markets and their influence on sustainability thinking among U.S. businesses. Private equity groups, as part of the leveraged buyout deal of TXU, agreed to scrap plans for eight coal-burning power plants, invest $400 million in consumer-side energy efficiency, build a pilot "clean-coal" plant, and increase alternate energy investment. The Environmental Defense Fund greeted the transaction, which reshaped TXU's business and environmental strategy, as a "watershed moment in America's fight against global warming."[56]

Progress Toward Sustainability Since Johannesburg: Three Case Studies

Wal-Mart

A meeting in Rogers, Arkansas, in October 2007 has already taken on legendary proportions. Wal-Mart CEO Lee Scott summoned the CEOs of 250 suppliers and told them Wal-Mart would be watching their carbon footprints.[57] The potential downstream consequences are huge: With revenues greater than $350 billion, Wal-Mart's action poses a powerful threat, approximating a privatized EPA, but with coercive powers beyond that of any government. "The EPA can levy a seven-figure fine; Wal-Mart can wipe out more than a quarter of a business in one fell swoop."[58]

Wal-Mart's initial announcement of its sustainability program, two years earlier in October 2005, had surprised and created doubts among its critics. Wal-Mart was viewed as an aggressive, sometimes "arrogant leviathan," out of touch with progressive social and environmental ideas.[59] Yet the giant retailer set "audacious" goals in three areas—climate, waste, and products:

1. 100 percent renewable energy;
2. Zero waste;
3. Sell products that sustain the resources and environment.[60]

As over 90 percent of Wal-Mart's sustainability footprint is in its supply chain, Wal-Mart's sustainability efforts focus squarely on its extended value chain, including its suppliers' operations.[61] The results can be staggering. For example, when Procter & Gamble sells Wal-Mart its Charmin 6 Mega Roll with the same amount of toilet paper as a regular 24-roll pack, Wal-Mart can ship about 40 percent more units on their trucks. This eliminates 90 million cardboard rolls, 360,000 pounds of plastic wrapping, and 54,000 gallons of fuel consumption.[62]

Wal-Mart readily concedes that its sustainability programs are a work in progress, but states they are still growing. The company is still developing a system to track waste through its supply chain, but has no accurate way to measure waste it may have already eliminated.[63] "We make no claims of being a green company," says CEO Scott, "We're not saying we're better than anyone, we're not saying we're doing it right. What we're saying is that we recognize an opportunity to make a difference in this world . . . , and it is worthwhile to do."[64]

General Electric

GE built on existing technologies and research to launch Ecomagination, its corporatewide sustainability initiative, in May, 2005. CEO Jeffrey Immelt stated that GE intends to "develop tomorrow's solutions such as solar energy, hybrid locomotives, fuel cells, lower-emission aircraft engines, lighter and stronger durable materials, efficient lighting, and water purification technology."[65] Ecomagination's goal is both to offer "a continuous stream of advancements to existing products" and to "serve as a catalyst for development of the next generation of 'clean' technologies."[66] GE committed to increasing its investment in research in air pollution, energy consumption, and water quality from \$900 million to \$1.5 billion by 2010.[67] In addition to doubling its annual cleaner technologies research investment, GE also plans to

- Double revenues from Ecomagination clean tech products to \$20 billion by 2010;
- Reduce absolute greenhouse gas emissions one percent by 2012 (a big goal given GE's business growth projections) and improve energy efficiency by 30 percent in the same time frame;
- Report publicly its progress in meeting these goals.[68]

GE has developed its own internal screening process to "certify" Ecomagination products' environmental benefits.[69] To date the company has launched 45 new products and technologies for customers that have produced \$12 billion in revenue.[70] The GE initiative is receiving mixed reviews, especially from critics who note that GE continues to sell "dirty" technology.[71] Others are more enthusiastic about Ecomagination, calling it "a bellwether in the quest for sustainable enterprise" because it uses growth strategies to deal with social and environmental issues.[72]

Coca-Cola

As the world's largest bottler, Coca-Cola operates in over 200 countries. Coke views its approach to corporate responsibility and sustainability (CRS) as "a way to balance all of the considerations that shape our decisions, weighing the possibility of growth today with the promise of sustainability in the future."[73] Coca-Cola identified the social and environmental issues of greatest concern to the business and its stakeholders as: health and wellness; water stewardship; energy and climate change; sustainable packaging and recycling; and diversity management and inclusion. These issues reflect Coca-Cola's strategic priorities, and it is developing a three-year plan with performance targets for each.[74]

Coke has linked sustainability to its core business at the most fundamental level: Without a reliable supply of water, the company cannot exist. Coke's Global Water Stewardship, perhaps the most sophisticated of its kind, includes four components:

- Global awareness and action;
- Plant performance;

- Support for community initiatives;

- Watershed protection.[75]

The goal of global awareness and action is to mobilize the international corporation to address water challenges. The goal of plant performance is to be the best in class in water management. Coca-Cola has established standards for efficient water use and wastewater management, and water usage has been reduced by 6 percent. Coca-Cola's community initiatives to protect the environment and promote sustainability are consistent with the company's longstanding efforts to build relationships in communities where plants are located and employ up to hundreds of local residents.[76]

Does this amount to a transformative strategy for Coca-Cola? CEO Brock says, "We still have a long way to go to embed [corporate responsibility and sustainability] in our business and are working hard to close the gaps."[77]

Recommendations for the Next Decade

The recommendations that follow are directed to business leaders. Because the discussion above is necessarily selective, these recommendations should not be seen as a comprehensive "to do" list. There are many other significant sustainability-related issues for business and industry, including the juxtaposition of globalization and "buy local" pressures, the emergence of green consumerism, the increasingly important role of international standards as an adjunct to regulation, the implications of retaining or eliminating perverse subsidies, and the need for sizeable investment in breakthrough technologies. These components of the multi-faceted sustainability dialogue will all need to be addressed going forward.

1. Develop multi-stakeholder "partnerships" within the framework of specific commitments made under international law. Since the inception of type II partnerships, it was understood that "partnerships would complement and work with global governance and international environmental law, not replace them."[78] However, Carl Bruch and Jay Pendergrass suggest that integrating existing international law with partnerships will require greater involvement of the United Nations and individual nations to instill a sense of accountability and coordination, and to identify the extent to which these partnerships seek to implement international agreements or achieve other sustainability goals as articulated, for example, in Agenda 21. Greater partnership reporting is essential to (1) discuss implementation plans and challenges, and partners' contributions to a specific partnership,[79] (2) identify partnership success and failure factors,[80] and (3) provide some external accountability, not through oversight but by giving the public data on the progress of the partnership.

   2. Embrace voluntary reporting on social and environmental effects or face mandatory reporting. Government can "instigate, catalyze, and hold accountable corporate social responsibility" reporting through a law.[81] In other countries, mandatory reporting is taking hold; in the United States, the components of such an approach are already available, including reporting guidelines such as GRI, and regulatory schemes such as the Sarbanes-Oxley Act.[82] The use of a standard reporting guideline provides the substantive values and indicators, while the regulatory nature of Sarbanes-Oxley opens management to external values. Mandatory reporting requirements could be avoided by establishing an external assurance mechanism to verify data and statements in voluntary reports.

   3. Determine the limits of private regulation. According to Vogel, "[c]ivil and government regulation both have a legitimate role to play in improving public welfare. The former reflects the potential of the market for virtue; the latter recognizes its limits."[83] Private regulation is well established but is still maturing, and new certification programs are emerging in various forms.[84] Of the various mechanisms moving into this governance gap, programs like the FSC potentially offer the most promise, beyond the "other non-state, hybrid and voluntary initiatives with which they have been conflated"[85] because they provide governance directly in markets, so long as they "contain purposeful social steering efforts."[86]

   4. Recognize that the financial sector will increasingly seek verifiable and comparable ESG information from businesses. The financial sectors are already incorporating ESG factors into their methodologies, and these nonfinancial aspects will only become more intimately woven into the operations of the capital markets. As Ross Gelbspan points out, because individual companies tend to focus on "shorter-term concerns about quarterly or annual [financial results]," it falls to financial institutions to ensure the health of the capitalist system by taking the longer view driven by their own strategic needs.[87]

   5. Use widely-accepted and comparable performance metrics in the implementation and recognition of sustainability and CSR ini-

tiatives. If sustainability reporting is the tail wagging the dog, as suggested above, then the key to the more sophisticated implementation strategies that will emerge over the next decade will be metrics. Numerous attempts have been made to develop sustainability metrics and indicators, not only at the organizational level but also for "sustainable communities" at the national level for use in domestic policy setting and at the international level to compare nations. As a significant stakeholder itself, business should engage in the development of metrics and indicators at each level of scale. At the enterprise level, the myriad sustainability reports and questionnaires from the investment community and other stakeholders will generate a need for greater comparability and transparency. If the disclosure rules of the U.S. Securities and Exchange Commission, which are limited to environmental liabilities, do not escape a decades' old time warp and expand to cover the broader scope of sustainability, the financial sectors will demand it. Moreover, it is not unreasonable to see currently distinct disclosure activities—such as GRI reporting, Sarbanes Oxley requirements and SEC materiality reporting—converging over time.

6. Understand how business can succeed in a carbon-constrained economy. Companies that manage their risks based on climate change and respond to new opportunities for profit will hold a competitive advantage over rivals in a carbon-constrained future. According to Jonathan Lash and Fred Wellington of the World Resources Institute, risks and opportunities include skill at hedging against physical climate risk, mitigating regulatory costs, avoiding expensive litigation and other threats to corporate reputation, managing climate risk in the supply chain, investing capital in low-carbon assets, and innovating around new technology and product opportunities.[88]

Conclusion

Borrowing Al Gore's reference to climate change as an "inconvenient truth," the future can be seen in the light of "inconvenient sustainability truths" expressed by three keen observers of the transition to sustainability.

First, Simon Zadek's truth: "[M]any companies have decided that the sustainability imperative is important, but they don't yet know how to exploit it . . . [;] smart strategies by innovative companies have not yet fed through to market performance . . . [a]nd . . . some aspects of sustainability, desirable as they may be, simply have no business case [for current markets]."[89]

Second, Tom Friedman's truth: "[G]reen has really gone Main Street—thanks to the perfect storm created by 9/11, Hurricane Katrina and the Internet revolution. The first flattened the twin towers, the second flattened New Orleans and the third flattened the global economic playing field." But "[w]e have not even begun to be serious about the costs, the effort and the scale of change that will be required to shift our country, and eventually the world, to a largely emissions-free infrastructure over the next 50 years."[90]

Third, Jonathon Porritt's truth: "What counts as CSR today will soon be seen as the palest imitation of genuinely sustainable [behavior and] . . . superficial add-on palliatives to inherently unsustainable business models" will not suffice.[91]

The greening revolution was indeed an important first step on the path to sustainable enterprise.[92] Today, corporations are being challenged to move beyond greening, first by pursuing new potentially inherently clean technologies (e.g., renewable energy, biomaterials, nanotechnology, wireless IT); and second, by extending the benefits of capitalism to the entire human community of 6.5 billion people, rather than merely the 800 million at the top of the economic pyramid.[93]

As the transition to sustainability continues, we will see increasing pressure to adopt sustainability measures, perhaps driven at first by carbon mitigation metrics, and we can anticipate that huge advantages will accrue to companies that adopt transformational business models. To achieve these advantages, Deloitte identifies an essential need "for a disciplined, structured approach tightly focused on strategic, operational, collaborative and governance drivers."[94] In conclusion, as Stuart Hart and Mark Milstein have noted, companies that lead this shift to sustainability will not only outperform competitors today, they will preempt competitors from tomorrow's markets and technologies, and speed up our rise to a sustainable world.[95]

ENDNOTES

The author acknowledges the insights and support of Douglas Weinfield, James Schaarsmith, William D'Alessandro, Joshua Kahan, Peter Soyka, Al Innes, and John Dernbach in the preparation of this chapter.

1. William Thomas, *Business and Industry, in* STUMBLING TOWARD SUSTAINABILITY, at 541 (John C. Dernbach ed., 2002).

2. *Id.*

3. BASD was a joint activity of the International Chamber of Commerce (ICC) and the World Business Council for Sustainable Development (WBCSD) at the WSSD; the partnership concluded shortly thereafter. The BASD website has been preserved and is available at http://basd.free.fr.

4. In 2001, EPA Administrator Christine Whitman promised, "You will hear a lot more about sustainability from this administration." James Connaughton, at CEQ, was an expert on the international consensus ISO 14000 processes and often alluded to NEPA as a "sustainability statute."

5. For Dupont, IBM, and Genencor, see case studies prepared by Ira Feldman included in Thomas, *supra* note 1, at 558-66. For DuPont's Sustainable Growth Excellence Award program, see www2.dupont.com/Sustainability/en_US/assets/downloads/2005%20SGEA%20brochure.pdf. For Interface, see also RAY ANDERSON, MID-COURSE CORRECTION (1998).

6. Joel Makower, *quoted in* Anita Huslin, *Sustainability Coach Takes Her Expertise to Market*, WASH. POST, Nov. 26, 2007, at D5, *available at* www.washingtonpost.com/wp-dyn/content/article/2007/11/25/AR2007112501272.html.

7. Achim Steiner, Global Business for the Environment Summit, Opening Speech at the UNEP and Global Compact, Singapore (Apr. 19, 2007) [hereinafter Steiner speech], *available at* www.unep.org/Documents.Multilingual/Default.asp?DocumentID=505&ArticleID=5565&l=en.

8. DuPont, Alcoa, BP America, General Electric, and PG&E joined with the Pew Center and other nonprofit groups to form the United States Climate Action Partnership. *See, e.g.*, Peter Baker, *In Bush's Final Year, The Agenda Gets Greener*, WASH. POST, Dec. 29, 2007, at A10.

9. The operationalization of sustainability since 2002 in U.S. business and industry is proceeding with the use of methods familiar to executive-level managers: strategic planning, training/capacity building, internal pilot projects, and engagement with external stakeholders, including voluntary reporting. The drivers for this increase include CEO epiphany (such as the well-known Ray Anderson example at Interface); supply chain pressure; NGO watchdogs; and consumer demand.

10. *See* Grocery Manufacturers Association's website at www.gmabrands.com/about/index.cfm, and the Sustainable Green Printing Partnership website at www.sgppartnership.org.

11. GLOBAL ENVTL. MGMT. INITIATIVE & BUS. FOR SOC. RESPONSIBILITY, SUSTAINABLE BUSINESS & STRATEGY; VIEWS FROM THE INSIDE (2006).

12. *See, e.g.*, CHRIS LASZLO, THE SUSTAINABLE COMPANY (2003); DANIEL ESTY & ANDREW WINSTON, GREEN TO GOLD (2006); ANDREW SAVITZ,

Triple Bottom Line (2006); and William Blackburn, The Sustainability Handbook (2007).

13. GEMI reports are available at www.gemi.org/docs/PubTools.htm; BSR reports are available at www.bsr.org/insight/reports.cfm; WBCSD reports are available at http://qpub.wbcsd.org/templates/TemplateWBCSD2/layout. asp?type=p&MenuId=ODU&doOpen=1&ClickMenu=RightMenu; and the Prince of Wales' Business and Environment Programme reports are available at www.cpi.cam.ac.uk/programmes/sustainable_development/business_ the_environment_pro/bep_network/reports_and_newsletters.aspx.

14. The Conference Board recently established the Center for Corporate Citizenship and Sustainability. *See* www.conference-board.org/knowledge/ citizenshipcenter.

15. The World Environment Center recently launched a series of dialogues on corporate sustainability practices. *See* www.wec.org/news/wec-establishes-washington-sustainability-forum.

16. Pew Center for Global Climate Change, Business Environmental Leadership Council (BELC), *available at* www.pewclimate.org/companies_ leading_the_way_belc.

17. *Id.*

18. David Victor, *Recovering Sustainable Development*, 85 Foreign Aff. 91 (Jan./Feb. 2006).

19. *See, e.g.*, *In Search of the Good Company*, Economist, Sept. 6, 2007, *available at* www.economist.com/business/displaystory.cfm?storyid= 9767615.

20. Aaron Chaterjee & Siona Listokin, *Corporate Social Irresponsibility*, Democracy (Winter 2007).

21. *See* GEMI, Exploring Pathways to a Sustainable Enterprise, at 3-4 (2002), stating that sustainability can be distinguished from these environmental management practices by its consideration of the socioeconomic dimension (i.e., social well-being) and by sustainability's link to marketplace competitive advantage as a strategic consideration.

22. Usage of the term "sustainability" in the business world remains inconsistent and confusing. Some organizations use the corporate sustainability terminology in a strictly financial sense, equating it solely with long-term financial success. Elsewhere, sustainability and CSR initiatives are co-opted by communications and public relations departments; in still others, corporate philanthropy or "corporate citizenship" programs take priority over efforts to infuse the core business with sustainability thinking.

23. Jennifer Howard-Grenville et al., *Who Can Act on Sustainability Issues? Corporate Capital and the Configuration of Organizational Fields*, in Organizations and the Sustainability Mosaic: Crafting Long-Term Ecological and Societal Solutions, at 197 (S. Sharma et al. eds., 2007).

24. Deloitte, Sustainability: Balancing Opportunity and Risk in the Consumer Products Industry, report to GMA/FPA (the Association of Food, Beverage, and Consumer Products Companies), June 10, 2007, at 10.

25. Steiner speech, *supra* note 7.

26. Thomas, *supra* note 1, at 571.

27. BLUSKYE SUSTAINABILITY CONSULTANTS, MAKING SUSTAINABILITY WORK (2007), *available at* www.bluskye.com/pdf/Making%Sustainability%20Work.pdf.

28. Traditional or "type I" agreements are between governments; "type II" agreements contemplate partnering agreements among combinations of governmental, private sector, and NGO entities. *See* Minu Hemmati, *Implementation Conference: Stakeholder Action for Our Common Future*, 3 STAKEHOLDER F. 8 (2002); and *Type 2s Explained*, both available at www.earthsummit2002.org. *See also* Ira Feldman, *The Stakeholder Convergence: Enhanced Public Participation and Sustainable Business Practices*, 33 ELR 10496, 10502 (July 2003).

29. U.N. Commission on Sustainable Development, 14th Session, May 1-12, 2006. Partnerships for Sustainable Development, Report of the Secretary-General, at 5, *available at* http://daccessdds.un.org/doc/UNDOC/GEN/N06/259/15/PDF/N0625915.pdf?OpenElement.

30. Karen Backstrand, *Multi-Stakeholder Partnerships for Sustainable Development: Rethinking Legitimacy, Accountability and Effectiveness*, 16 EUR. ENV'T 300 (2006).

31. Global Business Coalition, *see* http://www.gbcimpact.org/live/resources/action/bam.php.

32. Nicola Acutt & Ralph Hamann, *How Should Civil Society (and the Government) Respond to "Corporate Social Responsibility"? A Critique of Business Motivations and the Potential for Partnerships*, 20 DEV. S. AFR. 256 (June 2003).

33. Business Action for Sustainable Development, http://basd.free.fr/initiatives/viewproject.php.310.html.

34. *Id. See also* Juge Gregg & Jacob Scherr, *Johannesburg and Beyond: The 2002 World Summit on Sustainable Development and the Rise of Partnerships*, 18 GEO. INT'L ENVTL. L. REV. 425 (Spring 2006).

35. United Nations Partnership Database, http://webapps01.un.org/dsd/partnerships/public/browse.do.

36. Backstrand, *supra* note 30.

37. ACCOUNTABILITY, DEVELOPMENT AS ACCOUNTABILITY: ACCOUNTABILITY INNOVATIONS IN ACTION, at 19.

38. *Id.* at 16.

39. JULIA STEETS, GLOBAL PUB. POL'Y INST., DEVELOPING A FRAMEWORK: CONCEPTS AND RESEARCH PRIORITIES FOR PARTNERSHIP ACCOUNTABILITY (2005), at 9.

40. *Grading Sustainability Reports: Creating the Curve*, GREENBIZ, June 17, 2007, *available at* www.greenbiz.com/news/reviews_third.cfm?NewsID=35287.

41. Christine Parker, *Meta-Regulation: Legal Accountability for Corporate Social Responsibility?*, in THE NEW CORPORATE ACCOUNTABILITY: CORPORATE SOCIAL RESPONSIBILITY AND THE LAW (Doreen McBarnet et al. eds., 2007), at 42.

42. DAVID VOGEL, THE MARKET FOR VIRTUE (2005), at 162.

43. *Id.* at 9.

44. Benjamin Cashore et al., Governing Through Markets: Forest Certification and the Emergence of Non-State Authority (2004), at 4. Four features comprise an ideal type of NSMD governance system: role of state—the state does not use sovereign authority to directly require adherence to rules; role of market—products being regulated are demanded by purchasers further down the supply chain; role of stakeholders and civil society—authority is granted through an internal evaluation process; and enforcement—compliance must be verified. *Id.* at 20.

45. *Id.* at 23.

46. *Id.* at xi. *See also* Errol Meidinger, *The Administrative Law of Global Public-Private Regulation: The Case of Forestry,* 17 Eur. J. Int'l L. 47 (2006).

47. Cashore et al., *supra* note 44, at 15.

48. *Id.* at 17.

49. Steven Bernstein & Benjamin Cashore, Can Non-State Global Governance Be Legitimate? A Theoretical Framework, paper prepared for IDDRI Conference, The Role of Norms in the Governance of Economic Activities, Montpellier, France (June 2006), at 2.

50. Cashore et al., *supra* note 44, at 219.

51. Bernstein & Cashore, *supra* note 49, at 2.

52. Goldman Sachs' environmental policy is available at www2.goldmansachs. com/our_firm/our_culture/corporate_citizenship/environmental_policy_ framework/docs/EnvironmentalPolicyFramework.pdf.

53. Goldman Sachs' GS Sustain methodology, *available at* www.unglobal compact.org/docs/ summit2007/gs_esg_embargoed_until030707pdf.

54. Bruce Piasecki & Peter Asmus, *A Better Shade of Green for Wall Street,* Christian Science Monitor, Apr. 3, 2006, at 9. *See, e.g.,* Innovest Strategic Value Advisors, www.innovestgroup.com; and KLD Research and Analytics, www.kld.com.

55. Swiss Re's position on climate change is available at www.swissre.com/ pws/about%20us/knowledge_expertise/top%20topics/our%20position %20and%20objectives.html?contentIDR=c21767004561734fb900fb2ee 2bd2155&useDefaultText=0&useDefaultDesc=0.

56. Steven Mufson & David Cho, *Energy Firm Accepts $45 Billion Takeover; Buyers Made Environmental Pledge,* Wash. Post, Feb. 26, 2007, at A4.

57. Jack Neff, *Why Wal-Mart Has More Green Clout Than Anyone,* Advertising Age, Oct. 15, 2007, at 1.

58. *Id.*

59. Joel Makower, Wal-Mart's Sustainability Summit, *available at* http://makower. typepad.com/joel_makower/ 2007/10/wal-marts-susta.html.

60. Wal-Mart CEO Lee Scott announced these goals in a speech, Twenty-First Century Leadership, on Oct. 24, 2005. *See* Marc Gunther, *The Green Machine,* Fortune, July 31, 2006, *available at* http://money.cnn.com/magazines/ fortune/fortune_archive/2006/08/07/8382593/index.htm.

61. Chris Laszlo, Sustainable Value (2008), at 90.

62. Ylan Q. Mui, *At Wal-Mart "Green" Has Various Shades*, WASH. POST, Nov. 16, 2007, at D1, *available at* www.washingtonpost.com/wp-dyn/content/article/2007/11/15/ AR2007111502519.html.

63. *Id.*

64. Makower, *supra* note 59.

65. *General Electric's Ecomagination Finds Profit in Going Green*, STATES NEWS SERVICE, Sept. 14, 2007.

66. Stuart Hart & Mark Milstein, In Search of Sustainable Enterprise: The Case of GE's Ecomagination Initiative, *available at* www.policyinnovations.org/ideas/innovations/data/ecomagination.

67. GE, INVESTING IN A SUSTAINABLE FUTURE, 2007 Corporate Citizenship Report, *available at* www.ge.com/company/citizenship/2007_citizenship/index.html.

68. *Id.*

69. *Id.*

70. Business Wire, GE Ecomagination R&D Investment to Reach $1 Billion by Year End, Driving Expansion of Advanced Technology Pipeline, Oct. 23, 2007.

71. Kathryn Kranhold, *GE's Environment Push Hits Business Realities*, WALL ST. J., Sept. 14, 2007.

72. Hart & Millstein, *supra* note 66.

73. COCA-COLA ENTERS., CONTINUING OUR JOURNEY, 2006 Corporate Responsibility and Sustainability Report, at 1, *available at* www.cokecce.com/assets/uploaded_files/2006CCECRS.pdf.

74. *Id.*

75. Bruce Karas, The Coca-Cola Company and the Environment, Presentation to Georgia Chamber of Commerce, Savannah, Ga., Aug. 2007.

76. *Id.*

77. Coca-Cola 2006 Report, *supra* note 73, at 2.

78. Sustainable Development Issues Network (SDIN). "Questioning Partnerships," in *Taking Issue*, SDIN Paper No. 1 (2002), *available at* www.sdissues.net/SDIN/docs/TakingIssue-No1.pdf.

79. Carl Bruch & John Pendergrass, *The Road From Johannesburg: Type II Partnerships, International Law, and the Commons*, 15 GEO. INT'L ENVTL. L. REV. 855 (2003).

80. *Id.*

81. Parker, *supra* note 41.

82. Australia, Belgium, Canada, Denmark, the European Union, Finland, France, Germany, India, Japan, the Netherlands, Norway, South Africa, Spain, Sweden, and the United Kingdom have enacted mandatory reporting requirements, some more relevant to CSR than others. *See* KPMG, GLOBAL SUSTAINABILITY SERVICES AND UNITED NATIONS ENVIRONMENT PROGRAMME (UNEP): CARROTS AND STICKS FOR STARTERS: CURRENT TRENDS AND APPROACHES IN VOLUNTARY AND MANDATORY STANDARDS FOR SUSTAINABILITY REPORTING (2006), at 22-27.

83. VOGEL, *supra* note 42, at 173.

84. CASHORE ET AL., *supra* note 44, at 220.

85. Bernstein & Cashore, *supra* note 49, at 5.

86. *Id.* at 5.

87. Ross Gelbspan, author of THE HEAT IS ON, *quoted in* Piasecki & Asmus, *supra* note 54, at 9.

88. Jonathan Lash & Fred Wellington, *Competitive Advantage on a Warming Planet*, HARV. BUS. REV., Mar. 2007, at 94.

89. Simon Zadek, *Inconvenient But True: Good Is Not Always Profitable*, FORTUNE, Nov. 1, 2007, *available at* http://money.cnn.com/magazines/fortune/fortune_archive/2007/11/12/101012017/index.htm.

90. Thomas Friedman, *The Power of Green*, N.Y. TIMES SUNDAY MAGAZINE, Apr. 15, 2007, *available at* www.nytimes.com/2007/04/15/magazine/15green.t.html?_r=1&oref=slogin.

91. JONATHON PORRITT, CAPITALISM AS IF THE WORLD MATTERS 270 (2007).

92. Hart & Millstein, *supra* note 66.

93. *Id.*

94. DELOITTE, *supra* note 24, at 17.

95. Stuart Hart & Mark Milstein, *Creating Sustainable Value*, 17 ACAD. MGMT. EXEC. 14 (2003).

Chapter 7

Higher Education: More and More Laboratories for Inventing a Sustainable Future

Wynn Calder and Julian Dautremont-Smith

Sustainability is a growing imperative in higher education in America. Practitioners define sustainability both narrowly as the long-term protection and health of the natural environment, and broadly as the triple bottom line of environmental health, economic viability, and social well-being. A university fully committed to sustainability emphasizes an interdisciplinary and holistic approach to fostering the knowledge, skills, and attitudes needed to build a more sustainable world for present and future generations. Colleges and universities across the United States are increasingly practicing sustainability in campus operations, with climate change serving as a catalyst for energy conservation projects, renewable energy purchasing, recycling, and sustainable food initiatives. Departments of environmental studies and science remain strong or are increasing in popularity as general awareness of our environmental predicament grows. Specific courses and programs focused on sustainability are also increasingly evident, while sustainability as an academic discipline in its own right is at an early stage of development.

Fostering a more sustainable world is arguably the most logical outcome of the higher education endeavor. Nearly every college and university mission statement holds the institution to a purpose higher than simply the creation and dissemination of knowledge. Higher education consistently aspires to instill in graduates such qualities as good citizenship, moral integrity, leadership, critical thinking, and care for the environment. The work of building a sustainable world requires precisely these qualities and more. Because colleges and universities are uniquely equipped to help achieve sustainability through innovation in teaching, research, and institutional practice, it would seem incumbent upon them to rise to this challenge.

When deeply embraced by a college or university, sustainability is reflected in each of its core areas: curriculum; research; operations;

community outreach and service; student life; and institutional mission, policy, and planning. When embraced by higher education's external stakeholders, sustainability is supported by disciplinary and professional associations, governments, private foundations, nongovernmental organizations, and the business sector. This chapter assesses the state of progress in sustainability in higher education (SHE) and shows that increasing numbers of college and university campuses are becoming laboratories for inventing a sustainable future.

Curriculum

Despite the continuing trend toward specialization within traditional academic disciplines at U.S. colleges and universities, an increasing number of courses are being developed that incorporate sustainability concepts. There are also efforts underway to transform academic programs and create centers that foster interdisciplinary thinking, a hallmark of education for sustainability.[1] Programs in sustainability studies and related programs in sustainable design, sustainable agriculture, sustainability education, and sustainable business are emerging at several schools around the country. For instance, Arizona State University's new School of Sustainability began offering B.A., M.A., and Ph.D. programs in September 2007; Prescott College and Antioch New England began offering graduate degrees in education with a sustainability focus in 2005 and 2006, respectively.

Professional schools are also responding to the sustainability challenge. Some of the most promising are trends in law and business schools. Vermont Law School has an Environmental Tax Policy Institute, which, among other things, sponsors annual global symposia on environmental taxation.[2] The University of Washington School of Law offers a graduate program in the law of sustainable international development.[3] More law schools are offering seminars, courses, and symposia on sustainable development. To some degree, this is an outgrowth of international environmental law, which tends to use sustainable development as a conceptual framework, particularly when dealing with topics like biodiversity and climate change. More and more law schools, in fact, are offering courses on these specific topics, often in a sustainability context.

Beyond Grey Pinstripes, a biennial survey and ranking of business schools, highlights innovative full-time MBA programs that are integrating social and environmental stewardship into curricula and research. Of the more than 600 full-time MBA programs across six continents invited to participate in the survey, an increasing number (63 percent in 2007, up from 54 percent in 2005 and 34 percent in 2001) require one or more courses in ethics, corporate social responsibility, sustainability, or business and society.[4]

Despite clear progress in recent years, however, most college and university students still receive little or no exposure to sustainability within their academic coursework, and there are few rewards for faculty who integrate sustainability themes into their teaching. While evidence indicates a growing interest in sustainability, particularly the incorporation of environmental issues into standard academic subjects, there is much work still to be done to ensure that all students graduate with a basic understanding of sustainability concepts and an ability to implement them through critical thinking and problem solving.

Research

Sustainability-oriented research is increasingly funded in the sciences, but initiatives are also underway to include the social sciences and humanities. "Sustainability science" is emerging as a legitimate area of research, and the *Proceedings of the National Academies of Sciences* has even devoted a new section of the journal to the field.[5]

Likewise, the academic community has seen a growth in peer-reviewed journals and other publications focused on sustainability: the *International Journal of Sustainability in Higher Education* (Emerald) was launched in 2000; *Environment and Sustainable Development* (Inderscience) in 2002; and both the *Journal of Education for Sustainable Development* (Sage Publications) and *Sustainability: The Journal of Record* (Mary Ann Liebert, Inc.) in 2007. Business and law journals now discuss sustainable development or include sustainability themes. American University's Washington College of Law publishes a student-run journal called *Sustainable Development Law and Policy*.[6]

Along with the increasing number of publishing outlets for academic research on sustainability, many new research institutes focused on sustainability and related topics have been founded in recent years. The Georgia Institute of Technology, a leader in this area, hosts the Institute for Sustainable Technology and Development, a campus-wide advocate for sustainability in curriculum, research, and operations. Research at the Institute has focused on a range of issues: fuel cells, organic photonics and electronics, biologically inspired design, air pollution, and urban sprawl in U.S. cities.[7]

Higher education research will always tend to go where the money is. While few private foundations or government offices are funding SHE in classroom teaching or promoting sustainable operations of college facilities, they are showing increased interest in environmentally relevant research, especially as it relates to global warming and renewable energy technology.

Operations

"Campus greening," or sustainable campus operations, is the poster child of the SHE movement. New projects and programs are reported daily on e-mail discussion lists and e-bulletins devoted to this topic. Sustainable operations include recycling and waste minimization, energy and water conservation, green purchasing, transportation initiatives, sustainable landscaping, green buildings, and more. Such practices and technologies bring tangible, environmentally responsible results, and they can save money over time.

The 2008 *College Sustainability Report Card*, a study published by the Sustainable Endowments Institute, attests to steady growth in sustainable operations. The study evaluates the 200 colleges and universities with the largest endowments in the United States and Canada in eight categories,[8] including climate change and energy, food and recycling, green building, and transportation. Building on the 2007 report of the 100 richest institutions, the findings showed the strongest gains in sustainable food systems and recycling. For example, 70 percent of the schools evaluated commit a portion of their food budgets to purchasing from local farms and/or producers. To address climate change, nearly half of the schools have committed to carbon reduction, and almost one in three have committed to "climate neutrality" (having no net greenhouse gas emissions) in the long term. Over 60 percent of schools reported working on green building projects, though most lacked green building policies. Equally impressive were improvements in transportation programs, with hybrid or electric vehicles used in fleets at 42 percent of schools and biodiesel made or used at 31 percent of schools.[9] As a barometer of SHE initiatives in the rest of U.S. higher education, these results indicate significant gains over the past several years.

Climate change has indeed become the catalyst for many campus greening initiatives, especially in energy conservation and sustainable design. Tufts University was one of the first to use climate change as an organizing concept. The Tufts Climate Initiative, launched in 1999, supports a series of campus energy-reduction activities and programs designed to help the university meet its goal of cutting its emissions 7 percent below 1990 levels by 2012.[10] Yale University committed in 2005 to a reduction in greenhouse gas emissions to 10 percent below 1990 levels by 2020.[11] By spring 2008, over 500 U.S. college and university presidents had signed the American College & University Presidents Climate Commitment (described in more detail below).[12]

Sustainable design on campuses is one of the most promising new trends in the SHE movement. New buildings and existing building renovations are increasingly built to LEED (Leadership in Energy and Environmental Design) standards, a certification system administered by the U.S. Green Building Council.[13] Over 40 institutions have adopted green building policies requiring new construction to meet sustainability specifications, and public universities are increasingly subject to state regulations mandating green building techniques in publicly funded buildings.[14] Among professional schools, LEED certification is also catching on. In 2003, the University of Denver became the first law school in the country to achieve LEED gold status,[15] and the new law building at the University of Colorado at Boulder recently earned a gold rating.[16]

Green purchasing has also become increasingly popular, with some schools acting alone and others forming consortia to increase their purchasing power. A 2006 survey of professionals involved in purchasing decisions at 470 colleges and universities found that nine out of 10 campuses take sustainability into account in deciding upon new products, including consumables, furnishings, and building materials, and that three-quarters are switching to environmentally friendly janitorial products and equipment.[17]

While efforts to incorporate sustainability into campus operations are accelerating and recent advances are encouraging, most campuses are still a long way from operational sustainability. Most of the attention to date has focused on sustainability measures that save money, and yet only a small number of institutions have created mechanisms to ensure that these savings are used to help finance sustainability measures with lower rates of return. It remains to be seen how cam-

puses will respond once the most cost-effective sustainability measures have been implemented.

Community Outreach and Service

Numerous universities and colleges promote sustainable development in their surrounding communities and beyond. These efforts typically involve service learning projects, student internships, and student and faculty research. Now considered mainstream in higher education, service learning is also an effective pedagogical strategy for
integrating sustainability into class work.

Allegheny College, a small liberal arts institution in rural northwestern Pennsylvania, is working to improve the economic and social
dimensions of a struggling region through environmentally oriented
projects. The college created the Center for Economic and Environmental Development (CEED) in 1997. Wanting to be part of the solution to local and regional economic challenges, faculty members from
several departments founded CEED "to work with the community toward a forward-thinking vision for the region that is both economically inspiring and environmentally sustainable."[18] CEED focuses on
areas such as watershed protection, educational outreach, sustainable
energy, art and the environment, agriculture and forestry, and environmental justice. Each year, nearly 150 Allegheny students (out of approximately 1,900) work with over 100 community partners, such as
schools, landowners, and logging companies, on sustainable development in the region. Allegheny faculty and students engage with local
and regional community stakeholders in ways that will have lasting
practical as well as educational results. They are proving that the
health of both the institution and the surrounding community are ultimately interconnected.

Student Life

Student environmental activism has risen dramatically since 2002,
and students are often the major drivers of sustainability on their campuses. The Energy Action Coalition, which unites more than 40 student organizations from across the United States and Canada,
launched the Campus Climate Challenge campaign in 2005. This
youth-led campaign has catalyzed climate and energy initiatives on
many campuses, trained thousands of students, and held hundreds of
events focused on clean energy on campus. In November 2007, the

Coalition brought together more than 5,500 young people from all 50 states for Power Shift 2007,[19] the first national youth summit devoted to solving the climate crisis.

Student sustainability leaders have found that increasing student fees can be an effective way to fund campus sustainability initiatives. This strategy, which was started in 2000 by students at the University of Colorado at Boulder, has now been utilized successfully on over 50 campuses across the United States.[20] These fees range in size from $1 to $45 per student per semester but almost always receive wide approval in student elections. Generating as much as $350,000 annually at the largest institutions, the fees are used in various ways, including purchasing renewable energy, hiring sustainability staff, and supporting campus recycling programs.

Also increasingly popular at schools across the country are sustainable living programs, in which students engage in peer-to-peer education to encourage behaviors such as energy and water conservation, recycling, and waste reduction in dormitories. Harvard University's Green Campus Initiative has had success with this model, supporting a formal program in undergraduate dormitories.[21] Harvard's professional schools are also joining the effort; for example, the Harvard Law Green Living Program began its third year of operation in the fall semester of 2007.[22]

As with energy and climate issues, student interest in sustainable food and recycling initiatives continues to grow. Student demand for local, organic, and fair trade food options has led more than 200 campuses to initiate farm-to-college programs, which match up local farmers with area universities. Participation in RecycleMania—a friendly competition among campuses to increase recycling and reduce waste—has more than doubled annually, growing from two participants in 2001 to 400 in 2008.[23]

Though widespread, student support for sustainable campuses is still far from universal, and the fact remains that many students receive little extracurricular exposure to sustainability issues. As is often the case, however, it is student demand that will ultimately bring even greater commitment to sustainability within higher education.

Institutional Mission, Policy, and Planning

Various indicators show a strong shift toward sustainability at the administrative level of U.S. colleges and universities. The 2008 *Col-*

lege Sustainability Report Card examined four categories related to leadership and financial commitment, including administration, endowment transparency, investment priorities, and shareholder engagement. According to the study, more than one in three of the 200 schools evaluated have full-time staff dedicated to sustainability, focused primarily on campus operations and student engagement. Evidence suggests that many more colleges and universities have hired or are considering hiring sustainability coordinators and directors.[24] More than one in five schools reported having an office of sustainability, and more than 60 percent have a sustainability advisory committee. On questions concerning endowment, about 20 percent of respondents said they invest a portion of their endowment in renewable energy funds, but only about 6 percent invest in community development funds. Schools were weakest in the areas of shareholder engagement and endowment transparency.

Among the most promising campaigns by higher education leaders to advance sustainability is the American College & University Presidents Climate Commitment (ACUPCC). Initiated by a group of college and university presidents in 2006, the ACUPCC commits institutions to neutralizing their greenhouse gas emissions, and to accelerating research and educational efforts to equip society to restabilize the earth's climate.[25] As of June 2008, over 555 presidents and chancellors had signed the ACUPCC, which is expected to be a major driver of sustainability in higher education in the coming years.

Despite the success of the ACUPCC, too few leaders in higher education are willing to challenge the status quo. Colleges and universities tend to be reactive institutions. Climate change, increasingly seen as the fundamental environmental, economic, and indeed social challenge of our time, may one day prove to be the catalyst for a commitment to sustainability by a majority of higher education leaders.

External Forces Supporting Sustainability in Higher Education

Grassroots efforts and nonprofit organizations have consistently worked to strengthen sustainability in higher education in the United States. Several deserve mention here[26]:

- The Association for the Advancement of Sustainability in Higher Education (AASHE) is a membership-based association of colleges and universities in the United States and Canada committed to education for sustainability.[27]

Founded in 2005, AASHE has grown to become the largest organization of its kind, serving primarily as a clearinghouse for information about campus sustainability and offering a variety of professional development opportunities.[28]

- The Campus Consortium for Environmental Excellence, founded in 1997, maintains a network of environmental management professionals, develops resources and tools, and promotes innovative regulatory models.[29]

- The National Wildlife Federation's Campus Ecology Program, founded in 1989, supports climate leadership and student-led campus greening initiatives.[30]

- Second Nature, founded in 1993, promoted SHE in the 1990s through advocacy, faculty development workshops, and online resources, and now primarily helps initiate regional and national networks for SHE.[31]

- University Leaders for a Sustainable Future, founded in 1992, serves as the secretariat for signatories of the Talloires Declaration, which commits colleges and universities to advancing sustainability in teaching and practice.[32]

- The U.S. Partnership for Education for Sustainable Development was formed in 2004 to engage representatives from all levels of education and all sectors—business, government, and civil society—in support of the United Nations Decade of Education for Sustainable Development (2005-2014).[33]

State and regional networks supporting SHE are well established in the United States, including the New Jersey Higher Education Partnership for Sustainability (NJHEPS), founded in 1999,[34] and the Pennsylvania Environmental Resource Consortium, founded in 2000.[35] In recent years, similar networks have arisen in states such as California, Maine, Michigan, New York, and South Carolina, and in regions like the Upper Midwest and the Northeast. One of the most prominent regional groups is the Northeast Campus Sustainability Consortium (NECSC), which was established in 2004 to support the growing network of campus sustainability staff from institutions in northeastern United States and maritime Canada.[36]

In 2005, 14 mainstream national higher education associations formed the Higher Education Associations for Sustainability Consortium (HEASC), which works to advance sustainability among member constituencies, including facilities directors, business officers, campus planners, and student services officers.[37] Similarly, over twenty national disciplinary associations (including the American Society of Civil Engineers and the National Association of Biology Teachers) formed the Disciplinary Associations Network for Sustainability (DANS) in 2006 to promote education for sustainability via legislative briefings, public outreach, curricula, professional development, and accreditation standards.[38]

Historically, SHE has received little federal government support in the United States, except for modest interest from the Environmental Protection Agency, which houses an Office of Environmental Education and provides information on making campuses more eco-efficient. There are indications, however, that this may be changing. The Energy Independence and Security Act of 2007, which was signed into law in late 2007, included language authorizing $250 million annually in grants and another $500 million in direct loans for renewable energy and energy efficiency projects at higher education institutions, public schools, or local governments. Additionally, the Higher Education Sustainability Act of 2007 was introduced in both the House and Senate in fall 2007. The bill would amend the Higher Education Act to authorize a new $50 million grant program at the Department of Education to support sustainability projects at higher education institutions and consortia/associations. Though passage of this bill is uncertain, its introduction is a hopeful sign.

While there is evidence of a growing demand in the business sector for sustainability-literate graduates,[39] most of the external support for SHE in America continues to come from grassroots efforts and nonprofit organizations. To date, little external funding exists—either from private or corporate foundations or from government coffers—to help push higher education toward greater commitment to sustainability.

Recommendations

To enhance and build upon the successes of the past several years, a critical mass of internal and external stakeholders must mobilize in order to create the model sustainable institution of higher education envisioned here. To achieve this goal, we recommend the following actions within each of the core areas of university life, as well as among external stakeholders:

1. Curriculum: To ensure that all students achieve basic sustainability literacy, institutions need to create graduation requirements or core courses focused on sustainability. This requirement could take the form of a single required class or a menu of sustainability-focused courses from which students could choose.[40] To help faculty infuse sustainability into their teaching, institutions should offer sustainability course development workshops based on the successful peer-to-peer approaches pioneered in the Ponderosa and Piedmont projects.[41]

2. Research: To help meet the vast research needs for advancing sustainability and to capitalize on increasing demand for sustainability-related research, institutions should increase support for existing research centers and institutions related to sustainability, and should consider establishing new ones. Institutions should also restructure their academic reward systems to provide incentives for interdisciplinary research and teaching on sustainability topics. By providing students with research opportunities in sustainability-related subjects, institutions can prepare students for careers in emerging fields such as sustainable business, design, engineering, and agriculture.

3. Operations: Institutions should expand efforts to become more sustainable in their operations. To help finance sustainability projects on campus, institutions should investigate the creation of mechanisms to reinvest the savings from these projects into additional sustainability initiatives. Institutions should also work to connect campus sustainability activities with their educational and research efforts. The physical campus can be a powerful learning tool when students are given the opportunity to work with facilities staff and conduct studies on campus sustainability features such as green roofs and renewable energy technologies. Lastly, colleges and universities should hire full- or part-time sustainability directors to inspire and help coordinate these multi-constituency efforts.

4. Outreach and Service: Institutions should partner with their local communities and regions to promote sustainable development. Such partnerships break down the barriers between town and gown, support practical and experiential learning and research, and foster long-term sustainable community development.

5. Student Life: Sustainability can be made an integral part of campus culture through various new programs. Institutions can create peer-to-peer student sustainable living programs; incorporate sustainability into new student orientation and training for resident assistants; organize inter-dorm sustainability competitions; and endorse efforts, such as the Campus Climate Challenge, that foster active citizenship and leadership among students. For their part, students should work to conserve energy and water, reduce waste in their daily lives, and participate in sustainability outreach campaigns. Students should also support their institutions' sustainability efforts by approving increases in student fees for sustainability purposes. Finally, students should hold administrators accountable for meeting the sustainability commitments that their schools have made.

  6. *Institutional Mission, Policy, and Planning: Sustainability initiatives need upper-level support to flourish.* Signing presidential commitments like the American College & University Presidents Climate Commitment is an important way to signal this support since it integrates sustainability with strategic planning. However, to be truly effective, these commitments need to be backed up with real action. Higher education leaders should work to make good on their sustainability pledges, defend them publicly, and ensure that sufficient funding has been allocated to enable implementation.

  7. *External Stakeholders:*

  (a) Nonprofit organizations should continue to support sustainability in higher education by providing resources on best practices, facilitating information sharing between campuses, and improving the ability of schools to assess their progress. These organizations should also provide training and professional development opportunities to help strengthen the SHE community. National higher education associations should increase efforts to educate their members by incorporating sustainability into their programs, publications, and events. There is a continuing need for mechanisms like the Presidents Climate Commitment that encourage higher education leaders to express their commitment to sustainability, as well as programs, such as RecycleMania, that foster friendly competition among campuses.

  (b) Business has a critical role to play in supporting sustainability in higher education. Businesses that serve higher education should increase their sustainable product offerings, and work to support their clients' sustainability efforts. Businesses of all kinds can also partner with universities and provide funding for sustainability research.

Lastly, businesses that have an interest in hiring employees with knowledge of sustainability principles and practices should, in partnership with the nonprofit community, issue a joint declaration highlighting their desire for sustainability-literate employees and expressing support for sustainability in higher education.

(c) Government should work to create the regulatory conditions that will promote the growth of sustainability in higher education. For instance, regulation of carbon dioxide emissions and subsidies for renewable energy and other sustainable technologies provide incentives for higher education (and society at large) to move toward more sustainable energy sources. Likewise, state regulations requiring the achievement of ambitious efficiency standards for all publicly funded buildings (including those at public colleges and universities) provide further impetus for sustainability on campus. Voluntary programs that provide technical support and incentives for sustainability, such as the U.S. Environmental Protection Agency's Green Power Partnership, also have an important role to play. Finally, to enable American leadership in emerging sustainable industries, which include growth industries such as renewable energy, government should expand funding for sustainability research.

Conclusion

There has been significant progress in sustainability in higher education in the United States since 2002, particularly in campus operations. While only a few disciplines give legitimacy to teaching and research in this area, there is strong evidence that many are beginning to recognize sustainability as an important societal priority for the 21st century. Though little funding from either governments or foundations supports higher education initiatives in sustainability, a dynamic network of grassroots and nonprofit efforts is advocating effectively for this transition within U.S. colleges and universities.

American higher education can be very innovative and adaptive. Leaders at many institutions have grasped the critical need for a more sustainable society, and they have called for a variety of exemplary responses such as the American College & University Presidents Climate Commitment. Colleges and universities will ultimately respond to demands from both internal and external stakeholders. Higher education may be approaching a tipping point, when it will soon be unacceptable to ignore sustainability as a guiding principle.

ENDNOTES

1. For information on several new centers at U.S. colleges and universities devoted to interdisciplinary thinking around environmental and sustainability issues, see Claudia H. Deutsch, *A Threat So Big, Academics Try Collaboration*, N.Y. TIMES, Dec. 25, 2007.

2. Vermont Law School, Environmental Tax Policy Institute (last visited Oct. 15, 2007).

3. University of Washington Law School, Law of Sustainable International Development Graduate Program, *available at* www.law.washington.edu/SID (last updated May 19, 2005).

4. The Beyond Grey Pinstripes survey is managed by the Aspen Institute Center for Business Education. *See* www.beyondgreypinstripes.org.

5. *See* Proceedings of the National Academies of Sciences website, www.pnas.org/misc/sustainability.shtml.

6. American University, Washington College of Law, Sustainable Development Law & Policy, www.wcl.american.edu/org/sustainabledevelopment (last visited Oct. 15, 2007).

7. Georgia Institute of Technology, Institute for Sustainable Technology and Development website, www.sustainable.gatech.edu/research.

8. SUSTAINABLE ENDOWMENTS INST., COLLEGE SUSTAINABILITY REPORT CARD 2008, *available at* www.endowmentinstitute.org/sustainability. There are more than 4,000 colleges and universities in the United States, including community colleges, serving about 15,000,000 students.

9. *Id.*, at 5-6.

10. *See* www.tufts.edu/tci.

11. Press Release, Yale University, Yale to Reduce Greenhouse Gas Emissions (Oct. 11, 2005), *available at* www.yale.edu/opa/newsr/05-10-11-02.all.html.

12. *See* www.presidentsclimatecommitment.org.

13. U.S. Green Building Council website, www.usgbc.org.

14. Based on data gathered by the Association for the Advancement of Sustainability in Higher Education (AASHE) and posted at their website, www.aashe.org.

15. Press Release, University of Denver, Sturm College of Law, DU Law School Building Earns LEED Gold Certification, *available at* www.law.du.edu/news/story.cfm?ID=56 (last visited Oct. 15, 2007).

16. Press Release, University of Colorado at Boulder (Apr. 2, 2007), www.colorado.edu/news/releases/2007/121.html.

17. *See* INSTITUTIONS OF HIGHER EDUCATION: A STUDY OF FACILITIES AND ENVIRONMENTAL CONSIDERATIONS, Spring 2006, *available at* www.universitybusiness.com/uploaded/pdfs/HiEdGreenFacilitiesStudyECNN.pdf.

18. Allegheny College Center for Economic and Environmental Development website, http://ceed.allegheny.edu/.

19. *See* http://powershift07.org.

20. Based on data gathered by AASHE, *supra* note 14.

21. Harvard University's Green Campus Initiative website, www.greencampus. harvard.edu.

22. For more detail, see www.greencampus.harvard.edu/greenliving-hls.

23. *See* www.recyclemaniacs.org.

24. It is estimated there were no more than 20 such positions in the United States in 2002.

25. *See* www.presidentsclimatecommitment.org.

26. Due to lack of space, the authors cannot mention all organizations supporting SHE in the United States.

27. Association for the Advancement of Sustainability in Higher Education (AASHE) website, www.aashe.org.

28. AASHE's major projects include supporting the signatories of the ACUPCC and developing a rating system for campus sustainability.

29. Campus Consortium for Environmental Excellence website, www.c2e2. org.

30. National Wildlife Federation's Campus Ecology Program website, www. nwf.org/campusecology.

31. *See* www.secondnature.org.

32. Created in 1990, the international Talloires Declaration is signed by a university or college president, rector, or chancellor. As of May 2008, the total number of signatories stood at 375, with U.S. signatories numbering 142. *See* University Leaders for a Sustainable Future website, www.ulsf.org.

33. U.S. Partnership for Education for Sustainable Development website, www.uspartnership.org.

34. New Jersey Higher Education Partnership for Sustainability website, www.njheps.org.

35. Pennsylvania Environmental Resource Consortium website, www.pa consortium.state.pa.us.

36. *See* description of consortium at Yale University Office of Sustainability website, www.yale.edu/sustainability/consortium.htm.

37. Higher Education Associations for Sustainability Consortium website, www.heasc.net.

38. Information on Disciplinary Associations Network for Sustainability at AASHE website, www.aashe.net/dans.

39. Ray Anderson, founder of Interface, Inc., has made this claim regarding his company and others. *See* www.interfaceinc.com.

40. The University of Georgia's Environmental Literacy Requirement is one example. *See* http://bulletin.uga.edu/bulletin/prg/uga_req.html# Environmental.

41. Ponderosa Project at Northern Arizona University website, http://jan.ucc. nau.edu/ponderosa; and Piedmont Project at Emory University website, www.scienceandsociety.emory.edu/piedmont.

Chapter 8

Kindergarten Through Twelfth Grade Education: Fragmentary Progress in Equipping Students to Think and Act in a Challenging World

Carmela Federico and Jaimie Cloud

This chapter summarizes the development of education for sustainability (EFS) over the last five years at the K-12 level—changes in what children learn in classrooms from kindergarten through high school graduation that affects their ability to contribute to a healthy and abundant world. EFS includes the time-honored goals of environmental education, such as knowledge of Earth's systems and cycles and imbuing students with an ethic of environmental stewardship, and adds a few new goals:

- Comprehending the dynamic connections among economies, the values and practices of societies, and the ecosystems that sustain human life;
- Thinking systemically, critically, and across disciplines about issues, problems, and solutions;
- Valuing and seeking to nurture the well-being and specialness of home places;
- Gaining the skills and inclination to work in community with others, on scales from the personal to the global, to achieve a more sustainable world;
- Being able to learn continuously and to challenge assumptions and mental models in order to keep moving toward sustainability in a complex and ever-changing world.

Why reform our K-12 educational system to attain these goals? There is strong evidence that not only specific habitats but indeed our entire planet is in serious environmental crisis,[1] and that "business as usual"—continuing, around the globe, to grow our energy use, consumption, and waste—is the cause, rather than a few easily correctable flaws in the practices of human societies. Comprehensively reforming our educational system can redefine business as usual as it shapes the knowledge, attitudes, and values of every student in the United States—every future voter and worker in a country whose decisions disproportionately affect the state of the world. K-12 education offers a crucial opportunity to equip people to evolve new, life-sustaining modes of meeting human needs.

There has been remarkable success over the last five years in K-12 education for sustainability, although some threats and some serious challenges remain. More mainstream institutions and school systems (the Scarsdale, New York, system, for example) are embracing sustainability paradigms with positive effects on K-12 education. More educational efforts self-consciously and directly seek to imbue students with sustainability-enhancing knowledge, attitudes, and skills. A few new funding streams exist, and others promise to grow. Research results increasingly support the benefits of pedagogies and practices that support K-12 EFS, and both new and established educational materials that are attractive to teachers and useful in American educational settings help to advance many facets of K-12 EFS.

A current snapshot of K-12 education for sustainability, however, also has its shadows. Shorter-term trends in education pose some serious obstacles to advancing sustainability knowledge and practice, and the recent heightened focus on testing in traditional subjects makes it difficult for sustainability's interdisciplinary approach to gain a foothold. Needed changes in the K-12 teaching of many subjects, particularly economics, are slow to come. Religious traditions increasingly are elaborating and promulgating their particular understandings of humankind's relationship to nature, which has made some faith traditions active allies for EFS but others strenuous opponents. Progress toward K-12 EFS will remain fragmentary and incomplete until all positive trends fully flower and all these obstacles are overcome.

The National Zeitgeist

Americans increasingly acknowledge environmental problems and seek solutions to them, which has provided essential support for progress in EFS. While there has always been substantial room for maverick innovators in American education, the mainstream, in the United States and elsewhere, is generally conservative and normative: education serves to prepare students for success in a given society, as imagined and conceived by established experts in existing fields and as developed into training programs by educators. Progress in imbuing the general population with an understanding of how a healthy environment is relevant to our future wellbeing is therefore a prerequisite to widespread sustainability-supporting changes in our educational programs. Thankfully, such progress is finally occurring in the United States. The last five years have seen the publication of many credible and grim assessments of our global future[2]; the mounting evidence for global warming and its huge potential for harm has finally begun to affect the behavior of government institutions, businesses, faith traditions, and the public, thanks to the sheer weight of confirmatory data and to many recent successful educational efforts.[3] More college and graduate programs are evolving to include sustainability and environmental precepts and requirements, not just implicitly or peripherally but as clearly stated and central aspects of their mission.[4] All these changes are beginning to affect K-12 educational institutions as well, with even stronger impacts to follow as our institutions seek to accomplish their aims in ways that also safeguard the environment.

Although vague and more difficult to quantify, recent trends in work and lifestyle are also helping. More schools, responding to these trends, are critically addressing consumerism and its promised rewards.[5] Increasing job and income insecurity is making some educators focus on preparing students to obtain an adequate slice of a shrinking pie, but others are exposing students to the broader range of worklife and lifestyle choices currently abounding in America, some of which (e.g., voluntary simplicity, balancing work and personal/family goals) can serve as models for more sustainable and satisfying lives.[6]

Some American religious denominations pose obstacles to the goal of educating all American students to fashion a more sustainable world. In a 2005 Newsweek poll, an astonishing 55 percent of Americans claimed to believe in an imminent apocalypse[7]; believing that the world will end soon can make environmentalism seem pointless.[8] Some fundamentalist faiths oppose the teaching of evolution, which is critical for understanding Earth's systems and cycles, and some focus on the world to come and find little value in engaging with the material world. Many parents with such beliefs are homeschooling their children or sending them to independent schools lacking a strong EFS curriculum.[9] On a hopeful note, however, many American evangelical faith traditions are fostering "creation care" and are helping students in faith-based schools learn to safeguard the health of the environment.[10]

Standards and Capacity Building

Over the last five years, educational standards have increasingly supported EFS, and many states have launched new efforts to mobilize more resources to attain EFS-relevant goals, particularly in environmental education. Vermont continues to require schools to attain two explicit EFS standards,[11] and a growing number of states have adopted explicit environmental literacy standards, providing official requirements and expectations for this important component of K-12 education for sustainability. In the past, EFS goals have been addressed by science and social studies standards, but only indirectly and not comprehensively. Existing educational goals have hit some EFS "targets" without having EFS as a stated goal. Under explicit standards, not only is an EFS goal being achieved, but it is being *targeted* because an educational standards-setting board has acknowledged that it is important. For example, some environmental literacy was achieved with older science standards, but never was comprehensive environmental literacy a stated goal of a state's educational system. Occasionally, now, states have forthrightly stated that environmental literacy is a goal, and there are some educational standards that help students achieve it.

The Secretary's Advisory Group for Environmental Education (SAGEE) has been active in Massachusetts, having published benchmarks, promulgated effective environmental education models, and worked to implement the statewide Environmental Education Plan.[12] California is poised to begin implementing its Education and the Environment Initiative (EEI).[13] Numerous Oregon schools are active in the Sustainable Oregon Schools Initiative,[14] and Minnesota's Office of Environmental Assistance has developed a comprehensive and influential Environmental Literacy Scope and Sequence.[15] Washington State offers E3 Washington, an initiative "for an inclusive process to develop a comprehensive statewide environmental education plan that optimizes environmental education for everyone who lives, learns, works, and plays in Washington State."[16] An evolving partnership between the North American Association of Environmental Educators (NAAEE) and the National Council for Accreditation of Teacher Certification (NCATE) could have positive effects on teacher education: NAAEE will help shape the standards that apply to teacher education programs, which may prove to be a productive avenue for equipping more new teachers to cover environmental and sustainability topics effectively.[17]

Research and Funding

There has been a wealth of positive results supporting the benefits of EFS-relevant pedagogies and practices over the last five years, and some positive developments in funding EFS in schools. Recent research and reports in Washington State in 2004-2005 demonstrate positive correlations between environmental education and achievement on state tests.[18] New evidence also confirms many educational benefits of place-based education, which is EFS-supportive because it immerses students in an interdisciplinary study of, and connection to, the problems and potentials of their home places.[19] The National Environmental Literacy Assessment, an effort to benchmark current attainment of U.S. middle-school environmental literacy, is underway; this government-funded study should prove extremely useful in documenting the benefits and achievements of future environmental education and EFS initiatives.[20]

EPA grants continue to support environmental education, and sometimes even explicit K-12 EFS projects.[21] This funding, however, has been under threat over the last decade, and securing it has tied up much of the EFS community's fundraising efforts.

Recent concerns about children's health have supported efforts to educate children about food systems and healthy food choices. The Berkeley Food Systems Project's School Lunch Initiative, for example, provides mini-grants to area schools to link healthy lunch, experiential learning in gardens and kitchen classrooms, and formal academic study.[22] The National Farm to School Network was launched in 2007 to connect schools to local, healthier, and more sustainable food.[23] Some creative educators have used funding from the Centers for Disease Control and new school wellness mandates to support sustainable food systems education.[24]

Some promising new initiatives bode well for K-12 sustainability education to contribute to the health of children's minds and hearts as well as their bodies. An impressive collection of research is showing that experiences in nature that offer self-direction, play, free-ranging exploration, and contemplation are beneficial to children's emotional, psychological, and cognitive development,[25] and a new stream of funding to connect kids to the natural world is emerging as a result. Most notably, the National Forum on Children and Nature, a new co-alition of governors, mayors, corporate CEOs, heads of environmental organizations, and leaders from health and education institutions, "will invest several million dollars in projects with on-the-ground tangible results that address the issue of children's isolation from na-ture."[26] Meanwhile, a national coalition of environmental education advocates seeks to make "No Child Left Inside" part of the reauthorization of No Child Left Behind and to pass the No Child Left Inside Act in Congress (funding to train teachers and develop model environmental education programs).[27]

Overall, government grants have not abounded in recent years to support the interdisciplinary exploration of real-world issues from a sustainability framework, nor to prepare students to learn this approach. Independent foundations and corporations, however, are increasingly supporting sustainability projects, including those that involve children and K-12 education, and EFS activists are working to persuade sustainability-practicing companies to support efforts to train their future workforce.[28]

Systemic School Reform

There has been substantial growth in the number of schools whose central mission is to prepare students to advance sustainability. Many of these schools embody this commitment in their facilities and operations. A recent *Green Guide* article lists the top 10 green schools, offering eco-friendly buildings, green operations, and a consistent environmental infusion into teaching and activities.[29] A continued interest on the part of school-reform funders (for example, the New American Schools Corporation) to fund small, innovative schools and charter schools also has produced some new environment-focused schools, some of which operate in partnership with an environmental NGO.[30]

The long-term economic benefits of "high-performance" (energy and resource-efficient) construction are becoming evident to school building authorities across the country. In New Jersey, since 2002 all new state-funded school construction is required to follow the guidelines of the Leadership in Energy and Environmental Design (LEED) Green Building Rating System, although many criticize the spotty and inadequate implementation and enforcement of this mandate.[31] There is a wealth of new guidelines to support green school construction,[32] and many public school buildings fall under common regulations mandating that government buildings meet LEED standards.[33] Some state energy programs have set-asides to fund green energy in schools.[34] In California, the Green Schools Initiative seeks to employ green school practices and construction, seeking to avoid risks to student health.[35] Often, such school's green features are central to the school's curriculum—using the school, in David Orr's apt phrase, as "crystallized pedagogy."[36]

Given the vast numbers of independent schools in the United States, it is exciting that the National Association of Independent Schools (NAIS) has made a clear commitment to encourage and support education for sustainability in its member institutions, with diverse projects and capacity-building for its member institutions, teachers, and students.[37] Other noteworthy developments in independent K-12 sustainability education include the emergence of sustainability coordinators on independent school campuses[38] and the establishment of the E.E. Just Environmental Leadership Institute at the Kimball Union Academy in New Hampshire, serving as an EFS and environmental education resource for a growing network of independent schools.[39]

There has been a growth in the institutional support for place-based education and in the number of K-12 schools seeking to implement place-based education. Shelburne Farms (Vermont), The Rural Trust, the Center for Place-Based Education, and the Monadnock Institute of Nature, Place and Culture all continue to work to connect students to their home places and to foster connections to their local environment, traditions, and history,[40] and both urban and rural programs are coming to see the educational worth of connecting children to their world.[41]

NGOs whose mission is to foster K-12 education for sustainability have grown in both number and scope over the last five years. Shelburne Farms offers a summer Education for Sustainability Institute and a Sustainable Schools Project to help schools attain Vermont's EFS standards.[42] The Children's Environmental Literacy Foundation (CELF), a new organization based in Westchester County, New York, and the Wallerstein Collaborative for Urban Environmental Education, based at New York University, seek to support environmental and sustainability education in urban public schools.[43] The Cloud Institute for Sustainability Education has grown its programs regionally and nationally and helps school districts implement EFS.[44] Susan Santone's Creative Change Educational Solutions also works with more schools in a more geographically diverse swath of the United States.[45] The Marion Institute has sponsored teacher training to bring the ZERI Learning Initiative, a project of Gunter Pauli's Zero Emissions Research Initiative, more widely to the United States.[46] Facing the Future continues to offer teacher training and district support for implementing K-12 education for sustainability.[47] NAAEE offers workshops and symposia that are EFS-specific at its popular annual conference, and sustainability educators are appearing more frequently on the NAAEE board and its committees.[48] On-the-ground sustainability demonstration projects are increasingly common, and most offer curriculum and education to local K-12 schools—see, for example, New York City's Science Barge, a sustainable urban farm, which hosts visiting classes.[49]

Environmental education is also reaching faith-based independent schools. The Heifer Project's work is noteworthy; as they raise money for sustainable agriculture in developing countries, they effectively teach many faith communities about sustainability. In New Jersey, Green Faith (a regional NGO focused on green energy for congregations) and the Center for Health, Environment and Justice (founded by "Love Canal" heroine Lois Gibbs) have launched a project to green the operations of faith-based schools. Genesis Farm continues to be an important source for Catholic educators seeking to imbue their education with an "Earth literacy" approach.[50] While the Evangelical Environment Network focuses on communities of faith, camps, and colleges, its conferences and materials are undoubtedly having an impact on some evangelical K-12 schools and helping them to foster an ethic of creation care.[51]

Promising Programs and Projects

Over the last five years, there has been a growth in programs and projects to implement education for sustainability; opportunities for students to explore crucial aspects of EFS have become more numerous, more engaging and effective, and more diverse. While comprehensive reform of K-12 curriculum and practices must remain the long-term goal, individual programs and projects enable some progress and often serve as a first step toward schoolwide penetration and commitment.

Planners, whose job is to contribute to regional sustainability, are providing EFS content for schools and NGOs that work with schools. The Brooklyn Center for the Urban Environment, for example, has launched the Academy of Urban Planning, which organizes its curriculum around sustainable planning.[52] Moreover, EFS-focused NGOs also have been quick to connect to the burgeoning movement for regional sustainability planning. The Cloud Institute for Sustainability Education, most prominently, works with several regional authorities to create synergies between local sustainability planning and K-12 education; the city of Burlington, Vermont, includes its school system in the sustainability planning it undertakes.[53] The Sustainable Design Project, in Washington State, will soon be a public-private partnership that brings industry, business, and higher education partners together with K-12 classrooms to design sustainable solutions to real-world challenges.[54] The SoL Education Partnership fosters a national learning community of sites with school/community partnerships moving toward sustainability.[55]

Several NGOs, notably the Cloud Institute for Sustainability Education and Earth Day Network, work with schools to infuse sustainability content and approaches into their civics curricula and activities.[56] Green energy projects continue—for example, Junior Solar Sprint, Kidwind, and the Green Schools project.[57] Independent schools now offer several networkwide programs and projects that are noteworthy, such as the 2020 Challenge and the Interschool Green Cup Challenge.[58] Education about, and participation in, sustainable food systems continues to grow; NGOs such as the Heifer Project and the Food Project work with schools to help children grow local food and learn about healthy and sustainable food options.[59] Service learning continues to offer water-quality monitoring and beach/riparian cleanups as a prominent student activity.[60] Environmental justice organizations also work with schools.[61]

There has been a growth in international sustainability-related projects, and in U.S. participation in them. A U.S. partnership was formed, for example, to support participation in the U.N. Decade of Education for Sustainable Development.[62] The International Education and Resource Network (IEARN), an international organization of educators, reaches schools with its sustainability projects.[63] United States schools participate in the U.N.'s Water for Life project and in the U.S. Stockholm Junior Water Prize.[64] The National Science Foundation funds Global Challenge, in which United States and international high school students work in partnership to create global warming solutions.[65] EFS educators in the United States work with the Center for Environmental Education (CEE) in Ahmedebad, India, which publishes a journal and held an international EFS conference in 2007.[66]

There has been a promising surge in civic engagement among today's youth, some of which takes place in association with schools. The High School Ecological Literacy Project trains high school students to report on local environmental issues, and the Green Energy Council is seeking high school chapters.[67] Groups such as DoRight, a Westchester County middle school-run energy audit firm, are proliferating, and Eban Goodstein's Focus the Nation climate change campaign involves high school educational programs.[68]

On the negative side, budget constraints and the weight of increased testing focusing on math and reading skills have made it more difficult for off-campus trips to nature centers. Nature center staff are resourcefully adapting, making a convincing case that diverse and numerous standards are taught via on-site nature exploration, and equipping themselves to visit schools.[69]

Curriculum and Pedagogies

Progress continues in both the creation of exciting new material and the penetration of sustainability topics into what is taught in K-12 schools. The International Baccalaureate program, which is especially popular in high-performing schools, offers high school programs in design technology and environmental systems.[70] Advanced Placement World History includes the interaction between societies and the environment as one of its five major themes,[71] and the Environmental Literacy Council now offers environmental history modules for high school teachers.[72] Two new ecological economics textbooks suitable for use in both high schools and colleges now exist,[73] although their impact on the high school economics curriculum has not yet been felt. Nor have NGOs that promote entrepreneurship evolved to include "triple bottom line" thinking (assessing a company's impacts on society and the environment as well as its profitability) in the entrepreneurship training they undertake with American youth.

Facing the Future, The Cloud Institute, and Creative Change Educational Solutions offer a growing and diverse collection of resources to support K-12 education for sustainability.[74] The Center for a New

American Dream and the World Wildlife Fund have prepared *Smart Consumers: An Educator's Guide to Exploring Consumer Issues and the Environment* for middle-schoolers.[75] Great tools exist for the K-12 teaching of systems thinking, but this approach is still not widely found in K-12 schools, despite an established and active community of committed systems-thinking educators.[76]

High school earth science classes help students develop the knowledge base, critical thinking, and scientific reasoning needed to evaluate global warming arguments and evidence, and global warming appears more often in middle school science programming as well.[77] More than 50,000 classroom teachers received a free copy of Al Gore's climate change opus, *An Inconvenient Truth*, with a free downloadable educational guide.[78]

Mainstream curriculum organizations now offer curricula that are more supportive of K-12 education for sustainability. Project Learning Tree, for example, now offers *Exploring Environmental Issues: Places We Live*, illuminating the connections between environment, society, and economy, and the United Nations Association of the United States offers a new Model U.N. unit on the Commission on Sustainable Development.[79] Because these organizations have credibility and a broad client base, they will bring EFS to more and more schools and educators.

Recommendations for Future Progress

Five recommendations for future progress in EFS follow, based on the analysis and information in this chapter.

1. Standards and Capacity-Building. For decades now, support for EFS in existing standards and educational goals has been spotty and scattershot. K-12 education now needs to embrace EFS as a clearly-stated and central goal, and content and performance standards need to be redefined to attain this goal. More explicit support for sustainability in state-mandated and other influential content and performance standards would produce widespread improvement in EFS. Advocates for EFS in K-12 education must find new ways to encourage the national discipline-specific organizations and the state boards that establish standards to include EFS as a central goal throughout K-12 education. Guides to implementing standards can use EFS examples and content.[80] Work must advance in reforming testing regimes so that they are more attuned with EFS pedagogies, goals, and content knowledge. Successful statewide mobilizations for EFS, such as those in Massachusetts and Oregon, need to support fledgling efforts in other states.

2. Research and Funding. EFS advocates must secure funding to scale up current EFS efforts in the United States. The endeavor currently lacks consistent and sufficient funding for more than piecemeal attainment of its goals. Corporations, some of which are becoming sustainability leaders, must be persuaded to support the proper training of America's future workers and leaders. Foundations need to recognize the importance of funding EFS; it is a riskier and more long-term commitment than directly investing in environmental protection, but EFS is crucial to the future of our environment. The last 30 years have demonstrated how limited progress in laws and regulations can be without widespread popular commitment to environmental goals and values. EFS is crucial to providing the necessary broad support for all environmental progress; there is no shortcut. School reform remains a messy and inexact process, but there has been progress lately in compiling data to guide efforts to reform educational institutions to make them more supportive of EFS. EFS advocates must impress upon foundations the importance of EFS to all their goals, and must also help foundations recognize that money invested in EFS will produce tangible results. Securing government funds, through working with politicians and by electing EFS supporters to office, would also help immensely.

3. Systemic School Reform. Progress must occur in infusing EFS on a wide scale into the professional development of pre-service and working educators. This will require both the transformation of established professional development programs and the expansion of those teacher training offerings that already support EFS. National educational networks (NAIS is a shining example) need to share the best practices found in EFS model schools among their memberships. Established pedagogical models must be engaged and transformed so that they more explicitly and effectively support EFS. EFS practitioners must also form coalitions with other kinds of school reformers to advance pedagogies and goals that support EFS (e.g., students as lifelong learners, schools as learning institutions). An effort must be directed at engaging faith-based schools in realizing EFS goals in their educational programs; full weight must be given to the societal progress that can be result if this goal is achieved.

4. Curriculum and Programs. The producers of established and popular curricula and textbooks need to be further engaged to strengthen EFS in their offerings. EFS curricula must become even better at being teacher-friendly and being attuned to the realities of those who choose and use curriculum (e.g., providing activities that work for classes that mix mainstream and special needs students). Influential NGOs that offer K-12 school programs (e.g., Junior Achievement) must be engaged so that their popular and widespread offerings can support EFS.

5. The National Zeitgeist. Nothing will help to advance K-12 EFS more than growth in societal demand for educational programs that equip students to create a more sustainable world. All those with a role and a stake in our future (parents, universities, business, and government) must model sustainability, involve schools in their own efforts to progress toward sustainability, and advocate for EFS (and the funds to implement EFS) in our school systems.

Conclusion

Some piecemeal and some comprehensive progress has been made both in the preconditions needed for K-12 education for sustainability to flourish and in the institutions and materials needed to teach students what they need to know to contribute to a more sustainable world. Those committed to K-12 EFS feel immense pressure to achieve this important goal in time to safeguard the quality of human life. A groundswell in both public understanding of environmental problems and in societal commitment to sustainability-enhancing actions has opened doors and created new opportunities to transform institutions and reach our teachers and students. Efforts must continue to persuade school officials of the crucial importance of educating children so they can act sustainably as workers and citizens, and also to create quality and effective programs and curricula to achieve this goal.

ENDNOTES

1. INTERGOVERNMENTAL PANEL ON CLIMATE CHANGE (IPCC), FOURTH ASSESSMENT REPORT: CLIMATE CHANGE 2007, *available at* www.ipcc. ch/ipccreports/assessments-reports.htm (accessed Nov. 10, 2007); *see also* U.N. ENV'T PROGRAM, GLOBAL ENVIRONMENTAL OUTLOOK YEARBOOK 2007, *available at* www.unep.org/geo/yearbook/yb2007/ (accessed Nov. 10, 2007).

2. *See, e.g.*, the documents cited *supra*, note 1.

3. Notable recent films include Al Gore's *An Inconvenient Truth* and Leonardo DiCaprio's *The Eleventh Hour*; notable organizations include Bill McKibben's Step it Up (stepitup2007.org/) and Environmental Defense's Fight Global Warming campaign (www.fightglobalwarming.com).

4. Overall progress can be seen in the growth and work of the American Association for Sustainability in Higher Education (AASHE) (www.aashe.org); progress in business schools can be found in THE ASPEN INST., BEYOND GREY PINSTRIPES 2007-2008, *available at* www.beyondgreypinstripes. org/rankings/bgp_2007_2008.pdf (accessed Nov. 18, 2007); *see also* Wynn Calder & Julian Dautremont-Smith, *Higher Education: More and More Laboratories for Inventing a Sustainable Future*, Chapter 7 in this volume.

5. The Center for a New American Dream (www.newdream.org) leads the way, as does a growing movement in "character education"; *see* www. goodcharacter.com for an overview.

6. LOUIS UCHITELLE, THE DISPOSABLE AMERICAN: LAYOFFS AND THEIR CONSEQUENCES (2006); *see also* JULIET SCHOR, THE OVERSPENT AMERICAN (1999) (somewhat less up to date). There has also been substantial growth in "voluntary simplicity" websites and publications; *see, e.g.*, John Ewold, *More Make the Choice to Live With Less*, MINNEAPOLIS STAR TRIBUNE, *available at* www.startribune.com/1229/story/524491.html (accessed Nov. 20, 2007).

7. Colleen O'Connor, *Revelation Relevancy*, DENVER POST, Apr. 14, 2005, *available at* www.signonsandiego.com/uniontrib/20050414/news_lz1c14 revelat.html (accessed Sept. 1, 2007).

8. The view of Ted Haggard, then-president of the National Association of Evangelicals, *quoted in* O'Connor, *supra* note 7.

9. CHRIS HEDGES, AMERICAN FASCISTS 153 (2006). According to the National Center for Education Statistics, there was a 41 percent growth in enrollments at conservative Christian schools between 1992 and 2002, and it is estimated that the number of home-schoolers rose from 850,000 to 1.1 million between 1999 and 2003, with 72 percent of those surveyed citing religious reasons for their decision.

10. *See* "Systemic School Reform," *infra* in this chapter for details.

11. *See* Vermont Education for Sustainability Project, Vermont Education for Sustainability, *available at* www.vtefs.org/resources/standardsstory.html (accessed Sept. 30, 2007).

12. Secretary's Advisory Group for Environmental Education, www.sagee.org (accessed Sept. 15, 2007).

13. California Environmental Protection Agency, Education and the Environment Initiative Homepage (Cal. A.B. 1548), www.calepa.ca.gov/Education/EEI/ (accessed Sept. 15, 2007).

14. Zero Waste Alliance, Sustainable Oregon Schools Initiative, *available at* www.zerowaste.org/schools/index.htm (accessed Nov. 20, 2007) ("the next stage of a sustainable schools project that was initiated by the Governor and convened in 2003 by the Secretary of State as an Oregon Solutions project").

15. Standards available online at www.seek.state.mn.us/eemn_c.cfm; *see also* MINNESOTA OFFICE OF ENVTL. ASSISTANCE, ENVIRONMENTAL LITERACY SCOPE AND SEQUENCE, March 2002, www.seek.state.mn.us/publications/ScopeandSequence-Parts/Intro-ELSS-Basics.pdf (accessed Sept. 20, 2007).

16. Environmental Education Association of Washington, About E3 Washington, www.e3washington.org/about-e3-washington (accessed Sept. 20, 2007).

17. Michele Archie, *Setting High Standards: Environmental Education Builds a Home in Teacher Education Accreditation* (March 2006), *available at* http://eetap.org/media/pdf/accreditation.pdf (accessed Sept. 20, 2007).

18. CATHERINE TAYLOR ET AL., PACIFIC ED. INST., DEMONSTRATING THE EFFICACY OF ENVIRONMENTAL EDUCATION: USING CRITERION REFERENCED TESTS TO DEMONSTRATE STUDENT ACHIEVEMENT ON STATE DISCIPLINE BASED EXAMS, PEI Technical Report #7, *available at* www.pacificeducationinstitute.org/Research%20and%20Reports/PEI_Technical_Report_7_Cathy_Taylor.pdf (accessed Sept. 25, 2007); *see also* WASHINGTON STATE DEP'T OF ENVTL. RES., REPORT CARD ON THE STATUS OF ENVIRONMENTAL EDUCATION, *available at* http://aeoe.org/news/online/EEReportCard.pdf, 2004 (accessed Sept. 25, 2007).

19. See the list of recent research at www.peecworks.org/PEEC/PEEC_Research/, put together by the Place-Based Education Evaluation Collaborative (accessed Sept. 25, 2007). Also see "Preparing Youth for a Healthy and Sustainable Future: An Evaluation of the Cloud Institute's Business and Entrepreneurship Education for the 21st Century (BEE 21) and Inventing the Future (IF) Curricula, a Report to the Ewing Marion Kauffman Foundation, December 2007," prepared by Adria Gallup-Black et al., Academy for Educational Development.

20. Press Release, Nat'l Envtl. Literacy Assessment, Data Collectors Needed for National Education Study (Feb. 7, 2007), *available at* www.naaee.org/programs-and-initiatives/research/nela/nela-press-release.

21. For some recent EFS-funded projects, see www.socialstudies.org/discuss/msgReader$711; www.rprogress.org/training_manual/EPA_Grant_Summary.pdf; and www.blcse.org.

22. *See* School Lunch Initiative website, www.schoollunchinitiative.org/; and www.ecoliteracy.org/grants/index.html.

23. *See* National Farm to School Network website, www.farmtoschool.org/state-home.php?id=18.

24. Nancy Sing-Bock, New York City elementary school principal, personal communication, Sept. 12, 2007; Katie Ginsberg, Children's Environmental

Literacy Foundation Founder and Executive Director, personal communication, Sept. 29, 2007.

25. Dr. Nancy Allen's research has been noteworthy in this regard. *See* www.human.cornell.edu/che/bio.cfm?netid=nmw2 for publications. Richard Louv's recent book, LAST CHILD IN THE WOODS: SAVING OUR CHILDREN FROM NATURE DEFICIT DISORDER (2005), has galvanized the public, educators, and officials.

26. The Conservation Fund, The National Forum on Children and Nature, www.conservationfund.org/children_nature (accessed Sept. 25, 2007).

27. Chesapeake Bay Foundation, No Child Left Inside: Main EENCLB, www. Cbf.org/site/PageServer?pagename=act_sub_actioncenter_federal_NCLB& JServSessionIdr007=ghusq20jg3.app23a, (accessed Nov. 15, 2007).

28. Noteworthy: the Geraldine R. Dodge Foundation, www.grdodge.org; the Russell Family Foundation, www.trff.org; and the Bay and Paul Foundations, www.bayandpaulfoundations.org.

29. P.W. McRandle & Sara Smiley Smith, *The Top Ten Green Schools in the United States: 2006*, THE GREEN GUIDE, July/August 2005, *available at* www.thegreenguide.com/doc/115/toptenschools (accessed Oct. 2, 2007).

30. The Ridge and Valley Charter School and Genesis Farm in Blairstown, New Jersey, for example, www.ridgeandvalley.org, and The Green School and the Brooklyn Center for the Urban Environment in Brooklyn www.bcue.org/?go=joi.63. Other noteworthy examples are found in MICHELE L. ARCHIE, ASSOCIATION FOR SUPERVISION AND CURRICULUM DEVELOPMENT, ADVANCING EDUCATION THROUGH ENVIRONMENTAL LITERACY (2003), *available at* www.ascd.org/portal/site/ascd/template. Chapter/menuitem.b71d101a2f7c208cdeb3ffdb62108a0c/?chapterMgmtId= ca3b177a55f9ff00VgnVCM1000003d01a8c0RCRD (accessed Nov. 19, 2007).

31. *See* www.njsda.gov/Innovations/High_Performance_Schools/index.htm, although green advocates question overall compliance and enforcement.

32. *See, e.g.*, the Sustainable Buildings and Industry Council, High Performance School Buildings Program, www.sbicouncil.org/highperformance schoolbuildings.htm (accessed Oct. 15, 2007) and National Clearinghouse for Educational Facilities, NCEF Resource List: High Performance Green Schools, www.edfacilities.org/rl/high_performance.cfm (accessed Oct. 15, 2007).

33. New York City has such a standard. For example, see www.construction weblinks.com/Resources/Industry_Reports__Newsletters/Jan_15_2007/ newy.html.

34. For New Jersey, see www.eere.energy.gov/state_energy_program/project_ brief_detail.cfm/pb_id=955.

35. The Green Schools Initiative, About the Little Green Schoolhouse, www. greenschools.net/about.html (accessed Oct. 15, 2007).

36. David Orr, *What Is Education For?*, 27 IN CONTEXT 52 (Winter 1991), *available at* www.context.org/ICLIB/IC27/Orr.htm (accessed Nov. 20, 2007).

37. The National Association of Independent Schools website, www.nais.org, provides details on their diverse and comprehensive EFS work.

38. The Lawrenceville School and Newark Academy in New Jersey, for example (author campus visits).

39. The E.E. Just Environmental Leadership Institute, www.eejust.org (accessed on Nov. 20, 2007).

40. For more program information, see www.shelburnefarms.org, www.rural edu.org; www.anei.org/pages/89_cpbe.cfm; and www.fpc.edu/monadnock institute/.

41. For a great urban example, see El Puente Academy in Brooklyn, at www.elpuente.us/academy/index.htm.

42. Shelburne Farms, Shelburne Farms Professional Development Programs for Teachers, *available at* www.shelburnefarms.org/educationprograms/ professional.shtm (accessed Nov. 17, 2007).

43. Children's Environmental Literacy Foundation, www.celfoundation.org; Wallerstein Collaborative for Urban Environmental Education, http:// steinhardt.nyu.edu/wallerstein.

44. The Cloud Institute for Sustainability Education, www.sustainabilityed. org.

45. Creative Change Educational Solutions, What's New, www.creativechange. net/whatsnew/index.htm (accessed Nov. 8, 2007).

46. Marion Institute, The ZERI Educational Initiative, www.marioninstitute. Org/matriarch/MultiPiecePage.asp_Q_PageID_E_140_A_PageName_E_ programzeri (accessed Nov. 8, 2007).

47. Facing the Future, www.facingthefuture.org.

48. Jaimie P. Cloud, Founder and President, The Cloud Institute of Sustainability, personal communication, Sept. 19, 2007.

49. New York Sun Works, New York Sun Works: About the Barge, http://nysun works.org/science_barge/about_the_barge.html (accessed Nov. 10, 2007).

50. More information can be found at Genesis Farm's website, www.genesisfarm. org.

51. *See* the Evangelical Environment Network's website, www.creationcare. org, for updates and details.

52. Brooklyn Center for the Urban Environment, www.bcue.org/?go=joi.63 (accessed on Nov. 20, 2007).

53. Jaimie P. Cloud, Founder and President, The Cloud Institute of Sustainability Education, personal communication, Nov. 8, 2007; *see* Institute for Sustainable Communities section of City of Burlington, Vt. homepage, www.ci.burlington.vt.us/sistercities (accessed Nov. 19, 2007). Also noteworthy is the EfS Curriculum Development Project, a collaborative between the Putnam/Northern Westchester BOCES Curriculum Center, the curriculum council and educators from the 18 member school districts, and the Cloud Institute for Sustainability Education to develop K-12 EfS curriculum exemplars across the disciplines over the next several years, www.pnwboces.org.

54. Environmental Education Association of Washington, Job Opportunities—Environmental Education Association of Washington, www.eeaw. org/about/jobs/index_html (accessed Nov. 20, 2007).

55. Society for Organizational Learning, SoL Education Partnership Launches National Learning Community, www.solonline.org/news/item?item_id= 12391163 (accessed Nov. 19, 2007).

56. Earth Day Network, Civic Education, www.earthday.net/programs/CEP_ intro.aspx (accessed Nov. 19, 2007), and Inventing the Future: Leadership and Participation for the 21st Century, www.cloudinstitute.org..

57. For more information, visit www.nesea.org/education/jss/; www.kidwind. org; and www.ase.org/greenschools.

58. See www.nais.org/challenge2020 and www.exeter.edu/comm/866_4266. aspx for details.

59. See www.heifer.org/site/c.edJRKQNiFiG/b.734899; www.thefoodproject. org; and Vermont FEED, www.vtfeed.org, for information on these model programs.

60. See, e.g., the California Water Quality Service Learning Program, www. waterlessons.org.

61. Model programs include West Harlem Environmental Action, http://www. weact.org/programs/leadership/earthcrew.html, and Sustainable South Bronx, www.ssbx.org.

62. The U.S. Partnership website is at www.uspartnership.org.

63. IEARN website, www.iearn.org; Ed Gragert, IEARN Executive Director, personal communication, Sept. 5, 2007.

64. Water for Life website, www.un.org/waterforlifedecade; Stockholm Junior Water Prize website, www.wef.org/LearnAboutWater/ForStudents/SJWP.

65. The Arno Group, The Global Challenge, www.globalchallengeaward.org (accessed Nov. 12, 2007).

66. CEE's website is at www.ceeindia.org.

67. NPR and Living On Earth High School Ecological Literacy Project, www. basslinedesign.com/web.php?focus_cat=1&focus_item=2 (accessed Nov. 1, 2007); Green Energy Council spokesperson, personal conversation, Nov. 30, 2007.

68. Katie Ginsberg, CELF Executive Director, personal communication, Sept. 5, 2007; Focus the Nation, K-12 Schools, www.focusthenation.org/k-12.php (accessed Nov. 1, 2007).

69. The Meadowlands Environment Center, like many others, now brings a traveling experience to schools; personal observation, author, 2006.

70. International Baccalaureate, IB Diploma Programme Curriculum, Group 4: Experimental Sciences, www.ibo.org/diploma/curriculum/group4 (accessed Nov. 1, 2007).

71. The College Board, AP World History Course Description (May 2008 and May 2009), at 5, available at www.collegeboard.com/prod_downloads/ ap/students/worldhistory/ap-cd-worldhist-0708.pdf (accessed Nov. 2, 2007).

72. Environmental Literacy Council, Environmental History Modules for Teachers, www.enviroliteracy.org/subcategory.php/314.html (accessed Nov. 2, 2007).

73. MICHAEL COMMON & SIGRID STAGL, ECOLOGICAL ECONOMICS: AN INTRODUCTION (2005) and HERMAN DALY & JOSHUA FARLEY, ECOLOGICAL ECONOMICS: PRINCIPLES AND APPLICATIONS (2004). The Cloud Institute's "Business and Entrepreneurship for the 21st Century" (BEE 21) high school course remains a quality effort to attain these goals, as does their secondary unit on ecological economics entitled *The Paper Trail: Connecting Economic and Natural Systems. See* www.Sustainabilityed.org/what/services_for_educators/BEE21.html.

74. Publications on websites, *supra* notes 42-47.

75. WWF/Center for a New American Dream, www.ibuydifferent.org/educators.asp (accessed Nov. 15, 2007).

76. Systems-thinking educators network online at The Creative Learning Exchange, www.clexchange.org.

77. Marc Rogoff, e-mail communication, Sept. 6, 2006.

78. Techie Scientists, AN INCONVENIENT TRUTH DVD Available to Teachers, http://techiescientists.blogspot.com/2006/12/inconvenient-truth-dvd-available-to.html (accessed Nov. 15, 2007); Participate, AIT in the Classroom, www.participate.net/educators/node/1 (accessed Nov. 15, 2007).

79. UNA-USA, Global Classrooms Curriculum Units, www.unausa.org/site/pp.asp?c=fvKRI8MPJpF&b=324674 (accessed Nov. 15, 2007).

80. This has recently happened in New Jersey, thanks to the work of the New Jersey Department of Environmental Protection. Marc Rogoff, NJDEP, personal communication, Sept. 21, 2007.

Chapter 9

Religion and Ethics Focused on Sustainability

Dieter T. Hessel

Patterns of maldevelopment—unsustainable human production, consumption, and reproduction—threaten to undermine human development and the prospects for sustainable living. In fact, the problems resulting from maldevelopment portend massive species extinction, affecting the course of evolution itself. This perilous situation exposes a profound spiritual crisis and raises ethical questions that require urgent response from people of faith, especially those in the United States, during the next decade.

After presenting some examples of local and national faith-based engagement in "Earthkeeping," or eco-justice action, this chapter describes how religious responses to environmental dangers such as climate change have been more focused on lifestyle change than on policy reform. The ethics of a just and sustainable global community—featuring the four basic eco-justice norms of solidarity, sustainability, sufficiency, and participation that United Nations conferences anticipated and the Earth Charter articulated—have yet to be widely appreciated and applied.

The next steps for religious communities include teaching eco-justice ethics, emphasizing sustainable sufficiency in daily living, becoming energetic advocates for public policies and economic practices that build a just and sustainable community, acting in partnership with others who would also be responsible citizens of Earth, and nurturing members spiritually to journey with reverential gratitude and disciplined care for diverse creation.

Ethical and Religious Foundations of Sustainability

The overarching moral assignment of our time is to act personally, institutionally, and politically in ways that are both ecologically fitting and socially just. Earth community's health now depends on humans relating to the natural world so as to maintain its ecological health and aesthetic quality, or as Aldo Leopold wrote in *The Sand County Alma-*

nac, to attend to the "integrity, stability and beauty of the biotic community." We need a supportive ethos that melds respect for diverse life with justice for everykind and responsibility to future generations. Because sustainability links environmental health with socioeconomic well-being, sustainability ethics encompass concerns for both ecology and justice. Sustainability is served by doing several interrelated things:

- acting to protect the commons against pollution or enclosure;
- careful stewarding of scarce resources and fair distribution of their benefits;
- restraining production and trade;
- utilizing ecologically and socially appropriate technology;
- internalizing costs to the environment when pricing goods;
- fostering greater local/regional self-sufficiency;
- consuming frugally;
- preserving biodiversity; and
- delivering environmental justice to the vulnerable.

When will the norms of sustainability ethics, established through decades of international and ecumenical discourse, become operational among citizens and their governments? In 1972, the Declaration of the United Nations Conference on the Human Environment (also known as the Stockholm Conference) emphasized that environmental improvement "for present and future generations" must be accompanied by inter- and intra-generational equity among humans. The Stockholm Conference's two shifts in ethical sensibility—affirming transgenerational responsibility and understanding that there are holistic connections among humanity's social, ecological, and economic obligations—were restated in the Brundtland Commission's 1987 assertion that "sustainable development meets the needs of the present without compromising the ability of future generations to meet their own needs."[1]

All people are equally "entitled to a healthy and productive life in harmony with nature." The Earth Summit's action plan, Agenda 21, pushed for (1) distributive justice (fair sharing) of environmental resources, or "natural capital," and (2) moral constraint on human activities that, if not curtailed or redirected, will severely degrade ecosystem functioning and biodiversity. Excessive use of resources by affluent people and powerful corporations often makes these resources unavailable to those who most depend on them for sustainable living.

In authentic sustainable development, "neither the value of economic justice nor the value of ecological integrity is treated instrumentally."[2] It expresses a genuine sense of mutual relationship between humans and nature, and discards a mere use-value approach to the environment. It challenges the popular but false assumption that societies can wait until they develop economically to adopt measures for environmental protection. Neo-liberals and Marxists alike still assume that economic development comes first, to be followed eventually by ecological sustainability. But that is an impossible scenario for today's increasingly crowded and technologically toxic world, which faces severe biophysical limits and growing socioeconomic inequity. Ecology and justice are non-sequential, simultaneous requirements; otherwise, the world will have neither.

The vision of a just and sustainable Earth community resonates with major religious traditions of the West, East, South, and Indigenous Peoples, which, at their best, inculcate awareness of the sacred and visions of an interdependent Earth community pivoting around belief in a just, loving God or a benign cosmic order. Ecumenical Christianity, in particular, has played a reinforcing role in this regard by fostering a vision and principles of a "Just, Participatory, and Sustainable Society."

In 1975, theologians and ethicists at the Nairobi Assembly of the World Council of Churches discerned that there will be little environmental health without social justice, and vice versa. Having come to this realization, ecumenical gatherings and leaders began to express an inclusive vision of eco-justice—ecological health and social equity together. In subsequent deliberations and programs over the three decades, ecumenical thought and action highlighted a global ethic of just and sustainable Earth community emphasizing four interrelated norms:

- *solidarity* with other people and creatures;

- ecological *sustainability* in development, technology, and production;

- *sufficiency* as a standard of equitable consumption and organized resource-sharing with genuine floors and ceilings; and

- socially just *participation* in decisions about how to obtain sustenance and to manage community for the good of all.[3]

Solidarity comprehends the full dimensions of Earth community and of inter-human obligation. Sustainability highlights ecological integrity and wise behavior through the entire cycle of resource use. The norms of sufficiency and participation express the distributive and participatory requirements of social justice. As James B. Martin-Schramm and Robert L. Stivers have written, "Only an ethic and practice that stress sufficiency, frugality, and generosity will ensure a sustainable future"; in turn, "participation is concerned with empowerment and [removing] obstacles to participating in decisions that affect lives."[4]

Observance of each of these four ethical norms reinforces the others. All four are core values to guide personal practice, social analysis, economic life, and public policy. They express a moral posture of respect and fairness toward all creation, and underscore the proactive link between caring for otherkind's flourishing and humanity's well-being—for today and in the long term. These norms allow for plural expression and contextual application that are respectful of both biotic and cultural diversity.

The breadth and depth of these ethical norms are articulated in the sustainability ethics of the Earth Charter,[5] which has been endorsed by thousands of civil society groups on six continents and by government representatives at the World Conservation Union. Completed early in 2000, the Earth Charter is based on "the largest global consultation process ever associated with an international declaration," and is increasingly seen as representing a consensus position on the religious and ethical basis for sustainability.[6] The Charter is a holistic, layered document that articulates the inspirational vision, basic values, and essential principles needed in a global ethic for Earth community.

The first of the Earth Charter's four general principles—"Respect Earth and life in all its diversity"—affirms the interdependence and intrinsic worth of every kind. From that follow three more general principles that specify shared ethical responsibility: (2) human responsibility for otherkind , i.e., "care for the community of life with understanding, compassion, and love"; (3) responsibility within and among human societies, i.e., "build democratic societies that are just, participatory, sustainable, and peaceful"; and (4) responsibility for future as well as present generations, that is, "secure Earth's bounty and beauty for present and future generations." Humans are to care for and to conserve the community of life in all three spheres, sharing benefits and burdens, while recognizing that quality of life and relationships—among people and with nature—are the crucial criteria. In other words, the human goal is to have and share life abundantly. (See the words of Jesus in the Gospel of John 10:10.)

Sustainability ethics, when put into practice, embody a positive alternative to destructive economic maldevelopment and consumption. The eco-justice vision and the values characteristic of such ethics challenge us all—our energy, economic, and political leaders, as well as the public, religious communities, and each of us personally—to discern what should (and should not) be done to achieve sustainability with justice in a hotter, more crowded world.

Tragically, despite the solemn commitments to advance this agenda made by governments and NGOs at the world summits in Rio de Janeiro (1992) and Johannesburg (2002), there are still more than two billion poor people trying to live on less than $2 per day. The global money economy continues to treat natural resources and traditional communities ruthlessly, and ignores future costs.

Religious communities in the United States can play a key role by illuminating a more sustainable path and teaching their members about the impact of human actions or inaction on future generations as well as the present generation struggling to live with dignity. Americans, the great majority of whom are people of faith, constitute a significant part of the richest 20 percent of the world's population that has been consuming over 85 percent of what the world economy produces, much of it in the form of fossil fuels. (At the same time, the poorest 20 percent of the world's population has been consuming less than two percent.)[7]

What people, enterprises, and government at all levels in the United States do to consume and waste less while acting to share limited world resources equitably will make a big difference. If American society and the U.S. government continue to ignore sustainability requirements, and fail to set the pace toward a just and sustainable future, other nations that have been developing rapidly and polluting excessively will have little incentive to go green voluntarily and to accede to binding international agreements. The national and global situation of unsustainable human enterprise exposes a deep spiritual and ethical crisis requiring priority attention from people of faith in the United States.

Responsive Faith Communities in the United States

In the United States, many religious leaders and adherents have been as slow as the general populace at comprehending the urgency of the environmental crisis or grasping the linkages among ecology, justice, and faith. Some religious bodies[8] still deny that humans should act to reduce global warming. And although a growing number of Americans of every religious faith affirm the need to conserve energy resources and protect the environment, it is unclear how much they will do in their daily lives, occupations, and politics for ecological health and socioeconomic justice.

On the other hand, there is quite a story to tell about the rise of engaged religious environmentalism.[9] Perhaps as many as one in 10 congregations now have committees or action groups, as well as special moments of ritual life, that affirm the spiritual and ethical importance of "caring for creation." They participate in preservation struggles, ecological restoration projects, community-supported agriculture, and practices of sustainable living such as energy efficiency. Furthermore, networks have organized within major Christian denominations—Episcopalians, Lutherans, Methodists, Presbyterians, and Roman Catholics—to support Earthkeeping members and congregations.[10] Synagogues participate in a network called the Coalition on the Environment and Jewish Life. Finally, cadres of members in Earthkeeping congregations are networking effectively with each other and with environmental organizations to make a denominational, ecumenical, and public difference. Examples of interfaith alliances include Faith in Place (a Chicago cluster), Earth Ministry (a Seattle-based regional program), and Religious Witness for the Earth (active on the East Coast).

Religious environmental activists underscore contemporary humanity's ethical responsibility to respect and conserve Earth's ecological integrity and biodiversity while acting to achieve social and economic justice. The sustainability and justice being sought has both intra- and inter-generational dimensions. The objective is to journey toward a durable, healthy future for humans and otherkind by showing respect for all beings; consuming less; preserving more; and seeking distributive, participatory, and restorative justice for the Earth's most vulnerable occupants, both human and nonhuman.

Recognizing how environmentally and socially crucial the next few decades of the 21st century will be, more faith communities in the

United States intend to reduce their ecological footprint and to protect the commons by eating locally grown organic food (including humanely treated food animals), purchasing imported products that are "fair-traded," using appropriate technology, and conserving energy while reducing waste.[11] Those communities recognize the significance of what Bill McKibben calls "deep economy,"[12] and they are now much more aware of the urgent need to address the human causes of ominous ecological deterioration. They resonate with Al Gore's assertion in his documentary *An Inconvenient Truth*—shown in thousands of congregations and community groups as well as movie theaters—that global warming is a moral issue as well as a scientific-technical issue. In short, a growing segment of the faith community grasps how pervasive the problem is and wants to meet it with commensurate action. There are current, timely examples of people of faith taking action on behalf of sustainability.

Step It Up

Segments of the religious community joined the environmental studies and action community in the Step It Up grassroots organizing campaign initiated at Middlebury College. This campaign culminated in demonstrations across the country on April 14, 2007, to demand that Congress commit to cutting carbon emissions by 80 percent by 2050. Students in 60 evangelical colleges and seminaries participated, thanks to a call to action written and circulated by University of Wisconsin professor Cal DeWitt, who has organized a network of environmental studies professors in Christian colleges.

The Christian Century published a cover story by Bill McKibben on the campaign. Interfaith Power and Light, an interfaith ministry with state chapters and noted for fostering green power production and using energy-efficient light bulbs, put the Step It Up organizers in touch with numerous congregations. The National Council of Churches Eco-Justice Working Group alerted its network. Unitarian environmental activists and the Coalition on the Environment and Jewish Life also lent their energy to this effort. As the result of these efforts, at the April 14 demonstration the banners of environmentally engaged congregations were evident in many localities—a public expression of commitment to Earthkeeping that would have been unlikely five years earlier.

Live Earth Pledge

Another striking example of eco-justice activism by segments of organized religion was the inclusion in the 7/7/07 Live Earth Pledge promoted by Al Gore of places of worship (the United States has several hundred thousand) among the settings in which to work for a dramatic increase in energy efficiency. The pledge lists several settings, including "place of worship" (including churches, synagogues, temples, and mosques) that need to become energy efficient. This movement was due, in part, to the influence of organizations such as the National Religious Partnership for the Environment and Interfaith Power and Light. Such examples of engagement by organized religion suggest that "the day has passed when Americans of faith view environmentalism as either a luxury to be addressed once we've conquered war or poverty, or a sign of incipient paganism; people who disagree about how creation happened have agreed to make sure it is not destroyed."[13]

Advocating and Supporting Effective Policies

With awareness and opinion having moved beyond the tipping point, the question is not whether religious communities and citizens will *express concern*, but how seriously religious communities, ethicists, publics and politicians in affluent countries will *act* to grapple with climate change and other eco-social threats. Will the response go beyond becoming more efficient and conserving energy users? Will the response include shifting toward renewable ways of producing and more local patterns of consuming? Finally, will it express vigorous advocacy of collective action through public policies that set mandatory caps on CO_2 emissions or institute a significant carbon tax, while also taking steps to meet the plight of vulnerable human communities and ecosystems?

The shape of the problem is still perceived quite narrowly among economists and the mass media as an issue of energy efficiency and conservation that can be "solved" by moving to a low-carbon economy powered by green technology that large corporations want to provide for handsome profits. But global warming results from accumulating greenhouse gases, driven by a pervasive, destructive, market-driven pattern of overproduction and consumption, which must be displaced by systemically changing the way we do almost everything.

Voluntarily reducing energy consumption is a prominent aspect of what needs to be done to keep global warming from becoming catastrophic, but a response that is commensurate with the problem requires deeper and wider changes. As Barry Commoner observed when interviewed at age 90, "The only rational answer (to the climate crisis) is to change the way in which we do transportation, energy production, agriculture and a good deal of manufacturing. The problem originates . . . in the form of the production of goods. Action has to be taken on what's produced and how it's produced."[14] If the response is not systemic, we are likely to see an increasing green style among affluent consumers that actually does little to reduce overall CO_2 emissions.

Most of the public discourse and religious community response has stayed in the realm of fostering less wasteful lifestyles marked by better recycling, purchasing fair trade goods, eating locally grown food, reducing personal and household energy use, driving cars that get higher gas mileage, and planting trees. Responses of this kind are important and can become cumulatively significant, especially if religious communities assert their spiritual and moral priority. But individual lifestyle changes are not a sufficient response to entrenched patterns of maldevelopment; collective actions are also necessary to grapple effectively with the vast scale and looming planetary effects of the climate change scenarios so authoritatively projected by scientists of the U.N. Intergovernmental Panel on Climate Change.

At a minimum, the global community of nations must agree upon and implement binding reductions in CO_2 gas emissions, fairly allocated per capita, while rich countries also act to transfer appropriate technologies that enable poor and developing countries to adapt to or to mitigate the destructive impact of global warming that so disproportionately affects them. That latter ethical consideration of what the rich owe the poor and vulnerable deserves much more religious and political attention, now that we have better knowledge of the who, what, and where of climate change.

The special responsibility of the United States, where less than 5 percent of the world's population has been releasing 25 percent of all greenhouse gases, cannot be deflected by pointing at rapidly growing CO_2 emissions from China and India. The Earth community urgently needs accountable, collaborative action. People of faith in the United States will show that they are morally serious not only by reducing their driving, purchasing, energy use and waste, but also by advocating public policies that mandate major reductions in carbon emissions, and that deliver compensatory justice for the poor countries that are owed a large ecological and social debt by wealthy countries. The reality of recent history is that wealthy countries and corporations based in them have not only extracted or enclosed poor country resources; rich country production and consumption was the source of at least two-thirds of the CO_2 gas emissions that accumulated in the atmosphere through 2006. With China and India also becoming major CO_2 emitters, the rich countries must set an example by reducing emissions rapidly—particularly from coal-burning power plants and carbon fuel transportation systems. (U.S. action to rapidly reduce greenhouse gas emissions must not be postponed during the looming global recession.)

So far the federal government has responded weakly, and media campaigns for personal lifestyle change have not become robustly green. Purchasing expensive hybrid SUVs and carbon offsets for air travel while screwing in energy-efficient light bulbs offers false promises of sustainability—what the political philosopher Michael Sandel has called "a painless mechanism to buy our way out of the more fundamental changes in habits, attitudes and way of life that are actually required to address the climate problem."[15]

Next Steps

Faith communities, particularly those in the United States, should take the following five steps to move toward ecological and social justice.

1. Teach the vision and values of eco-justice ethics informed by insights from green sciences and rooted in the sacred texts of religion. To offer just one example of invoking sacred texts, the scriptural portrayal of the fifth and sixth days of creation (Genesis 1:20-31), which Jews and Christians traditionally viewed as a mandate from God for human domination of nature, actually underscores human interdependence with, and stewardship of, the vast community of diverse life. Rereading the Genesis saga now with awareness of Earth's evolution and current human devolution, we see that other creatures had prior place and were mandated to "be fruitful and multiply" before humans even came on the scene.

2. Continue to emphasize the simpler living, energy saving, Earth-community-building initiatives that are expected of all who claim to care for creation. Sustainable energy use is already the focus of networks such as Interfaith Power and Light, which was preceded by a 1990s project, initiated in California, called Episcopal Power and Light. A promising example of organized religious response to global warming, now active in a majority of the states, Interfaith Power and Light supports green energy producers and fosters energy-efficient lighting, heating, and cooling of households and congregations.

3. Communities of faith must advocate energetically for environmentally responsible public policies. Members of faith-based communities can connect with the Interfaith Climate and Energy Campaign, supported by the Eco-Justice Working Group of the National Council of Churches and the National Religious Partnership for the Environment.[16] The campaign's goal is to move beyond changing lifestyles and light bulbs to advocating public polices that put mandatory caps on carbon emissions and internalize environmental costs of greenhouse gas emissions occurring throughout the economy. It remains to be seen whether faith communities will also push for concrete steps of compensatory justice designed to help the most vulnerable, to whom we owe a large ecological debt. A small percentage of revenues from a carbon tax could be earmarked for international assistance to help poor countries and communities adapt effectively to the severe effects of climate change.

4. Because sustainability with justice involves changing our daily lives, our institutions, our economics, and our politics, religious communities should not try to go it alone. People of faith need to act in partnership with others who also want to be responsible Earth citizens.[17] In the last few years, environmental organizations have become less diffident about reaching out to religious bodies that care for creation and want to build Earth community. Congregations should reciprocate by collaborating with others to protect or restore special places, reduce individual and institutional consumption, build community, support local food systems, foster renewable energy and corporate responsibility, and influence public officials.

5. Religious bodies awakening to the sustainability challenge must nurture their members spiritually to continue a difficult (if it's easy it won't be fulfilling) eco-justice journey. Because the deepening environmental crisis is cultural as well as ecological, one of the religious communities' most significant contributions is to inspire reverence, gratitude, repentance, and self-discipline—to the benefit of Earth community. As one religiously resonant sentence in the Earth Charter Preamble puts it, "The spirit of human solidarity and kinship with all life is strengthened when we live with reverence for the mystery of being, gratitude for the gift of life, and humility regarding the human place in nature."

Conclusion

In 2004, I joined 10 other theologians and activists gathered by the National Council of Churches to craft *God's Earth Is Sacred*,[18] an open letter to church and society in the United States. We admitted to becoming "un-Creators" and underscored the urgency of addressing environmental degradation:

> To continue to walk the current path of ecological destruction is not only folly; it is sin. . . . The imperative first step is to repent of our sins, in the presence of God and one another. This repentance of our social and ecological sins will acknowledge the special responsibility that falls to those of us who are citizens of the United States. Though not even five percent of the planet's human population, we produce one-quarter of the world's carbon emissions, consume a quarter of its natural riches, and perpetuate scandalous inequities at home and abroad. . . .
>
> The second step is to pursue a new journey together, with courage and joy. We can share in renewal by clinging to God's trustworthy promise to restore and fulfill all that God creates and by walking, with God's help, a path different from our present course. To that end, we affirm our faith, propose a set of guiding (eco-justice) norms, and call on our churches to rededicate themselves to this mission.

ENDNOTES

1. WORLD COMM'N ON ENV'T & DEV. (BRUNDTLAND COMM'N), OUR COMMON FUTURE 43 (1987).

2. J. Ronald Engel, *The Ethics of Sustainable Development, in* ETHICS OF ENVIRONMENT AND DEVELOPMENT: GLOBAL CHALLENGE, INTERNATIONAL RESPONSE 11 (J. Ronald Engel and Joan Gibb Engel eds., 1990).

3. These norms are discussed in Dieter T. Hessel, *Ecumenical Ethics for Earth Community*, VIII THEOLOGY & PUB. POL'Y, Nos. 1 & 2 (1996); WILLIAM E. GIBSON, ECO-JUSTICE — THE UNFINISHED JOURNEY 26-29 (2004); and JAMES B. MARTIN-SCHRAMM & ROBERT L. STIVERS, CHRISTIAN ENVIRONMENTAL ETHICS: A CASE METHOD APPROACH (2003), ch. 2.

4. MARTIN-SCHRAMM & STIVERS, *supra* note 3, at 41-42.

5. Earth Charter International, based in Sweden and Costa Rica, is an up-to-date Internet source of information about the Earth Charter text, related programs, and resources. My earlier essay, Chapter 25, in STUMBLING TOWARD SUSTAINABILITY (John C. Dernbach ed., 2002), unpacks the 16 ethical principles of the Earth Charter, which was issued in 2000 by the World Conservation Union (IUCN).

6. EARTH CHARTER INTERNATIONAL COUNCIL, THE EARTH CHARTER INITIATIVE, *available at* http://earthcharterinaction.org/about_charter.shtml (last visited Sept. 8, 2007).

7. U.N. DEV. PROGRAMME, HUMAN DEVELOPMENT REPORT 2 (1998).

8. For example, on June 13, 2007, the Southern Baptist Convention, meeting in Fort Worth, Texas, refused to ask the federal government to do something about climate change, claiming that "scientific evidence does *not* support computer models of catastrophic human-induced global warming," and then asserting that major efforts to reduce greenhouse gases would unfairly impact the world's poorest people. Reported in *The Christian Century*, July 10, 2007, at 16.

9. ROGER S. GOTTLIEB, A GREENER FAITH: RELIGIOUS ENVIRONMENTALISM AND OUR PLANET'S FUTURE (2006).

10. *See, e.g.*, PRESBYTERIANS FOR RESTORING CREATION, PRC UPDATE (quarterly newsletter), *available at* www.prcweb.org. The newsletter is in its 13th year.

11. Earth Ministry in Seattle, Wash., and Green Faith in New Brunswick, N.J., are two outstanding regional organizations offering newsletters and interfaith educational resources on sustainable living.

12. BILL MCKIBBEN, DEEP ECONOMY: THE WEALTH OF COMMUNITIES AND THE DURABLE FUTURE (2007).

13. Bill McKibben, *Stepping It Up to Save the Earth*, 36 SOJOURNERS MAGAZINE No. 7 (July 2007), at 16.

14. Thomas Vinciguerra, *A Conversation With Barry Commoner*, N.Y. TIMES, June 19, 2007, at D2.

15. Comment by political philosopher Michael Sandel, quoted in an op-ed column by Thomas Friedman, *Live Bad, Go Green*, N.Y TIMES, July 8, 2007.

16. In addition to the website of the Interfaith Climate and Energy Campaign, *see* EARTH MINISTRY, THE CRY OF CREATION: A CALL FOR CLIMATE JUSTICE (2006).

17. Dieter Hessel, *Becoming a Church for Ecology and Justice, in* THE PROPHETIC CALL: CELEBRATING COMMUNITY, EARTH, JUSTICE, AND PEACE (Hugh Sanborn ed., 2004), reviews what mainline churches in the United States have been doing and how congregations can become more engaged.

18. The full text of the theologians' letter, *God's Earth Is Sacred*, is reprinted in the appendix to EARTH AND WORD (David Rhoads ed., 2007) at 291-300. An optional study guide is available from the Eco-Justice Working Group of the National Council of Churches of Christ in the U.S.A., at www.nccecojustice.org.

III. Consumption, Population, and Poverty

CHAPTER 10

Sustainable and Unsustainable Developments in the U.S. Energy System

Mark D. Levine and Nathaniel T. Aden

Over the course of the 19th and 20th centuries, the United States developed a wealthy society on the basis of cheap and abundant fossil fuel energy. As fossil fuels have become ecologically and economically expensive in the 21st century, America has shown mixed progress in transitioning to a more sustainable energy system. From 2000 to 2006, energy and carbon intensity of GDP continued favorable long-term trends of decline. Energy end-use efficiency also continued to improve; for example, per capita electricity use was 12.76 MWh per person per year in 2000 and again in 2006, despite 16 percent GDP growth over that period. Environmental costs of U.S. energy production and consumption have also been reduced, as illustrated in air quality improvements. However, increased fossil fuel consumption, stagnant efficiency standards, and expanding corn-based ethanol production have moved the energy system in the opposite direction, toward a less sustainable energy system.

This chapter reviews energy system developments between 2000 and 2006 and presents policy recommendations to move the United States toward a more sustainable energy system.

Sustainable Development

To paraphrase the Brundtland Commission, sustainability is defined as meeting the needs of the present without compromising the ability of future generations to meet their needs.[1] Regarding energy production and consumption, sustainability primarily addresses issues of the environment, economics, and the political system. The criteria for measuring sustainable energy usage constantly shift in response to resource availability, costs, and new technologies. Likewise, the meaning of sustainable energy varies by geographic area: What is sustainable for the United States through its energy imports is unsustainable for the rest of the planet. Aside from moral and ethical questions of resource distribution, increased energy sustainability in the United States assumes adoption of global-scale definitions.

Governments can play a central role in the development of sustainable energy by guiding market forces and acting as a bulwark against human avarice. Policies can encourage increased use of renewables on the supply side and improved efficiency and conservation on the demand side. The European Union, Japan, and China have articulated national and international targets for sustainable energy. In June 2006 the European Council adopted a Sustainable Development Strategy for all EU countries. In Asia, Japan has adopted its 3R Initiative for Building a Sound Material-Cycle Society, and China has developed its Circular Economy Development Strategy. However, the issue of sustainability has not yet risen to such a level in energy discussions in the United States.

Sustainability of the U.S. Energy System: 2000-2006

From 2000 to 2006, the U.S. energy system moved both toward and away from sustainability. Positive developments include diminishing the carbon and energy intensity of GDP, increased energy end-use efficiency, and improved air quality. Trends away from sustainability include increased combustion of fossil fuel, particularly coal, failure to implement improved energy efficiency standards (especially stagnant standards for appliances and vehicles), and increased production of corn-based ethanol.

Following is a discussion of three trends in U.S. energy sustainability: declining carbon emissions as a fraction of GDP; increased energy end-use efficiency/declining energy intensity; and improved energy-related air quality. In the absence of other quantitative metrics, these trends serve as indicators of U.S. energy system sustainability.

Declining Carbon Emissions as a Fraction of GDP

In order to measure the sustainability of economic growth in the United States, annual energy-related carbon emissions are divided by GDP to calculate carbon intensity. While carbon intensity does not portray changes in absolute carbon emissions levels or sources of emissions, it does provide a useful indicator of economic and environmental sustainability.

As illustrated in Figure 1, the carbon intensity of U.S. GDP has declined intermittently since 1970. While the economy continued to expand, carbon intensity was reduced through economic restructuring (i.e., the shift of economic growth from industrial production to the service sector) and improved energy end-use efficiency (including reduced electricity requirements for home appliances). The trend during the past five years has been similar to the long-term trend in which the carbon intensity of the United States economy declined by 54 percent between 1970 and 2006.

Figure 1
Carbon Intensity of U.S. GDP, 1970-2006

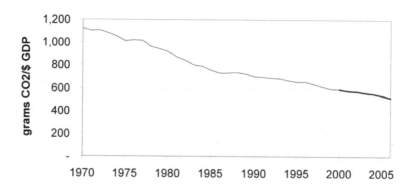

Source: EIA, AER 2006; IEA, Carbon Emissions From Fossil Fuel Combustion.

The decline in carbon intensity has been 2.0 percent per year over the last six years, comparable to the long-term trend since 1970. This decline in U.S. carbon intensity needs to be seen in the context of global CO_2 emissions. Acceptable levels of CO_2 concentrations correspond to a very wide variety of emissions profiles and distribution of emissions between industrialized and developing countries.[2] Almost all scenarios of CO_2 emissions worldwide predict a much higher contribution from developing than from industrialized nations. As a result, a slope of -3 to -4 percent per year on Figure 1 is more likely to be a number that, when combined with comparable actions by other industrialized countries and energy efficiency policies in developing countries, could result in a more sustainable energy future.

Table 1 shows the absolute value of CO_2 emissions in the United States. Partially as a result of declining industrial-sector energy use, emissions have grown at a slower pace—0.2 percent annually—than occurred over the preceding eight years or in the 20 years after the oil embargo of the 1970s.

Table 1
U.S. CO_2 Emissions From Fossil Fuel Combustion by Sector (Mt CO_2), 1972–2006

	1972	1992	2000	2006	AAGR 1972–1992	AAGR 1992–2000	AAGR 2000–2006
Residential	891.37	970.60	1,171.90	1,197.00	0.4%	2.4%	0.4%
Commercial	575.30	783.30	1,006.40	1,046.00	1.6%	3.2%	0.6%
Industry	1,237.13	1,720.80	1,778.00	1,669.00	1.7%	0.4%	-1.0%
Transportation	1,783.10	1,566.30	1,854.00	1,965.00	-0.6%	2.1%	1.0%
Total	4,486.90	5,041.00	5,810.20	5,877.00	0.6%	1.8%	0.2%

Source: EIA, AER 2006.
Note: 2006 data are preliminary; AAGR=Average Annual Growth Rate (%).

Table 2 presents the same information for energy use. A comparison between Tables 1 and 2 illustrates how closely CO_2 emissions and energy track one another.

	1972	1992	2000	2006	AAGR 1972– 1992	AAGR 1992– 2000	AAGR 2000– 2006
Residential	15.7	18.4	21.6	22.2	0.8%	2.0%	0.5%
Commercial	9.6	14.2	18.1	19.0	1.9%	3.1%	0.8%
Transportation	18.7	23.6	28.0	30.0	1.2%	2.1%	1.1%
Industry	32.7	34.5	36.7	34.2	0.3%	0.8%	-1.2%
Total Energy	76.7	90.7	104.4	105.4	0.8%	1.8%	0.2%

Source: EIA, AER 2006.
Note: Final energy use; 2006 data are preliminary; AAGR=Average Annual Growth Rate (%).

Increased Energy End-Use Efficiency and Declining Energy Intensity

Between 2000 and 2006, energy use in the United States grew at historically low rates in both absolute terms and in relation to the economy and population. There are various aggregate indicators that can be used to describe improving energy efficiency and declining energy intensity:

- *Annual energy consumption per capita* (in units of primary energy per year) declined from 371 GJ/capita in 2000 to 352 GJ/capita (giga-joules per person per year) in 2006. This occurred while per capita GDP grew from $34,883 in 2000 to $38,122 in 2006 (in deflated year 2000 dollars).

- During the same period, *per capita electricity consumption*, which usually rises faster than overall energy use because electricity is the energy form of choice for expanding energy uses in developed countries, remained constant (12,765 kWh/capita in 2000 compared to 12,758 kWh/capita in 2006).

- Decline in *energy intensity of GDP* of 2.0 percent per year (equal to that of the decline in CO_2 emissions, as previously noted).

Improved Energy-Related Air Quality

A large portion of air pollution is caused by combustion of fuel; as such, it is useful to note trends in local emissions to the air and air quality throughout the United States. Overall, air quality in the United States improved in the period 2000-2005. This trend was seen at local air quality and emissions monitoring stations throughout the nation. During 1999-2001, monitoring stations showed 4.5 percent of air quality readings to be in excess of standards for ozone. This percentage dropped to 2.1 percent for 2003-2005. Similarly, measurements showing small particulate ($PM_{2.5}$) violations of air quality standards declined from 2.1 percent in 1999-2001 to 1.4 percent in 2003-2005.

Below, we describe total emissions trends in the United States. In some cases, data are only available through 2002; in others, they are available to 2005. The data summarized here are either for 2000-2002 or 2003-2005, and are compared to the data from the 1990s.[3]

Emissions of carbon monoxide (CO), of which more than 90 percent comes from vehicles, declined 33 percent from 1990 to 2002; the decline from 2000 to 2002 was at roughly the same rate.

All nitrogen oxide (NO_x) emissions are caused by the combustion of fuels. NO_x emissions declined about 10 percent from 1996 to 2000 and roughly another 10 percent from 2000 to 2002. Ambient concentrations throughout the country declined through 2004. All regions of the country are in compliance with NO_x standards.

Emissions of anthropogenic volatile organic compounds (VOCs), which along with NO_x are an important input to ozone concentrations, have declined steadily on the order of 2 to 3 percent per year since 1990 and at a higher rate from 2000 to 2002. Fifty percent of anthropogenic VOCs come from fuel combustion; the remainder is from industrial processes.

Emissions of particulate matter with mass median diameter less than 2.5 micrometers ($PM_{2.5}$), 60 percent of which are from vehicles or stationary fuel combustion, showed no decline from 2000 to 2002.

Sulfur dioxide (SO_2) emissions declined 34 percent from 1990 to 2002. The major source of SO_2 emissions is coal-fired power plants (two-thirds of the total); such plants showed the greatest reduction. As a result of the decrease in ambient levels of SO_2, considerable progress has been made since 1990 in reducing acid rain deposition, especially in the mid-Appalachian region and the Ohio River Valley, where its impacts have been most serious.

Mercury levels from municipal and medical wastes and incinerators have been reduced substantially. Mercury from coal-fired power plants, however, has declined little, and it increased as a portion of total mercury emissions from 25 percent in 1990-1993 to more than 40 percent in 2002 because of the decline in emissions from other sources.

Continued High Levels of Fossil Fuel Combustion

Since 1992, coal has retained a steady 23 percent share of total primary energy consumption (see Table 3). Over the past six years, noncarbon energy sources have not significantly increased in the energy mix. In 2006, fossil fuels provided 85 percent of the U.S. energy supply; in 2000, the fraction was 86 percent. In contrast to the past six years, from 1972 to 1992 the United States did diversify its energy sources away from an even stronger reliance on fossil energy. During the same period renewables showed significant relative increases in wind and biofuels. Still, the share of renewables and of nuclear energy—the two nonfossil fuel energy sources—remained virtually unchanged from 1992 to 2006.

Table 3
U.S. Fossil, Nuclear, and Renewable Energy Consumption, 1972–2006

	Energy Consumption (EJ)				Share of Total			
	1972	1992	2000	2006	1972	1992	2000	2006
Hydroelectric	3.02	2.76	2.97	3.05	4%	3%	3%	3%
Biomass	1.59	3.09	3.18	3.46	2%	3%	3%	3%
Wood	1.58	2.44	2.39	2.23	2%	3%	2%	2%
Waste	0.00	0.50	0.54	0.43	0%	1%	1%	0%
Biofuels	-	0.15	0.25	0.80	0%	0%	0%	1%
Geothermal	0.03	0.37	0.33	0.37	0%	0%	0%	0%
Solar/PV	-	0.07	0.07	0.07	0%	0%	0%	0%
Wind	-	0.03	0.06	0.27	0%	0%	0%	0%
Total Renewables	4.64	6.32	6.61	7.17	6%	7%	6%	7%
Nuclear	0.62	6.84	8.29	8.66	1%	8%	8%	8%
Fossil Fuels	71.42	77.43	89.39	89.42	93%	85%	86%	85%
Coal	12.74	20.17	23.82	23.75	17%	22%	23%	23%
Total	**76.70**	**90.68**	**104.42**	**105.37**	**100%**	**100%**	**100%**	**100%**

Source: EIA, AER 2006.
Note: Total final energy use; 2006 data are preliminary; wood, waste, and biofuels are components of biomass.

The trend of reduced carbon intensity of energy use from 1970 to 2000 reversed in 2000.

Figure 2 shows that since 2000 emissions of carbon dioxide per unit of energy consumed have exceeded the 36-year trend line, as well as the absolute value of carbon intensity over the previous 10 years. If the United States had maintained the earlier trend for this indicator, CO_2 emissions would have declined more rapidly than energy use. Increased coal use partially explains why carbon intensity of energy consumption in 2000-2006 was above the 36-year trend.

Figure 2
Carbon Intensity of U.S. Energy Consumption, 1970-2006

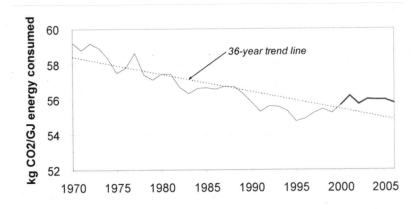

Source: EIA, AER 2006; IEA, Carbon Emissions From Fossil Fuel
Combustion.
Note: Total final energy use; 2006 energy data are preliminary.

High Energy Use and CO_2 Emissions Relative to Other Industrialized Nations

It is important to recognize how far outside the norm of energy use and carbon emissions per capita the United States is in comparison with other industrialized countries. Figure 3 shows that the United States is responsible for 2.5 times the per capita CO_2 emissions of the major European Union nations. The ratio has changed little over the past 35 years. Recent data are not available to make comparisons for all of the past six years.

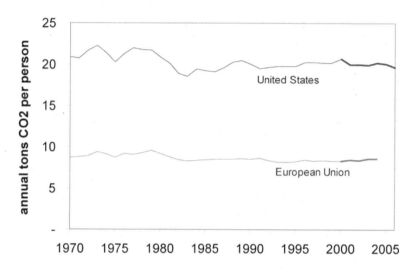

Figure 3
Annual Energy-Related Per Capita CO$_2$ Emissions in the EU
and the United States, 1970-2006

Source: IEA and U.S. EIA.
Note: EU data cover the EU 15: Austria, Belgium, Denmark, Finland, France,
Germany, Greece, Ireland, Italy, Luxembourg, Netherlands, Portugal, Spain,
Sweden, and the United Kingdom.

Lack of Federal Engagement in Energy Efficiency Policy

The two major federal policies to increase energy efficiency in the
United States are appliance standards and the corporate auto fuel
economy (CAFE) standards. However, only recently has the federal
government begun to address new standards for appliance efficiency
and to update the 1975 corporate automobile fuel standards.

The Energy Policy and Conservation Act (EPCA), as amended,[4] required the U.S. Department of Energy (DOE) to undertake rulemakings for appliance standards on specified schedules. On September 7, 2005, the Natural Resources Defense Council, 15 states, and the
city of New York filed a lawsuit against DOE in the U.S. District Court
for the Southern District of New York, alleging that DOE failed to
comply with deadlines and other requirements for publishing final
rules concerning energy efficiency standards for 22 categories of
products. On January 31, 2006, DOE published a report to Congress
containing a five-year schedule, to be completed by June 2011, to is-

sue the final rules required by EPCA. In November 2006, the district court issued a consent decree, which the parties had agreed to, stating that "[f]or each product covered by the Complaints, DOE shall publish a final rule by the deadlines set forth," with the last due in June 2011. The DOE completed five *Federal Register* notices in this area in 2006, and two final rules in 2007, and other rulemakings are in process.

Because light trucks have become a large portion of the U.S. vehicle fleet, their fuel economy is significant. In 2007, a standard was set for light trucks at 22.2 mpg in 2008, increasing to 23.5 mpg in 2010. However, the Ninth Circuit found these new light-truck rules to be arbitrary and capricious, and directed NHTSA to prepare a new standard as quickly as possible.

The standards for automobiles remained at the level of 27.5 mpg as mandated in 1975 (and achieved by 1985) until 2007. In December of that year, Congress passed the Energy Independence and Security Act,[5] which requires increases in fuel efficiency during the model years 2011 to 2020, reaching at least 35 mpg in 2020 for the total fleet of passenger and non-passenger automobiles. For the years 2021 to 2030, the standards require mpg to be the "maximum feasible" fuel economy.

In comparison, Japan and the European Union have set voluntary standards in the range of 50 mpg by 2020. It remains to be seen whether the voluntary approach will be effective in these countries; however, it is virtually certain that fuel economy in new vehicles in the United States will lag behind many or most other industrialized countries. China recently adopted standards that are tighter than U.S. standards.

Burgeoning Biofuels

Biomass plays a growing role in the U.S. transition from reliance on fossil fuel to a more diversified energy system. Between 2000 and 2006, biomass consumption grew at an average annual rate of 1 percent. Within biomass energy usage, wood diminished by 7 percent and biofuel consumption more than tripled.

Biomass and particularly biofuel consumption only have the potential, at best, to marginally increase the sustainability of the U.S. energy system. However, the current American production of biofuels through corn-based ethanol is unsustainable for four reasons:

- low energy return on energy investment;
- low energy density;
- inflationary impact on food and energy prices;
- ecological limitations on the feasible scale of U.S. and global corn production.

Whereas petroleum production generates an energy return of approximately 15:1 on energy investment (i.e., 15 units of energy returned for each unit of required energy input), the ratio for corn-based ethanol varies between only 1.2:1 and 1.6:1.[6] Corn-based ethanol's low energy return on investment means that vastly more energy is required to produce the same given amount of liquid transport fuel.

This low energy return is compounded by the low energy density (unit of energy per unit volume) of ethanol. On a volumetric basis, ethanol contains only 65 percent of the energy of an equivalent amount of gasoline. Despite these limitations of corn-based ethanol production, the U.S. government has provided a generous production subsidy in the form of a $0.51 tax credit per gallon of ethanol used as motor fuel.

Further, growth of biofuel demand has had a negative effect on food and oil prices. Although U.S. maize production increased to historic levels over the past three years, maize prices rose from $78/ton in December 2000 to $142/ton in December 2006.[7]

Finally, the capacity of the United States for biofuel production is limited. Dedication of all U.S. corn and soybean production to biofuels would meet only 12 percent of gasoline demand and 6 percent of diesel demand.[8] While domestic biofuel production presents an attractive political alternative to fossil fuel imports, current production technologies are not sustainable.

Increased biofuel production, particularly from palm oil, corn, and sugarcane, further demonstrates that renewable energy sources are not necessarily sustainable. Given the scale of biofuel production necessary to offset liquid transport fuel demand, current programs for renewable cultivation are detrimental to sustainable energy production. Soil nutrient depletion, fertilizer consumption, water consumption, carbon-intensive land use change, and high primary energy requirements for ethanol production all undermine the sustainability of existing renewable fuel initiatives.[9]

Policy Recommendations for More Sustainable U.S. Energy

In response to developments in the U.S. energy system between 2000 and 2006, this chapter presents five federal-level policy recommendations to improve sustainability:

1. Increase energy end-use efficiency through applied standards and improved technology. This can be achieved by substantially tighter appliance efficiency standards for many products and an aggressive policy to require more efficient automobiles, light-duty vehicles, and heavy-duty vehicles.

2. Support research, development, and demonstration of energy-efficient commercial buildings to prepare the way for net zero-energy buildings. This area of research and demonstration has been underemphasized for years and offers large energy savings opportunities.

3. Implement taxation on energy production and consumption of carbon or a cap-and-trade system of carbon emissions. Taxation or a cap-and-trade system would internalize costs and align private incentives with social costs.

4. Support biofuel research to supplant inefficient and inflationary corn-based ethanol production. Biomass will play an important role in the transition to a modern solar energy system. However, it is important to make the transition from corn to more sustainable energy sources (e.g., woody crops).

5. Set targets for industrial-sector CO_2 emissions in advance of establishing a carbon tax or cap and trade system. Despite the absolute decline in industrial energy use over the past six years, U.S. industry remains less energy efficient, in many cases by a substantial margin, than industry in other developed countries.

ENDNOTES

1. WORLD COMM'N ON ENV'T & DEV. (BRUNDTLAND COMM'N), OUR COMMON FUTURE 43 (1987).

2. INTERGOVERNMENTAL PANEL ON CLIMATE CHANGE (IPCC), WORKING GROUP I (2007).

3. All data in this section are from the U.S. EPA SCIENCE ADVISORY BOARD DRAFT REPORT ON THE ENVIRONMENT (2007), Chapter 2. The original source of the information was in most cases the National Emissions Inventory, maintained by EPA.

4. 42 U.S.C. §§6291-6317.

5. Pub. L. No. 110-140, 121 Stat. 1492 (2007).

6. Alexander E. Farrell et al., *Ethanol Can Contribute to Energy and Environmental Goals*, 311 SCIENCE 506-08 (2006).

7. Kenneth G. Cassman & Adam J. Liska, *Food and Fuel for All: Realistic or Foolish?*, 1 BIOFUELS BIOPRODUCTION, BIOREFINING 18-23 (2007).

8. Jason Hill et al., *Environmental, Economic, and Energetic Costs and Benefits of Biodiesel and Ethanol Fuels*, PROCEEDINGS OF THE NAT'L ACAD. OF SCIENCES 103(30): 11206-11210 (2006).

9. Timothy Searchinger et al., *Use of U.S. Croplands for Biofuels Increases Greenhouse Gases Through Emissions From Land-Use Change*, 319 SCIENCE 1238-40 (2008).

Chapter 11

Materials: From High Consumption to More Sustainable Resource Use

Amit Kapur and Thomas E. Graedel

An aspect of sustainability that has received increased attention since the Earth Summit at Rio in 1992 is the material resources that are vital for economic growth. Sustainability with respect to use of resources has three components:

- The relationship between rate of resource utilization and overall stock of available virgin resources;
- Effectiveness of resource use in providing essential services;
- The proportion of resources that leak from the economy and the impact of that leakage on the environment.[1]

The first two topics reflect the sustainability of supply, and the third affects the sustainability of the receiving ecosystems (a combination of loss rate and ecosystem sensitivity). This chapter reports on trends in resource use in the United States, focusing on the 15 years following the Rio Earth Summit, and particularly the years since 2002. It concludes with suggestions for approaches that can improve sustainability in the use of materials.

The United States leads the world in the consumption of natural resources and, in most cases, in the use of natural resources per capita, including fossil fuels and materials.[2] In many cases, those resources are imported from other countries and other continents,[3] and sustainability on the supply side requires that those resources remain sufficient and that the countries holding them remain willing to supply them. On the demand side, it is imperative at the same time to reduce the need for nonrenewable resources and to make the use of those resources more efficient and less harmful to the environment.

The sustainability movement in the United States is slowly shifting attitudes on both the demand and supply sides. Consumers are asking for greener products and cleaner technologies. Simultaneously, a shift is occurring in our approach to production systems. The life cycle analysis of products, processes, and materials is providing feedback to product designers on how to improve the sustainability of everything from washing machines to factories.[4]

Life Cycle Assessment

Life cycle assessment (LCA) uses a systems approach to evaluate a product's environmental burden over its entire life cycle from raw material acquisition to production, use, and ultimate disposal. Life cycle assessment of industrial processes, energy systems, emerging technologies, new materials, and consumer products is critical to the U.S. economy because it evaluates the environmental impacts associated with production and consumption of natural resources and identifies opportunities for businesses and government to mitigate the impacts on the U.S. economy.

Sustainability of Resources

Nonrenewable resources are finite. Sperm oil, once used widely for lighting and other purposes, became so depleted in the 19th century that it ceased to be a factor in commerce. We are capable of doing the same with any of the Earth's stock of nonrenewable resources.

The wealth of modern society is based in part on the availability of an abundance of the materials we choose to employ—be it zinc, copper, or lead—in order to provide the products and services that we desire. One approach to sustainability of resources is through a policy of *strong sustainability*, in which a particular resource is conserved so that its availability is guaranteed far into the future. Another approach is *weak sustainability*, in which the function provided by a given resource is guaranteed, perhaps by alternative resources, but the supply of the resource itself is not. It will run out, but the function it served will still be available through other means and materials. There is debate as to whether strong sustainability is universally required to maintain modern technology, but there are some materials with unusual physical or chemical properties—heat tolerance or corrosion resistance, for example—that appear difficult or impossible to replace.[5] In other words, when they run out, their functions will be lost.

A sustainable-resource policy involves both increasing supply and restricting rates of usage. On the supply side, all of the needed resources for modern society do not have to come from virgin stock; instead, some may come from recycled materials. Supplies can thereby be supplemented from these in-use resources when they are discarded.

On the demand side, the need for some materials can be minimized. As a result, resource sustainability is ultimately an effort that involves all of the stages from mining engineering to product design and other technological activities, along with improved recycling and reuse, and perhaps considerations on how to reduce the material intensity[6] of the "consumption society" that is driving the rates of resource consumption.

Trends in Resource Use: Looking Back and Thinking Ahead

Profiles of resource use for renewable materials (agriculture, wood products, and primary paper) and nonrenewable materials (primary metals, industrial minerals, and materials used in construction) indicate that raw material use in the United States in the 20th century rose sharply, even though the corresponding increase in population was less than one-half as great.[7,8] More recently, from 1992 to 2005 the apparent consumption[9] of primary metals, except for aluminum, has remained more or less stable (see Figure 1). The increase in consumption of aluminum is attributed to its enhanced use in the construction and automotive sectors. The substitution of aluminum for iron and steel in these sectors resulted in an increase in aluminum consumption by approximately 10 percent, whereas iron and steel consumption declined by approximately 12 percent. Aside from aluminum, this flat pattern contrasts with that of Asia in general and China in particular, where rates of metal use have increased rapidly in the last few years, substantially driving those commodity prices.[10]

Figure 1
Apparent Consumption of Primary Metals in the United States, 1992-2005

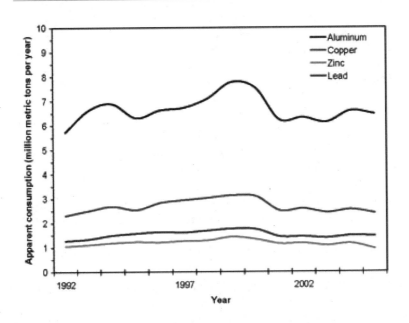

Source: THOMAS D. KELLY & GRECIA R. MATOS, U.S. GEOLOGICAL SURVEY, HISTORICAL STATISTICS FOR MINERAL AND METAL COMMODITIES IN THE UNITED STATES, *available at* http://minerals.usgs.gov/ds/2005/140.

The consumption of construction materials accounts for the largest share of the materials footprint of the United States. Figure 2 illustrates trends in consumption of crushed stone, sand and gravel, and cement from 1992 to 2005. Unlike the metals shown in Figure 1, consumption of each of the primary construction materials increased more than 50 percent over the last 15 years, and use of crushed stone and sand and gravel (and to a lesser extent cement) rose notably from 2002 to 2005. That pattern can be attributed to the exponential growth of the U.S. housing sector during the same period (see Figure 3 for the trends in the growth of privately owned housing units in the United States). Not only is the number of housing units in the United States increasing, but the floor areas of those units are larger (see Table 1).

Figure 2
Apparent Consumption of Primary Construction Materials in the United States, 1992-2005

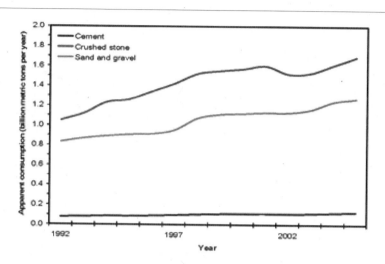

Source: Thomas D. Kelly & Grecia R. Matos, U.S. Geological Survey, Historical Statistics for Mineral and Metal Commodities in the United States, *available at* http://minerals.usgs.gov/ds/2005/140.

Figure 3
Trends in the Number of Privately Owned Housing Units in the United States, 1992-2006

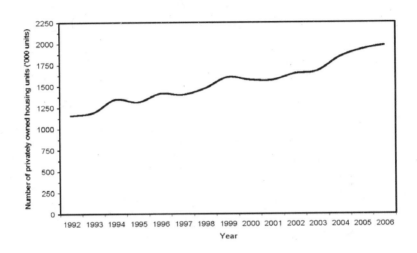

Source: U.S. Census Bureau, *available at* www.census.gov/hhes/www/ housing.html.

Table 1
Number of single-family housing units (< 1,200 sq. ft. and > 3,000 sq. ft.) in the United States, 1992-2006 (in thousands of units)

Year	Units < 1,200 sq.ft.	Units > 3,000 sq.ft.
1992	93	128
1993	95	136
1994	101	154
1995	103	141
1996	98	153
1997	88	164
1998	83	182
1999	88	216
2000	78	225
2001	71	247
2002	66	256
2003	73	276
2004	69	311
2005	60	381
2006	69	400

Source: U.S. Census Bureau, *available at* www.census.gov/hhes/www/housing.html.

Similarly, production of larger and more material-intensive (and less energy-efficient) vehicles increased from 2002 to 2005, as shown in Figure 4. (At this writing, the high price of gasoline was beginning to reverse this trend, at least temporarily.)

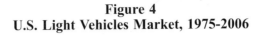

Figure 4
U.S. Light Vehicles Market, 1975-2006

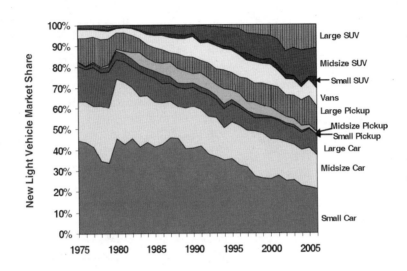

Source: Center for Transportation Analysis, *available at* http://cta.ornl.
gov/data/tedb26/Edition26_Chapter04.pdf

Forward Directions

The path toward sustainability has been debated in many forums.
Part of the debate is caused by the fact that the present system of measuring and tracking environmental performance does not quantify the
attributes that define sustainability.[11] Goals and perceptions of
sustainability vary significantly from one stakeholder to the other in
terms of achieving the triple bottom line—environmental, economic,
and social sustainability. In addition, there is usually a lack of unified
will, vision, and strategy to address the issue.

In the absence of quantifiable standards, some would argue, it is not
possible to set policy goals. In Chapter 1 of this volume, John
Dernbach writes:

> Of course, there continue to be questions about the meaning of sus-
> tainable development. . . . [It] may not be open to a more specific

meaning any more than concepts like freedom or democracy. We all have a general idea of what freedom and democracy mean; each embraces a set of core principles, and we can surely identify obvious examples of unsustainable development or the absence of democracy. . . . We will define and further sustainable development, in other words, by the actions we take and by what we learn from those actions.

In that spirit, the authors have elsewhere outlined a framework for the future[12] that provides a comprehensive set of actions and strategies to move toward sustainability in the use of materials, even in the absence of quantified goals. These actions and strategies include:

1. Materials conservation. "Reduce, reuse, recycle, and remanufacture" should be the motto of producers and consumers in order to supplement virgin supplies of nonrenewable resources, even though the relatively flat trends in consumption of primary metals shown in Figure 1 might provide a false sense of resource efficiency. Currently, 30 percent of municipal solid waste in the United States is recovered for recycling or composting; these actions divert more than 68 million tons of material from landfills and incinerators.[13] However, much remains to be done to effectively manage resource discards.

2. Change the material composition of products. Consumer products should be largely made with recycled materials, should be readily recyclable themselves, and should employ the more abundant of the nonrenewable resources such as iron and aluminum. This goal requires manufacturers to design for all stages of the life cycle, and to do so with the environment in mind.

3. Reduce material intensity. Advances in technology can help reduce the material intensity of products, thus reducing resource demand. Aluminum cans are 52 percent lighter today than they were two decades ago, thus enabling the production of more cans from the same amount of aluminum—from 22 cans per pound of aluminum in 1972 to about 34 cans per pound in 2002.[14]

4. Develop composite materials with reuse in mind. There is an increasing trend to use advanced composite materials in products of all types in order to enhance performance and fuel efficiency. However, these materials are very difficult to recycle; thus, from a long-term perspective their use is definitely a trade-off. Designers of products, especially high-technology products, should consider the recycling and reuse of products as well as their performance when new.

5. Encourage use of renewable materials. Increase the use of renewable materials for construction supplies (such as insulation, roofing, etc.). For example, polylactic acid, a biodegradable polymer derived from corn, can provide performance characteristics similar to petroleum-based plastics, but has lower environmental impacts.[15] The growing popularity of LEED (Leadership in Energy and Environmental Design) certification of buildings by the U.S. Green Building Council has the potential to promote the use of such materials as they are evaluated and judged satisfactory from the perspectives of both performance and environmental impact.

6. Design to limit energy and water use. Ultimately, the life cycles of all resources are linked. For example, the mining of ore requires energy, water, and land. Good design of products and processes can minimize the use of those enabling resources at all life-cycle stages as well as minimize the use of the basic resources themselves.

7. Promote product stewardship. Appropriate policy and regulatory measures, such as the European Union's Directive on Waste Electronic and Electrical Equipment (WEEE)[16] can make product manufacturers responsible for environmentally conscious management at the end of the useful life and eventual reuse of consumer goods and perhaps construction materials.[17]

Conclusion

It is no longer wise to assume adequate supplies of nonrenewable resources, if indeed it ever was. Some resources are limited in abundance, some resource use requires associated energy and water requirements, and there are environmental impacts from resource extraction and use. Sustainability for humans is ultimately based upon providing a desired level of services (food, housing, transportation, and other needs) in a sustainable manner. In almost all cases, these services rest upon a base of nonrenewable resources that must be sustained in one way or another. As technologists and as a society, we need to pay more attention to minimizing rates of resource use and retaining resources already in use. Without those resources, the concept of sustainability has no future.

ENDNOTES

1. Amit Kapur & Thomas E. Graedel, *Resource Use and Sustainability*, 33 ELR 10143-54 (Feb. 2003); UNIV. MICH. CTR. FOR SUSTAINABLE SYS., U.S. MATERIAL USE, *available at* http://css.snre.umich.edu/css_doc/CSS05-18.pdf.

2. PRESIDENT'S COUNCIL ON SUSTAINABLE DEV., POPULATION & CONSUMPTION TASK FORCE REPORT (1996).

3. U.S. GEOLOGICAL SURVEY, MINERAL COMMODITY SUMMARIES 2007.

4. U.N. ENV'T PROGRAMME, WHY TAKE A LIFE CYCLE APPROACH? (2004).

5. COMM. ON CRITICAL MATERIAL IMPACTS ON THE U.S. ECON., MINERALS, CRITICAL MINERALS, AND THE U.S. ECONOMY (2007).

6. Material intensity of use is defined as the amount of materials required to produce goods and services. *See* www.eoearth.org/article/Material_intensity_of_use (accessed June 2008).

7. Grecia Matos & Lorie Wagner, *Consumption of Material in United States: 1900-1995*, 23 ANN. REV. ENERGY & ENV'T 107-22 (1998).

8. Kapur & Graedel, *supra* note 1.

9. Apparent consumption is defined as production plus imports minus exports.

10. U.S. GEOLOGICAL SURVEY, *supra* note 3.

11. ORGANISATION FOR ECON. CO-OPERATION & DEV. (OECD), ENVIRONMENTAL PERFORMANCE REVIEWS—UNITED STATES (2005); CTR. FOR ENV'T & POPULATION, U.S. NATIONAL REPORT ON POPULATION AND THE ENVIRONMENT (2006); Thomas M. Parris & Robert W. Kates, *Characterizing and Measuring Sustainable Development*, 28 ANN. REV. ENV'T & RES. 559-86 (2003).

12. Kapur & Graedel, *supra* note 1.

13. *See* U.S. EPA's website, Municipal Solid Waste page, *available at* www.epa.gov/epaoswer/non-hw/muncpl/facts.htm).

14. Data available from the Aluminum Association, www.aluminum.org.

15. Steven C. Slater & Tillman U. Gerngross, *How Green Are Green Plastics?*, SCI. AM., August 2000, 36-41.

16. WEEE includes electronic and electrical equipment (such as computers, washing machines, vacuum cleaners) discarded by consumers at the end of the products' useful life.

17. Bill Sheehan & Helen Spiegelman, *Extended Producer Responsibility Policies in the United States and Canada: History and Status, in* GOVERNANCE OF INTEGRATED PRODUCT POLICY—IN SEARCH OF SUSTAINABLE PRODUCTION AND CONSUMPTION (Dirk Scheer & Frieder Rubik eds., 2005).

Chapter 12

The Importance of Curbing and Ending Population Growth to Achieve Sustainability

Anne H. Ehrlich and James Salzman

Population growth is a fundamental obstacle to sustainable development. Indeed, the forms of environmental degradation seen around the world—climate change; losses of natural capital, biodiversity, and ecosystem services; collapsing fisheries; air and water pollution; and other harms—cannot be addressed effectively without addressing human population growth as well.

Over the last decade, the U.S. population grew more than in any other 10-year period in the nation's history, resulting in significant environmental impacts both at home and abroad. Yet the government asserts that it has no population policy. In its submission to the 2002 World Summit on Sustainable Development, in Johannesburg, the U.S. report stated:

> The U.S. does not have an official population policy, in part because population density is low in the United States and large regions of the country are sparsely populated.... In addition, there is little public consensus about either the need for population-based policies or their nature.[1]

The facts belie this claim. Population growth in the United States is due to a number of policies that have demographic effects, ranging from immigration regulations and restrictions on abortions to the tax code and foreign aid policies. Since 2002, there have been no major changes to this de facto U.S. population policy. More than ever, the U.S. government needs to engage in a serious consideration of the nation's population-carrying capacity and the related issues of resource consumption and development. Unless we confront these physical facts and corresponding ethical implications, we cannot establish a meaningful or effective policy for managing population growth in the United States.

Why Should the World Care About Population Size and Growth?

No poor country can increase its standard of living and raise its per capita income while also wrestling with the problems of trying to feed and care for a rapidly expanding population. Experience has confirmed the importance of investing in family planning along with other human development programs, such as health and education, as part of the economic development process in developing nations. The longer that basic development and reductions in birthrates are deferred, the more difficult they will be to achieve, and the greater and more irreversible the cumulative environmental impacts will be. Beyond purely humanitarian concerns, these trends in developing countries affect fundamental American interests: immigration management, international political and economic stability, economic development and growth of foreign markets, losses of biodiversity, and degradation of ecosystem services such as climate stability.

The world population has tripled since 1940, reaching 6.7 billion in 2008, and is still growing at about 1.2 percent per year.[2] The most recent medium projection from the United Nations Population Division estimates a world population of about 8 billion in 2025 and 9.2 billion in 2050.[3] Despite the growing numbers, the rate of increase has been declining in most countries around the globe. Nonetheless, the world's poorest countries still have the highest population growth rates, frustrating efforts to reduce poverty and protect the environment.[4]

The Rio Declaration on Environment and Development in 1992 addressed population growth in Principle 8, stating that "[t]o achieve sustainable development and a higher quality of life for all people, States should reduce and eliminate unsustainable patterns of production and consumption and promote appropriate demographic policies."[5] This text reflects the compromise between developing countries' concerns about overconsumption in the North and developed countries' concerns about overpopulation in the South. Subsequent international conferences and declarations have emphasized the importance of curbing population growth not by setting numerical targets and focusing solely on birth-control efforts but, rather, by addressing underlying social issues—improving people's education, health, and social standing (particularly young women's)—on the theory that this would lead to smaller families.[6] These aspirations have also been expressed most recently in the eight Millennium Development Goals (most significantly the goal to promote gender equality and empower women).

Why Should Americans Care About Population Growth?

For decades, the population "problem" has been described chiefly as an issue for developing countries, particularly for countries with huge populations, such as China or India, or those wracked by poverty, such as Bangladesh. If one considers a nation's per capita environmental impact, however, the issue becomes more complex. Because most environmental damage is caused directly or indirectly by the use of energy, a useful measure of environmental impact is commercial energy use. Using per capita energy use as a rough index, in 2000, it was calculated that each American on average consumed an estimated 45 times as much as the average sub-Saharan African, and four times as much as the average Chinese.[7] Therefore, the key lesson is that when considering the impact of increased population on the environment *at the margin*, i.e., the environmental impact caused by the addition of one more person to the population, population growth is a more pressing issue in the United States than in China or India. The simple reason is that each additional American's level of consumption is so much greater than that of an additional Chinese or Indian.

In addition to contributing to increases in poverty, resource consumption, and environmental deterioration, population growth plays a critical role in generating urbanization and migration, and (in certain instances) political instability. By exacerbating poverty and resource depletion, population increase has helped to spur the migration of people seeking better social and economic opportunities from rural to urban communities. This internal migration today occurs mainly in developing regions. By 2010, for the first time in human history, more people will be living in cities than in rural communities. Including international and within-country migrants, the total number of people on the move worldwide may be as high as one billion.[8] Although few compared with internal migration, a new class of "environmental refugees" is having a significant geopolitical impact.[9] Most environmental refugees are subsistence farmers, impoverished and vulnerable to soil degradation and water scarcity, with little or no political influence. Many of the current illegal migrants to the United States are effectively environmental refugees. Indeed, in coming decades, as global warming leads to sea level rises, the number of environmental refugees will grow far higher as low-lying islands and coastal areas are submerged, forcing their current populations to move.

Status of U.S. Population

Population growth in the United States raises substantial environmental concerns because of the country's high level of per capita consumption. Since the Rio Summit in 1992, the U.S. population has grown by about 18 percent, the only major industrialized country in the world experiencing population growth on a significant scale.[10] The U.S. Census Bureau reported that the population reached 281.4 million in 2000, the largest increase in a 10-year period in U.S. history. The population passed 300 million in 2006, so the first decade of the 21st century may well surpass the 1990s as growth continues. Mirroring the global trend of urbanization, more than 80 percent of Americans live in a metropolitan area.[11]

In 2007, the average number of children born per woman in the population (known as the total fertility rate, or TFR) in the United States was slightly below the replacement rate of 2.1,[12] and the TFR has been near or below that level for about 35 years. Yet the population continues to grow significantly, in part because of the "population momentum" resulting from the higher birthrates of previous generations,[13] and in part because of immigration, which currently contributes roughly 40 percent of the annual population growth. The natural increase (births minus deaths) of the U.S. population is 0.6 percent annually (without taking immigration into account), but it is growing at approximately 1.0 percent or more when immigration is included. Projections of population size by demographers vary because they adopt differing assumptions about future immigration and fertility trends. Assuming no significant change in either factor, most indicate a population of about 420 million by 2050[14] with no hint of an end to growth in the following decades.

The sustainability of the current population of the United States can be questioned on a variety of grounds. It is less than credible to assert that an increase of 40 percent in the number of Americans within a half century, even with no increase in per capita consumption rates, might be sustainable. Under eco-footprint analysis, an American draws on as much as 25 to 30 acres (or 10 to 12 hectares) per person of productive land or surface water to support his or her lifestyle.[15] Moreover, our energy use is a major component of global environmental change.[16] With just 4.5 percent of the world's population, the United States accounts for roughly 23 percent of the world's fossil fuel energy use. Consumption of other materials and resources, largely drawn from the rest of the world, is similarly disproportionate.[17] The consumption and population patterns in the United States contribute to increasingly evident global impacts: widespread soil erosion and degradation of land, drawdown of ancient aquifers, collapses of oceanic fisheries, tropical deforestation, climate change, and desertification.[18] A U.S. population with unchanged consumption patterns slated to grow by 10 percent per decade or more while striving to increase per capita consumption even further is not a recipe for sustainability.

U.S. Population Policies

Although the United States has no explicit policy regarding population size or growth, it does have one in practice. Immigration laws and policies play a large role in determining overall population size. The tax code and laws relating to inheritance, women's rights, minimum wage, and labor, for example, constitute a de facto population policy that indirectly influences people's choices regarding family size. The legality and availability of family planning and abortion services have direct influences on family sizes. And the nation's trade policies influence immigration rates, while foreign aid policies have important implications for population size and growth in many developing countries.

Immigration

Given the nation's history of welcoming immigrants, the importance of immigration to population growth in the United States is hardly surprising. But the relative contribution of immigration to U.S. population growth has long been an extremely controversial subject, with different groups providing conflicting data depending on their agenda. The bitter disputes over revising immigration laws show no sign of abating.

Despite uncertainty surrounding the numbers of undocumented immigrants, the most reliable data indicate that more than one-third of annual U.S. population growth is due to immigration. Immigration law, then, is an important determinant of U.S. population policy. And it has become even more important since 1990, when Congress revised immigration laws, changing immigration patterns and allowing greater numbers of legal immigrants.[19] The illegal influx has also increased; by 2006, an estimated 10 to 12 million undocumented immigrants resided in the United States.[20] Despite the current and past administrations' stated commitment to sustainable development, considerations of population size have not, and still do not, play a role in the immigration debate.[21]

Abortion

Before 1969, abortion was almost completely illegal in the United States, although roughly a million American women had abortions each year, either clandestinely (and very unsafely) or in other countries where it was legal. In recent years abortions have averaged about 1.2 to 1.3 million annually in the United States.[22] If those pregnancies were carried to term, the U.S. birthrate would be 28 percent higher, boosting the rate of natural increase to about 1.0 percent. The population growth rate, including net immigration, would then be over 1.4 percent, a rate more typical of a developing nation.

Since 1973, abortion has been one of the most contentious issues in American politics. Violent protests at abortion facilities and even murders of abortion providers have caused many providers to cease practicing. Indeed, 87 percent of U.S. counties now lack abortion providers,[23] and few hospitals even teach safe abortion procedures. "Pro-life" advocates have introduced bills in every Congress since 1973 to prohibit abortions. While no outright prohibition has been successfully enacted, Congress and state legislatures have greatly restricted access to abortions by banning the use of federal funds for performing abortions, imposing consent requirements, outlawing "partial-birth" abortions, and other measures. Courts have upheld many of these restrictions.[24]

Today, 17 states pay for medically necessary abortions for Medicaid recipients, and 29 states will cover Medicaid recipients if the mother's life is in danger or in cases of rape or incest.[25] Many states restrict private insurance coverage of abortions. Among other widespread restrictions, 44 states require abortion reporting, 34 require parental consent or notification for minors, and many require state-directed counseling afterward with or without a mandatory delay.[26]

Another abortion-related controversy surrounds mifepristone, better known as the abortion pill, or RU-486. A synthetic steroid, mifepristone functions by blocking a hormone necessary for fetal development.[27] The Food and Drug Administration (FDA) delayed approval for four years, partly because of pressure from anti-abortion advocates and partly because of the lack of a U.S. manufacturer.[28] In September 2000 the FDA finally approved RU-486, but with restrictions. A similar controversy and delay of approval attended introduction of Plan B, the "day-after" pill, an oral dose of hormones that can prevent implantation of an early embryo if taken within five days after unprotected intercourse. When finally approved for over-the-counter sale in 2006, prescriptions for Plan B were required for women under the age of 18.

Tax Code

As Prof. Mona Hymel has argued, "the symbolic aspect of tax policies makes the tax system a particularly well-suited tool for sending messages and encouraging individuals to reform attitudes and behaviors."[29] In fact, domestic tax policies indirectly influence population size. Historically, they have supported childbearing, providing government subsidies to families.[30] Most important, the per-child dependency exemption has translated into "more children equals more tax relief." This policy was furthered in President George W. Bush's Agenda for Tax Relief law of 2001, which doubled the tax credit per child from $500 to $1,000 for the next 10 years.[31]

Foreign Aid for Family Planning

Both bilateral and multilateral funding from industrial nations are essential for successful efforts to address population growth in developing nations. The United States has supported international family planning since 1965 and has been the largest donor, providing more than $8 billion of aid over this period. This aid has almost certainly played a role in the significant decline in population growth rates in developing countries, from an average growth rate of roughly 2.4 percent in the 1960s to 1.5 percent in 2006.[32] Some developing countries such as China, South Korea, Thailand, and several Caribbean nations now have below-replacement reproduction, but others—such as sub-Saharan African and many Middle Eastern nations—have seen little or no decline in birthrates. And because population growth rates lag decades behind birthrate changes due to population momentum, global population growth is likely to continue throughout the 21st century.

Population assistance has proven extremely contentious, however, since the Reagan Administration, with the domestic abortion debate serving as a lightning rod. After the *Roe v. Wade* decision in 1973, Congress banned the use of foreign aid for abortions and involuntary sterilizations. Thus, the U.S. Agency for International Development (USAID) has long been prohibited from directly supporting abortion as a method of family planning, although it was still allowed to provide foreign aid to family planning organizations that relied on *other* funds to support or counsel about abortion. Worldwide, an estimated 42 million abortions take place each year, of which some 20 million occur in nations where the procedure is illegal or restricted.[33] If the 42 million pregnancies ending in abortion each year were carried to term, the global population growth rate today would be 1.9 percent per year, not 1.2 percent.

In 1984, the Reagan Administration banned U.S. foreign aid for organizations (though not governments) that provided abortions, even if supported by non-U.S. funds. The Reagan Administration and first Bush Administration withheld aid to the United Nations Population Fund (UNFPA) and limited family planning assistance mostly to bilateral programs through USAID. Previously, the United States had provided almost one-third of UNFPA's budget. In 1993, President Bill Clinton restored funding for family planning assistance and UNFPA, but in 2001, President George W. Bush reinstated the policy. New USAID guidelines ban foreign aid to organizations and international agencies that perform or promote abortions, defined as providing information or advice on availability of abortion, except in cases of rape or incest or to save the mother's life.[34]

Abortion is an important method of birth control in many countries where contraceptives are not reliably available, especially in the nations of the former Soviet bloc and in many developing countries. Abortions occur in every country, although the rate is usually much lower when contraceptives are readily available. Until family planning services are universally available and affordable, abortion will remain an important avenue by which couples can limit their reproduction and will be a significant factor in curbing population growth.

The Millennium Development Goals, subscribed to at the World Summit on Sustainable Development at Johannesburg in 2002, failed to mention family planning or reduction of population growth, although they did include related goals such as universal primary education, promotion of gender equality, and improvement of maternal health.[35] Global funding for family planning services dropped by nearly two-thirds between 1995 and 2003, overtaken by accelerated funding to combat sexually transmitted diseases, especially HIV/AIDS. Consequently, adoption of modern contraception in the least developed countries has lagged or stalled altogether. Because of that, and new estimates of the prevalence and treatment of HIV/AIDS, the United Nations in 2006 revised its population projections for 2050 slightly upward.[36]

Conclusion and Recommendations

It is useful to repeat here the extraordinary statement of the United States at the 2002 Johannesburg Summit:

> The U.S. does not have an official population policy, in part because population density is low in the United States and large regions of the country are sparsely populated. . . . In addition, there is little public consensus about either the need for population-based policies or their nature.[37]

In the context of Agenda 21, the Rio Declaration, and subsequent conferences, the U.S. claim that it does not have a population policy is a remarkable statement. The principal purpose of the 1992 Rio conference was to highlight the relationship between environmental sustainability and development. Population size and growth are inescapable components of this dynamic, but the U.S. statement reflected no such awareness. Parts of the United States could be considered "sparsely populated" only by the simple measurement of people per square mile, certainly not in relation to local resources such as supplies of freshwater. While some population redistribution might be environmentally desirable, local incentives and disincentives have played a dominant role in determining settlement patterns. Ordinarily, municipalities try to lure businesses and potential employees to their areas; development of infrastructure and support systems comes later, and environmental concerns later still.

Further, it is disingenuous to assert that there is no public awareness of the impact of population growth. In most areas of the country, environmental impacts associated with population growth have impinged on public consciousness through concerns about urban sprawl, traffic congestion, and water supplies.

Official government statements notwithstanding, the United States clearly *does* have de facto population policies, although some of them contradict each other. The provision of family planning means and facilities, legalized abortion, access to reproductive health facilities, equal treatment (if imperfectly applied) in the job market and economic independence for women, compulsory education for all, and subsidized higher educational institutions all influence couples to decide to have smaller families. These small-family influences are counterbalanced by other policies, such as income tax deductions for children and the increasing difficulty of access to abortion services, that encourage larger families. The most obvious U.S population policy is immigration policy. As the intensifying debate makes clear, the topic remains very controversial, and how it will be resolved remains to be seen. It is striking, however, that this debate rarely considers, even implicitly, the context of national demographic trends and a national population policy. This surely represents an impediment to intelligent discussion of the complex topic.

As the government's report to Johannesburg suggests, the U.S. government has been reluctant, to put it mildly, to recognize the connections between population size and growth rates and the resultant impacts on the environment and resource availability. This was true for the Clinton Administration, and the second Bush Administration has been even more overtly neglectful of the links. Little wonder the public ignores the connections and many of the problems they underlie.

There are three major steps the United States should take to fulfill the goals of the Rio Summit domestically and internationally:

1. Deepen the nation's commitment to the international agreements on population, development, and the environment that our government has signed. Taken together, these agreements add up to a common understanding that population stability, environmental integrity, prudent resource use, and considerations of equity must all be inextricably linked in any design for a sustainable human future. Yet this perception is far from instilled in the American consciousness. While the vast majority of citizens consider themselves pro-environment, believe that they use resources prudently, and honor equity, their practice belies this self-perception. Most important, overpopulation is believed to be a problem for developing nations, not the United States. Although much could be done to incorporate goals of sustainability into domestic and international policies, the Bush Administration has shown little inclination to do so. Nor, until recently, has Congress, although the 110th Congress has shown renewed interest in developing such policies.

2. Commit to a serious examination of the nation's carrying capacity. This review should be set in a global context and include considerations of equity in a globalizing world.[38] The U.S. government cannot claim that it is taking steps toward sustainable development without first analyzing its environmental resource base and developing policies to ensure that its population does not exceed its carrying capacity, including its ability to draw on foreign resources. The United States clearly has failed in this admittedly difficult and complex obligation. Piecemeal analyses have been undertaken, often supported with government funds, but there has been no government-sponsored attempt to make such an assessment on a comprehensive national scale. In some cases, Congress and the administration have discouraged such research by cutting budgets for work by government agencies on such relevant topics as renewable energy or a national inventory of biodiversity. Nor has any government-sponsored research been conducted on a desirable population size for the United States from an environmental standpoint, although President Clinton's Council on Sustainable Development at least raised the question.[39]

3. Address the complex problem of global warming. This step, sure to dominate policy discussions for the foreseeable future, includes not only efforts to reduce emissions of greenhouse gases and retard the processes of climate change and the rise of sea levels, but also measures to mitigate the anticipated effects on various sectors of the economy. Population growth is related, directly and indirectly, to national rates of fossil fuel use and land use changes, both of which are major sources of greenhouse gas emissions. Population size and distribution are related to degrees of vulnerability to the consequences of climate change. And the consequences may well lead to mass movements of people from severely affected areas; indeed, populations of low-lying islands threatened by rising sea level have already begun to relocate. Today's huge migrations might be dwarfed by those a few decades from now.

The sustainability of the human population through the 21st century will be problematic, given a projected population increase of 30-50 percent by mid-century and the continuing depletion of the world's natural capital.[40] Providing sufficient food, water, and other necessities, amenities, and employment for 9 billion or more people without further degrading Earth's already profoundly impacted life support systems would be more than enough of a challenge, even without the added risks due to climate change and rising sea level. It should also be noted that the populations most vulnerable and least able to adapt to climate change are among the poorest and most rapidly growing ones. Given those risks, intelligently addressing population growth becomes all the more essential. Clearly, the need for international cooperation to tackle humanity's common dilemma has never been greater, and neither has the need for American leadership in this common endeavor.

ENDNOTES

1. United Nations Johannesburg Summit 2002: United States of America Country Profile [hereinafter U.S.A. Country Profile], *available at* www.un.org/esa/agenda21/natlinfo/wssd/usa.pdf.

2. POPULATION REFERENCE BUREAU, 2007 WORLD POPULATION DATA SHEET.

3. U.N. SECRETARIAT, DEP'T OF ECON. & SOC. AFFAIRS, WORLD POPULATION PROSPECTS: THE 2006 REVISION.

4. U.N. COMM'N ON SUSTAINABLE DEV., DEMOGRAPHIC DYNAMICS AND SUSTAINABILITY (2001) (E/CN.17/2001/PC/2).

5. U.N. Conference on Environment & Development, Rio Declaration, U.N. Doc. A/CONF.151/5/Rev.1 princ. 8, *reprinted in* 31 I.L.M. 874.

6. *See, e.g.*, the Cairo Conference on Population and Development in 1994 and the Beijing Conference on the Status of Women in 1995.

7. *See* WORLD RES. INST., *Population and Environment Development, in* WORLD RESOURCES 2000-2001—PEOPLE AND ECOSYSTEMS: THE FRAYING WEB OF LIFE.

8. JANET N. ABRAMOVITZ ET AL., VITAL SIGNS 2001 (2001); Philip Martin & Elizabeth Midgley, *Immigration: Shaping and Reshaping America*, 58 POP. BULL. 2 (June 2003).

9. *See* NORMAN MYERS & JENNIFER KENT, ENVIRONMENTAL EXODUS (1995); Jessica Tuchman Mathews, *Redefining Security*, 68 FOREIGN AFF. 162 (Spring 1989).

10. PRESIDENT'S COUNCIL ON SUSTAINABLE DEV., POPULATION & CONSUMPTION TASK FORCE REPORT, *Chapter 1: Population Issues, History of the U.S. Population Issue* [hereinafter PCSD].

11. U.S. CENSUS BUREAU, POPULATION CHANGE AND DISTRIBUTION: CENSUS BRIEF 2000, at 5, 7.

12. *See* POPULATION CONNECTION, SILENCE & MYTHS: A RESPONSE TO THE "BIRTH DEARTH," *available at* www.populationconnection.org/Communications/Reporter/winter2004/birthdearth.pdf. This is a significant reduction from the 1950s and 1960s.

13. If a previously growing population reaches replacement level, the population growth will continue for roughly a lifetime—about 70 years. This phenomenon is known as the momentum of population growth.

14. The Population Reference Bureau projects a U.S. population size of 419.9 million in 2050, a 40 percent increase over the 2006 population of 300 million. *See* POPULATION REFERENCE BUREAU, 2006 WORLD POPULATION DATA SHEET (2006).

15. MATHIS WACKERNAGEL & WILLIAM E. REES, OUR ECOLOGICAL FOOTPRINT: REDUCING HUMAN IMPACT ON THE EARTH (1996); Mathis Wackernagel et al., *National Natural Capital Accounting With the Ecological Footprint Concept*, 29 ECOLOGICAL ECON. 375 (1999).

16. P.M. Vitousek et al., *Human Domination of Earth's Ecosystems*, 277 SCIENCE 494 (1997).

17. Am. Ass'n for the Advancement of Sci., AAAS Atlas of Population & Development, *available at* http://atlas.aaas.org/index.php?part=2.

18. Millennium Ecosystem Assessment, Ecosystems and Human Well-being: General Synthesis (2005).

19. PCSD, *supra* note 10.

20. Brad Knickerbocker, *Illegal Immigrants in the US: How Many Are There?*, Christian Science Monitor, May 16, 2006.

21. Paul R. Ehrlich et al., The Golden Door: International Migration, Mexico, and the United States (1981).

22. Guttmacher Inst., An Overview of Abortion in the United States, 2005, *available at* www.guttmacher.org/media/presskits/2005/06/28/abortionoverview.html (accessed May 10, 2007)

23. *Id.*

24. *See, e.g.,* Gonzales v. Carhart, 127 S. Ct. 1610 (2007) (upholding the Partial-Birth Abortion Ban Act).

25. Guttmacher Inst., The Status of Major Abortion-Related Laws and Policies in the States (2001).

26. These data are from a May 31, 2001 survey by the Alan Guttmacher Institute. *Id.*

27. Press Release, U.S. Dep't Health & Human Servs., FDA Approves Mifepristone for the Termination of Early Pregnancy (Sept. 28, 2000).

28. *See* Planned Parenthood, Mifepristone: A Brief History, *at* www.ppatp.org/MifeHistory.htm (accessed July 18, 2008).

29. Mona L. Hymel, *The Population Crisis: The Stork, the Plow, and the IRS*, 77 N.C. L. Rev. 13, 45 (1998).

30. *Id.* at 49.

31. Radio Address by the President to the Nation, June 2, 2001, *available at* www.whitehouse.gov/news/releases/2001/06/20010602.html. Professor Hymel further argues that revisions are necessary to the earned income credit, which seeks to subsidize low-wage parents. Under the present tax code, "the addition of a qualifying child increases both the credit percentage and the eligible wage base." The problem with this policy is that there is no guarantee that the money is actually spent on the child. Thus, Hymel supports a subsidy "more closely tied to amounts actually spent on children." In contrast, the child care credit more closely resembles the type of tax policy that is narrowly targeted toward the amount parents actually spend on their children and treats children as a "consumption choice." Hymel, *supra* note 29, at 65-68.

32. Population Reference Bureau, 2006 World Population Data Sheet. The following section is largely based on Larry Nowels, Cong. Research Serv., *Population Assistance and Family Planning Programs: Issues for Congress* (2001) [hereinafter Nowels].

33. In 2001, Stanley Henshaw estimated that 46 million women annually have abortions. Carl Haub, Population Reference Bureau, personal communication, Nov. 29, 2001. The rate appears to have dropped more recently. *See* Guttmacher Inst., Facts on Induced Abortion Worldwide

(2007), *available at* www.guttmacher.org/pubs/fb_IAW.html (accessed July 18, 2008).

34. It should be noted that, despite the debate over abortion funding, the United States remains the largest single donor to family planning programs in developing countries at roughly $425 million annually, though this is well below the commitment made by donor nations (including the United States) at the 1994 Cairo Conference to provide one-third of the family planning and reproductive health care costs in developing countries (about $5.7 billion annually then, but expected to rise to $18.5 billion in 2005). ALL PARTY PARL. GROUP ON POPULATION, DEV. & REPROD. HEALTH, RETURN OF THE POPULATION GROWTH FACTOR: ITS IMPACT UPON THE MILLENNIUM DEVELOPMENT GOALS (Jan. 2007).

35. *Id.*

36. U. N. POPULATION DIV., WORLD POPULATION PROSPECTS: THE 2006 REVISION (2006).

37. U.S.A. Country Profile, *supra* note 1.

38. Gretchen C. Daily & Paul R. Ehrlich, *Population, Sustainability, and Earth's Carrying Capacity*, 42 BIOSCIENCE 761 (1992); PAUL R. EHRLICH & ANNE H. EHRLICH, ONE WITH NINEVEH: POLITICS, CONSUMPTION, AND THE HUMAN FUTURE (2004).

39. PCSD, *supra* note 10.

40. NATURE'S SERVICES: SOCIETAL DEPENDENCE ON NATURAL ECOSYSTEMS (Gretchen C. Daily ed., 1997); GRETCHEN C. DAILY & KATHERINE ELLISON, THE NEW ECONOMY OF NATURE (2002).

Chapter 13

Poverty: Greening the Tax and Transfer System to Create More Opportunities

Jonathan Barry Forman

The relationship between poverty and sustainable development is complex. The global scale of environmental degradation is unprecedented in human history, and the United States bears a great deal of the responsibility for that degradation.[1] Although the United States has less than 5 percent of the world's population, our economy accounts for more than 28 percent of the world's production of goods and services.[2]

While the relationship between poverty and sustainable development is probably more important in the developing world than in developed countries,[3] there are important issues in the developed countries as well. This chapter considers the relationship between poverty and sustainable development in the United States.

The chapter begins with an overview of economic inequality and poverty in the United States. It then discusses the relationship between poverty and environmental justice, and explains the role of government in the distribution of economic resources. The chapter closes with suggestions for using refundable tax credits to reduce poverty and inequality in the United States and for using "green" tax credits to offset the regressive impact of pollution taxes.

Economic Inequality and Poverty in the United States

Growing economic inequality and high levels of poverty are major problems for the U.S. economy, for our democratic institutions, and for our environment. The maldistribution of economic resources results in inefficient allocation and utilization of resources, as well as in social disharmony.[4] A more equal distribution of economic resources could help to promote sustainable consumption and production. For example, with greater economic resources, those with modest incomes, not just the rich, could afford the initial upfront investment for more energy-efficient automobiles and homes.

There is substantial inequality in the distribution of earnings, income, consumption, and wealth in the United States today.[5] Table 1 shows that in 2005 the bottom 20 percent of consumer units (households) had an average income of $9,676 and average consumption of goods and services of $19,120, while the top 20 percent of consumer units had an average income of $147,737 and average consumption of $90,469. Inequality in consumption is smaller than inequality in income because (1) consumers tend to maintain their levels of consumption even when their incomes fluctuate temporarily, (2) transfer programs increase the consumption levels for low-income households, and (3) higher-income families save a relatively greater percentage of their income and pay relatively more in taxes.

Table 1
Quintiles of Income Before Taxes: Average Annual Expenditures, Consumer Units, 2005

	All consumer units	Lowest quintile	Second quintile	Third quintile	Fourth quintile	Highest quintile
Income before taxes	$58,712	$9,676	$25,546	$42,622	$66,813	$147,737
Average annual expenditures	46,409	19,120	28,921	39,098	54,354	90,469

Source: BUREAU OF LABOR STATISTICS, U.S. DEP'T OF LABOR, CONSUMER EXPENDITURES IN 2005 (Report No. 998, Feb. 2007), tbl. 1.
Note: A consumer unit generally includes all members of a household related by blood, marriage, adoption, or some other legal arrangement.

To be sure, the numbers in Table 1 do not capture some of the most remarkable aspects of inequality in America. For example, earnings inequality in the United States is fairly large, even among year-round, full-time workers. In 2006, for example, the typical chief executive officer (CEO) in a major U.S. company made 364 times as much as the average production worker, according to a recent survey of 386 *Fortune* 500 companies.[6] With roughly 260 work days per year, that means that the typical CEO earns more in a day than an average worker earns in a full year.[7] Of course, CEOs are by no means the only American workers who earn extraordinary compensation. Movie stars and athletes often have multimillion dollar contracts.[8]

Economic inequality has also increased significantly in recent decades. One measure of income inequality is the Gini index, a mathematical measure of income inequality that can range from 0.0, indicating perfect equality (where everyone has the same income), to 1.0, indicating perfect inequality (where one person has all the income and the rest have none). According to the Census Bureau, the Gini index of household income inequality in 2005 was a fairly sizeable 0.469, up from just 0.428 in 1990, 0.403 in 1980, and 0.394 in 1970.[9]

Pertinent here, income inequality in the United States also tends to be larger than in other industrialized nations. For example, according to one recent survey, the most recent Gini indices of household income inequality were just 0.243 for Sweden, 0.273 for France, and 0.326 for the United Kingdom, compared with 0.357 for the United States in that survey.[10]

Of particular note, in recent years, the wealthiest Americans have seen an extraordinary increase in their share of household income. For example in 2000, the top 400 individual taxpayers received 1.09 percent of all the income in America, up from just 0.52 percent in 1992.[11]

Earnings inequality has also increased significantly in recent decades. For example, from 1979 to 2003 the real wages of high earners (those in the 95th percentile of earnings) increased by 31.1 percent; on the other hand, workers in the 50th percentile saw their wages grow by just 10.2 percent over that period, and workers in the 10th percentile saw an increase of only 0.9 percent. Along the same lines, the Gini index of earnings inequality for full-time, year-round workers rose from 0.326 in 1970 to 0.409 in 2005.[12]

One of the primary reasons for these recent increases in earnings (and income) inequality is that the rewards for education have grown. In particular, the gap between the average wages of high school and college graduates has widened significantly in recent years; college graduates age 25 and over now earn almost twice as much as workers who stop their education with a high school diploma.[13] The increased wage premiums for skilled and educated workers reflect the underlying shift from a manufacturing economy to a services economy. As the years go by, there are fewer good jobs in the U.S. manufacturing sector, and good jobs in the services sector tend to require high levels of education or experience.

Poverty is also a major problem in the United States. In 2008, the poverty level is $10,400 for a single individual, $17,600 for a single parent with two children, and \$21,200 for a married couple with two children.[14] In 2005, 12.6 percent (37 million people) lived in poverty, up from 11.1 percent (23 million people) in 1973.[15]

Poverty, Health, and Inequality

We know that the environment has a significant impact on human development, health, and disease. In particular, hazardous agents in our air, water, and soil are major contributors to illness, disability, and death. The poor in the United States, as well as throughout the world, typically face higher risks of ill health and environmental exposure than the rich,[16] in part because they are more likely to live near hazardous wastes and toxic products. Tables 2 and 3 illustrate some of the inequities in the United States regarding exposure to selected environmental hazards.[17]

Table 2
Proportions of African American, Hispanic, and White Populations Living in Air Quality Nonattainment Areas, 2004 (Percent)

	Demographic Breakdowns		
Pollutant	African American	Hispanic or Latino	White
Particulates (fine)	6	28	7
Carbon monoxide	4	20	4
Ozone	43	59	33

Source: U.S. Dep't of Health & Human Servs., Healthy People 2010 Database (Focus area: 08-Environmental Health), *available at* http://wonder.cdc.gov/data2010/focraceg.htm (visited June 25, 2008).

Table 3
Proportions of Certain Racial and Ethnic and Lower Socioeconomic Populations in Census Tracts Surrounding Waste Treatment, Storage, and Disposal Facilities (TSDF) Compared With the Proportions of These Groups in Other Census Tracts, 1994

Location of TSDFs	Demographic Breakdowns		
	African Americans	Hispanics	Persons Living Below the Poverty Line
Census tracts with either TSDFs or at least 50 percent of their area within 2.5 miles of a tract with TSDF	24.7	10.7	19.0
Census tracts without TSDFs	13.6	7.3	13.1

Source: U.S. Dep't of Health & Human Servs., Healthy People 2010: Understanding and Improving Health (2d ed., 2000), vol. 1, tbl. 8-B.

We made some progress cleaning up our environment and promoting environmental justice in the 1990s, but there clearly is more to be done.[18] In the meantime, the poor will bear a disproportionate share of the burdens of pollution.

The Government's Role in Reducing Poverty and Inequality

In a complex society like ours, economic rewards are determined by a combination of market forces and government policies. Markets arise automatically from the economic interactions among people and institutions. Here and there, government policies intervene to influence the operations of those markets and to shape the outcomes that result from market transactions.

Needless to say, policymakers cannot do much about market forces per se. But they can influence market outcomes through a combination of regulation, spending, and taxation. Government regulation defines and limits the range of markets, and so influences the shape of the initial distribution of economic resources. Government taxes and spending also have a significant impact on the distribution of economic resources. Most clearly, government taxes and transfers are the primary tools for the redistribution of economic resources and the mitigation of economic inequality.

The Major Federal Transfer Programs

Dozens of federal transfer programs provide assistance to individuals for retirement, disability, health, education, housing, public assistance, employment, and other needs. The vast majority of these programs transfer cash or in-kind benefits (e.g., food or medical care) directly to individuals. Social welfare analysts generally differentiate between transfer programs that are "means-tested" and those that are not. For programs that are means-tested (e.g., family support, Medicaid, and food stamps), eligibility and benefits depend upon an individual's need, as measured by the individual's income and assets. For programs that are not means-tested (e.g., social insurance programs like Social Security and Medicare), eligibility is based on other criteria such as age and work history. Table 4 shows the federal government's outlays for the principal federal transfer programs.

Table 4
Outlays for the Principal Federal Benefit Programs
(Billions of Dollars)

	2007 actual	2013 estimate
Social Security	$581	$842
Medicare	372	500
Medicaid	191	287
Unemployment compensation	32	44
Supplemental Security Income	33	49
Earned income tax credit	38	44
Food assistance	49	60
Family support	24	25
Housing assistance	17	15
Retirement and disability programs for civilians, military and veterans	149	197

Source: Exec. Office of the President and Office of Mgmt. & Budget, Historical Tables, Budget of the United States Government, Fiscal Year 2009 (2008), tbl. 8.5.

Measuring the Impact of Government on Inequality and Poverty

Most government operations have only a slight or indirect impact on the distribution of earnings and income. Spending on the military and other government operations, for example, probably has relatively little impact on economic inequality. Even among entitlement programs, relatively few programs are means-tested, and only about 10-15 percent of the federal budget is spent for such explicit redistribution. All in all, government tax and transfer policies currently reduce household income inequality by about 20 percent, as shown in Table 5.[19]

Table 5
Share of Aggregate Household Income by Quintiles and the Gini Index, 2005

	Market income	*Disposable income*
Quintiles		
Lowest	1.50	4.42
Second	7.26	9.86
Middle	14.00	15.33
Fourth	23.41	23.11
Highest	53.83	47.28
Gini Index	0.493	0.418

Source: U.S. Census Bureau, The Effect of Taxes and Transfers on Income and Poverty in the United States: 2005 (Current Population Report No. P60-232, Mar. 2007), tbl. 3.

Transfer programs reduce household income inequality much more than taxes. According to a recent Census Bureau report, subtracting taxes and including the earned income tax credit lowered the Gini index of household income inequality by just 4.6 percent in 2003 (from 0.498 to 0.475), while transfer programs lowered the Gini index by 17.0 percent (from 0.475 to 0.394).[20]

To be sure, high income households pay the lion's share of taxes, but they also receive an ever-increasing share of household income. In that regard, Table 6 shows estimates by the Congressional Budget Office (CBO) of the share of income, share of federal tax liabilities, and effective federal tax rates for all households in 2004.[21]

Table 6
Shares of Income, Shares of Federal Tax Liabilities,
and Effective Federal Tax Rates by Household Income
Category, 2004

	Share of pretax income	Share of federal tax liabilities	Total effective federal tax rate
Quintiles			
Lowest	4.1	0.9	4.5
Second	8.9	4.5	10.0
Middle	13.9	9.7	13.9
Fourth	20.4	17.6	17.2
Highest	53.5	67.1	25.1
All quintiles	100.0	100.0	20.0
Top 10 percent	38.8	52.3	26.9
Top 5 percent	29.0	41.3	28.5
Top 1 percent	16.3	25.3	31.1

Source: CONG. BUDGET OFFICE, HISTORICAL EFFECTIVE FEDERAL TAX
RATES: 1979 TO 2004 (2006), at 5-6.

There is some dispute about how much the U.S. tax and transfer systems affect poverty levels. As already mentioned, some 37 million Americans (12.6 percent) were poor in 2005 using the official estimate of poverty (based on money income).[22] Based on market income, however, the Census Bureau estimated that 18.9 percent of Americans were poor before taxes and transfers.[23] After taxes and transfers, the Census Bureau estimated that just 10.3 percent of Americans had disposable income that left them in poverty.

On the other hand, a recent comparative study by the economist Timothy M. Smeeding found that our tax and transfer systems had more modest effects.[24] His study estimated that our current tax and transfer systems reduced the poverty rate of two-parent families by just 0.5 percentage points in 2000, from 13.7 to 13.2 percent. That was a mere 3.6 percent reduction in two-parent poverty rates, compared with an average reduction of 44 percent across all 11 high-income countries studied (including the United States).

Recommendations for Reducing Poverty

Two recommendations for reducing poverty and enhancing sustainability flow from an analysis of the current U.S. tax and transfer systems.

1. Reform the Current Welfare System. The current system of transfer and tax programs for low-income workers is unnecessarily complicated, inequitable, and expensive to administer, and it needs to be reformed. The House Committee on Ways and Means recently identified 85 programs that provide everything from cash aid to energy assistance[25]—each with its own eligibility criteria and administrative system. Not surprisingly, many low-income Americans never receive the benefits to which they are entitled. For example, less than 60 percent of those eligible for food stamps actually receive them.[26]

The bottom line is that we are unlikely to achieve any meaningful reform of the welfare system by simply, in Edgar K. Browning's words, "trying to patch up each one of the innumerable and uncountable programs."[27] Instead, we should replace the current system with a *comprehensive and unified* tax and transfer system. This goal could be achieved by "cashing out" as many welfare programs as possible and using that money to help pay for a system of refundable tax credits.

Refundable tax credits could replace personal exemptions, standard deductions, and the many other child and family benefits in the current income tax system, and these tax credits could also replace all or a large portion of most welfare benefits. This new tax and transfer system would not necessarily cost any more than the current system, as costs could be managed by adjusting the size of the refundable tax credits and by adjusting the structure of tax rates. Moreover, the money generated as a result of administrative savings from combining these tax breaks and welfare programs into refundable tax credits could also be used for financing these credits.

For example, imagine a simple, integrated tax and transfer system with $2,000 *per person* refundable tax credits, $2,000 *per worker* refundable earned income credits (computed as 20 percent of the first $10,000 of earned income), and two tax rates: 20 percent of the first $50,000 of income, and 35 percent on income above $50,000.

A single mother with two children who earns $10,000 a year would be entitled to three $2,000 refundable tax credits and a $2,000 worker credit. She would owe $2,000 in taxes on her $10,000 of pre-transfer earnings, and that would leave her with $16,000 of disposable income after taxes and transfers.[28]

Those refundable tax credits should be paid out on a monthly basis. Each individual would present something like the current IRS Form W-4, Employee's Withholding Allowance Certificate, to her employer—or to a bank. Employees would then receive advance payment of their credits from their employers in the form of reduced withholding, while other beneficiaries would have their payments directly deposited into their bank accounts.

This comprehensive tax and transfer system would be simpler than the current system, would encourage low-skilled workers to enter and remain in the workforce, and would minimize marriage penalties. And it would help ensure that low-income families actually get their benefits. The Temporary Assistance for Needy Families program currently reaches just 52 percent of eligible families.[29] On the other hand, the Earned Income Tax Credit reaches 86 percent of eligible households, and it does so without any welfare stigma or loss of privacy.

As noted above, much of the cost of this new system could be paid for by cashing out current programs. As an initial step, we should cash out the food stamp program. Like most welfare programs, it has arcane eligibility criteria, baffling administrative procedures, and high administrative costs. Repealing the food stamp program would free up its $33 billion annual appropriation to instead pay for the refundable tax credits.[30]

Next, we should cash out low-income housing programs and get rid of the Low Income Home Energy Assistance Program. Instead of providing rental subsidies, mortgage-interest subsidies, and home energy assistance to just a fraction of low-income families, we should give *all* low-income families $2,000 per person tax credits and let them choose their own energy-efficient housing.

To be sure, it would take more than just a system of refundable tax credits to solve the problem of poverty in America. We would need to provide additional benefits to individuals who are not able to work. For example, many elderly and disabled individuals would need additional cash benefits. The additional benefits that these recipients need could continue to come in the form of SSI benefits, or they could be distributed through additional refundable tax credits.

Finally, an effective welfare system would also need to provide some services to beneficiaries. Education, training, job search and placement, counseling, and a clean environment are but a few that come to mind.

We also need to redesign our health care system to provide universal health care coverage.[31] Under a plan proposed by the New America Foundation,[32] the federal government would guarantee access to adequate and affordable health insurance for everyone. In exchange, each person would be required to maintain health insurance and to pay for that insurance with a combination of employer and employee contributions and government assistance based on ability to pay. An adequate but basic level of health care coverage would be required, and community insurance pools would offer individuals a choice among plans. Government assistance would be provided in the form of refundable tax credits calculated on a sliding scale based on need.

All in all, a comprehensive system of $2,000 per person refundable tax credits, $2,000 per worker tax credits, health care tax credits, and other work supports would lead to dramatic reductions in poverty and inequality in the United States.

2. Promote Sustainable Development. An integrated tax and transfer system could also be used to promote sustainable development. For example, once we accept the logic inherent in refundable tax credits, we could use them to distribute rebates of environmentally sensible polluter taxes.[33]

Many people oppose gasoline excise tax hikes and carbon emissions taxes on the grounds that these taxes would hurt poor people.[34] In tax parlance, such taxes are said to be regressive as opposed to progressive. One solution is to impose those environmental taxes on polluters but offset their regressive impact with refundable "green" tax credits for consumers.[35] Americans would get a cleaner environment, the costs of pollution would be internalized in the financial accounting of companies that pollute, and polluters would bear the true costs of the damage they cause.

For example, a carbon emissions tax could be made progressive by coupling it with rebates paid out in the form of refundable tax credits. Modest rebates (or "prebates" if paid ahead of time) would protect low-income families from any carbon tax burden and would reduce the burden on middle-income taxpayers, too. For example, we might impose a carbon tax that costs modest consumers of energy $500 per year and then rebate $500 a year to low-income families.

Alternatively, we could impose whatever pollution taxes and regulations we believe are necessary to achieve sustainable development and then increase the amount of the personal tax credits described above to offset any additional burdens on consumers. In short, we could use refundable tax credits to mitigate any economic burdens on households that result from pollution taxes or regulation.

Finally, we need to redouble our efforts to improve air, water, and soil quality, and we need to better manage the effects of toxics and waste. In particular, we need to minimize the risks to human health posed by hazardous sites, which are so often situated in or close to poor communities.

Conclusion

The Constitution of the United States created a new American government to, among other things, "establish Justice" and "promote the general Welfare."[36] The American experiment has worked because it has encouraged its citizens to be productive. But America can work even better. The way to make America work better is to make the government's responsibility to "promote the general Welfare" work better. We should redesign our tax, transfer, and regulatory policies to reduce poverty and promote sustainable development.

ENDNOTES

1. John C. Dernbach, *Sustainable Development: Now More Than Ever*, 32 ELR 10003 (Jan. 2002).

2. Author's computations from the World Bank's Quick Reference Tables Web page (2007), *available at* www.worldbank.org/data/quickreference/quickref.html.

3. *See, e.g.*, DAVID REED, ESCAPING POVERTY'S GRASP: THE ENVIRONMENTAL FOUNDATIONS OF POVERTY REDUCTION (2006); REDUCING POVERTY AND SUSTAINING THE ENVIRONMENT: THE POLITICS OF LOCAL ENGAGEMENT (Steve Bass et al. eds., 2005); ECONOMIC DEVELOPMENT AND ENVIRONMENTAL SUSTAINABILITY: POLICIES AND PRINCIPLES FOR A DURABLE EQUILIBRIUM (José I. dos R. Furtado et al. eds., 2000); and JACK M. HOLLANDER, THE REAL ENVIRONMENTAL CRISIS: WHY POVERTY, NOT AFFLUENCE, IS THE ENVIRONMENT'S NUMBER ONE ENEMY (2003).

4. In that regard, according to the United Nations' recent report on sustainable development:

   > At the domestic level, sound environmental, social and economic policies, democratic institutions responsive to the needs of the people, the rule of law, anti-corruption measures, gender equality and an enabling environment for investment are the basis for sustainable development.

   U.N. REPORT OF THE WORLD SUMMIT ON SUSTAINABLE DEVELOPMENT 8 (2002).

5. *See generally* JONATHAN BARRY FORMAN, MAKING AMERICA WORK 28-37 (2006).

6. SARAH ANDERSON ET AL., EXECUTIVE EXCESS 2007: THE STAGGERING SOCIAL COST OF U.S. BUSINESS LEADERSHIP (14TH ANNUAL CEO COMPENSATION SURVEY) 5 (2007).

7. LAWRENCE MISHEL ET AL., THE STATE OF WORKING IN AMERICA: 2004-2005, at 214 (2005).

8. *See, e.g.*, *What People Earn: Our Annual Report on the Economy and You*, PARADE: THE SUNDAY NEWSPAPER MAGAZINE (in THE SUNDAY OKLAHOMAN, Apr. 15, 2007) (showing that 43-year-old actor Steve Carrell made $9 million in 2006 and 31-year-old NASCAR driver Jimmie Johnson made $15.8 million).

9. U.S. CENSUS BUREAU, HISTORICAL INCOME TABLES, tbl. H-4 (updated May 15, 2007), *available at* www.census.gov/hhes/www/income/histinc/ie2.html.

10. MICHAEL FÖRSTER & MARCO MIRA D'ERCOLE, ORGANISATION FOR ECON. CO-OPERATION & DEV. (OECD), INCOME DISTRIBUTION AND POVERTY IN THE OECD COUNTRIES IN THE SECOND HALF OF THE 1990s (2005).

11. Michael Parisi & Michael Strudler, *The 400 Individual Income Tax Returns Reporting the Highest Adjusted Gross Incomes Each Year, 1992-2000: Data Release*, STAT. INCOME BULL. 7 (Spring 2003).

12. U.S. CENSUS BUREAU, HISTORICAL INCOME TABLES, tbl. IE-2 (updated Mar. 7, 2007), *available at* www.census.gov/hhes/www/income/histinc/h04.html.

13. *See, e.g.*, Press Release, U.S. Census Bureau, College Degree Nearly Doubles Annual Earnings, Release CB05-38 (Mar. 28, 2005), *available at* http://www.census.gov/Press-Release/www/releases/archives/education/004214.html. Over a lifetime, one recent study estimated that a college degree is worth more than $1,000,000 in additional lifetime earnings. KENT HILL ET AL., THE VALUE OF HIGHER EDUCATION: INDIVIDUAL AND SOCIETAL BENEFITS (WITH SPECIAL CONSIDERATION FOR THE STATE OF ARIZONA) (2005).

14. U.S. DEP'T OF HEALTH & HUMAN SERVS., ANNUAL UPDATE OF THE HHS POVERTY GUIDELINES, 73 Fed. Reg. 3971 (Jan. 23, 2008) [hereinafter HHS POVERTY GUIDELINES], *available at* http://aspe.hhs.gov/POVERTY/08fedreg.htm.

15. U.S. CENSUS BUREAU, INCOME, POVERTY, AND HEALTH INSURANCE COVERAGE IN THE UNITED STATES: 2005 (Census Population Report No. P60-231, Aug. 2006), tbl. B-1.

16. *See, e.g.*, Emily Cooper, *Health, Environment, and Poverty, in* WORLD RES. INST., WORLD RESOURCES 2005: MANAGING ECOSYSTEMS TO FIGHT POVERTY (2005), *available at* http://earthtrends.wri.org/features/view_feature.php?fid=57&theme=4; Amy K. Glasmeier & Tracey Farrigan, *Poverty, Sustainability, and the Culture of Despair: Can Sustainable Development Strategies Support Poverty Alleviation in America's Most Environmentally Challenged Communities?*, 590 ANNALS AM. ACAD. POL. & SOC. SCI. 131 (2003).

17. U.S. Dep't of Health & Human Servs. (HHS), Healthy People 2010 Database (Focus area: 08-Environmental Health), *available at* http://wonder.cdc.gov/data2010/focraceg.htm (last visited June 25, 2008); HHS, HEALTHY PEOPLE 2010: UNDERSTANDING AND IMPROVING HEALTH (2d ed., 2000), vol. 1, tbl. 8-B. *See also* HHS, CTRS. FOR DISEASE CONTROL & PREVENTION, NAT'L CTR. FOR ENVTL. HEALTH, FACT BOOK (Mar. 2000). For Table 3, more current data are hard to find, despite the fact that the federal government says that it is committed to environmental justice. *See, e.g.*, Nov. 4, 2005, letter of EPA Administrator Stephen L. Johnson reaffirming the Agency's and the Bush Administration's commitment to environmental justice, *available at* www.epa.gov/compliance/resources/policies/ej/admin-ej-commit-letter-110305.pdf; *but see* U.S. EPA OFFICE OF INSPECTOR GEN., EPA NEEDS TO CONDUCT ENVIRONMENTAL JUSTICE REVIEWS OF ITS PROGRAMS, POLICIES, AND ACTIVITIES, Report No. 2006-P-00034 (Sept. 18, 2006), *available at* www.epa.gov/oig/reports/2006/20060918-2006-P-00034.pdf; and U.S. GOV'T ACCOUNTABILITY OFFICE, ENVIRONMENTAL JUSTICE: EPA SHOULD DEVOTE MORE ATTENTION TO ENVIRONMENTAL JUSTICE WHEN DEVELOPING CLEAN AIR RULES (GAO-05-289, 2005), *available at* www.gao.gov/new.items/d05289.pdf. EPA provides its Environmental Justice Geographic Assessment Tool on its website, which provides information to assess adverse health or environmental impacts by location, *available at* www.epa.gov/compliance/whereyoulive/ejtool.html. *See also* ROBERT D. BULLARD ET AL., TOXIC WASTES AND RACE AT TWENTY: 1987-2007: GRASS ROOTS STRUGGLES TO DISMANTLE ENVIRONMENTAL RACISM IN THE UNITED STATES (2007), *available at* www.ejrc.cau.edu/TWART-light.pdf; Pollution Locator/Environmental Burdens Web Page on Scorecard: The Pollu-

tion Information Site, www.scorecard.org/env-releases/def/ej_burdens.
html.

18. HHS, HEALTHY PEOPLE 2010, *supra* note 17, vol. 1, ch. 8. EPA defines environmental justice as "fair treatment for people of all races, cultures, and incomes, regarding the development of environmental laws, regulations, and policies." U.S. EPA, ENVIRONMENTAL JUSTICE, FREQUENTLY ASKED QUESTIONS, FAQ No. 2 (last updated Mar. 23, 2006), *available at* www.epa.gov/compliance/resources/faqs/ej/index.html#faq2.

19. U.S. CENSUS BUREAU, THE EFFECTS OF GOVERNMENT TAXES AND TRANSFERS ON INCOME AND POVERTY: 2005 (Current Population Report No. P60-232, Mar. 2007), tbl. 3. The second column of Table 5 shows the Census Bureau's estimates of the market's initial distribution of household income before government taxes and transfers, by quintiles of population ("market income"). Before government taxes and transfers, the richest 20 percent of American households received 53.83 percent of household income, while the poorest 20 percent received just 1.50 percent. That is a rather unequal distribution of income. The Gini index for the market distribution of household income in the United States in 2005 was a sizeable 0.493.

The third column of Table 5 shows the "disposable income" shares that households end up with after government taxes and transfers in the year 2005. Taxes and transfers increased the relative share of income held by the bottom three quintiles at the expense of the share of income held by the top two quintiles, and the Gini index fell to 0.418.

20. ROBERT W. CLEVELAND, U.S. CENSUS BUREAU, ALTERNATIVE INCOME ESTIMATES IN THE UNITED STATES: 2003, Current Population Report No. P60-228 (2005), at 4-5.

21. CONG. BUDGET OFFICE, HISTORICAL EFFECTIVE FEDERAL TAX RATES: 1979 TO 2004 (2006), at 5-6.

22. U.S. CENSUS BUREAU, INCOME, POVERTY, AND HEALTH INSURANCE COVERAGE IN THE UNITED STATES: 2005, *supra* note 15.

23. U.S. CENSUS BUREAU, THE EFFECTS OF GOVERNMENT TAXES AND TRANSFERS ON INCOME AND POVERTY: 2005, *supra* note 19, tbl. A-2.

24. Timothy M. Smeeding, *Poor People in Rich Nations: The United States in Comparative Perspective*, 20 J. ECON. PERSPECTIVES 69 (2006).

25. U.S. HOUSE OF REPS., COMM. ON WAYS & MEANS, 2004 GREEN BOOK: BACKGROUND MATERIAL AND DATA ON PROGRAMS WITHIN THE JURISDICTION OF THE COMMITTEE ON WAYS AND MEANS (2004), K-10 to K-12.

26. U.S. DEP'T OF AGRIC., MAKING AMERICA STRONGER: A PROFILE OF THE FOOD STAMP PROGRAM (2005).

27. Edgar K. Browning, *Commentaries, in* INCOME REDISTRIBUTION 207, 209 (Colin D. Campbell ed., 1977).

28. Recall that the poverty level for a single parent with two children is $17,600 in 2008. HHS POVERTY GUIDELINES, *supra* note 14.

29. Leonard E. Burman & Deborah I. Kobes, *EITC Reaches More Families Than TANF, Food Stamps*, TAX NOTES, Mar. 17, 2003, at 1769.

30. *See* U.S. Dep't of Agric., Food Stamp Program Participation and Costs Web page, www.fns.usda.gov/pd/fssummar.htm.

31. *See, e.g.*, Jonathan Barry Forman, *Making Universal Health Care Work*, 19 ST. THOMAS L. REV. 137 (2006). According to the Census Bureau, 44.8 million people, 15.3 percent of the population, were without health insurance in 2005, including 27.3 million Americans between 18 and 64 years of age who worked during the year. Press Release, U.S. Census Bureau, Census Bureau Revises 2004 and 2005 Health Insurance Coverage Estimates (Release No. CB07-45, 2007).

32. Michael Calabrese & Lauri Rubiner, *Universal Coverage, Universal Responsibility: A Roadmap to Make Coverage Affordable for All Americans* 6 (New Am. Found., Working Paper No. 1, 2004).

33. Under the polluter-pay principle, governments should require polluters to bear the costs of their pollution.

34. *See, e.g.*, CONG. BUDGET OFFICE, BUDGET OPTIONS (2007) (Option 48 would increase excise taxes on motor fuels by 50 cents per gallon, and option 53 would impose an "upstream" tax on carbon emissions). *See also* Juliet Eilperin & Steven Mufsaon, *Tax on Carbon Emissions Gains Support*, WASH. POST, Apr. 1, 2007, at A5.

35. *See, e.g.*, LAURENCE S. SEIDMAN, POURING LIBERAL WINE INTO CONSERVATIVE BOTTLES (2006).

36. U.S. CONST. pmbl.

IV. Conservation and Management
of Natural Resources

Chapter 14

Freshwater: Sustaining Use by Protecting Ecosystems

Robert W. Adler

In 2002, the United Nations Committee on Economic, Social, and Cultural Rights determined that access to water is a fundamental human right.[1] Yet billions of people around the world lack access to clean water and sanitation, and millions of people each year die of waterborne diseases.[2] Over a billion people lack access to an improved water supply within one kilometer of their homes, and over two-and-one-half billion people have no access to modern sanitation.[3] Virtually the entire population of the United States, by contrast, has access to relatively safe drinking water and modern sanitation.[4] Nevertheless, freshwater resources and aquatic ecosystems in the United States face serious threats.[5] Global warming now poses new threats to those resources and ecosystems.

This chapter addresses freshwater resources and ecosystems that depend on freshwater flows, such as rivers, streams, lakes, and inland wetlands, as opposed to saltwater resources and ecosystems in the ocean, estuaries, and coastal waters. (Those resources are discussed in Chapter 15.) Freshwater also includes groundwater, water stored in underground aquifers but usually connected hydrologically to surface water systems. The chapter summarizes the state of U.S. freshwater resources and ecosystems. It then evaluates changes in U.S. water law and policy since 2002, and presents policy recommendations to address the threats to the nation's water.

Assessment of U.S. Freshwater Resources and Ecosystems

Surface Water Quality

It is difficult to identify long-term trends in U.S. water quality based on the limited available data. Water quality standards, as well as methods and frequency of monitoring, have evolved and vary from state to state. Water quality and environmental conditions change with climate and other factors that are not directly related to land use or human sources of pollution. Because monitoring and assessment resources are inadequate, little or no information is available for many water bodies, or for all of the characteristics necessary to assess water quality fully.[6]

Notwithstanding these limitations, the data are sufficiently clear to show that U.S. rivers, lakes, wetlands, and other water bodies remain seriously degraded due to chemical pollution, physical alterations to aquatic ecosystems, habitat loss and degradation, invasive species, and other factors. The EPA requires states to identify all water bodies that are impaired for one or more reasons.[7] According to EPA, in 2004, states reported a total of 38,886 impaired water bodies throughout the country, and a total of 64,581 causes of impairment.[8] Leading sources of impairment were pathogens, mercury, sediment, other metals, nutrients, oxygen depletion, pH levels, temperature, habitat alteration, polychlorinated biphenyls (PCBs), turbidity, pesticides, and salinity.[9]

The U.S. Geological Survey (USGS) conducts a monitoring and assessment program to provide baseline information on water pollutants such as pesticides, nutrients, volatile organic compounds (VOCs), and radon, as well as indicators of aquatic ecosystem health. These data cannot yet be used to evaluate more recent water quality trends because the decadal timeframes for the studies (1991-2001 and 2002-2012) have not elapsed. Still, the program does provide useful information to judge the quality of a scientifically selected sample of water bodies with a more consistent record than is possible using disparate sets of data from all 50 states.[10]

In the 51 study units assessed, USGS found that most water bodies were suitable for most common uses (such as swimming and other recreation, public drinking water supply, and support of fish and aquatic life), but also widely contaminated—especially in agricultural and urban areas—by nutrients, pesticides, VOCs and their breakdown products, and other chemicals. Water quality varied with land use and management, as well as natural variables such as geology, hydrology, soils, and climate.[11] Streams and groundwater in agricultural and urban regions almost always contained mixtures of contaminants (including pesticides, organic chemicals, and nutrients), often with seasonally high concentrations.[12] USGS found toxics such as mercury, pesticides, and PCBs in virtually all fish samples from urban streams, frequently at levels exceeding guidelines for the protection of human health and wildlife; and organochlorine compounds in sediments from most agricultural and urban watersheds, often in concentrations exceeding guidelines.[13]

Trends in chemical water pollution can also be gleaned from patterns in releases of toxic chemicals as reported in EPA's Toxic Release Inventory (TRI). Between 2001 and 2005, total releases of chemicals covered by the TRI decreased by 22 percent, largely due to reductions in releases to air and land. However, during the same period the release of TRI chemicals to underground injection wells and surface waters increased, by 7 percent and 3 percent, respectively.[14]

Threats to Human Health

The USGS detected toxic metals and organic chemicals in a large percentage of surface waters in urban and agricultural watersheds. Drinking water contaminants were also found widely in drinking water wells. In a survey of 3,497 wells, at least one VOC was detected in about 18 percent of all samples (623 well samples). Levels exceeding drinking water standards—the enforceable maximum contaminant levels (MCLs) established by EPA under the federal Safe Drinking Water Act[15]—were found in about one percent of all wells tested (45 samples out of the 623 in which VOCs were found).[16] In tests for microbiological contaminants from 22 basins, USGS found coliform bacteria and other pathogens in nearly 30 percent of all wells sampled, with higher frequency and generally higher contaminant levels in domestic as opposed to public water supply wells.[17]

U.S. public health officials have maintained statistics since 1920 on outbreaks of water-borne disease.[18] Over that period, modern sanitation and drinking water treatment have dramatically reduced the incidence of illnesses and deaths from water-borne pathogens.[19] Nevertheless, from 1991 to 2002 an average of 17 outbreaks per year due to inadequately treated water and distribution-system contamination were reported, and experts believe that many water-borne disease outbreaks are undetected or unreported.[20] Those outbreaks caused almost one-half million reported illnesses, and 73 reported deaths.[21]

Chemical and biological contaminants also continue to pose threats to consumers of freshwater fish. The 2004 EPA listing of fishing advisories around the United States indicates that the number of fish advisories continues to grow, although many of the new listings reflect improved monitoring for mercury and other contaminants.[22] The 2004 listing identifies 3,221 advisories, which collectively report contamination in more than one-third of the nation's total lake acreage, and about one-quarter of its total river miles (over 14 million lake acres and about 840,000 river miles).[23] Reported bioaccumulative contaminants, which are stored in fish tissue and concentrate at higher levels over time, include mercury, PCBs, chlordane, dioxins, and DDT.[24] EPA detected mercury, PCBs, dioxins and related compounds, DDT, chlordane, and dieldrin in lake fish taken from 486 sites out of 500 lakes sampled from 2000 to 2003.[25]

Integrity of Aquatic Ecosystems

Chemical pollution has been the main focus of efforts to control water pollution. Significantly less attention has been paid to serious physical and hydrological changes and other adverse impacts to aquatic habitats.[26] In a recent survey of the nation's wadeable streams, the first in a series of evaluations that will later include rivers, lakes, and other surface waters, EPA concluded that 42 percent of the nation's stream length is in poor biological condition, 25 percent in fair condition, and only 28 percent in good biological condition (5 percent not assessed).[27] The most significant causes of impairment were nutrients, riparian disturbance, streambed sediments, and loss or alteration of in-stream fish habitat and riparian vegetation.[28]

Some progress has been made in protecting critical wetlands in the United States, although these gains should be interpreted with caution. After decades of steady losses in the acreage of wetlands identified by the U.S. Fish and Wildlife Service (FWS) in the National Wetlands Inventory program, FWS recently reported the first-ever net gain in wetlands acreage, with a national gain of nearly 200,000 acres of wetlands between 1998 and 2004.[29] These data reflect steady improvement, reversing a trend in which net wetlands acreage declined at a rate of almost half a million acres per year between the mid-1950s and the mid-1970s, about 290,000 acres a year from the mid-1970s to the mid-1980s, and about 58,000 acres a year between 1986 and 1997.[30] But net wetland acreage does not necessarily translate to the functions and values of wetlands. Most wetlands gains from 1998 to 2004 reflected artificial freshwater ponds created as mitigation for the loss of natural wetlands. Such open ponds typically do not provide the same range of wetland values and functions as the wetlands they replaced.[31]

Rivers and streams in urbanized areas exhibit some of the most serious ecological changes due to the impacts of urbanization on water quality and temperature, runoff timing and volumes, river and stream profiles, sediment flow and streambed composition and morphology, riparian vegetation, and other physical, chemical, and hydrological characteristics.[32] USGS studies of urban stream ecosystems throughout the United States indicate significant adverse ecological and hydrologic impacts even in areas of moderate urbanization (based on factors such as percent impervious cover in a watershed), although the degree of impact varied depending on climate, geology, topography, and other physical variables.[33] Hydrologic changes in urbanized areas may pose more substantial barriers to aquatic ecosystem restoration than chemical pollution.[34]

Water Supply

Compared to many countries, the United States has ample renewable freshwater resources.[35] Although total U.S. water withdrawals are much larger than in most other countries, on both an absolute and per capita basis,[36] the United States withdraws less than one-sixth of its renewable water supplies every year on a national basis (meaning *in theory* that those supplies could support a population six times as many people as the current U.S. population, assuming unrealistically that all of that water was available for use in the correct places, without causing dramatic environmental harm).[37] However, drought causes relative and often severe shortages in both western and eastern parts of the country[38] as increased population combined with high rates of water use strain regional water supplies.[39] Although drought in the United States does not lead to famines and the massive number of drought-related deaths that occur in other parts of the world, economists estimate that drought causes at least $6-8 billion in economic costs per year.[40]

Global Warming and Freshwater Resources

Scientists predict that global warming will have significant impacts on water resources around the world, including the United States. Some areas will become wetter and others drier, leading to more frequent and more severe droughts and related famines in some regions, and higher flood risks in others.[41] For example, decreased runoff into reservoirs in the Colorado River basin could exacerbate droughts in a region that is already experiencing serious water shortages.[42] Shifts in temperature and precipitation are also expected to have serious adverse effects on water quality, as are ecological disruptions to fish, plant, and wildlife populations, blooms of nuisance algae, and losses or impairments to both coastal and inland wetlands.[43]

Programs and Policies to Protect Freshwater

Federal government laws and programs to protect and manage freshwater resources have not changed significantly for several decades. For example, the Clean Water Act, which governs federal and state programs to protect the chemical, physical, and biological integrity of surface waters, was last amended significantly in 1987. Likewise, the basic structure of the Safe Drinking Water Act has not changed substantially since 1986, although Congress adopted incremental changes in 1996.

EPA's current strategic plan to protect water resources reflects an approach of working within the existing statutory system.[44] For example, EPA recently adopted new regulations to protect drinking water from certain pathogens and disinfection byproducts.[45] Similarly, EPA adopted new rules to reduce pollution from concentrated animal feeding operations (CAFOs).[46] Although the CAFO rule was controversial in some respects and subject to litigation and subsequent changes, it does represent conceptual progress in trying to fill in the gaps between EPA's relatively stringent control of industrial and municipal sources of water pollution and the absence of significant controls on most kinds of agricultural pollution.

In many respects, EPA's approach is to try to do a better job of implementing its long-standing regulations and existing programs.[47] Those efforts show some improvement in program implementation even where actual gains in water quality and aquatic ecosystem health have not yet been documented. For example, since 2000 the states and EPA have completed over 20,000 total maximum daily loads (TMDLs), which are calculations of how much pollution particular water bodies can accept without exceeding water quality standards, and accompanying plans to clean up specific impaired water bodies around the country.[48] TMDLs are supposed to identify additional measures to reduce pollution from a combination of point and nonpoint sources so that water quality standards are met.[49] Whether TMDLs will achieve improvements in significant numbers of waterways, however, remains to be seen. In fact, EPA's current goal is to restore by 2012 only 2,250 out of the almost 40,000 impaired water bodies identified by the states.[50]

EPA continues to support local and regional watershed-based programs to protect and restore water bodies,[51] as do various nongovernmental organizations.[52] As a result, much of the progress in watershed protection since 2002 has occurred at the state, local, and private levels. Island County, Washington, for example, is preparing a more comprehensive water resources monitoring and protection initiative than required by federal law.[53] The county is implementing watershed protection efforts through a shoreline management plan, best management practices linked to a permitting process, and other end-use measures.[54] Private land trusts and other conservation organizations play an increasing role in protecting wetlands, riparian zones, and other critical aquatic areas. In its first five years, for example, Montana Wetlands Legacy conserved over 27,000 acres of wetlands and more than 800,000 acres of watershed lands through conservation easements, leases, cooperative agreements with landowners, and fee title acquisitions.[55] Programs to restore instream, riparian, and other aquatic habitats are being implemented throughout the country, with varying levels of success.[56]

As with other watershed-based restoration and protection initiatives, raw numbers of watershed restoration efforts do not necessarily translate to program effectiveness absent valid monitoring and assessment. A comprehensive review of over 38,000 restoration projects around the United States, for example, found that fewer than 10 percent included written documentation of effectiveness monitoring.[57]

Impact of the Judiciary

State, local, and private efforts to protect and restore wetlands and other aquatic ecosystems may become even more critical given recent decisions by federal courts that could reduce dramatically the scope of water bodies subject to regulation under the federal Clean Water Act (CWA). In 2001, the U.S. Supreme Court ruled in *Solid Waste Agency of Northern Cook County v. U.S. Army Corps of Engineers* that CWA jurisdiction does not extend to ponds used as habitat by migratory birds but whose waters were isolated (not adjacent to or connected directly to rivers, streams, or other surface waters covered by the Act).[58] That decision led to confusion and differences among lower courts regarding the extent to which the CWA applies to water bodies with less direct connection to waters that meet the traditional test of navigability for purposes of federal authority under the Commerce Clause of the U.S. Constitution, although most lower courts read the 2001 decision narrowly.[59]

In 2006, however, in a fragmented decision in which no single opinion was joined by a majority of the justices, the Supreme Court decided two related cases in a way that further calls into question the scope of federal regulatory control over non-navigable waters, and that further confuses decisions by federal regulators and lower courts.[60] Writing for a plurality of four justices in *Rapanos v. United States*, Justice Scalia concluded that the CWA applies only to "relatively permanent, standing, or continuously flowing bodies of water" and only to wetlands with a "continuous surface water connection" to other waters of the United States.[61] In a concurring opinion, Justice Kennedy would find CWA jurisdiction over any water body with a "significant nexus" to navigable waters,[62] while four dissenting justices would find jurisdiction over a far broader scope of waterways, deferring to the professional and scientific judgments of the responsible federal agencies.[63] Given the highly divided nature of the decision, lower courts continue to disagree about the test to apply in deciding which waters are covered by the CWA.[64]

Water Resource Policies

Water use and supply policies in the United States have also remained relatively constant since 2002. Most efforts to improve water efficiency and otherwise better manage water resources have evolved at the state and local levels, consistent with the historic policy of Congress that water resources are most appropriately left to state control.[65] Total freshwater use in the United States varied very little between 1985 and 2000 despite increased population, indicating improvements in water use efficiency over recent decades, especially in irrigated agriculture.[66] Some urban areas have also improved water efficiency dramatically,[67] although highly drought-prone regions could reap significant efficiency savings in both agricultural and urban areas using current technologies and prices.[68]

The Importance of Sustainable Freshwater and Aquatic Ecosystems

For a nation with virtually universal access to modern sanitation and potable freshwater at the turn of the faucet, it seems almost trite to assert that clean, adequate supplies of freshwater are essential to a sustainable lifestyle and economy. As suggested by the many ongoing and potential future problems discussed above, however, defining and achieving sustainability for those resources is a serious and complex issue.

In regard to freshwater for direct human use, sustainability suggests adequate—and adequately treated—supplies of water for all legitimate human economic uses, including agricultural, industrial, and municipal purposes. "Adequate supply" no longer means what it has in the past—that is, as much water as one can use, on demand, and at trivial costs. Rather, to reconcile population and economic growth with increasingly scarce water resources, the concept of sustainable water use must entail *sufficient* supplies to accomplish necessary and legitimate purposes, using the most efficient means possible.[69]

Moreover, those resources must be supplied in amounts and in ways that avoid the massive loss and degradation of freshwater aquatic ecosystems that has occurred in the past. Stated most simply, we must leave enough water, in the right places and at the right times, in the natural system to sustain healthy aquatic ecosystems. Sustainability of freshwater resources also demands that we continue to reduce all sources of water pollution to acceptable levels of risk to human health, to fish and aquatic life, and to the integrity of aquatic ecosystems. Likewise, that goal requires that we pay more attention to the physical as well as the chemical integrity of aquatic ecosystems, so that we can restore and protect aquatic and aquatic-dependent biodiversity and other resources.

Policy Recommendations

Although U.S. residents enjoy enviable access to ample supplies of safe freshwater resources, pollution continues to pose risks to human health, aquatic ecosystems remain significantly impaired throughout the country and face increasing risks due to urbanization and other development, and water supplies will become increasingly scarce as population continues to grow and as global warming affects the amount and distribution of water supplies. The following four policy changes could enhance the sustainability of freshwater resources.

1. Make new, smarter investments in water resources. Although U.S. water supply and sanitation systems remain among the best in the world, many systems are aging and require significant repairs or upgrades, and growth will require additional investments. EPA's 2002 Gap Analysis Report stated that between 2000 and 2019, U.S. communities will have to spend approximately $100 billion on capital infrastructure for drinking water and $120 billion in wastewater infrastructure—almost a quarter of a trillion dollars over two decades.[70] Those investments are essential to maintain public health and other benefits. However, future investments should focus on sustainable uses of land and water. "Least-cost first" policies will promote investment in water conservation where it is more cost-effective than increasing supplies. Zoning requirements designed to ensure that water and sewer services are in place before development can occur will help to prevent sprawl, which ultimately imposes more strain on resources and aquatic ecosystems. Pricing policies that ensure that consumers pay the full costs of providing safe water, with lifeline rate exceptions for purposes of equity, will encourage new investments to be made as wisely as possible. It also makes sense to consider a twenty-first century water supply and distribution system in which water used for household uses (drinking, bathing, cooking) is separate from outside irrigation water, so that the huge investment necessary to treat drinking water is not wasted on water that only irrigates lawns and golf courses. Likewise, more systems should be devised to divert treated gray water (household water from sinks and tubs that is only mildly contaminated, as opposed to wastewater flushed from toilets), recycled but treated sewage effluent, and stormwater runoff, for non-drinking water uses.

   2. Control polluted runoff. Although pollution from industrial and municipal point sources (water pollution that enters waterways through pipes or other discrete conveyances) requires continued vigilance and additional standards and enforcement, runoff from more dispersed sources (often called "nonpoint sources") is still the leading source of water pollution in the United States. For the most part, those pollution sources remain subject to a patchwork of state and local control programs, most of which are voluntary or poorly enforced. Although watershed programs are a promising way to coordinate efforts to address all sources of impairments within watersheds, those programs will remain limited if the methods to address the largest remaining source of harm remain vague and largely unenforceable. A mandatory system of enforceable best practice standards for sources of runoff pollution remains the biggest gap in U.S. Water pollution programs. Such standards should be sufficiently flexible to account for differences in climate, soils, topography, land uses, and other factors, but the inherent variability in conditions is not a sufficient reason to leave this major source of pollution unregulated.

3. Undertake comprehensive aquatic ecosystem restoration and protection. Although the stated goal of the Clean Water Act is to restore the chemical, physical, and biological integrity of the nation's waters,[71] habitat loss and degradation and other causes beyond chemical pollution contribute widely to the significant ecological impairment of U.S. waterways. To date, CWA implementation has focused largely on chemical pollution. While the Act aspires to a broader focus on other forms of aquatic ecosystem restoration and protection, it lacks the kinds of specific programs or provisions to address those kinds of impairments as apply to chemical pollution. Those issues might be addressed more effectively through a separate, broadly focused aquatic ecosystem restoration and protection statute. Just as additional investment is needed in traditional water and wastewater infrastructure, the nation should invest in aquatic ecosystem restoration efforts that can produce healthier aquatic ecosystems, provide opportunities for skilled employment (such as riparian revegetation or restoration of natural stream channels), and generate significant economic returns in the form of reduced flooding, increased property values, and other benefits. Strategies for aquatic ecosystem restoration need to focus on the full range of chemical, physical, and biological impairments, including factors such as flow amounts and timing, instream and riparian habitat structure and quality, and invasive species, as well as more traditional forms of pollution.

4. Impose comprehensive federal jurisdiction over aquatic ecosystems. Despite the impressive array of state, local, and private conservation efforts, recent Supreme Court decisions that would eliminate an unknown but potentially large percentage of the nation's waters from CWA jurisdiction could eviscerate important federal safeguards and undermine the incentives for successful voluntary approaches to aquatic ecosystem restoration and protection. All components of aquatic ecosystems are integrally connected, via surface water, groundwater, and other hydrological and ecological connections. But some interpretations of the divided Supreme Court opinion in *Rapanos* would eliminate CWA jurisdiction over wetlands with no direct surface water connections to other waters, and many waterways in the western states that do not flow year-round. The concept of navigability as the defining line for federal jurisdiction under the Commerce Clause of the U.S. Constitution is a remnant of an era when the main federal purpose for protecting waters was interstate commerce and navigation, and has long outlived its purpose. Federal authority over watershed protection and restoration should be clarified to include the full range of aquatic ecosystem resources and their many other linkages to interstate commerce.

Conclusion

The United States continues to enjoy some of the safest and most abundant supplies of freshwater in the world, and has built a nationwide system of infrastructure to deliver safe water to most of its citizens, and to treat wastewater properly before discharging it back into the environment. The sustainability of that luxury is by no means certain, and to date water development infrastructure has carried significant economic costs as well as human health risks and ecological harm. In order to attain sustainable water uses and to ensure healthy freshwater aquatic ecosystems, we can no longer afford to take water for granted. We need to understand that water is a limited rather than an infinite resource, and to strike a more reasonable balance between water systems as natural resources to be used and as natural ecosystems to be protected.

ENDNOTES

1. U.N. Econ. & Soc. Council, Comm. on Econ., Soc. & Cultural Rights, Substantive Issues Arising in the Implementation of the International Covenant on Economic, Social and Cultural Rights. The Right to Water (E/C.12/2002/11) General cmt. 15, 29th Sess., Geneva, Nov. 26, 2002.

2. Meena Palaniappan et al., *Environmental Justice and Water, in* The World's Water 2006-2007, The Biennial Report on Freshwater Resources 117 (Peter H. Gleick ed., 2007).

3. *Id.* at 124.

4. Gleick, *supra* note 2, at 242, 251.

5. *See* Robert W. Adler, *Fresh Water, in* Stumbling Toward Sustainability 197 (John C. Dernbach ed., 2002).

6. *See* Robert M. Hirsch et al., *U.S. Geological Survey Perspective on Water-Quality Monitoring and Assessment*, 8 J. Envtl. Monit. 512 (2006).

7. 33 U.S.C. §1313(d).

8. U.S. EPA, 2004 National Assessment Database, *available at* http://www.epa.gov/waters/305b/index_2004.html (visited June 6, 2007).

9. *Id.*

10. U.S. Geological Survey, Circular 1265, Water Quality of the Nation's Streams and Aquifers—Overview of Selected Findings, 1991-2001, at 2 (2004).

11. *Id.*

12. *Id.* at 8.

13. *Id.* at 14, 16.

14. U.S. EPA, Toxics Release Inventory Reporting Year 2005 Public Data Release, *available at* http://www.epa.gov/tri/tridata/tri05 (visited June 7, 2007).

15. *See* 42 U.S.C. §300g-1(b)(1)(C).

16. U.S. Geological Survey, Fact Sheet 2006-3043, Volatile Organic Compounds in the Nation's Drinking-Water Supply Wells—What Findings May Mean to Human Health (Revised June 2006).

17. U.S. Geological Survey, Scientific Investigations Report 2006-5290, Microbial Quality of the Nation's Ground-Water Resources, 1993-1994, *available at* http://pubs.usgs.gov/sir/2006/5290/section1.html (visited June 8, 2007).

18. Michael F. Craun et al., *Waterborne Outbreaks Reported in the United States*, 4 J. Water & Health (Supp. 2) 19 (2006).

19. Michael F. Craun et al., *Assessing Waterborne Risks: An Introduction*, 4 J. Water & Health (Supp. 2) 3 (2006).

20. *Id.*

21. Craun et al., *supra* note 18, at 22-23.

22. U.S. EPA, 2005 NATIONAL LISTING OF FISH ADVISORIES, FACT SHEET (Sept. 2005), *available at* www.epa.gov/waterscience/fish/advisories/ fs2004.html (visited June 6, 2007).

23. *Id.*

24. *Id.*

25. U.S. EPA, OFFICE OF WATER, FACT SHEET: 2005 UPDATE, THE NATIONAL STUDY OF CHEMICAL RESIDUES IN LAKE FISH TISSUE, EPA-823-F-05-012 (2005).

26. *See* Robert W. Adler, *The Two Lost Books in the Water Quality Trilogy: The Elusive Objectives of Physical and Biological Integrity*, 33 ENVTL. L. 29-77 (2003).

27. U.S. EPA, WADEABLE STREAMS ASSESSMENT: A COLLABORATIVE SURVEY OF THE NATION'S STREAMS, EPA 841-B-06-002, at ES-5 (2006).

28. *Id.* at ES-6.

29. THOMAS E. DAHL, U.S. DEP'T OF INTERIOR, STATUS AND TRENDS OF WETLANDS IN THE CONTERMINOUS UNITED STATES 1998 TO 2004, at 15 (2006).

30. *Id.*

31. *Id.* at 16-17.

32. Larry R. Brown et al., *Introduction to Effects of Urbanization on Stream Ecosystems*, 47 AMER. FISH. SOC. SYMP. 1-2 (2005).

33. U.S. GEOLOGICAL SURVEY, FACT SHEET FS-042-02, EFFECTS OF URBANIZATION ON STREAM ECOSYSTEMS (2002); JAMES F. COLES ET AL., U.S. GEOLOGICAL SURVEY, THE EFFECTS OF URBANIZATION ON THE BIOLOGICAL, PHYSICAL, AND CHEMICAL CHARACTERISTICS OF COASTAL NEW ENGLAND STREAMS, Professional Paper 1695 (2004); Faith A. Fitzpatrick et al., *Urbanization Influences on Aquatic Communities in Northeastern Illinois Streams*, 2004 J. AM. WATER. RES. ASS'N 461 (2004); LORI A. SPRAGUE ET AL., U.S. GEOLOGICAL SURVEY, EFFECTS OF URBAN DEVELOPMENT ON STREAM ECOSYSTEMS ALONG THE FRONT RANGE OF THE ROCKY MOUNTAINS, COLORADO AND WYOMING, Fact Sheet 2006-3083 (2006).

34. Christopher P. Konrad & Derek B. Booth, *Hydrologic Changes in Urban Streams and Their Ecological Significance*, 47 AM. FISH. SOC. SYMP. 157 (2005).

35. Gleick, *supra* note 2, at 223-27.

36. *Id.* at 232.

37. *Id.* at 224, 232.

38. *See* Robert W. Adler, Restoring Colorado River Ecosystems, A Troubled Sense of Immensity 114-15 (2007) (regarding drought in the Colorado River Basin); SUSAN S. HUTSON ET AL., U.S. GEOLOGICAL SURVEY, ESTIMATED USE OF WATER IN THE UNITED STATES IN 2000, Circular 1268 (2004); U.S. GEOLOGICAL SURVEY, RECORD LOW WATER LEVELS IN MAY FOR GEORGIA RIVERS (June 1, 2007), *available at* www.usgs.gov/ newsroom/article.asp?ID=1687 (visited June 8, 2007); U.S. GEOLOGICAL SURVEY, RECORD LOW WATER LEVELS IN MAY FOR NORTH CAROLINA

RIVERS (June 8, 2007), *available at* www.usgs.gov/newsroom/article.asp?ID=1690 (visited June 8, 2007).

39. Heather Cooley, *Floods and Droughts, in* Gleick, *supra* note 2, at 91, 92.

40. *Id.* at 96-97.

41. INTERGOVERNMENTAL PANEL ON CLIMATE CHANGE, CLIMATE CHANGE 2007: IMPACTS, ADAPTATION, AND VULNERABILITY, SUMMARY FOR POLICYMAKERS 5 (Apr. 2007).

42. *See* Adler, *supra* note 38, at 247; Kenneth Strzepek & Davis N. Yates, *Assessing the Effects of Climate Change on the Water Resources of the Western United States, in* WATER AND CLIMATE IN THE WESTERN UNITED STATES (William M. Lewis Jr. ed., 2003).

43. N. LeRoy POFF ET AL., PEW CTR. ON GLOBAL CLIMATE CHANGE, AQUATIC ECOSYSTEMS & GLOBAL CLIMATE CHANGE, POTENTIAL IMPACTS ON INLAND FRESHWATER AND COASTAL WETLAND ECOSYSTEMS IN THE UNITED STATES (2002).

44. *See* U.S. EPA, 2006-2011 Strategic Plan: Charting Our Course 35-57 (2006) [hereinafter EPA STRATEGIC PLAN] (Goal 2, Clean and Safe Water).

45. *Id.* at 38; 71 Fed. Reg. 4644 (Jan. 27, 2006).

46. EPA STRATEGIC PLAN, *supra* note 44, at 46; 68 Fed. Reg. 7175 (Feb. 12, 2003); *but see* Waterkeeper Alliance v. EPA, 399 F.3d 486 (3d Cir. 2005) (remanding to EPA for amendments).

47. *See* EPA STRATEGIC PLAN, *supra* note 44, at 42 (better implementation of existing policy for combined sewer overflows); 45-47 (better implementation of existing regulations using a watershed approach).

48. *Id.* at 47.

49. *See* 33 U.S.C. §1313(d).

50. *Id.*

51. *See* U.S. EPA, HANDBOOK FOR DEVELOPING WATERSHED PLANS TO RESTORE AND PROTECT OUR WATERS, EPA 841-B-05-005 (2005).

52. *See, e.g.,* KAREN CAPPIELLA ET AL., CTR. FOR WATERSHED PROT., USING LOCAL WATERSHED PLANS TO PROTECT WETLANDS (2006).

53. *See* PAUL ADAMIS & JOSEPH EILERS, ISLAND COUNTY DEP'T OF PLANNING & COMMUNITY DEV., DRAFT WATER QUALITY DATA SYNTHESIS AND RECOMMENDATIONS FOR A SURFACE FRESHWATER MONITORING PROGRAM, *available at* www.islandcounty.net/planning/IC-WQmonitor Plan_FinalDraft.pdf.pdf (visited June 26, 2007).

54. *See* Island County's website, Planning Department page, *at* www.island county.net/planning (visited June 26, 2007).

55. *See* Montana Wetlands Legacy website, www.wetlandslegacy.org (visited June 26, 2007).

56. For case studies in the western United States, *see, e.g.,* Montana State University's Wild Fish Habitat Initiative, *available at* www.wildfish. montana.edu/Cases/default.asp (visited June 26, 2007).

57. E.S. Bernhardt et al., *Synthesizing U.S. River Restoration Efforts,* 308 SCIENCE 636-37 (2005).

58. Solid Waste Agency of Northern Cook County v. U.S. Army Corps of Engineers, 531 U.S. 159 (2001) [hereinafter *SWANCC*].

59. *Compare, e.g.,* United v. Deaton, 332 F.3d 698 (4th Cir. 2003), *cert. denied*, 124 S. Ct. 1874 (2004) (reading *SWANCC* narrowly and finding CWA jurisdiction over all waters with a hydrological connection to navigable waters), *with* In re Needham, 354 F.3d 340 (5th Cir. 2003) (finding CWA jurisdiction over only navigable waters and water bodies immediately adjacent thereto).

60. Rapanos v. United States, 126 S. Ct. 2208 (2006).

61. *Id.* at 2225-26.

62. *Id.* at 2236.

63. *Id.* at 2253.

64. *Compare, e.g.,* Northern Cal. River Watch v. City of Healdsburg, 457 F.3d 1023 (9th Cir. 2006) (finding CWA jurisdiction based on Justice Kennedy's "significant nexus" test), *with* United States v. Chevron Pipe Line Co., 437 F. Supp. 2d 605 (N.D. Tex. 2006) (rejecting CWA jurisdiction absent clear connection between oil spill and navigable water).

65. *See* 33 U.S.C. §1251(g).

66. HUTSON ET AL., *supra* note 38, at 1-2.

67. *See, e.g.,* Southern Nevada Water Authority's aggressive water conservation programs, *available at* www.snwa.com/html/cons_index.html (visited June 26, 2007).

68. *See* Adler, *supra* note 38, at 252-54.

69. *See* A. Dan Tarlock & Sarah B. Van de Wetering, *Western Growth and Sustainable Water Use: If There Are No "Natural Limits," Should We Worry About Water Supplies?*, 27 PUB. LAND & RES. L. REV. 33 (2006).

70. EPA STRATEGIC PLAN, *supra* note 44, at 39, 48.

71. 33 U.S.C. §1251(a).

Chapter 15

Oceans and Estuaries: The Ocean Commissions' Unfulfilled Vision

Robin Kundis Craig

Agenda 21, the action plan of the United Nations Conference on Environment and Development, addresses the myriad ways that human activity affects the global environment. Chapter 17 of the plan specifically focuses on sustainable development of oceans and estuaries. It outlines seven program areas for marine resources: integrated management and sustainable development of coastal areas, marine environmental protection, marine living resources of the high seas, marine living resources under national jurisdiction, climate change, international cooperation, and the particular concerns of small nation states.[1] In the years preceding the 1992 Rio Conference, the United States was a world leader in addressing the first four of these programs and international cooperation.

Since 2002, however, the complexity of U.S. ocean regulation has prompted two ocean commissions to recommend substantial changes to U.S. law to better pursue an *integrated, ecosystem-based, sustainable policy* for its marine resources. Moreover, the United States has lagged behind the rest of the world in addressing global climate change, an issue that has now become critical to the sustainable use of ocean and coastal resources.

This chapter provides a brief review of the importance of the oceans, the general goals of Chapter 17, and U.S. progress in meeting those goals. It emphasizes the 2003 report of the Pew Ocean Commission and its recommendations for the U.S. living marine resources, the U.S. Commission on Ocean Policy's more expansive 2004 report and recommendations, and recent discoveries regarding the threats that climate change and ocean acidification from increasing carbon dioxide concentrations pose to ocean sustainability.

Oceans, Agenda 21, and Sustainable Development

Oceans cover more than 70 percent of our planet,[2] support immense reserves of biodiversity (in all senses),[3] produce at least half of Earth's

atmospheric oxygen,[4] drive the planet's hydrological cycle,[5] sequester carbon dioxide,[6] and play a significant role in Earth's climate and
weather.[7] As such, oceans and estuaries are critical providers of ecosystem services—the "myriad . . . life support functions, the observ-
able manifestations of ecosystem processes that ecosystems provide
and without which human civilizations could not thrive . . . ."[8] A
comprehensive study that appeared in *Nature* in 1997 reported that
"[a]bout 63% of the estimated value [of the world's ecosystem ser-
vices] is contributed by marine ecosystems," especially coastal
ecosystems.[9] Specifically, "[c]oastal environments, including estuaries, coastal wetlands, beds of sea grass and algae, coral reefs,
and continental shelves . . . cover only 6.3% of the world's surface,
but are responsible for 43% of the estimated value of the world's
ecosystem services."[10]

Small wonder, then, that Chapter 17 of Agenda 21 recognizes that
"[t]he marine environment—including the oceans and all seas and adjacent coastal areas—forms an integrated whole that is an essential
component of the global life-support system and a positive asset that
presents opportunities for sustainable development."[11] The overall
goal of Chapter 17 is to develop "new approaches to marine and
coastal areas management and development, at the national, subre-
gional, regional, and global levels . . . *that are integrated in content
and are precautionary and anticipatory in ambit . . . .*"[12]

Chapter 17's integrated approach requires a management system
that identifies and protects marine ecosystems and the services that
they provide or should be providing, as opposed to just regulating the
taking of specific goods. Specifically:

> Sustainable use of the oceans requires that all activities, individu-
> ally and collectively, both coastal and deepwater, preserve water
> quality sufficient to support the biological, chemical, and physical
> processes of the ocean without stress, so that oceans can support a
> variety of healthy ecosystems; nurture the plankton (small, some-
> times microscopic, plants and animals that drift near the surface of
> oceans) that generate much of the earth's atmospheric oxygen and
> form the basis of all ocean food chains; deter outbreaks of patho-
> gens and other harmful organisms; dissolve excess CO_2 from the at-
> mosphere; and circulate in currents that aid human navigation, drive
> relatively predictable weather patterns, and cycle heat and nutrients
> throughout the depths and around the world. Sustainable develop-
> ment further requires that humans remove only the amount of bio-

logical resources—algae/seaweed, fish, marine mammals, corals, etc.—that those species can comfortably replace between human harvests and that will not disrupt the greater food webs and ecosystems of which those species are a part. In addition, species that are already overexploited need to be allowed to recover. Finally, sustainable use of the oceans requires that humans plan for their uses of the oceans, not just season to season but also through decades-long programs that recognize that human populations are increasing, especially along the coast; that many ocean and coastal ecosystems are fragile and easily stressed or destroyed; that the transition to sustainable use will require restriction and even elimination of jobs in overcapitalized sea-related industries; and that lack of information cannot be an excuse for business as usual but rather should serve as a warning that we really do not know what we are doing to ocean resources.[13]

Moreover, it has become increasingly clear since the 1992 Rio Conference on sustainable development,[14] and even since the 2002 follow-on summit in Johannesburg,[15] that sustainable development of the oceans will have to account for the effects of climate change.

Ocean Resources of the United States

The United States has over 13,000 miles of coastline,[16] and, in concert with the provisions of the Third United Nations Convention on the Law of the Sea,[17] it asserts national jurisdiction over a 200-nautical-mile-wide Exclusive Economic Zone.[18] As a result, the United States controls "more than 4 million square miles of ocean territory, the largest and richest in the world."[19] Indeed, the marine areas subject to the United States' jurisdiction are "23 percent larger than the land area of the nation . . . ."[20]

The United States' ocean and coastal territories contribute significantly to the nation's cultural and economic identity. For example, more than half of the nation's population lives in coastal counties, an area comprising only 17 percent of the nation's land area,[21] a testimony to the aesthetic and lifestyle values of this resource. The U.S. coastal and marine resources have substantial economic value: commercial fishing was worth $28 billion per year to the United States in 2004, recreational fishing was worth $30 billion, and trade in ornamental fish was worth $3 billion.[22] And the value of fish is not just in capture. In 2005, processed fisheries products were worth over $7.5

billion.[23] Beyond fisheries, annual offshore production of oil and gas was "valued at $25-$40 billion" in 2004.[24]

Americans value marine ecosystem services, as well. "Nationwide, retail expenditures on recreational boating alone exceeded $30 billion in 2002,"[25] much of which occurs along seacoasts and in the Great Lakes. Caribbean coral reefs provide fisheries, tourism, and shoreline protection benefits worth $3.1 to $4.6 billion per year, and degradation of these ecosystems will cost several hundred million dollars in yearly income by 2015.[26] Hawaiian coral reefs provide "added value" of $364 million per year, most of which derives from the net business revenues from snorkeling and diving (however, that added value also includes $40 million per year in increased property values).[27]

In light of these benefits, developing a sustainable, comprehensive, and integrated marine regulatory and management regime is critical to the continued wealth, quality of life, and national security of the United States. However, the country has yet to transition to a fully integrated, ecosystem-based approach to ocean management.

Before Johannesburg: Fragmented Regulation

In some respects, the United States has been a world leader in addressing many impacts on the marine environment, and long before the Rio Conference it had addressed many of the problems identified in Chapter 17. For example, in 1972 the United States enacted the contemporary version of the Federal Water Pollution Control Act,[28] better known as the Clean Water Act, which protects coastal and ocean waters from discharges of pollutants.[29] Pursuant to the Coastal Zone Management Act (CZMA),[30] also enacted in 1972, 30 states and five U.S. territories had federally approved coastal zone management plans in place by 1992.[31] Moreover, the CZMA's National Estuarine Research Reserve System and the Clean Water Act's National Estuary Program extended special protections to estuaries.[32] The Marine Mammal Protection Act of 1972 (MMPA)[33] protects all marine mammals and specifically addresses the impacts of fishing on marine mammals, while the Endangered Species Act of 1973 (ESA)[34] extends additional protections for species, including marine species, that face threats of extinction. The Magnuson-Stevens Fishery Conservation and Management Act of 1976[35] required fisheries management plans for all over-harvested fish stocks, while the Sustainable Fisheries Act of 1996[36] added principles of precaution and sustainable development to the United States' fisheries management law.

However, from the beginning of the federal government's significant involvement in environmental regulation in the 1960s, the United States did a much better job of addressing obvious problems with easy-to-identify causes, such as point sources of water pollution (contained and controlled sources such as effluent in a pipe), than longer-term, more complex problems such as land-based nonpoint source pollution (diffuse sources of water pollution such as run-off)) and atmospheric deposition of mercury and nutrients. Moreover, the United States pursued—and continues to pursue—fragmented rather than integrated management of marine resources. Federal statutes related to marine resources regulate on a medium- or resource-specific basis, as their titles indicate. Moreover, pursuant to many of these statutes—most notably, the ESA, MMPA, and Magnuson-Stevens Act—living marine resources have been managed on a species-by-species, rather than ecosystem, basis, with limited legal bases for cross-correlation.[37]

Regulation of ocean ecosystems also was, and remains, fragmented jurisdictionally, on at least three levels.[38] First, regulatory jurisdiction is divided between the state and federal governments, most sharply at three nautical miles out to sea, as emphasized in the Submerged Lands Act.[39] Second, within state waters, regulatory jurisdiction is divided among the states, with state borders generally being extended out into the coastal waters. Finally, within the federal government, regulatory authority over marine resources is divided among 11 of the 15 cabinet-level departments and four independent agencies,[40] including NOAA and its subagency, the National Marine Fisheries Service (NMFS) (Department of Commerce), the Environmental Protection Agency (EPA), the U.S. Fish and Wildlife Service (Department of the Interior), the U.S. Army Corps of Engineers (Department of the Army), the Minerals Management Service (Department of the Interior), the Coast Guard (Department of Homeland Security), and the National Park Service (Department of the Interior).

This multi-level regulatory fragmentation has impeded, and continues to impede, the development and implementation of an integrated, sustainable, ecosystem-based marine management program in the United States. However, developments since 2002 provide reason to hope that U.S. management of oceans and estuaries may evolve to better promote the sustainability and healthy functioning of marine ecosystems.

After Johannesburg: A Movement Toward Integrated Management?

Since 2002, two commissions have reviewed U.S. ocean policy and made comprehensive recommendations for improvement: (1) the Pew Oceans Commission, which issued *America's Living Oceans: Charting a Course for Sea Change*[41] in May 2003; and (2) the U.S. Commission on Ocean Policy, which President George W. Bush appointed pursuant to the Oceans Act of 2000[42] and which issued its report, *An Ocean Blueprint for the 21st Century*,[43] in July 2004. As Prof. Donna Christie has emphasized, the two reports are "largely in agreement on some very fundamental issues," including the need for an integrated, ecosystem-based approach to ocean management.[44]

As the title of its report suggests, the Pew Oceans Commission focused on the marine *living* resources of the United States. It identified eight major threats to these resources: nonpoint source pollution, point source pollution, invasive species, aquaculture, coastal development, overfishing, habitat alteration, bycatch (the unintended catching of nontarget species, such as when shrimp trawlers catch sea turtles), and climate change.[45] From this list alone, the need for integrated management—the coordination of pollution regulation, land-based activities, fisheries regulation, and atmospheric regulation—becomes obvious. The Pew Commission

> identified three primary problems with ocean governance. The first is a focus on exploitation of ocean resources with too little regard for environmental consequences. The second is its fragmented nature—institutionally, legislatively, and geographically. Thirdly, our ocean governance has focused on individual species as opposed to the larger ecosystems that produce and nurture all life in the sea.[46]

It concluded that the United States needs a "fundamental change in values" with respect to its ocean resources and "an ethic of stewardship and responsibility toward the oceans and their inhabitants."[47] Moreover, "[e]xtending environmental protection beyond a single medium—such as air, or water, or a single species of plant or animal—to entire ecosystems is both a practical measure and our moral obligation as stewards of the planet."[48] Thus an integrated, ecosystem-based approach is at the core of the Pew Commission's recommendations.

The U.S. Commission on Ocean Policy had a broader focus, encompassing all U.S. marine resources and interests, including energy, transportation, and international relations. Nevertheless, in its vision of future ocean management, "[m]anagement boundaries correspond with ecosystem regions, and policies consider interactions among all ecosystem components. In the face of scientific uncertainty, managers balance competing considerations and proceed with caution. Ocean governance is effective, participatory, and well coordinated among government agencies, the private sector, and the public."[49] Moreover, like the Pew Commission, the Commission on Ocean Policy espoused a stewardship ethic, relying on "lifelong education" to make "all citizens . . . better stewards of the nation's resources and marine environment."[50]

Despite these commissions' broad agreement regarding necessary changes, neither the executive branch nor Congress has embraced their vision of integrated, ecosystem-based ocean management. Moreover, given the prominent federal role in the oceans,[51] until the federal government acts to change its structure for managing and regulating marine resources and ecosystems, state and local governments will be limited in their abilities to do so.

On December 17, 2004, the Bush Administration both created, through an executive order, the cabinet-level Committee on Ocean Policy[52] and responded to the U.S. Commission's Report with the U.S. Ocean Action Plan.[53] The Action Plan announced 88 specific steps the Administration intended to take to improve federal regulation of marine resources. However, nowhere did the Action Plan even contemplate an integrated, ecosystem-based approach to ocean management.[54] Instead, it largely reinforced the existing fragmented regulatory structure—for example, dividing into separate actions coral reef conservation; conservation of marine mammals, sharks, and sea turtles; improvement of marine managed areas; and conservation and restoration of coastal habitat.[55] Moreover, in its January 2007 update to the Action Plan, the Bush Administration essentially declared its task complete, emphasizing that "we have met the [Plan's] commitment for 73 of the 88 actions and nearly met the commitments in 4 larger multi-action items."[56] This despite the fact that NOAA still lacked an organic act; the United States still lacked any overarching national oceans policy, established management priorities, or regulatory regime; and regulatory fragmentation remained the law of marine resources.

Congress has been equally unresponsive to the commissions' reports. The Marine Turtle Conservation Act of 2004[57] became law in July 2004, but it only extended limited aid to the international conservation of sea turtles. The House passed H.R. 5450,[58] an organic act for NOAA, on September 20, 2006, but the Senate has failed to act on it. The reauthorization of the Magnuson-Stevens Fishery Conservation and Management Act[59] in December 2006 and January 2007 was perhaps the most singular rejection of the two commissions' recommended new vision of ocean policy, as both chambers of Congress passed over bills that would have made ecosystem-based management a part of the nation's fisheries regulation in favor of legislation that barely tweaks the established fisheries management regime. In particular, with respect to the recommended ecosystem-based regulatory approach, the reauthorized Act merely notes that "[a] number of Fishery Management Councils have demonstrated significant progress in integrating ecosystem considerations in fisheries management using the existing authorities provided in this Act"[60] and allows, as discretionary measures in fisheries management plans, "management measures . . . to conserve target and non-target species and habitats, considering the variety of ecological factors affecting fishery populations."[61]

Nevertheless, there are some indications that the tide may be turning in the federal government. On June 15, 2006, President Bush used his authority under the Antiquities Act[62] to establish the Northwestern Hawaiian Islands Marine National Monument, since renamed the Papahānaumokuākea Marine National Monument.[63] The new monument protects almost 140,000 square miles of coral reef ecosystem,[64] and NOAA's management vision for it is "[t]hat the vast coral reefs, ecosystems, and resources of the Northwestern Hawaiian Islands—unique in the world—remain healthy and diverse forever."[65] In January 2007 the Bush Administration released its Ocean Research Priorities Plan and Implementation Strategy, emphasizing that one of the three critical roles for science and technology in ocean management is "providing scientific support for ecosystem-based management."[66]

Finally, senators and representatives continue to introduce legislation that could begin to transform the philosophical and regulatory underpinnings of U.S. ocean policy and management.[67] In April and May 2007, the House began hearings on H.R. 21, the latest version of the Oceans Conservation, Education, and National Strategy for the 21st Century Act.[68] Responding explicitly to the call by both commissions for "a more comprehensive and integrated ecosystem-based management approach to address current and future ocean and coastal challenges,"[69] H.R. 21 acknowledges that "[h]ealthy marine ecosystems provide more goods and services, such as seafood and tourism opportunities, than degraded marine ecosystems" and that "a unified national oceans policy is needed to govern the range of human activities affecting the health and productivity of marine ecosystems."[70] The act would establish a national policy "to protect, maintain, and restore the health of marine ecosystems in order to fulfill the ecological, economic, educational, social, cultural, nutritional, recreational and other requirements of current and future generations of Americans."[71] "Marine ecosystem health" would mean "the ability of a marine ecosystem to support and maintain a productive and resilient community of organisms, having a species composition, diversity, and functional organization resulting from the natural habitat of the region, such that it provides a complete range of ecological benefits . . . ."[72]

Federal agencies would have to ensure that any activities authorized, funded, or carried out by them that could affect ocean or coastal waters or resources were "conducted in a manner that is consistent with the protection, maintenance, and restoration of healthy ecosystems" after certification from the administrator of NOAA, subject to judicial review.[73] In addition, H.R. 21 would provide for regional management planning on the basis of the United States' 10 biogeographically distinct large marine ecosystems, with special protections accorded to important ecological areas within each such ecosystem.[74] Finally, H.R. 21 would provide NOAA with statutory authority for the first time in the agency's existence, commanding it to "conserve and manage coastal, ocean, and Great Lakes resources and ecosystems to meet national economic, social, and environmental needs, and promote the ecologically sustainable use of these resources so such future needs of the nation can be met" by "protecting, restoring, and maintaining the health and sustainability of the coasts, oceans, and Great Lakes through ecosystem-based research, development, demonstration, and management . . . ."[75]

The Looming Challenge: Climate Change and the Oceans

The need to manage oceans on a comprehensive, integrated, eco-system-based, and adaptive basis has become even more urgent since 2002 as a result of the widespread acknowledgement that global climate change is affecting both the physical and chemical integrity of the oceans and the services and goods that marine ecosystems provide.[76] With the release by the Intergovernmental Panel on Climate Change (IPCC) of its *Fourth Assessment Report*,[77] it is nearly impossible for governments to claim that climate change is not occurring or that human emissions of greenhouse gases, especially carbon dioxide, are not a significant cause.

Two effects of carbon dioxide emissions are particularly important for marine ecosystems. First, rising ocean temperatures are likely to change—and may already be changing—important ecosystem functions and services. Scientists have suggested that the oceans reached temperatures of up to 107°F millions of years ago when there were extremely high levels of carbon dioxide,[78] and coral reefs in particular "are vulnerable to thermal stress and have low adaptive capacity. Increases in sea surface temperature of about 1-3°C [~1 to 5°F] are projected to result in more frequent coral bleaching events and widespread mortality, unless there is thermal adaptation or acclimatization by corals."[79] More widespread ecological effects are also most likely already occurring. The IPCC expressed "high confidence . . . that observed changes in marine . . . biological systems are associated with rising sea temperatures, as well as related changes in ice cover, salinity, oxygen levels, and circulation," including "shifts in ranges and changes in algal, plankton, and fish abundance in high-latitude oceans."[80] Other reports have noted more specifically that "[e]vidence is starting to accumulate that global warming may contribute to—or even trigger—troubling ecological changes taking place in . . . key regions of coastal upwelling," including areas off the coasts of northern California and Oregon "where some of the world's richest fisheries exist," collectively accounting for 20 percent of the world's fish catch.[81] Finally, ocean temperature increases also contribute to sea level rise, which in turn is expected to lead to coastal erosion, loss of coastal wetlands, and increasingly violent storms such as hurricanes.[82]

Second, the Royal Society reported in June 2005 that increased carbon dioxide levels in the atmosphere are acidifying the oceans.[83] This acidification most directly puts coral reefs and pelagic plankton at risk because both sets of species need to form shells, a process with which acidification interferes.[84] The IPCC similarly concluded that "[t]he progressive acidification of oceans due to increasing atmospheric carbon dioxide is expected to have negative impacts on marine shell forming organisms (e.g., corals) and their dependent species."[85] As such, ocean acidification threatens the biodiversity that coral reefs support and maintain, the planktonic basis of all ocean food webs, and the oceans' ability (through phytoplankton) to contribute oxygen to the planet's atmosphere.

The IPCC report states that "[s]ustainable development can reduce vulnerability to climate change by enhancing adaptive capacity and increasing resilience."[86] Conversely, it says, "climate change can slow the pace of progress toward sustainable development either directly through increased exposure to adverse impact or indirectly through erosion of the capacity to adapt."[87] Addressing sustainable ocean management sooner rather than later will increase the ability of the United States to adapt to changes in its ocean resources and in the services that its marine ecosystems provide.

Recommendations

The two oceans commissions provided recommendations to the federal government regarding improvements in ocean governance. Implementing the recommendations of the commissions' reports should be the nation's highest priorities for the oceans. Five of these recommendations are particularly important and garnered the support of both commissions.

1. The United States needs to improve the coordination of its regulation of ocean activities and resources.[88] Preferably this would be done through a comprehensive national oceans policy that will govern all ocean activities across regulatory jurisdictions. This policy should be founded on sustainable use and a stewardship ethic, and should mandate ecosystem-based management of marine resources.

2. The United States should enhance regional authority over marine resources,[89] *subject to the national oceans policy.*

3. The United States needs to realize that marine resources both depend upon and are damaged by land-based activities. Thus, legislation should be enacted that will regulate land-based activities with the oceans in mind, preferably on a watershed basis.[90]

4. The United States needs to enact more comprehensive protections for its living marine resources. This should include measures to prioritize both the health of fish stocks and the health of the ecosystems that support those stocks in fisheries management, measures to reduce bycatch and other unintended incidental killing of marine organisms, and measures to encourage increased use of marine protected areas and marine reserves to protect marine (and especially coastal) habitats and ecosystems, such as coral reefs and kelp forests.[91]

5. Perhaps most important, the United States needs to embark on a pervasive, thorough educational campaign. This should be undertaken at all levels of society and include increased investments in marine scientific research, so that Americans will understand why their marine resources are important and how their individual choices can contribute to a sustainable ocean future.[92]

Conclusion

The U.S. Commission on Ocean Policy estimated that "in 2000, ocean-related activities directly contributed more than $117 billion to American prosperity and supported well over two million jobs. By including coastal activities, the numbers become even more impressive; more than $1 trillion, or one-tenth of the nation's annual gross domestic product, is generated within the relatively narrow strip of land immediately adjacent to the coast . . . ."[93]

Regardless of one's moral or ethical perspective on ocean stewardship, it is difficult to rationalize the federal government's continued willingness to put such a large portion of the U.S. social and economic well-being at risk. Two blue-ribbon commissions have concluded that the United States needs to reform its fragmented approach to ocean management, integrate its marine resource goals, and manage its marine resources on an ecosystem basis. Scientists worldwide are concluding that the stresses on these ecosystems and resources have not abated and in fact will only increase. In light of this evidence, there can be only one recommendation for the next 5 to 10 years: *GET IT DONE.*

ENDNOTES

1. U.N. Conference on Environment & Development (UNCED), Agenda 21, U.N. Doc. A/CONF.151.26 (1992) [hereinafter Agenda 21], at ¶ 17.98.

2. THOMAS E. SVARNEY & PATRICIA BARNES-SVARNEY, THE HANDY OCEAN ANSWER BOOK 3, 6 (2000).

3. PEW OCEANS COMM'N, AMERICA'S LIVING OCEANS: CHARTING A COURSE FOR SEA CHANGE: SUMMARY REPORT 5 (May 2003) [hereinafter PEW SUMMARY REPORT] ("The genetic, species, habitat, and ecosystem diversity of the oceans is believed to exceed that of any other Earth system."), *available through* www.pewoceans.org.

4. John Roach, *Source of Half Earth's Oxygen Gets Little Credit, available at* http://news.nationalgeographic.com/news/2004/06/0607_040607_phytoplankton.html (June 7, 2004).

5. SVARNEY & BARNES-SVARNEY, *supra* note 2, at 76.

6. *Id.* at 77.

7. *Id.* at 78-86.

8. NAT'L RESEARCH COUNCIL, COMM. ON ASSESSING & VALUING SERVS. OF AQUATIC & RELATED TERRESTRIAL ECOSYSTEMS, VALUING ECOSYSTEM SERVICES: TOWARD BETTER ENVIRONMENTAL DECISION-MAKING 17 (2005) (*citing* Gretchen C. Daily, *Introduction: What Are Ecosystem Services?, in* NATURE'S SERVICES: SOCIETAL DEPENDENCE ON NATURAL ECOSYSTEMS 1-10 (Gretchen C. Daily ed., 1997)); S. Naeem et al., *Biodiversity and Ecosystem Functioning: Maintaining Natural Life Support Processes*, 4 ISSUES IN ECOLOGY (1999).

9. Robert Costanza et al., *The Value of the World's Ecosystem Services and Natural Capital*, 387 NATURE 253, 259 (May 15, 1997).

10. Robert Costanza, *The Ecological, Economic, and Social Importance of the Oceans*, 31 ECOLOGICAL ECON. 199, 201 (1999).

11. Agenda 21, *supra* note 1, at ¶ 17.1.

12. *Id.* (emphasis added).

13. Robin Kundis Craig, *Oceans and Estuaries, in* STUMBLING TOWARD SUSTAINABILITY 227, 228 (John C. Dernbach ed., 2002) [hereinafter *Oceans & Estuaries*].

14. U.N. Conference on Environment & Development (UNCED), Earth Summit, Rio de Janeiro, Brazil (1992). Papers available at www.un.org/esa/sustdev/documents/docs_unced.htm (last visited Apr. 30, 2007).

15. U.N. Johannesburg Summit 2002, Johannesburg, South Africa (Aug. 26-Sept. 4, 2002). More information available at www.un.org/jsummit/html/basic_info/basicinfo.html (last visited Apr. 30, 2007).

16. NAT'L MARINE FISHERIES SERV., THE UNITED STATES IS AN OCEAN NATION, *available at* www.nmfs.noaa.gov/mediacenter/aquaculture/docs/12a_USCOP_EEZ_map_3.pdf (last visited Apr. 28, 2007).

17. *See* UNITED NATIONS CONVENTION ON THE LAW OF THE SEA III, arts. 2.1, 2.2., 3, 57, 56.1 (1982) (in force Nov. 16, 1994).

18. Exclusive Economic Zone of the United States of America, Proclamation No. 5030, 48 Fed. Reg. 10605 (R. Reagan, Mar. 10, 1983).

19. Lisa Tewell, *Oceans Act Allows Public Input*, SEATTLE POST-INTELLIGEN-CER, Aug. 16, 2000, at C5. *See also* NAT'L MARINE FISHERIES SERV., *supra* note 16 (noting that the United States' EEZ encompasses "3.4 million square nautical miles of ocean," where a square nautical mile equals 1.3 square miles).

20. PEW SUMMARY REPORT, *supra* note 3, at 5.

21. *Id*. at 10.

22. U.S. COMM'N ON OCEAN POLICY, AN OCEAN BLUEPRINT FOR THE 21ST CENTURY: FINAL REPORT 2 (Sept. 2004) [hereinafter OCEAN BLUEPRINT].

23. NAT'L MARINE FISHERIES SERV., FISHERIES OF THE UNITED STATES 2005, at 43 (Feb. 2007), *available at* www.st.nmfs.gov/st1/fus/fus05/fus_2005. pdf.

24. OCEAN BLUEPRINT, *supra* note 22, at 2.

25. *Id*.

26. ROYAL SOCIETY, OCEAN ACIDIFICATION DUE TO INCREASING ATMO-SPHERIC CARBON DIOXIDE 33 (June 2005), *available at* www.royalsoc. ac.uk/displaypagedoc.asp?id-13314.

27. *Id*.

28. 33 U.S.C. §§1251-1387.

29. *Id*. §§1311(a), 1343, 1362(7), (8), (9), (10).

30. 16 U.S.C. §§1451-1464.

31. Craig, *Oceans & Estuaries*, *supra* note 13, at 233.

32. 16 U.S.C. §1461(a) (NERRS); 33 U.S.C. §1330 (NEP).

33. 16 U.S.C. §§1361-1421h.

34. 16 U.S.C. §§1531-1544.

35. 16 U.S.C. §§1801-1882.

36. Pub. L. No. 104-297, 110 Stat. 3559-3621 (Oct. 11, 1996).

37. *See* Robin Kundis Craig, *Regulation of Marine Resources: An Overview of the Current Complexity*, 19 NATURAL RES. & ENV'T 3, 3-7 (Summer 2004).

38. *Id*.

39. 43 U.S.C. §§1301-1303, 1311-1315.

40. COUNCIL ON ENVTL QUALITY, U.S. OCEAN ACTION PLAN: THE BUSH ADMINISTRATION'S RESPONSE TO THE U.S. COMMISSION ON OCEAN POL-ICY 18 (Dec. 17, 2004), *available at* http://ocean.ceq.gov/actionplan.pdf [hereinafter OCEAN ACTION PLAN].

41. PEW SUMMARY REPORT, *supra* note 3.

42. Pub. L. No. 106-256, §2, 114 Stat. 644 (Aug. 7, 2000).

43. OCEAN BLUEPRINT, *supra* note 22.

44. Donna R. Christie, *Implementing an Ecosystem Approach to Ocean Man-agement: An Assessment of Current Regional Governance Models*, 16 DUKE ENVTL. L. & POL'Y F. 117, 117-18 (Spring 2006); *see also id*. at

120-23 (discussing the Pew Oceans Commission Report), and 123-29 (discussing the U.S. Commission on Ocean Policy's Report). *See also generally* Josh Eagle, *Regional Ocean Governance: The Perils of Multiple Use Management and the Promise of Agency Diversity,* 16 DUKE ENVTL. L. & POL'Y F. 143 (Spring 2006); Andrew A. Rosenberg, *Regional Ocean Governance and Ecosystem-Based Management of Ocean and Coastal Resources,* 16 DUKE ENVTL. L. & POL'Y F. 179 (Spring 2006).

45. PEW SUMMARY REPORT, *supra* note 3, at 7-8.

46. *Id.* at 15-16. *See also generally* Linda M.B. Paul, *The 2003 Pew Oceans Commission Report: Law, Policy, and Governance,* 19 NATURAL RES. & ENVT. 10 (Summer 2004) (summarizing the Commission's recommendations).

47. PEW SUMMARY REPORT, *supra* note 3, at 16.

48. *Id.* at 19. *See also generally* Hope M. Babcock, *Grotius, Ocean Fish Ranching, and the Public Trust Doctrine: Ride 'Em Charlie Tuna,* 26 STAN. ENVTL. L.J. 3 (Jan. 2007); Kristen M. Fletcher, *Regional Ocean Governance: The Role of the Public Trust Doctrine,* 16 DUKE ENVTL. L. & POL'Y F. 187 (Spring 2006) (both invoking the public trust doctrine to discuss the larger, public stewardship aspects of marine regulation and use).

49. OCEAN BLUEPRINT, *supra* note 22, at 4.

50. *Id.* at 5.

51. *United States v. California,* 332 U.S. 19, 34 (1947) ("Not only has acquisition, as it were, of the [territorial sea] been accomplished by the national government, but protection and control of it has been and is a function of national external sovereignty.").

52. Exec. Order No. 13366, 69 Fed. Reg. 76591 (Dec. 17, 2004).

53. OCEAN ACTION PLAN, *supra* note 40.

54. *See, e.g.,* Helen V. Smith, *A Summary Analysis of the U.S. Commission on Ocean Policy's Recommendations for a Revised Federal Ocean Policy, and the Bush Administration's Response,* 14 SOUTHEASTERN ENVTL. L.J. 133, 155-56 (Fall 2005) (discussing how the Bush Administration has largely avoided ecosystem-based management, especially in its fisheries bill).

55. OCEAN ACTION PLAN, *supra* note 40, at 20-21, 21-22, 23-24, 27-29, respectively.

56. U.S. COMM'N ON OCEAN POLICY, U.S. ACTION PLAN IMPLEMENTATION UPDATE i (Jan. 2007), *available at* http://ocean.ceq.gov/oap_update 012207.pdf.

57. Pub. L. No. 108-266, 118 Stat. 791 (July 2, 2004).

58. National Oceanic and Atmospheric Administration Act, H.R. 5450, 109th Cong. (2005).

59. Magnuson-Stevens Fishery Conservation and Management Reauthorization Act of 2006, Pub. L. No. 109-479, 120 Stat. 3575 (Jan. 12, 2007).

60. *Id.* §3(a).

61. *Id.* §105(7).

62. Act of June 8, 1906, 16 U.S.C. §431.

63. Information on Papahānaumokuākea Marine National Monument *available at* www.hawaiireef.noaa.gov (last updated Mar. 26, 2007).

64. *Id. See also generally* Robin Kundis Craig, *Are Marine National Monuments Better Than National Marine Sanctuaries? U.S. Ocean Policy, Marine Protected Areas, and the Northwest Hawaiian Islands*, 7 SUSTAINABLE DEV. L. & POL'Y 27 (Fall 2006) (discussing the relative advantages of the Antiquities Act in protecting marine ecosystems).

65. NAT'L OCEANIC & ATMOSPHERIC ADMIN., NORTHWESTERN HAWAIIAN ISLANDS PROPOSED NATIONAL MARINE SANCTUARY: DRAFT ENVIRONMENTAL IMPACT STATEMENT AND MANAGEMENT PLAN: DRAFT MANAGEMENT PLAN, Vol. II, at iii (April 2006), *available through* www.hawaiireef. noaa.gov/management/mp.html.

66. NAT'L SCI. & TECH. COUNCIL JOINT SUBCOMM. ON OCEAN SCI. & POLICY, CHARTING THE COURSE FOR OCEAN SCIENCE IN THE UNITED STATES FOR THE NEXT DECADE: AN OCEAN RESEARCH PRIORITIES PLAN AND IMPLEMENTATION STRATEGY ii (Jan. 26, 2007), *available at* http://ocean.ceq. gov/about/docs/orppfinal.pdf.

67. *See, e.g.*, Oceans Conservation, Education, and National Strategy for the 21st Century Act, §2(6), H.R. 2939, 109th Cong. (introduced June 16, 2005) (proclaiming that "[h]ealthy and productive coastal and marine ecosystems are the keys to securing the full range of benefits from ocean resources, including important economic uses such as productive fisheries, for the people of the United States"); National Oceans Protection Act of 2005, §2(4), (7) S. 1224 (introduced June 9, 2005) (proclaiming that "[o]cean resources are the property of the people of the United States, are held in trust for them by Federal, State, local, and tribal governments, and should be managed in a precautionary manner to preserve the full range of their benefits for present and future generations" and that "[a]ctivities harming coastal and marine ecosystems jeopardize the economies and social structure of coastal communities dependent on these resources."). *See also generally* AMY A. FRAENKEL, U.S. SENATE, *Oceans Legislation Before the Senate Commerce Committee: Status for the 109th Congress*, ALI-ABA CLEAN WATER ACT LAW & REG. 41 (Oct. 18-21, 2005) (summarizing extant Senate ocean-policy-related bills).

68. H.R. 21, 110th Cong. (introduced Jan. 4, 2007).

69. *Id.* §2(3)(A).

70. *Id.* §§2(12), 2(14).

71. *Id.* §101(a).

72. *Id.* §4(12).

73. *Id.* §§4(4), 101(b)(2), 101(d), 101(f).

74. *Id.* §§401(3), (4), (6).

75. *Id.* §§201(b)(3), (c)(3).

76. *See generally* Magdalena A.K. Muir, *Oceans and Climate Change: Global and Arctic Perspectives*, 7 SUSTAINABLE DEV. L & POL'Y 50 (Fall 2006) (discussing the various effects of climate change on the oceans).

77. INTERGOVERNMENTAL PANEL ON CLIMATE CHANGE, CLIMATE CHANGE 2007: CLIMATE CHANGE IMPACTS, ADAPTATION, AND VUL-

NERABILITY: SUMMARY FOR POLICYMAKERS (Apr. 6, 2007) [hereinafter 2007 IPCC REPORT].

78. LONNY LIPPSETT & AMY E. NEVALA, WOODS HOLE OCEANOGRAPHIC INST., AN OCEAN WARMER THAN A HOT TUB, *available at* www.whoi. edu/page.do?pid=12455&tid=282&cid=10366 (Feb. 17, 2006).

79. 2007 IPCC REPORT, *supra* note 77, at 9.

80. *Id.* at 3.

81. Peter N. Spotts, *Climate Change Brews Ocean Trouble: Scientists Tie Global Warming to Increased Upwelling of Deep Ocean Water, Which Can Create Crippling Aquatic Dead Zones*, THE CHRISTIAN SCIENCE MONI-TOR, *available at* www.csmonitor.com/2007/0308/p13s01-sten.html (Mar. 8, 2007).

82. 2007 IPCC REPORT, *supra* note 77, at 9.

83. ROYAL SOCIETY, OCEAN ACIDIFICATION DUE TO INCREASING ATMO-SPHERIC CARBON DIOXIDE (June 2005), *available at* www.royalsoc.ac. uk/displaypagedoc.asp?id=13314.

84. *Id.* at 25-28, 33 (coral reefs), and 28-29 (pelagic plankton).

85. 2007 IPCC REPORT, *supra* note 77, at 8.

86. *Id.* at 19.

87. *Id.*

88. PEW SUMMARY REPORT, *supra* note 3, at 21; OCEAN BLUEPRINT, *supra* note 22, at 5-8.

89. PEW SUMMARY REPORT at 21; OCEAN BLUEPRINT at 8-9.

90. PEW SUMMARY REPORT at 26-28; OCEAN BLUEPRINT at 14-16.

91. PEW SUMMARY REPORT at 21, 23-25; OCEAN BLUEPRINT at 20-22.

92. PEW SUMMARY REPORT at 15-16, 20, 22 box 3, 24 box 4; OCEAN BLUE-PRINT at 11-14.

93. OCEAN BLUEPRINT at 2.

Chapter 16

Air Quality: The Need to Replace Basic Technologies With Cleaner Alternatives

David M. Driesen

Since 2002, the United States has failed to make the fundamental technological changes that are needed to meet the ambitious goals established in the Rio Declaration.[1] Still, we continue to stumble toward sustainability in many areas, as many indicators of air quality and emissions have continued to show improvement after 2002.

This chapter begins by explaining sustainable development's meaning for air quality under Agenda 21 and the Rio Declaration.[2] It then assesses progress since 2002 toward these commitments by looking at emission trends, recent regulatory developments, and movement toward sustainable technology. The chapter closes with recommendations for improving U.S. conformity to the Rio Declaration and Agenda 21.

Sustainable Development and Air Quality

The Rio Declaration, the statement of principles promulgated by the U.N. Conference on Environment and Development in 1992, states that "human beings . . . are entitled to a healthy and productive life in harmony with nature."[3] Because air pollution damages both human health and the environment, air quality implicates both environmental and health concerns.[4] To support this principle, Agenda 21, the action plan to implement the Rio Declaration, establishes an objective of eliminating "unacceptable or unreasonable" risks from air pollution "to the extent economically feasible."[5] The Rio Declaration suggests further that we must eliminate unreasonable risks not only for this generation but for future generations as well.[6] In order to meet this objective, the Rio Declaration states that countries "should reduce and eliminate unsustainable patterns of production and consumption."[7] The elimination of unsustainable production and consumption patterns requires integrated decisionmaking[8] that incorporates air quality considerations into key economic decisionmaking processes, so that important production and consumption choices lead to achievement of air-quality goals.

Most air pollution comes from a single class of activities: burning fossil fuels. As a result, Agenda 21 aims to reduce "adverse effects on the atmosphere from the energy sector" through, among other things, the increased use of renewable energy and energy efficiency.[9]

The current pattern of fossil fuel consumption in the United States is not sustainable. Because we will eventually run out of fossil fuels, we face a choice. We can either continue to warm the atmosphere and inflict this generation and subsequent generations with serious health and environmental problems, and in so doing delay facing up to the need for substitutes for fossil fuels only after scarcity makes fossil fuels uneconomical. Or we can act now, while we still have a chance to avert some of climate change's worst impacts upon future generations and ameliorate conventional air pollutants' impacts upon this generation. We may better serve our economic and environmental interests by starting to move away from fossil fuels now.

Progress Toward Sustainable Development Since 2002

The United States has reduced pollution, but it has often not achieved the goals that the Rio Declaration suggests for these activities. We have generally failed to substitute clean sustainable technologies for the basic dirty technologies in use when the modern Clean Air Act was passed more than 30 years ago.

Pollution Trends

Emissions of most pollutants have decreased since 2002. Still, the United States has failed to meet the ambitious goals implicit in the Rio Declaration, namely the goals of granting all human beings a healthy and productive life and of avoiding damage to the environments of other states.[10] With respect to urban air pollution, the United States has failed to meet Clean Air Act requirements governing the scope and timing of reductions. While the United States has probably met its obligations respecting ozone-depleting chemicals, the country increased, rather than decreased, its greenhouse gas emissions.

By the time of the most recent major overhaul of the Clean Air Act in 1990, almost every area in the country had met National Ambient Air Quality Standards for lead, sulfur oxides, and nitrogen oxides. But the failure to achieve the standards for ozone, particulate, and carbon monoxide left approximately 103 million people still prey to un-healthy air quality in 2006.[11]

Since 2002, efforts to address air pollution have continued to produce incremental progress, despite strong economic growth and increasing population. In the most recent five-year period for which data exist (2002-2006), emissions of carbon monoxide declined by 10 percent, volatile organic compound (an ozone precursor) by 8 percent, nitrogen oxide by 14 percent, and hazardous air pollutants for sources reporting to the EPA's Toxic Release Inventory by 8 percent (2001-2005).[12]

But with respect to particulate matter, which is associated with tens of thousands of deaths annually, the progress has been barely detectable, with fine particulate (PM 2.5), likely the most serious health hazard, declining by less than 1 percent, and coarse particulate (PM 10) declining by just 4 percent. Over the most recent five-year period for which data is available (2002-2006), atmospheric concentrations of tropospheric ozone declined by 4.5 percent, carbon monoxide by 19 percent, fine particulate by 7 percent, coarse particulate by 11 percent, lead by 44 percent, sulfur dioxide by 13 percent, and nitrogen dioxide by 17 percent.[13] These data suggest that air quality has improved since 2002.

With respect to acid rain, the United States has made progress, but has not fully protected the ecosystem. The federal government has implemented a well-designed emissions trading program to address this issue.[14] Power plant sulfur dioxide emissions fell 6 percent from 2002 to 2006. But this program has not fully met the goals the Rio Declaration suggested for transboundary programs, as remaining emissions are adversely affecting aquatic and terrestrial ecosystems.[15]

The United States has generally made substantial progress toward sustainable development goals for stratospheric ozone depletion. It has ratified the Montreal Protocol and subsequent amendments, and virtually ended production of chlorofluorocarbons, carbon tetrachloride, methyl chloroform, and halons.

Since 2002, however, the EPA has delayed completion of the contemplated phaseout of methyl bromide, another ozone depleting substance.[16] Even more significantly, greenhouse gas emissions have risen—a major failure to move toward sustainable development.

Some Key Regulatory Developments

While some of the data on pollution trends may reflect regulatory developments since 2002, most key regulatory measures taken recently will only influence pollution trends and technological development in future years. In an effort to protect public health, EPA replaced its .12 parts per million (ppm) standard for ground-level ozone with a .08 ppm standard (averaged over an eight-hour period) in 1997, and took some initial steps toward implementing it in recent years.[17] Scientists have called for additional tightening of this standard because data indicate that the current standards do not adequately protect public health, but EPA has so far not acted on this call. EPA also revised its standards for fine particulates in 2006. Because it takes a long time for states to develop rules limiting the emissions of the pollution sources creating violations of these ambient air quality standards, these revisions will influence future air quality.[18]

EPA had an opportunity to address mercury, a bioaccumulative pollutant having transboundary impacts, through a rule addressing power plant mercury emissions. Because this rule delays mercury reductions and demands less reduction than many states thought technologically feasible, more significant mercury reductions may stem from individual state decisions to adopt more stringent standards.[19] But the U.S. Court of Appeals for the District of Columbia Circuit recently reversed EPA's lax mercury rule as inconsistent with the Clean Air Act, so EPA may belatedly take the opportunity to significantly reduce emissions.[20]

The Clean Air Act's new source-review program offers perhaps the major forum for the type of integrated decisionmaking called for in the Rio Declaration. Generally, the Clean Air Act uses pollution control requirements to ameliorate the effects of technological decisions made privately, often with no consideration of sustainable development. But the new source review program requires integration of environmental decisions with technological choices when a major "stationary source" (such as a factory or power plant) is created or modified. Generally, it requires incorporation of state-of-the-art pollution control in such major changes.

Since 2002, EPA has sought to exempt existing sources from new source review by manipulating the definition of *modification*. While this effort has met a mixed reception in court,[21] EPA has probably succeeded in creating a disparity between treatment of existing sources, which will largely be exempt from this integrated planning requirement, and treatment of new greenfield sources, which remain subject to strict new source review. This disparity, while ostensibly intended to advance movement to more sustainable technology, may actually retard its development.[22]

On the positive side, EPA produced an ambitious rule limiting non-road vehicle emissions that should begin to protect public health this year. EPA has also produced a rule generally instituting a cap-and-trade program to further reduce nitrogen oxide and sulfur dioxide emissions in 28 eastern states and the District of Columbia, which should provide modest emissions reductions after an unusually long time lag.[23] A federal court recently invalidated this regulation.

Movement Toward Sustainable Technology

The United States has moved to more sustainable patterns of production for refrigeration, solvents, and other applications that prior to the Earth Summit depended heavily upon ozone-depleting substances.[24] In these areas, the United States has unleashed substantial technological change, including some very simple changes, such as substituting soap and water for CFCs, and some more complicated ones, substituting substances with less severe, but still real, environmental downsides.[25]

Little change has occurred in the power sector. The United States continues to rely predominantly upon coal-fired power production, a very dirty energy source contributing to acid rain, climate change, and urban air pollution, just as it did prior to the Earth Summit.[26] Renewable technologies, such as wind power, fuel cells, and solar power, produce power with no direct air pollution at all, but have not led to a decline in coal-fired generation.[27] Similarly, we remain dependent upon the internal combustion engine, which burns petroleum, thereby contributing significantly to urban air pollution and climate change.

Since 2002, however, we have seen some changes developing with respect to vehicle technology. For example, the California Air Resources Board Low Emission Vehicle (LEV-II) Program tightened and expanded the scope of standards that led to the introduction of hybrid vehicles.[28] The program demands significant emission reductions, which effectively forces significant technological change. California also enacted standards requiring a 33 percent cut in carbon dioxide emissions from new passenger vehicles and a 25 percent reduction from new light-duty trucks by 2030,[29] which would significantly improve vehicle efficiency.[30] However, in late 2007, EPA denied California's request for a waiver to implement this standard.[31] California has filed a petition for review of that decision in federal court.[32]

Recommendations for the Next Decade

We must move away from our dependence upon fossil fuels, especially the fossil fuels that produce the largest contributions to acid rain, global warming, and urban air pollution. The need for this transition becomes apparent when we consider a broad range of environmental factors with an eye toward the long-term economic and environmental good. Following are key actions that should be undertaken for this transition.

1. Move toward phasing-out fossil fuels. We must begin the process of phasing out the nonrenewable fossil fuels that lie at the heart of so many serious environmental problems. We have begun to take steps that might lessen our dependence on oil through the introduction of hybrid and alternative-fuel vehicles. A movement toward phasing out oil would not only catalyze the development of lower or zero emissions vehicles, it would also lessen dangers from oil drilling, oil spills, petroleum refinery emissions, and leaking underground storage tanks, while improving national security by lessening our dependence on Middle East oil. A good first step would be to cap the amount of oil that can be produced or imported at or near current levels.[33]

This approach builds on the model we used successfully to address ozone depletion and lead in gasoline, limiting the use of substances with proven serious hazards. Such limits will encourage the investments we need to develop substitutes for fossil fuels and allow us to plan gradually for the day when they will disappear, instead of being quickly forced away from them by price shocks created by scarcity beyond our control.

Phasing down coal-fired power would not only have an enormous impact on global warming and conventional air pollution, it would also limit the enormous damage that coal mining does to land and water. A phaseout of coal would produce enormous health and environmental benefits.[34] While we may be able to address global warming more cost effectively through carbon capture and storage,[35] this approach would not prove as effective as a phaseout, since carbon capture likely would leave some residual emissions. These emissions would be added to the cumulative atmospheric concentrations and remain in the atmosphere, trapping heat for hundreds if not thousands of years.[36] Also, carbon capture does nothing to address problems like mountaintop removal and the degradation of water in coal mining areas.[37] Furthermore, storage of the captured carbon poses some risks to groundwater.[38] If carbon capture and storage is used, we should still be developing the alternatives that can make modernization of our basic energy infrastructure politically feasible in the future.

A phaseout of fossil fuels would catalyze enormous innovation in the production of substitutes. While predicting the complete nature and extent of this innovation is difficult, experience with previous phaseouts suggests grounds for optimism. For example, Britain replaced 40 percent of its coal-fired generation with natural gas plants in the 1990s and experienced a 30 percent decline in electricity prices in real terms.[39]

If steps toward phasing out fossil fuel raised costs significantly, the price increases would probably stimulate much-needed investment in energy efficiency, which would bring down the cost. Governments should, however, support movement toward a phaseout with programs to support energy efficiency[40] and, if the need arises, with subsidies for low-income citizens to cope with short-term energy price increases.

From a long-term perspective, massive investment in end-of-the-pipe controls to handle fuels that will run out anyway constitutes a waste. In the long run we will be better off economically and environmentally if we become an economic leader in technologies and fuels that can make it possible to live with little or no fossil fuels. Fossil fuel prices will inevitably rise in the future as they become scarce. By contrast, renewable energy sources rely on fuel sources that will not run out and, in some cases, are free. The world is moving toward cleaner energy, and countries that remain saddled with antiquated infrastructure are unlikely to prosper in the long run.

2. Redesign the regulatory system to encourage advanced technology. With or without a phaseout, government must create an economic dynamic that encourages innovative technologies to meet environmental needs. We should experiment with new economic incentive mechanisms, such as an "environmental competition" statute,[41] which would authorize polluters who clean up to collect the costs of that cleanup, plus a set premium, from competitors with higher pollution levels. This would stimulate a race to improve environmental quality.

It circumvents a key problem with environmental regulation—the tendency of government to set overly modest pollution reduction goals because the government does not have full knowledge of all of the reduction possibilities.[42] This approach would make the achievements of those with the greatest technological capability the measuring rod for compliance.

Such an approach emulates the dynamic that rewards innovation in free markets. In highly competitive markets, innovators can take market share from their competitors, thereby increasing their revenues while decreasing those of their competitors. An environmental competition statute allows improvements in environmental quality to generate rewards at the expense of unsuccessful environmental competitors. This creates a free market dynamic that relies on greed (the hope of gain) and fear (the risk of loss) to motivate environmental cleanup.

Such an approach would need enforceable anti-collusion rules, lest potential competitors for environmental quality conspire not to compete.[43] And it would require a dispute settlement mechanism, so that low-polluting firms could quickly and reliably collect from more-polluting competitors even if a dispute arose about who has the lowest emission levels.[44]

3. Improve monitoring and enforcement of the Clean Air Act. All economic incentive programs, including taxes, emissions trading, and environmental competition statutes, require good monitoring to be effective.[45] EPA should require use of the best available monitoring absent a showing that such monitoring is prohibitively expensive. In most cases, we know too little about emissions to regulate effectively, especially if we make wider use of economic incentives. EPA must enforce state compliance with the Clean Air Act. It has usually failed to do this,[46] so Congress should examine alternative means of securing state compliance and adopt its own standards for more nationally significant pollution sources, such as electric utilities.

Conclusion

The United States has made incremental progress toward sustainability since 2002. But it has fallen far short of the more ambitious goals underlying the Rio Declaration. Meeting these goals requires a substantial movement toward more sustainable technology and phasing out of the dirtiest fossil fuels. We must create an economic dynamic favoring much greater use of sustainable technology.

ENDNOTES

1. U.N. Conference on Environment and Development (UNCED), Rio Declaration, U.N. Doc. A/CONF.151/5/Rev.1, 31 I.L.M. 874 (1992) [hereinafter Rio Declaration].

2. U.N. Conference on Environment and Development (UNCED), Agenda 21, U.N. Doc. A/CONF.151.26 (1992) [hereinafter Agenda 21].

3. Rio Declaration, *supra* note 1, princ. 1.

4. Agenda 21 seeks to avoid impairment of human health and "yet encourage development to proceed." Agenda 21, *supra* note 2, at ¶ 6.40.

5. *Id.*

6. Rio Declaration, *supra* note 1, at princ. 3.

7. *Id.* at princ. 8.

8. *Id.* at princ. 4.

9. *See* Agenda 21, *supra* note 2, at ¶¶ 9.9, 9.12; David M. Driesen, *Air Pollution, in* STUMBLING TOWARD SUSTAINABILITY 261, 811 n.59 (John C. Dernbach ed., 2002) (parsing the relevant language in Agenda 21).

10. Rio Declaration, *supra* note 1, at princs. 1, 2.

11. See EPA website, Air Trends page, *available at* www.epa.gov/air/airtrends/sixpoll.html (last visited on June 27, 2007).

12. Except for the hazardous air pollutant data, this data comes from a Microsoft Excel file obtained from EPA, containing the data reflected in various online graphs. The hazardous air pollution data was generated at ww.epa.gov/triexplorer/chemical.htm. The information respecting hazardous air pollutants represents reporting by a small subset of toxic emitters (albeit ones with especially large emissions) using estimation methods of the operators' choosing. *See* U.S. EPA, TOXIC RELEASE INVENTORY 1999: EXECUTIVE SUMMARY, E-10-11 (2001).

13. These figures were derived using data supplied by EPA focusing on the top 10 percentile of emissions, a frequently used metric for measuring air quality. The subsequent numbers in this paragraph use the same metric from the same source. The fine particulate numbers are based on 24-hour averages.

14. *See* Byron Swift, *Command Without Control: Why Cap-and-Trade Should Replace Rate Standards for Regional Pollutants*, 31 ELR 10330 (Mar. 2001).

15. *See* U.S. GOV'T ACCOUNTABILITY OFFICE (GAO), ACID RAIN: EMISSIONS TRENDS AND EFFECTS IN THE EASTERN UNITED STATES (GAO/RCED-00-47) 18-20 (2000).

16. *See* Natural Res. Defense Council v. EPA, 464 F.3d 1 (D.C. Cir. 2006) (allowing EPA to broaden exemptions for methyl bromide); 42 C.F.R. §§82.6, 82.7 (2001); 42 U.S.C. §§7671a(b), 7671d(b). *Cf.* Lee Anne Duval, *The Future of the Montreal Protocol: Money and Methyl Bromide*, 18 VA. ENVTL L.J. 609 (1999) (arguing that developed countries have failed to meet a legal obligation to fund developing country phaseout of methyl bromide).

17. National Ambient Air Quality Standards for Ozone, 62 Fed. Reg. 38835 (July 18, 1997) (codified at 40 C.F.R. §§50.9, 50.10). These standards were upheld in *Whitman v. Am. Trucking Ass'n*, 531 U.S. 457 (2001).

18. *See* South Coast Air Quality Mgmt. Dist. v. EPA, 472 F.3d 882 (D.C. Cir. 2006); Air Quality Designations and Classifications for the 8-Hour Ozone National Ambient Air Quality Standards; Early Action Compact Areas With Deferred Effective Dates, 69 Fed. Reg. 23858 (Apr. 30, 2004) (to be codified at 40 C.F.R. pt. 81).

19. *See* E. Donald Elliott et al., *Recent Clean Air Act Developments*—2006, 37 ELR 10274, 10279 (Apr. 2007).

20. *See* New Jersey v. EPA, 517 F.3d 574 (D.C. Cir. 2008).

21. *See* New York v. EPA, 413 F.3d 3 (D.C. Cir. 2005) (upholding some revisions of the definition of an "emission" increase causing a modification, while striking down others); New York v. EPA, 443 F.3d 880 (D.C. Cir. 2006) (rejecting an EPA effort to broaden the exemption from NSR for routine maintenance). *Cf.* Envtl. Defense v. Duke Energy Corp., 127 S. Ct. 1473 (2007) (upholding EPA decision to apply prevention of significant deterioration requirements to sources that increase their tons of emissions per year, but not their hourly emissions rate).

22. *See* DAVID M. DRIESEN, THE ECONOMIC DYNAMICS OF ENVIRONMENTAL LAW 187-92 (2003). *See generally* Richard L. Revesz & Jonathan Nash, *Grandfathering and Environmental Regulation: The Law and Economics of New Source Review*, 101 Nw. U. L. REV. 1677 (2007). The author of this chapter represented several U.S. senators in an amicus brief challenging one of the relevant rules, but this article's statements about new source review reflect the author's views, not necessarily those of his former clients.

23. Rule to Reduce Interstate Transport of Fine Particulate Matter and Ozone (Clean Air Interstate Rule), 70 Fed. Reg. 25162 (May 12, 2005) (to be codified at 40 C.F.R. pts. 51, 72-74, 77, 78 & 96).

24. *See* WORLD RESOURCES INST., OZONE DEPLETION IN THE UNITED STATES: ELEMENTS OF SUCCESS (Elizabeth Cook ed., 1996).

25. *Id.* at 14-15, 23-26, 58-60, 90-94, 98-104, 109. For example, some companies have substituted HCFCs for CFCs. HCFCs deplete the ozone layer, albeit less severely than CFCs. While some of the substitutes for CFC-based solvents are benign, many are toxic.

26. See EPA's website, Clean Energy page, EGrid2006Version 2.1 Year 2004 Summary Tables (April 2007), *available at* www.epa.gov/cleanenergy/egrid/index.htm (showing coal as providing more than 50 percent of electricity generation).

27. *See* Pace University's Power Scorecard website, www.powerscorecard.org/technologies.cfm.

28. *See* CAL. CODE REGS. tit. 13 §1960.1(g) (1998).

29. *See* CAL. AIR RES. BD., INITIAL STATEMENT OF REASONS FOR PROPOSED RULEMAKING, PUBLIC HEARING TO CONSIDER ADOPTION OF REGULATIONS TO CONTROL GREENHOUSE GAS EMISSIONS FROM MOTOR VEHICLES vi (2004).

30. *Id.* at xi (stating that many measures that manufacturers will employ to meet the California standards will make the vehicles more efficient).

31. John M. Broder & Micheline Maynard, *E.P.A. Denies California Emission's Waiver*, N.Y. TIMES, Dec. 19, 2007.

32. Petition for Review of Decision of the U.S. EPA, California v. U.S. EPA, (9th Cir. filed Jan. 2, 2008), *available at* http://ag.ca.gov/cms_attachments/press/pdfs/n1514_epapetition-1.pdf.

33. *See generally* David M. Driesen & Amy Sinden, *The Missing Instrument: Dirty Input Limits*, 22 HARV. ENVTL. L. REV. (2009) (forthcoming).

34. *See* ELI, CLEANER POWER: THE BENEFITS AND COSTS OF MOVING FROM COAL GENERATION TO MODERN POWER TECHNOLOGIES 16 (2001) (projecting enormous benefits from just a 50 percent reduction in coal).

35. *See generally* KEN BERLIN & ROBERT M. SUSSMAN, GLOBAL WARMING AND THE FUTURE OF COAL: THE PATH TO CARBON CAPTURE AND STORAGE (2007), *available at* www.americanprogress.org.

36. *See Greenhouse Gas in* Wikipedia.

37. *See* Ohio Valley Envtl. Coalition v. U.S. Army Corps of Eng'rs, 479 F. Supp. 2d 607, 614-15, 629-42 (S.D. W. Va. 2007) (describing mountaintop removal and reviewing its impacts).

38. *See* Jeff Goodell, *The Dirty Rock: Can Coal Clean Up Its Act?*, 284 THE NATION 30, 32 (May 7, 2007) (discussing how carbon dioxide can dissolve minerals and thereby contaminate drinking water).

39. *See* ELI, CLEANER POWER, *supra* note 34, at 10.

40. *See* John C. Dernbach et al., *Stabilizing and Then Reducing U.S. Energy Consumption: Legal and Policy Tools for Efficiency and Conservation*, 37 ELR 10003 (Jan. 2007).

41. *See* Driesen, *supra* note 22, at 151-61.

42. *Id.* at 104-05 (explaining why government has trouble writing sufficiently ambitious regulations).

43. *Id.* at 154.

44. *Id.* at 156.

45. *Cf.* Envtl. Integrity Project v. EPA, 425 F.3d 992 (D.C. Cir. 2005).

46. *See e.g.*, Natural Res. Defense Council v. EPA, 22 F.3d 1125 (D.C. Cir. 1994); Natural Res. Defense Council v. EPA, 475 F.2d 968 (D.C. Cir. 1973); Sierra Club v. EPA, 719 F.2d 436, 469 (D.C. Cir. 1983).

Chapter 17

Climate Change: The Unmet Obligation to Reduce Greenhouse Gas Emissions

Donald A. Brown

This chapter summarizes the performance of the U.S. government in reducing the threat of climate change since 2002,[1] focusing on U.S. responsibilities under the United Nations Framework Convention on Climate Change (UNFCCC).[2] For several reasons, the U.S. obligations under the UNFCCC can be understood to constitute minimum sustainability requirements:

- The United States has ratified the UNFCCC, which means that it is legally binding under international law.
- Other federal obligations on sustainable development that relate to climate change, including those in Agenda 21, are "soft law," that is, nonbinding promises of the United States.
- Only the UNFCCC contains express obligations in regard to greenhouse gas emissions.
- The UNFCCC includes provisions that are understood to be the building blocks of an international climate change regime that likely will continue to structure national responses to climate change.
- Almost all climate change programs adopted by the United States can be understood as consistent with U.S. commitments under the UNFCCC to implement climate change policies and measure their effectiveness.

Because climate change is a global problem that requires international cooperation for a solution, a nation's responsibility for climate change must be thought of in terms of its fair share of global emissions. That is, national climate change actions must be judged in relation to international climate change obligations. In addition, the UNFCCC contains binding obligations of party nations, including the United States, on such matters as the goal of the treaty, obligations of rich nations to poor nations, and international reporting requirements. Taking stock of how the United States has lived up to its UNFCCC obligations is therefore central to any evaluation of the U.S. performance on climate change.

The UNFCCC took effect in 1994, and now has 189 parties.[3] Many Americans are unaware of, or have forgotten, the fact that the United States is party to the UNFCCC. Yet the treaty is likely to continue to be relevant to the U.S. international obligations on climate change even if the nation decides not to join an international regime that sets specific greenhouse gas (GHG) reduction targets such as those specified in the Kyoto Protocol. In 2001, President George W. Bush specifically reaffirmed a U.S. commitment to the UNFCCC, despite the Bush Administration's unwillingness to participate in the Kyoto Protocol.[4]

The analysis in this chapter concludes that the United States has failed to live up to its climate change obligations in regard to reductions in greenhouse gas emissions, although it has done much better on many other international climate change obligations. The failure of the United States to meet its emissions-reductions obligations can be traced to the U.S. unwillingness to put into place legally binding restrictions on GHG emissions. At this time, the United States is virtually isolated from the rest of the developed world in committing itself to binding international obligations to reduce these emissions. Although the federal government has implemented a host of voluntary energy programs and a few mandatory energy-efficiency requirements, the country has failed to meet its commitments under the UNFCCC because energy demand in the United States has outpaced gains in energy efficiency.

Why is it important for the United States to live up to its obligations under the UNFCCC? As discussed later in this chapter, the Bush Administration, at the UNFCCC negotiations in Bali in 2007, finally agreed to rejoin the rest of the world under the UNFCCC and negotiate a second commitment period to follow the Kyoto Protocol. Because the Kyoto Protocol creates emissions reductions obligations from 2008 to 2012, the international community will need to establish a new framework for a period after 2012. Given the now universal international agreement among countries to work within the UNFCCC, the treaty and its implementing protocols are very likely to constitute the structure of the international climate change regime in the years ahead. For this reason, if the United States has any desire to show leadership in solving the enormous problem of climate change, it will need to reconnect with the rest of the world under the UNFCCC and its protocols and comply with the commitments made thereunder.

By cooperating with the international UNFCCC regime, the United States can help solve the enormous threat to life, human health, property, biodiversity, plants, animals, species, and ecosystems posed by climate change because this regime is likely to define the global solution so urgently needed. Climate change threatens people around the world with rising seas, reduced agricultural production, decreases in water supply, drought, floods, lethal heat waves, and increases in vector-borne disease. Because these problems threaten to destabilize large parts of the world, it is in the United States' interest to lead the international community working within the UNFCCC framework.

The U.S. Record on Reduction of Greenhouse Gas Emissions

The United States has failed to comply with its GHG reductions obligations under the UNFCCC. Under the Convention, the United States agreed with other developed countries to the nonbinding commitment to "aim" at reducing greenhouse gas emissions to 1990 levels by 2000.[5] The UNFCCC also contains additional goals and commitments relevant to the emissions policies of member nations, including the United States. For instance, the United States agreed to take steps to stabilize greenhouse gas emissions in the atmosphere by working with other nations "to prevent dangerous anthropocentric interference with the climate system."[6] The United States also agreed to take the lead along with other developed nations to protect the climate system on the basis of equity.[7] Therefore, the United States has agreed that it will consider what its fair share of safe GHG global emissions is when setting national policy, and not simply justify its climate change policy based upon national interest alone.

Another important provision of the UNFCCC relating to reductions of U.S. greenhouse gas emissions is Principle 3 in Article 3, in which the United States agreed that it would not use scientific uncertainty as the basis for delaying action in regard to its emissions obligations.[8] Thus, the United States has obligated itself under what is generally referred to as the "precautionary principle" of the UNFCCC to begin to reduce its emissions to safe levels notwithstanding some scientific uncertainty about the timing and magnitude of climate change impacts. Yet we continue to hear arguments in the United States against government action to reduce GHG emissions on the basis of scientific uncertainty. It would appear that those making these arguments are not aware of U.S. promises in regard to scientific uncertainty.

The Kyoto Protocol

The parties to the UNFCCC understood that in later years new obligations would need to be negotiated in order to stabilize GHG levels in the atmosphere at safe levels. In other words, as its name implies, the UNFCCC was understood to be a "framework" convention—that is, a document that would need to be supplemented by more tightly focused and specific global warming commitments. Future negotiations would be required to specify more precise national obligations. In this regard, beginning in 1993 the United States participated in negotiations that led up to agreement on the Kyoto Protocol in 1997.[9] Under the Kyoto Protocol, developed countries agreed to reduce their net GHG emissions by at least 5 percent from 1990 levels by 2008-2012.[10] No comparable commitment was included for developing countries. The Protocol contains somewhat different commitments for individual developed countries. For instance, the U.S. commitment is 7 percent below 1990 levels, while other nations with commitments under the Protocol average 5 percent.[11]

The Clinton Administration eventually agreed to the terms of the Kyoto Protocol, but because Congress was hostile to the Protocol, it was never submitted to the Senate for ratification.

On February 16, 2005, following Russia's ratification, the Kyoto Protocol went into effect.[12] After Australia's announcement that it would comply, the United States remained the only developed country not committed to compliance.

On March 13, 2001, President George W. Bush announced that he would abandon his campaign promise to regulate CO_2 emissions from electrical generation facilities.[13] A week later, the Bush Administration announced that it was repudiating the Kyoto Protocol.[14] In making this announcement, the president pointed to the same three reasons that had become an American refrain for refusing to take serious action to reduce domestic emissions—namely, scientific uncertainty, cost to the United States economy, and the failure of the developing world to make commitments. The scientific uncertainty excuse for the unwillingness of the United States to commit to binding targets has been used with varying consistency since 2002 despite the UNFCCC's adoption of the precautionary principle in Article 3.

Greenhouse Gas Emission Levels in the United States

Despite promises by the United States in the UNFCCC to "aim" to stabilize GHG emissions at 1990 levels by 2000, by the end of 2005 the United States was almost 17 percent above 1990 levels. See Figure 1.

Figure 1
U.S. Greenhouse Gas Emissions, 1990 to 2005

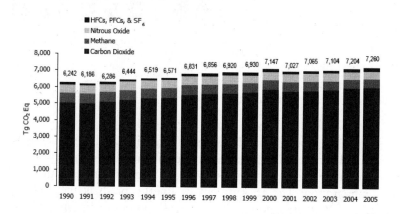

Source: U.S. Environmental Protection Agency.[15]

The trend data in Figure 1 does not include recent 2006 emissions which represent a 1.5 percent decrease from 2005.[16] With the exception of the 2006 decrease, which may be explained by a warm winter, year in and year out GHG emissions in the United States have continued to rise despite considerable improvements in energy efficiency. The cause of this increase is that energy demand in the United States is outpacing efficiency gains.

Figure 2
U.S. Greenhouse Gas Emissions Changes Relative to 1990

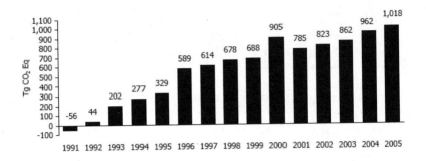

Source: U.S. Environmental Protection Agency.[17]

Because energy demand has been increasing, GHG emissions are expected to rise in the United States despite numerous, mostly voluntary, climate change programs that have been initiated by the Bush Administration. The Department of Energy predicts that between 2000 and 2020 greenhouse gases from all sources in the United States will rise by 42.7 percent above 2000 levels. This projection demonstrates that the programs adopted thus far by the Bush Administration will fall far short of the goal the United States agreed to in the UNFCCC to aim to stabilize GHG at 1990 levels by 2000, as well as the UNFCCC goal of stabilizing atmospheric greenhouse gas concentrations at levels to prevent dangerous anthropocentric interference with the climate system. (See Table 1.)

Table 1
Potential U.S. Greenhouse Gas Emissions From
All Sources, 2000-2020 (TgCO$_2$ Equivalent)

Between 2000 and 2020, total net U.S. greenhouse gas emissions are projected to rise by 42.7 percent. However, the rate of increase in emissions is projected to diminish over the same period, reflecting the development and implementation of cleaner, more efficient technologies; the substitution of fuels that emit lower volumes of greenhouse gases; and changes in the composition of GDP to goods and services with fewer fuel inputs.

All Covered Sources	2000	2005	2010	2015	2020
Energy-Related CO$_2$	5,726	6,210	6,727	7,206	7,655
Non-energy CO$_2$	132	138	145	153	161
Methane	623	633	630	625	611
Nitrous Oxide	433	447	464	483	504
High GWP Gases	124	170	208	290	410
Sequestration Removals	-1,205	-1,175	-1,144	-1,096	-1,053
Adjustments	- 59	- 58	- 59	- 57	- 51
Total	5,773	6,366	6,972	7,604	8,237

GWP = global warming potential.

Notes: These total U.S. CO$_2$ equivalent emissions correspond to carbon weights of 1,574 teragrams (Tg) for year 2000; 1,901 Tg for 2010; and 2,246 Tg for 2020. Totals may not sum due to independent rounding.

Source: U.S. Environmental Protection Agency.[18]

For the most part, the Bush Administration has resisted capping emissions at a specific level, preferring instead to pursue policies that improve energy efficiency or create incentives for sustainable energy. In February 2002, President Bush announced a program to reduce the economy's greenhouse gas intensity (i.e., how much we emit per unit of economic activity) by 18 percent by 2012.[19] Improvements in energy efficiency have been the cornerstone of the Bush Administration's approach to its GHG commitments under the UNFCCC. The Administration has sought to achieve this goal with numerous programs, policies, and voluntary partnerships, and some revisions to energy law; however, none of these strategies include either enforceable GHG emissions targets or carbon taxes.

As a matter of energy law, a key element in the Bush strategy relating to climate change has been the Energy Policy Act of 2005,[20] which included new testing procedures for a standardized determination of energy efficiency, energy use, and estimated annual operating cost for particular products.[21] The Act also requires new or more stringent standards for a variety of products[22] as well as commercial and industrial equipment.[23] It includes required improvements in product labeling[24] and a variety of other provisions such as an obligation to reduce energy consumption in federal buildings by 20 percent from fiscal year 2003 levels.[25] The Act contains additional requirements relating to renewable energy, including a provision that the EPA establish regulations requiring the volume of renewable fuel sold or introduced into commerce in the United States annually to increase from 4.0 billion gallons in 2006 to 7.5 billion gallons in 2012.[26]

To achieve its goal of decoupling increases in GHG emissions from economic growth, the Bush Administration adopted a series of voluntary programs and initiatives: (1) energy partnerships with state governments and individual corporations; (2) combined heat and power partnerships; (3) the Energy Star program to promote energy-efficient products and appliances; (4) programs to increase energy efficiency in the transportation sector; (5) green power purchasing programs; (6) voluntary programs to reduce emissions of high global warming potential gases; (6) methane gas reduction programs; (7) programs to reduce the volume of waste; (8) programs to reduce emissions from particular industrial sectors including the agricultural sector; and (9) a voluntary GHG emissions reporting system.[27]

These programs are the cornerstone of the U.S. program to improve carbon intensity. Figure 3 describes the projected improvement in energy efficiency under these programs.

Figure 3
Energy Use Per Capita and Per Dollar of Domestic
Product, 1980-2030 (1980 = 1)

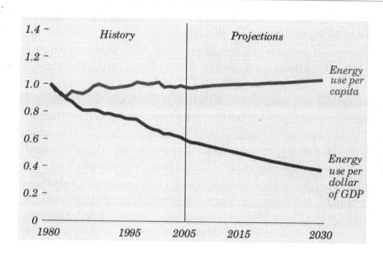

Source: U.S. Energy Information Agency.[28]

   As we have seen, however, even if the United States achieves its efficiency targets, it still expects large increases in total greenhouse gas
emissions—that is, it expects increases in GHG emissions to rise by
42.7 percent above 2000 levels by 2020. Because future emissions are
expected to continue to rise so steeply, the United States has failed to
meet its commitments under the UNFCCC in this regard and is not on
a path to reverse the trend.

   On February 2, 2007, the United Nations Intergovernmental Panel
on Climate Change (IPCC) declared that the evidence of a warming
trend is "unequivocal," and that human activity has "very likely" been
the driving force in that change over the last 50 years.[29] The IPCC report, along with other mounting scientific evidence of human causa-
tion of climate change, appears to have added momentum in the
United States toward future adoption of more specific climate change
law and policies. Support for more specific action on climate change
also appeared to increase in reaction to former Vice President Al
Gore's documentary *An Inconvenient Truth*. And the U.S. Supreme
Court made its first global warming-related decision, ruling 5-4 that

EPA had not justified its position that it was not authorized to regulate carbon dioxide.[30] For whatever reasons, the Bush Administration took several steps in 2007 that signaled a growing willingness to take more concrete steps on climate change; nonetheless, as of the date this chapter went to press there has been no stated willingness to commit to legally binding emissions limitations.

At the G-8 Summit in Germany in June 2007, the Bush Administration unveiled a long-term strategy for dealing with climate change that called for 15 of the world's largest-polluting industrial nations to reach an agreement by the end of 2008 on goals for reducing GHG emissions globally.[31] Under this program, America and other nations will set a long-term global goal for reducing greenhouse gases. To help develop this goal, the United States announced that it would convene a series of meetings of nations that produce most GHG emissions, including nations with rapidly growing economies such as India and China.[32] Although this announcement appears to be a change in course for the United States, it seems that the Bush Administration is still unwilling to submit to binding GHG reductions targets, and wants to rely instead on inspirational goals. Nor is it clear what domestic policies the Bush Administration is willing to adopt to achieve serious targets. Any serious plan to reduce greenhouse gas emissions will need to make major changes in U.S. law.

In Bali, Indonesia, in December 2007, the Bush Administration agreed to the Bali Action Plan, a roadmap under the UNFCCC to put into place an agreement to replace the Kyoto Protocol, which terminates in 2012.[33] In agreeing to the Bali Action Plan, the Bush Administration seemed to be signaling a willingness to rejoin the rest of the world in an international regime to combat climate change under the UNFCCC. Yet it is not clear that the Administration is willing to agree to enforceable caps on U.S. emissions under a treaty that replaces the Kyoto Protocol.

On December 18, 2007, President Bush signed the Energy Independence and Security Act of 2007, the first significant piece of legislation during his presidency relevant to climate change.[34] The major provisions of this law include: (1) a requirement to improve vehicle fuel efficiency of the U.S. transportation sector by setting a national fuel economy standard of at least 35 miles per gallon by 2020 for automobiles, an improvement of 40 percent over existing standards; (2) adoption of the Renewable Fuel Standard (RFS) requiring fuel producers to use at least 36 billion gallons of biofuel in 2022; (3) an amendment to the Energy Policy and Conservation Act to set new appliance efficiency standards that will save Americans money and energy; (4) a phaseout of widely-used incandescent bulbs in favor of more energy-efficient fluorescent bulbs and LEDs (light emitting diodes); and (5) incentives for more energy-efficient buildings, including green government buildings by 2030.[35]

U.S. Compliance With Non-Emissions Reductions Commitments of the UNFCCC

In addition to its promise to curb emissions, the United States made several other commitments under the UNFCCC. Specifically, the United States agreed to: (1) assist developing nations to finance some of their obligations under the treaty; (2) report to the secretariat of the UNFCCC on GHG emissions and programs; (3) educate Americans about climate change; and (4) support scientific research on climate change. For the most part, the United States has lived up to these obligations.

Financing Developing Country Commitments

Since 2002, the United States has continued a variety of programs and partnerships designed to support the introduction of technologies that are climate-friendly in developing countries.[36] Between 2001 and 2006, U.S. funding for climate change in developing countries totaled approximately $1.4 billion, including $209 million to the Global Environmental Facility in support of climate change programs.[37] For this reason, an argument can be made that the United States has continued to achieve its commitments to finance and transfer climate change technologies in developing countries. In the last four years, however, there has been a growing call from developing countries, which are starting to experience damages from human-induced climate change, that those developed nations most responsible for climate change have a duty to pay more of the costs of adapting to climate change and of ameliorating its unavoidable damages. Following this line of argument, a case can be made that the United States has a responsibility to make larger contributions to adaptation funds.

Reporting Requirements

Under the UNFCCC the United States has agreed to report regularly to the United Nations on compliance with its many commitments, including on national emissions; policies and measures adopted; projected GHG emissions; impacts and adaptation; financial resources and transfer of technology; research and systematic observation; and education, training, and outreach.[38] In 2006, the United States prepared its fourth comprehensive report to the UNFCCC secretariat on these matters. For this reason, the United States can be said to have complied with its reporting obligations under the UNFCCC. In the past, the secretariat for the UNFCCC has said that the U.S. reports are "generally transparent, well-documented, presented in accordance with the reporting requirements of Annex 1 Parties, and had been put together with the use of major resources."[39]

Education, Training, and Public Awareness[40]

Under UNFCCC Article 4, all parties must promote education, training, and public awareness of global warming and encourage the widest participation in the policy process.[41] The 2006 U.S. report to the UNFCCC secretariat identified a host of educational and outreach programs by the U.S. Agency for International Development, the U.S. Departments of Agriculture, Energy, and Interior, and the Environmental Protection Agency, National Science Foundation, and Climate Change Science Program.[42] It can be concluded that the United States has complied with its educational obligations under the UNFCCC.

Scientific Research

Under Article 5 of the UNFCCC the United States agreed to support and further develop research on global warming while taking into account the particular needs of developing nations on technical issues.[43] The United States has been the undisputed leader in scientific research on climate change, investing over $1.5 billion annually in scientific monitoring and predicting global change.[44] In 2002, President Bush launched the U.S. Climate Change Science Program, which coordinates and prioritizes the scientific research on climate change among 13 federal agencies and their national and international partners.[45] The Program's goals are: (1) improving knowledge of Earth's climate system, (2) improving quantification of the forces changing Earth's climate, (3) reducing uncertainty about future projections, (4) understanding the adaptability of natural and human systems to climate change, and (5) improving our ability to manage the "risks and opportunities" of climate change.[46] A case can be made, therefore, that the

United States performed well on most of its scientific research commitments under the UNFCCC.[47]

Recommendations for the Next Decade

The analysis in this chapter leads to four recommendations.

1. As soon as possible, the United States must adopt programs for the reduction of greenhouse gas emissions to 1990 levels. This is an explicit promise made by the United States in ratifying the UNFCCC and must be immediately honored. Because U.S. emissions are currently more than 14 percent above 1990 levels and because those emissions are increasing by over 1 percent per year, the United States will need to adopt strong programs to return to 1990 emissions levels in the near future. The record of the Bush Administration's voluntary global warming programs has demonstrated that they cannot alone be relied upon to achieve the emissions reductions required. Therefore the United States needs to adopt both emissions caps for various sectors and a mix of financial incentives and regulatory requirements that will achieve the reductions needed to return to 1990 levels within the next few years. In selecting legal instruments to achieve these reductions, the United States needs to take some obvious steps while also identifying other programs through careful strategic thinking and public outreach. Some of the obvious steps that need to be enacted into law include:

- Eliminate subsidies for fossil fuel while increasing subsidies and/or tax incentives for renewable energy;
- Modify federal spending on transportation so that a much higher percentage of transportation spending is dedicated to transportation programs based on non-fossil fuels;
- Require that all generators of electric power provide at least 20 percent of electric generation supply through renewable energy;
- Adopt tax incentives that support the various forms of energy that do not release greenhouse gases;
- Provide federal grants for transportation, energy, and environmental protection to states and municipalities contingent upon the adoption by state and local governments of GHG emissions reduction strategies;
- Launch a public education campaign about global warming that helps Americans understand not only how U.S. emis-

sions of greenhouse gases affect them but also others around the world.

2. The United States should take leadership in the effort to achieve an international consensus on what constitutes safe atmospheric concentrations of greenhouse gases. Although the UNFCCC created a goal to stabilize atmospheric concentrations at safe levels, the international community must soon achieve a better definition of what constitutes a safe atmospheric target, so that all nations can understand what their individual obligations will be to prevent dangerous interference with the climate system.

3. The United States must openly declare that it will take steps to substantially reduce its greenhouse gas emissions regardless of whether the developing world accepts targets in the first commitment period. Such an approach would communicate to the world that the United States is willing to live up to its obligations under the UNFCCC and to accept its responsibility as one of the world's largest emitters of greenhouse gases. In this regard, the United States should also state that over the next few decades it will work to reduce its emissions to an equitable portion of total world emissions, a level that will achieve the lowest possible atmospheric concentrations of greenhouse gases.

4. The United States needs to put greenhouse gas emissions reduction at the very top of its domestic and foreign policy agenda. The world needs the United States to take leadership on this issue, and the United States must accept its responsibility as the world's largest emitter of greenhouse gases. This country can lead the world on global warming policy because of its great technical and innovative ability and resources.

Conclusion

The United States has complied with many of its promises made on global warming in 1992 at Rio. It has met its obligations to report domestic GHG emissions and policies, support scientific research, and financially help developing nations abide by their commitments under the UNFCCC. Yet the United States has failed to take adequate steps to reduce spiraling domestic GHG emissions and has not worked cooperatively with other nations to stabilize greenhouse gases in the atmosphere at safe levels.

ENDNOTES

1. This chapter will not review the considerable climate change developments that are taking place in individual states, municipalities, businesses, and organizations. Climate change developments at the nonfederal level can be found in Chapter 29.

2. United Nations Framework Convention on Climate Change, U.N. Doc. A/AC.237/18 (1992), *reprinted in* 31 I.L.M. 849 (1992) [hereinafter UNFCCC].

3. *Id.*

4. Press Release, President Bush Discusses Global Climate Change, June 11, 2001, *available at* www.whitehouse.gov/news/releases/2001/06/20010611-2.html (last visited June 14, 2006); Kyoto Protocol to UNFCCC [hereinafter Kyoto Protocol], Dec. 10, 1997, U.N. Doc. FCCC/CP/197/L.7/Add. 1, art. 3.1 & Annex B, *reprinted in* 37 I.L.M. 22 (1998).

5. UNFCCC, *supra* note 2, art. 4.2(a).

6. *Id.* art. 2.

7. *Id.* art. 3.

8. *Id.* art. 3, princ.3.

9. Kyoto Protocol, *supra* note 4.

10. *Id.* art. 3.1. The Annex I, or developed, countries also agreed to make "demonstrable progress" by 2005 in meeting their commitments. *Id.* art. 3.2.

11. *Id.* Annex B.

12. The Protocol could not become effective until countries accounting for 55 percent of the carbon dioxide generated by "Annex I" industrialized nations had ratified it. Kyoto Protocol, *supra* note 4, art. 24.1. After the United States declined to ratify the Protocol, it could only become effective if Russia ratified it.

13. Douglas Jehl & Andrew C. Revkin, *Bush Reverses Vow to Curb Gas Tied to Global Warming*, N.Y. TIMES, Mar. 14, 2001.

14. William Drozdiak & Eric Pianin, *U.S. Angers Allies Over Climate Pact: Europeans Will Ask Bush to Reconsider*, WASH. POST, Mar. 29, 2001, at A01.

15. U.S. EPA, GREENHOUSE GAS EMISSIONS AND SINKS 1990-2005, *available at* www.epa.gov/climatechange/emissions/downloads06/07CR.pdf.

16. U.S. DEP'T OF ENERGY, ENERGY INFO. ADMIN., EMISSIONS OF GREENHOUSE GASES IN THE UNITED STATES (2007), *available at* www.eia.doe.gov/pub/oiaf/1605/cdrom/pdf/ggrpt/057306.pdf.

17. *Id.*

18. U.S. EPA, PROJECTED GREENHOUSE GAS EMISSIONS, *available at* www.epa.gov/climatechange/emissions/downloads/ch5.pdf (last visited Nov. 12, 2007).

19. Press Release, President Bush Announces Clear Skies & Global Climate Change Initiative, www.whitehouse.gov/news/releases/2002/02/20020214.html (last visited Dec. 23, 2007).

20. For a thorough review of recent U.S. energy law, see John C. Dernbach et al., *Stabilizing and Then Reducing U.S. Energy Consumption: Legal and Policy Tools for Efficiency and Conservation*, 37 ELR 10003 (Jan. 2007).

21. 42 U.S.C. §6293. For showerheads, faucets, water closets, and urinals, the test procedures are required to cover water use. *Id.* §6293(b).

22. Energy Policy Act of 2005 §135; 42 U.S.C. §§6291-6297.

23. *Id.* §136; 42 U.S.C. §§6311-6316.

24. *Id.* §137; 42 U.S.C. §6294(a)(2)(F).

25. *Id.* §102(a)(1); 42 U.S.C. §8253(a)(1).

26. *Id.* §1501; 42 U.S.C. §7545.

27. U.S. EPA, CURRENT AND NEAR-TERM GREENHOUSE GAS REDUCTION INITIATIVES, *available at* www.epa.gov/climatechange/policy/nearterm ghgreduction.html (last visited Dec. 25, 2007).

28. U.S. ENERGY INFO. AGENCY, U.S. ENERGY OUTLOOK, *available at* www.eia.doe.gov/bookshelf/brochures/aeo2006/aeo2006.html.

29. INTERGOVERNMENTAL PANEL ON CLIMATE CHANGE (IPCC), FOURTH ASSESSMENT REPORT, *available at* www.ipcc.ch/ (last visited Dec. 22, 2007).

30. Massachusetts v. U.S. EPA, 549 U.S. 1438 (2007).

31. CNN, *G8 Backs Climate-Change Science, Sets No Hard Goals*, *available at* http://edition.cnn.com/2007/WORLD/europe/06/07/g8.climatechange (last visited July 4, 2007).

32. Fact Sheet, President Bush Announces U.S. Support for an Effort to Develop a New Post-2012 Framework on Climate Change, *available at* www.state.gov/g/oes/rls/or/85846.htm.

33. *See* website for U.N. Climate Change Conference in Bali, http://unfccc. int/meetings/cop_13/items/4049.php (last visited Dec. 24, 2007).

34. Energy Independence and Security Act of 2007, Pub. L. No. 10-140, 121 Stat. 1492 (2007); *see also* John Broder, *Bush Signs Broad Energy Law*, N.Y. TIMES, Dec. 19, 2007, *available at* www.nytimes.com/2007/12/19/ washington/19cnd-energy.html?_r=1&hp&oref=slogin.

35. *Id.*

36. U.S. Fourth Climate Action Report to the UNFCCC, [hereinafter U.S. Fourth CAR] *available at* http://www.state.gov/g/oes/rls/rpts/car/ (last visited July 8, 2007).

37. *Id.*

38. *Id.*

39. UNFCCC, United States of America: Report on the In-Depth Review of the Second National Communication of the United States of America, FCCC/IDR.2/U.S.A, 12 May 1999, *available at* unfccc.int/resource/docs/ idr/usa02.htm.

40. UNFCCC, *supra* note 2, art. 4.2(a).

41. *Id.* art. 4(1)(a)-(j).

42. U.S. Fourth CAR, *supra* note 36.

43. UNFCCC, *supra* note 2, art. 5.
44. U.S. Fourth CAR, *supra* note 36.
45. *Id.*
46. *Id.* at 3-4.
47. *Id.*

Chapter 18

Biodiversity Conservation: An Unrealized Aspiration

A. Dan Tarlock and Andrew Zabel

Biodiversity conservation remains an elusive goal in the United States. The most that one can say is that our biodiversity loss is less pronounced than in tropical regions.[1] In addition to the inherent technical and institutional obstacles, conservation has not been a priority of the administration of President George W. Bush, although it remains a formal domestic and policy objective.[2] The 1992 Biodiversity Convention remains unratified by the United States, and the Bush Administration has been generally hostile to environmental protection and mandatory greenhouse gas reduction. Further, its successful efforts to open large amounts of public lands, much of them important wildlife habitats, to energy exploration and production have compromised the country's public and private biodiversity.

The federal government has actively diluted its biodiversity conservation duties in many crucial areas. For example, in 2005 the Forest Service eliminated the duty to assure the survival of "viable populations" because the focus on viability diverted attention from ecosystem management.[3] A similar effort to weaken the Endangered Species Act is underway in the U.S. Department of the Interior.

Still, there are several bright spots. The most promising prospect is the conservation of marine biodiversity. Large new state and federal marine reserves have been established in territorial waters and in the 200-mile Exclusive Economic Zone.[4] Another bright spot is the acceleration of the private acquisition of large amounts of undeveloped land and the dedication of this land to uses that are generally consistent with biodiversity conservation.

This chapter surveys efforts since 2002 to conserve biodiversity in the United States. It concentrates on four areas: the evolving rationale for biodiversity conservation and new developments in the relevant science; federal legislation and administrative regulations; federal judicial decisions; and state actions.

What Is Sustainable Development and Why Does It Matter to the United States?

Biodiversity conservation should be understood as an integral component of sustainable development rather than, as it often is in practice, merely a factor to be considered and traded off against economic development. Otherwise, sustainable development is simply development that leaves no natural legacy for the future. Despite advances in understanding the impacts and effects of humans, the succinct definition from the 1987 Brundtland Commission report remains a benchmark: "Sustainable development is development that meets the needs of the present without compromising the ability of future generations to meet their own needs."[5]

The evidence suggests that we are far from the goal of effective biodiversity conservation. No standard, systematic assessment of the state of biodiversity exists in the United States.[6] The most ambitious and closest effort is the 2002 Heinz Center survey of the state of our ecosystems.[7] This survey, which was updated in 2008, is a scientific work in progress and applies a wide range of disciplines and technologies to identify the major characteristics of ecosystems and the available information as well as crucial information gaps. Even without a comprehensive assessment, the clear message from a variety of sources is that we are squandering our rich heritage of species and ecosystem diversity through continued habitat destruction. The degradation of freshwater aquatic ecosystems[8] and the spread of exotic species[9] remain especially challenging, but ineffectively addressed, problems.

The science of biodiversity assessment continues to evolve but not always in ways that make it easy to apply the findings to actual efforts to conserve biodiversity. Article 2 of the Convention on Biological Diversity defines biodiversity as "the variability among living organisms from all sources including, inter alia, terrestrial, marine and other aquatic ecosystems and the ecological complexes of which they are a part; this includes diversity within species, between species and of ecosystems." Despite this broad legal definition, biodiversity remains an artificial construct with no coherent meaning. Scientists continue to struggle both to define and to measure biodiversity. These scientific debates have important consequences for law and policy. For example, if two or more species perform the same ecological function, do we conserve the individual species or the function?[10] Species viability is, of course, crucial, but biodiversity conservation requires that ecosystems be viewed as functioning units rather than a discrete collection of species. Put differently, all species and the natural processes that support them are equally important. However, scientists continue to warn that we should focus on "the biological structure that maintains ecosystems," although it is easier to do species counts than "to document their interactions."[11]

Biodiversity conservation has taken on a greater urgency in recent years in light of the recognition that global climate change will have major impacts on the distribution and density of biodiversity. In general, it is expected that species will migrate northward and habitats will be altered to become suitable for previously unknown species, but we do not know if species will be able to migrate and adapt to new terrestrial habitats.[12] Aquatic ecosystems face a discrete set of stresses which include the loss of coastal wetlands from the rise of sea levels and warmer freshwaters. As a recent study points out, avian species may be able to migrate, but "resident fish and plants are less likely to be able to disperse to new locations, even over several generations."[13]

The warnings of science suggest a duty to conserve but do not compel it. A variety of rationales have been offered for biodiversity conservation, but in the past few years a utilitarian theory has emerged as a compelling argument: the role that ecosystems play in providing useful services to humans. The utilitarian rationale reflects two powerful recent trends. First, the emphasis on ecosystem services reflects the emergence of biodiversity as an organizing concept for a variety of uncoordinated resource management objectives.[14] Second, the pure utilitarian rationale for ecosystem and biodiversity protection reflects the increased role that science and welfare economics has come to play in the environmental policy discourse.[15] The emphasis on the provision of ecosystem services offers some positive advantages over appeals to ethics. The strongest case for environmental protection remains the ability to show that such protection can be justified by hard numbers. Science-based, utilitarian solutions have the potential to appeal to a wide variety of interests and make it harder to trade off "soft" benefits for "hard" ones. They are less polarizing than appeals to higher spiritual and aesthetic values. Despite heroic efforts to create a workable system of environmental ethics that encompasses nonhumans, environmental protection remains relentlessly anthropocentric. It is also harder to argue against a policy with dollar values attached to different options. A study of the costs of providing sufficient water in the South Platte River to support wildlife habitat concluded that the total cost of acquiring the necessary water would be $18.96 million compared to the $29 million value of the enhanced ecosystem services.[16] Finally, because ecosystem service provision is tied either to a functioning market or to government subsidies, it can be a fair and equitable way of reallocating resources.

Progress Since 2002

Legislation

There has been no effort to enact a general biodiversity conservation statute at the federal level. Federal public land law, the principal legal framework that intentionally and unintentionally preserves biodiversity, remains as dysfunctional as ever.[17] Instead, biodiversity conservation remains a secondary objective of other legislation. There are three facets to biodiversity-related legislation between 2002 and 2007. The first is a short, positive story about the 2002 Farm Bill,[18] which continued the conservation reserve program inaugurated in 1985.[19] The Wildlife Habitat Incentives Program (WHIP) supports biodiversity conservation on private lands through the Conservation Security Program, which paid farmers $2 billion a year between 2002 and 2007 to enhance wildlife habitat. Although the program was drastically underfunded, some 3.2 million acres of wildlife habitat have been established.[20]

The second facet is a longer and sadder story. Congress cut back various statutes that promote the consideration of biodiversity, such as the National Environmental Policy Act of 1969 (NEPA), by limiting judicial review for certain agency decisions.[21] Congress' efforts were complemented by numerous successful efforts by the George W. Bush Administration to inject political influence for lobbying groups into the science-based processes that exist to assess and protect biodiversity.

The third story is about what did not happen. Beginning in 2001, there have been persistent efforts to gut the Endangered Species Act (ESA), especially after the Bureau of Reclamation shut off the head gates of an agricultural irrigation project in 2001 to protect several listed fish species.[22] These congressional efforts appear to have ended when the Democrats took control of both houses of Congress in the November 2006 midterm election, but the administration tried to achieve the same result through administrative regulations.[23]

Administrative Regulation (or Deregulation)

The Bush II Administration's hostility to environmental regulation and to the use of relatively neutral science has impacted the goal of biodiversity conservation because many of its initiatives directly or indirectly undermine conservation. This section offers three examples. The best example of a direct compromise is the Bush II Administration's endangered species habitat-protection policy. The continued subsidization of public land grazing fees is an example of indirect compromise. Finally, the Administration's efforts to undermine the use of science is not good for biodiversity conservation.

Habitat Protection

The Clinton Administration's efforts to protect habitat have been significantly reduced by the Bush Administration. The ESA lists species at risk, and then gives the Departments of Commerce and the Interior limited discretion to decide whether to list critical habitat, i.e., the geographical area inhabited or likely to be inhabited by the listed species.[24] The Bush Administration is the only administration since the enactment of the ESA that has not designated a single critical habitat except under court order. And the critical habitats it has designated are dramatically smaller than those of the Clinton Administration, which designated 115 million acres of critical habitat for 50 endangered species. In contrast, the Interior Department under President George W. Bush has designated just 40 million acres for 195 species.[25] The Clinton Administration reduced the size of 64 percent of the critical-habitat proposals of the Fish and Wildlife Service (FWS), and the average size of reduction was 9 percent. The Bush Administration has reduced the size of 92 percent of FWS proposals; the average reduction was 76 percent. Suffering most under the Bush directives were Hawaiian plants (99 percent were reduced, average size reduction was 89 percent) and Texas invertebrates (100 percent were reduced, average size reduction was 89 percent). Critical habitat for the spectacled eider in Alaska was cut by 22.7 million acres. Eastern states lost 2.0 million acres of protection for the piping plover.

FWS biologists in the Southwest were ordered to slash 8.9 million acres out of its proposal for the Mexican spotted owl's critical habitat. The result was a designation that excluded 95 percent of all known owls, 80 percent of owl habitat, and virtually all timber areas sought after by the timber industry. A FWS biologist objected that "the designation would make no biological sense if the [U.S. Forest Service land] was excluded since these lands are the most essential for the owl." Two years later a federal court in Arizona agreed, calling the designation "nonsensical"; the agency's final rule was ultimately upheld.[26] Habitat protection for the San Bernardino kangaroo rat in California was slashed by 40 percent, even though four scientific peer reviewers warned that the proposal must be expanded. Scientific peer reviewers also recommended an expansion of critical habitat for the Riverside fairy shrimp.[27] In all, the Bush Administration removed 42 million acres of critical habitat from the FWS's proposed designations.

Grazing on Public Lands

Grazing on public land has long been identified as a serious threat to biodiversity, but the long tradition of masking the social costs of this activity through subsidies continues. Grazing fees for cattle on national forest and Bureau of Land Management lands have been lowered, even though the program continues to run a budget deficit.

A recent study by the University of Colorado shows that grazing has degraded the environment and produced significant dust, which has numerous ecological impacts. Grazing on public land has long been questioned as economically irrational.[28] Its persistence is a tribute to the cowboy myth and the disproportionate political influence enjoyed by western states with comparatively small populations.

Manipulation of Science

The manipulation of scientific reports by political appointees at the Interior Department has threatened species protection. In 2006, the Union of Concerned Scientists asked the Fish and Wildlife Service's southwest regional director to rescind a policy that prohibited FWS biologists from considering the use of genetic information to maximize the diversity of existing populations of endangered species. It is common practice in captive breeding programs to use genetic information to determine the most suitable management of remnant populations and to ensure a higher rate of survival because of the genetic diversity.[29] In 2007, the assistant secretary of the office of Fish, Wildlife and Parks, which administers the ESA, was forced to resign after it was revealed that she used her position to aggressively compromise protection of endangered species by rewriting scientific reports, browbeating FWS employees, and colluding with industry lawyers to generate lawsuits against the FWS.[30]

The Judiciary

The judiciary continues to play an important, albeit limited, role in biodiversity conservation. Biodiversity issues come to the courts after an administrative agency has taken a decision alleged to compromise the objective. Courts cannot reconsider the merits of an agency's decision. The judicial role is limited to three important policing functions. First, a court can ensure that the agency has correctly interpreted the legislative language it is acting pursuant to. In theory, construing statutory language is an exclusively judicial function, but courts accord varying degrees of deference to an agency's construction of its authority.[31] The second function is to test agency regulations against legislative mandates to ensure that the regulation is authorized and consistent with the statute. The third function is to determine if an agency's explanation is logical and follows from the available evidence. The following discussion describes some of the more important cases that have come before the courts in which administrative regulations were used to unravel previous biodiversity conservation initiatives.

Federal circuit courts hear many challenges under the ESA, NEPA or the federal land use planning statutes alleging that biodiversity protection is inadequate. In general, courts have only been willing to police federal agencies when they have deliberately undermined the statutory mandates. Courts have generally deferred to the agencies on science-based questions of protection methodology. These cases generally involve a mix of the first and second judicial functions mentioned above, i.e., to review an agency's construction of a statute and to test an agency's regulations against a legislative mandate. Cases in the first category increased as the George W. Bush Administration became bolder in issuing public land regulations that attempted to eliminate environmental protection standards that had been in place, with varying decrees, since the 1970s. A Ninth Circuit opinion held that a FWS rule that defined critical habitat destruction as changes that would "appreciably diminish" its value for species survival and recovery was inconsistent with the ESA's mandate to conserve species.[32] Other opinions include the invalidation of a Biological Opinion that postponed for 8 to 10 years the guarantee of adequate Coho salmon protection flows,[33] the adoption of grazer-sponsored grazing rules that threatened species protection,[34] and a Habitat Conservation

Plan that required but had not secured the participation of several cities.[35] The Forest Service's abandonment of planning guidelines in place since 1982 has also been invalidated.[36] In contrast, the courts generally defer to the debatable economic and scientific methodologies used to make decisions. Courts have generally deferred to the FWS's presumption that critical habitat designations will not impose additional economic costs,[37] and the agency's use of habitat proxies rather than on-the-ground species counts to determine jeopardy.[38]

The Supreme Court's role is simpler to define. Commentators have observed that the Court has been generally indifferent or hostile to environmental issues, and its opinions that involve biodiversity conservation generally follow this trend, but with one limited exception. The ever-controversial issue of what constitutes a wetland reached the Court for the third time in 2006. A split Court (4-1-4) held in *Rapanos v. United States* that only wetlands with a continuous surface connection to navigable waters are subject to federal jurisdiction.[39] Justice Kennedy's solo concurring opinion proposed a more functional standard closer to the position of the four dissenters. Some lower courts followed the Kennedy concurrence,[40] as did the first proposed Environmental Protection Agency/Army Corps of Engineers joint policy guidance. However, in July 2007 the Administration proposed a narrow, exclusionary definition of a wetland,[41] adding a new constraint on an already ecologically dysfunctional program. In the 2007 term, another divided (5-4) Court held in *National Association of Home Builders v. Defenders of Wildlife* that an EPA transfer of Clean Water Act authority to a state did not trigger ESA consultation even though the FWS was concerned that there would be an increase in discharge permits that would potentially harm listed species by promoting more intense development in their remaining habitats.[42] *Massachusetts v. EPA* is the limited exception to the Court's anti-environmental tradition.[43] In a 5-4 decision the Court upheld the right of Massachusetts to sue the EPA for failing to regulate automobile greenhouse gas emissions and decided that the EPA had the power to regulate emissions. The majority's ringing endorsement of the dangers posed by global warming suggests that states may have standing to challenge a wide range of federal inactions that include threats to a state's biodiversity.

State, Local, and Private Protection

Biodiversity conservation requires large land reserves to serve as habitat for species. Thus, state and local governments have a crucial role to play in biodiversity conservation because the control of land rests with the states. The federal government can only manage its retained public lands, but it has the further authority to prevent activities on nonfederal lands that directly interfere with the relevant agency's management objectives. State control is becoming more important as large amounts of private land are withheld from development through the purchase of fee title or conservation easements. This process has largely been unsupervised by any level of government, but much more scrutiny must be devoted to the way in which private land reserves do and can contribute to biodiversity conservation.[44]

State biodiversity conservation laws and programs fall into two strategic categories. First, there are a number of laws that could promote biodiversity conservation but do not necessarily do so in actuality. These range from state wildlife conservation laws to state land use laws that permit the conservation of sensitive areas.[45] The second strategic category is development of programs that directly address the problem of biodiversity conservation. No state has enacted a comprehensive statutory framework for biodiversity conservation. Instead, states have begun to develop conservation strategies that try to use existing statutory authorities and agency structures to produce a new focus. A 2007 survey describes this strategy as "processes [which] vary from planning efforts within government agencies to collaborate planning efforts involving a wide range of partners." The initiatives range "from providing an inventory of state wildlife and habitat requirements, to analyzing laws and policies that could be used to effectuate change . . . ."[46]

In the 1990s, Florida became one of the first states to develop a biodiversity conservation strategy.[47] If actually implemented, it could serve as a model for other states. Florida identified species representative of the state's biodiversity and assessed the adequacy of public lands to protect them. After the inevitable protection gaps were revealed,[48] a strategic habitat map was developed to include the minimum amount of private land necessary to ensure the long-term survival of a majority of the state's biodiversity. The total amount of mapped land came to 13 percent of the state's acreage. In 2001, Florida voters approved Florida Forever, a $3 billion land and water resource acquisition program, and a gap assessment program is being used to guide and monitor land and water purchases. Conservation easements are the primary land acquisition tool. No new state legislation has been passed, and implementation beyond land or easement acquisition depends on local governments complying with the conservation element mandated by the state's weakened growth management act.[49]

Private land acquisition (in fee and through conservation easements) is gaining momentum across the United States. A 2005 survey by the Land Trust Alliance reported that national, state, and local conservation organizations held an amount of land equal to the size of the state of Georgia, some 37 million acres, a 54 percent increase from 2000.[50] The pace of private land conservation is also accelerating; state and local land trust organizations conserved three times as many acres between 2000 and 2005 as they did between 1995 and 2000.[51]

Recommendations

1. The United States should ratify the Convention on Biological Diversity. The Biological Diversity Convention's broad objective is to encourage national biodiversity conservation at large geographic scales, preferably by *in situ* rather than *ex situ* (zoos, for example) conservation, and it requires an integrated ecosystem approach. Ratification alone will not advance biodiversity conservation in the United States because the treaty is weak and the United States can meet its minimal standards. However, ratification will establish biodiversity conservation as an official overarching legal objective in the United States and stimulate the development of a comprehensive national biodiversity conservation strategy. It will also focus attention on effective compliance with the substantive objective.

2. Congress should authorize and adequately fund a national commission on biodiversity conservation. The commission should be charged with three major tasks. The first is to synthesize the existing science of biodiversity conservation to develop biodiversity measurements and conservation indices so that the status of biodiversity can be tracked and the efficacy of programs evaluated. The second function would be to survey the existing legal mandates of the major federal land management and regulatory agencies to determine how well they promote biodiversity conservation and what revisions are required to enable them to conserve biodiversity to the maximum extent possible consistent with due process and the sustainable use of natural resources. All of the current laws were enacted before biodiversity conservation emerged as a legislative objective and long before the Rio Summit of 1992, and they need to be revised to provide federal land management agencies with express biodiversity conservation mandates and duties.[52] This will be difficult, but there are precedents, such as the 1970 report of the Public Land Law Review Commission[53] and the 1973 report of the National Water Commission,[54] both of which stimulated new legislative and policy approaches to resource management.

3. The role of private land acquisition in biodiversity conservation should be assessed. Rather than just count the number of acres added to private conservation, we need to measure the amount of biodiversity conserved on these lands and understand how private reserves relate to state and federal public land reserves.[55] One pressing question is the impact of global climate change on land private reservations. Much land was purchased on the assumption it would conserve a specific ecosystem, but components of the system may disappear. National conservation organizations are beginning to reassess their land holding and acquisition policies in light of projected species migration patterns.

4. The United States should create a Biological Survey equal to the U.S. Geological Survey. The purpose of the new agency would be to inventory the nation's biodiversity heritage and to provide the necessary scientific support for the establishment of biodiversity indices and conservation performance standards. Effective conservation will not be possible until we have substantive criteria to establish conservation goals and performance measures. Too often, major biodiversity conservation initiatives such as the California Bay Delta Process have been long on process and short on substance. The creation of a Biodiversity Survey should be complemented by providing support to state land-grant universities for biodiversity conservation research, in order to bring such research into parity with agricultural research.

5. Although biodiversity conservation is primarily a national responsibility, private land stewardship must be recognized and supported. There are many innovative private efforts underway, and these must be encouraged by appropriate public incentives.[56] A guideline is provided by the 2005 OECD (Organisation for Economic Co-operation and Development) environmental performance review of the United States, which recommended further integration of nature protection into forestry and agricultural practices, the expansion of incentives for voluntary wildlife cooperation, the sharing of knowledge among the major sources of data about the state of eco-

systems, and better information on the effectiveness of different policy responses.[57]

Conclusion

Effective biodiversity conservation remains an aspiration rather
than a reality in the United States. The need to take more aggressive
steps to conserve our legacy has taken on a greater urgency as we begin to focus on the landscape and ecosystem changes that may result
from global climate change. There are many promising public and private initiatives, especially at the local level, but these need to be integrated into a larger national strategy.

ENDNOTES

1. MILLENNIUM ECOSYSTEM ASSESSMENT, ECOSYSTEMS AND HUMAN WELL-BEING: BIODIVERSITY SYNTHESIS 46 (2005).

2. A 2004 presidential order emphasizes state, local government, tribal, and private partnerships for cooperative conservation measures. *See* Exec. Order No. 13352, 69 Fed. Reg. 52989 (Aug. 30, 2004) ("Facilitation of Cooperative Conservation").

3. U.S. Forest Service, Department of Agriculture, National Forest System Land and Resource Management Planning; Final Rule, 70 Fed. Reg. 1023 (2005). It is hard to know how to interpret Forest Service assessments of the state of the nation's private and public forests. U.S. DEP'T OF AGRIC., FOREST SERV., SUSTAINABILITY ASSESSMENT HIGHLIGHTS FOR THE NORTHERN UNITED STATES vii concludes that the "majority of native plants and animals evaluated in the Northern United States are doing well," at the same time that species are being restricted to portions of their former ranges, some species are presumed extinct, and forests are being degraded by exotic flora and fauna.

4. In 2006, President Bush invoked the Antiquities Act of 1906, 16 U.S.C. §431, to create the Northwestern Hawaiian Islands Marine National Monument. The Monument expands on the efforts of President Clinton and is the largest protected marine area in the world.

5. WORLD COMM'N ON ENV'T & DEV., OUR COMMON FUTURE, 43 (1987). The report is informally known as the Brundtland Report for the chair, Gro Harlem Brundtland.

6. An effort to evaluate the success of the ESA concluded that it may be "several decades before we can fully assess the success of the Endangered Species Act in preventing the loss of species on this planet." J. Michael Scott et al., *By the Numbers, in* THE ENDANGERED SPECIES ACT AT THIRTY: RENEWING THE PROMISE OF CONSERVATION 16, 35 (Dale D. Gobel et al. eds., 2006).

7. H. JOHN HEINZ III CTR. FOR SCI., ECON. & ENV'T, THE STATE OF THE NATION'S ECOSYSTEMS: MEASURING THE LANDS, WATERS, AND LIVING RESOURCES OF THE UNITED STATES (2002).

8. ORGANISATION FOR ECON. CO-OPERATION & DEV. (OECD), ENVIRONMENTAL PERFORMANCE REVIEWS: UNITED STATES 23 (2007) noted that "[p]articularly at risk are freshwater and andronomous fish . . . ." Review *available at* http://www.oecd.org/dataoecd/7/53/2452410.pdf.

9. Bruce A. Stein et al., PRECIOUS HERITAGE: THE STATUS OF BIODIVERSITY IN THE UNITED STATES (2000).

10. Fred Bosselman, *A Dozen Biodiversity Puzzles*, 12 N.Y.U. ENVTL. L.J. 364, 440-54 (2004).

11. Kevin McCann, *Protecting Biostructure*, 446 NATURE 29 (March 2007).

12. Thomas J. Lovejoy & Lee Hannah, *Global Greenhouse Gas Levels and the Future of Biodiversity, in* CLIMATE CHANGE AND BIODIVERSITY, 387, 390 (2005).

13. NATURAL RESOURCES DEFENSE COUNCIL, WATER MANAGEMENT STRATEGIES TO WEATHER THE EFFECTS OF GLOBAL WARMING 13 (2007).

14. *See* DAVID TACKAS, THE IDEA OF BIODIVERSITY: PHILOSOPHIES IN PARA-
DISE (1996), for an informative history of the construction of the term. A recent United Nations report links biodiversity conservation and ecosystem
services. *See* MILLENNIUM ECOSYSTEM ASSESSMENT, LIVING BEYOND
OUR MEANS: NATURAL ASSETS AND WELL-BEING 12 (2005).

15. The best example of this capture is LIVING BEYOND OUR MEANS, *supra*
note 14. *See also* J.B. RUHL ET AL., THE LAW AND POLICY OF ECOSYSTEM
SERVICES (2007); Roundtable, *Law and Policy for Ecosystem Services*, 37
ELR 10573 (July 2007).

16. John B. Loomis, *Can Environmental Valuation Techniques Aid Ecological
Economics and Wildlife Conservation?*, 28 WATER RES. BULL. 52 (2000).

17. *E.g.*, Jamison E. Colburn, *Habitat and Humanity: Public Land Law in the
Age of Ecology*, 39 ARIZ. ST. U. L.J. 145 (2007).

18. Farm Security and Rural Investment Act of 2002 (Farm Bill), Pub. L. No.
107-171, 116 Stat. 134 (2002), at §2502.

19. *See* U.S. Dep't of Agric., Natural Res. Conservation Serv., Wildlife Habitat
Incentives Program, Final Rule, codified at 7 C.F.R. Part 636; *see also* discussion of rule *available at* www.nrcs.usda.gov/programs/farmbill/1996/
WHIPfinal.html. The current WHIP program grew out of the 1985 Conservation Reserve Program of the Food Security Act, 16 U.S.C. §§3831 et seq.

20. J.B. RUHL ET AL., *supra* note 15, at 192.

21. The Safe, Accountable, Flexible, Efficient Transportation Equity Act of
2005, Pub. L. No. 109-59, 119 Stat. 1144 (2005) (alternative selection and
judicial review limited).

22. Holly D. Doremus & A. Dan Tarlock, *Fish, Farms, and the Clash of Cultures in the Klamath Basin*, 30 ECOLOGY L.Q. 279 (2003).

23. Rebecca Claren, *Inside the Secretive Plan to Gut the Endangered Species
Act*, SALON.COM, Mar. 27, 2007, *available at* www.salon.com/news/
feature/2007/03/27/endangered_species/index.html.

24. While a species must be listed if the science establishes that it is at risk, critical habitat need only be designated "to the maximum extent prudent and
determinable." 16 U.S.C. §1533(a)(3).

25. *See* Craig Welch, *Bush Switches Nation's Tack on Protecting Species*, SE-
ATTLE TIMES, Sept. 27, 2004, *available at* http://seattletimes.nwsource.
com/html/nationworld/2002047271_bushesa27m.html.

26. Center for Biological Diversity v. Norton, 240 F. Supp. 2d 1090 (D. Ariz.
2003) (calling designation nonsensical). The final rule was upheld in Arizona Cattle Growers Ass'n v. Kempthorne, 2008 WL 435488 (D. Ariz.
2008).

27. EARTH JUSTICE, POLICY FACT SHEET: BUSH ADMINISTRATION ATTACKS
ENDANGERED SPECIES ACT, undated, *available at* www.earthjustice.org/
library/policy_factsheets/CHFactSheet.pdf.

28. *See* http://www.nature.com/ngeo/journal/vaop/ncurrent/abs/ngeo133.
html.

29. Press Release, Union of Concerned Scientists, Scientists Challenge Restrictions on Use of Genetic Studies for Endangered Species Review (Dec.
11, 2006), *available at* http://www.ucsusa.org/scientific_integrity/interference/

endangered-species-genetics.html. *See also* 8 CONSERVATION BIOLOGY 613 (Sept. 1994).

30. Juliet Eilperin, *Bush Appointee Said to Reject Advice on Endangered Species,* WASH. POST, Oct. 30, 2006, at A3, *available at* www.washington post.com/wp-dyn/content/article/2006/10/29/AR2006102900776.html.

31. Chevron U.S.A. v. Natural Res. Defense Council, Inc., 467 U.S. 837 (1984); Babbitt v. Sweet Home Chapter of Communities for a Greater Oregon, 515 U.S. 687 (1995).

32. Gifford Pinchot Task Force v. U.S. Fish & Wildlife Serv., 378 F.3d 1059 (9th Cir. 2004). The Fish and Wildlife Service regulation only required an agency to consult with it, which, as the court noted, requires appreciable diminishment of the habitat *before* any duty to prevent destruction or adverse modification. Thus the regulation "offends the ESA because the ESA was enacted not merely to forestall the extinction of species . . . but to allow a species to recover to the point where it may be delisted."

33. Pacific Coast Fishermen's Ass'n v. U.S. Bureau of Reclamation, 426 F.3d 1082 (9th Cir. 2005). Biological Opinions ("Biops") are the formal determinations of whether a federal action will jeopardize the survival of a listed endangered species. *See generally* HOLLY D. DOREMUS & A. DAN TARLOCK, WATER WARS IN THE KLAMATH BASIN: MACHO LAW, COMBAT BIOLOGY, AND DIRTY POLITICS (2008).

34. Western Watersheds Project v. Kraayenbrink, Slip. Op. CV-05-297-E-BLW (D. Idaho June 8, 2007) (new regulations reach far beyond that prosaic purpose and the Fish and Wildlife Service objected to them because the new regulations "fundamentally change the way BLM lands are managed," and "could have profound impacts on wildlife resources").

35. Nat'l Wildlife Fed'n v. Babbitt, 128 F. Supp. 3d 1274 (E.D. Cal. 2000). The revised plan was upheld in Nat'l Wildlife Fed'n v. Norton, 2005 WL 2175874 (E.D. Cal. 2005).

36. The agency substantially revised the regulations in 2000, but the U.S. Court of Appeals for the Ninth Circuit held that it had violated the National Environmental Policy Act (NEPA) in developing those regulations. Citizens for Better Forestry v. U.S. Dept. of Agric., 341 F.3d 961 (9th Cir. 2003). The Forest Service revised the regulations in 2005, but a federal district court found that in doing so the agency had violated NEPA, the Endangered Species Act, and the Administrative Procedures Act. Citizens for Better Forestry v. U.S. Dept. of Agriculture, 481 F. Supp. 2d 1059 (N.D. Cal. 2007). The court therefore issued a nationwide injunction prohibiting the Forest Service from implementing its 2005 regulations. On April 27, 2007, in response to the court's injunction, the Forest Service issued national direction to all regions to revert to the 2000 regulations, even though these regulations had also been found to be illegal by the Ninth Circuit.

37. Cape Hatteras Access Preservation Alliance v. U.S. Dep't of Interior, 334 F. Supp. 2d 108 (D.D.C. 2004).

38. Gifford Pinchot Task Force v. U.S. Fish & Wildlife Service, 378 F.3d 1059, 1066-67 (9th Cir. 2004).

39. Rapanos v. United States, 547 U.S. 715 (2006).

40. United States v. Johnston, 437 F.3d 157 (1st Cir. 2006).

41. John M. Broder, *After Lobbying, Wetlands Rules Are Narrowed*, N.Y. TIMES, July 5, 2007, at 1. EPA's guidance for its Clean Water Act jurisdiction in the wake of *Rapanos, supra* note 39, can be found at www.epa. gov.owow/wetlands/pdf/RapanosGuidelines6507.pdf.

42. Nat'l Ass'n of Home Builders v. Defenders of Wildlife, 127 S. Ct. 2518 (2007).

43. Massachusetts v. EPA, 549 U.S. 497 (2007).

44. *See* Jamison E. Colburn, *Localisms Ecology: Protecting Habitat in the Suburban Nation*, 33 ECOLOGY L.Q. 945 (2006).

45. *See* ENVTL. L. INST. & DEFENDERS OF WILDLIFE, PLANNING FOR BIODIVERSITY: AUTHORITIES IN STATE LAND USE LAWS (2003); BIODIVERSITY CONSERVATION HANDBOOK; STATE, LOCAL & PRIVATE PROTECTION OF BIOLOGICAL DIVERSITY (Robert B. McKinistry et al. eds., 2006).

46. Susan George, *The State of the States: An Overview of State Biodiversity Programs*, 37 ELR 10631, 10633 (Aug. 2007).

47. *See* Closing the Gaps in Florida's Wildlife Habitat Conservation System: Recommendations to Meet Minimum Conservation Goals for Declining Wildlife Species (1994), *available at* www.biodiversitypartners.org/state/fl/gaps.shtml.

48. *Id.*

49. FLA. STAT. ANN. §163.3177[6][d].

50. LAND TRUST ALLIANCE, NATIONAL LAND TRUST CENSUS REPORT 3 (2005).

51. *Id.*

52. Jamison E. Colburn, *The Indignity of Federal Wildlife Law*, 57 ALA. L. REV. 417 (2005), is a thoughtful effort to test the teaching of modern conservation biology against the law of public land management.

53. PUBLIC LAND LAW REVIEW COMM'N, ONE THIRD OF THE NATION'S LAND: A REPORT TO THE PRESIDENT AND TO CONGRESS (1970).

54. NAT'L WATER COMM'N, WATER POLICIES FOR THE FUTURE (1973).

55. *See* Symposium, *Private Property and Nature Conservation: Land Ownership in the 21st Century*, 26 J. LAND RES. & ENVTL. L. 1-81 (2005); and Jamison E. Colburn, *Bioregional Conservation May Mean Taking Habitat*, 37 ENVTL. L. 249 (2007), articulating the case for monitoring more closely the consequences of private conservation land and easement acquisition. SALLY K. FAIRFAX & DARK GUENZLER, CONSERVATION TRUSTS (2001), is a useful survey of the different forms of private land preservation and their strengths and weaknesses.

56. *See* Barton H. Thompson Jr., *The Endangered Species Act: A Case Study in Takings & Incentives*, 49 STAN. L. REV. 305 (1997).

57. OECD, ENVIRONMENTAL PERFORMANCE REVIEWS: UNITED STATES, *supra* note 8, at 24.

Chapter 19

Sustainable Forestry: Moving From Concept to Consistent Practice

Federico Cheever and Ward J. Scott

Forests cover roughly one-third of the United States. Of the 2.3 billion acres in the nation (including Alaska),[1] 651 million acres (28.8 percent) are "forest use" lands,[2] and 98 million acres (4.5 percent) are forest land in parks and other protective designations.[3] Any significant progress toward sustainable land use will therefore require progress toward sustainable forest management.

While the population of the United States more than doubled between 1929 and 2000, the aggregate area of forest land remained relatively stable through that period.[4] This does not mean that the forest mosaic of 2008 looks like the forest mosaic of 1929. Dramatic increases in second-growth eastern woodlands in rural areas and southeastern pine plantations[5] have replaced the woodlands destroyed by the expansion of the nation's suburbs.[6]

The nature and the extent of the U.S. forest mosaic will continue to change in the decades to come, dramatically affecting the nation's ability to preserve native ecosystems, soils, and watersheds; to sequester carbon from the atmosphere; and to maintain a stable forest products industry. Sustainable forest management provides the strongest foundation for shaping that future change in positive ways.

For two reasons, it is difficult to gauge the progress in the United States toward a structure of law that supports (much less requires) sustainable practices in forest management: The notion of sustainability itself is difficult to define, and the concept has not been incorporated directly into any significant forestry law. Entities at every level of government and in the private sector have declared their commitment to the concept of sustainable forest management. Although encouraging, the full significance of these declarations remains unclear.

This chapter discusses recent developments in sustainable forest management law in the United States. It begins by discussing the relatively new concept of "sustainable forest management." The chapter then examines sustainability practices in the three types of forests that, for the most part, make up the nation's forested areas: private forests, state forests, and federally controlled forests. These three ownership regimes are subject to discrete and largely unconnected regulatory structures. The chapter deals with each ownership regime in turn.

Sustainable Forest Management

Two broad concepts dominate the field of forestry management. The relatively new concept of *sustainable forest management*, which came to the fore at the Rio Earth Summit in 1992, exists in an unsettled relationship with its century-old forebear, *sustained yield* forestry. The federal Multiple Use-Sustained Yield Act of 1960, which still governs activities on the 192-million-acre National Forest System,[7] defines "sustained yield of the several products and services" as "the achievement and maintenance in perpetuity of a high-level annual or regular periodic output of the various renewable resources of the national forests without impairment of the productivity of the land."[8] On the other hand, the influential U.N. Brundtland Commission Report of 1987 observed that sustainable development "implies meeting the needs of the present without compromising the ability of future generations to meet their own needs."[9] The U.S. Department of Agriculture's *National Report on Sustainable Forests—2003* asserts that "sustainability should be viewed as more of a journey than a destination."[10]

Both sustained yield forestry and sustainable forest management emphasize the use of resources in a way that preserves their utility for future generations. To the degree that there is a difference between the two approaches, it is in the range of the resource and outputs that are to be preserved for future generations. The founding documents of sustained yield forestry in the United States, including the Forest Service Organic Act of 1897, consider only timber, range, and watershed as resources to be maintained in perpetuity. The 1960 Multiple Use-Sustained Yield Act intentionally broadens that list of relevant resources to include "outdoor recreation, range, timber, watershed, and wildlife and fish purposes."[11] The international process initiated at the Rio Earth Summit in 1992 embraces a much broader set of resources and resource indicators.

In a presidential directive in November 1993, President William Clinton committed the United States to the goal of sustainable forest management.[12] While that document shied away from defining "sustainable" forestry, it did indicate that "[o]ur national objectives are that: our nation's forest should be healthy and productive; the growth of our timber should exceed harvest; and our forests should be reservoirs of biological diversity and carbon."[13]

Building on the Forest Principles adopted at the 1992 Earth Summit, various countries began to meet to consider what sustainable forestry really meant. The United States participated in one post-Rio discussion: the Montreal Process in 1995. The Montreal Process member countries—Argentina, Australia, Canada, Chile, China, Japan, the Republic of Korea, Mexico, New Zealand, the Russian Federation, the United States, and Uruguay, which together represent about 90 percent of the world's temperate and boreal forests[14]—reached a nonbinding agreement identifying "criteria" and "indicators" for the conservation and sustainable management of temperate and boreal forests. This "Santiago Declaration" identified seven criteria and 67 indicators. The seven criteria were: "Conservation of Biological Diversity," "Maintenance of Productive Capacity of Forest Ecosystems," "Maintenance of Forest Ecosystem Health and Vitality," "Maintenance of Soil and Water Resources," "Maintenance of Forest Contribution to Global Carbon Cycles," "Maintenance and Enhancement of Long-term Multiple Socio-Economic Benefits to Meet the Needs of Societies," and "Legal, Institutional, and Economic Framework; Capacity to Conduct and Apply Research and Development for Forest Conservation and Sustainable Management."

Because the concept of sustainable forest management implies active management, it is important to make a distinction between "forest use lands," where commercial logging occurs and where we can evaluate a management process, and forested lands that are protected but not actively managed. While protected lands cannot, in a strict sense, be subject to sustainable forest management, the qualities they preserve may render overall forest management more sustainable. The presence of protected forest lands in a landscape may significantly further *all* of the seven Montreal Process criteria.

Private Forest Land

Private forests make up 57.6 percent of the forest area of the United States.[15] Three forces are moving private forest management toward more sustainable practices: state and federal forestry laws, the continued increase of land conservation transactions on private forest land, and the growth in forest product certification.

Several states have adopted laws addressing forestry practices on private lands. Largely inspired by concerns surrounding timber production, these laws attempt to promote principles of sustainability, such as forest regeneration, sustained timber production, and the protection of forest resources, including wildlife habitat, soil and water quality, and the recreation and aesthetic value of forested areas.[16] The actions by state governments take many forms, including regulation, incentives, and planning mandates. The administration and design of each program varies greatly. Not surprisingly, the diverse actions taken by state and local governments have seen mixed success and varying responses from landowners and other interested stakeholders throughout the country.[17]

Private forestry regulation has roots in common law trespass and nuisance. It is an exercise of the traditional police power. The authority to regulate activities on private land is limited by the Takings Clause of the Fifth Amendment to the United States Constitution and by various similar clauses in state constitutional and statutory law.[18] Counties and municipalities, often delegated with zoning authority to control land use in forested areas, may be preempted from interfering with timber operations when states have expressly reserved authority to regulate the industry.[19]

State forestry regulations began to appear in the early 1970s, and were initially adopted by many western states.[20] Several states have endeavored to promote sustainable forestry practices, including ensuring regeneration after harvest,[21] protecting watercourses and soil,[22] promoting responsible road construction and maintenance,[23] and limiting the practice of clear-cutting.[24] Some argue these regulations may produce negative effects for sustainability because landowners overburdened by regulations may abandon forestry altogether and convert their land to higher impact, less-regulated uses.[25]

State legislatures have also chosen to promote sustainable forestry practices by providing landowners with financial incentives, usually in the form of tax advantages, when they practice measures that promote the health of the forests. Several forms of legislation are currently in place, extending tax breaks for a variety of conservation-oriented actions on private land.[26] These incentives give landowners reason to come to the government, rather than giving them a reason to avoid interaction, as strict regulatory schemes sometimes do.[27] A number of states have also enacted voluntary programs for landowners who wish to protect land.[28] These programs tend to enjoy higher success when compliance is relatively convenient and landowners believe that participation is worthwhile.[29]

The United States has witnessed an historically unprecedented explosion in the amount of land protected by land conservation transactions. From a handful of land trusts (nonprofit organizations committed to conservation) in 1960 that protected a few acres of land, the movement has grown to more than 1,800 land trusts nationwide[30] protecting an area roughly the size of Georgia. According to the 2005 National Land Trust Census Report prepared by the Land Trust Alliance (LTA), the total number of acres conserved by local, state, and national land trusts increased by 54 percent since 2000 and now totals 37 million acres.[31] This includes both land purchased in fee simple by land trusts and land subject to conservation easement (a negative servitude protecting conservation values). All 50 states now authorize conservation easements by statute.

Federal and state tax benefits encourage land trust acquisition of property rights for preservation. The Internal Revenue Code authorizes a charitable tax deduction for land owners who grant away property, including perpetual conservation easements,[32] to land trusts. A number of states provide additional deductions and tax credits.[33] In addition, both state and federal governments provide direct funding grants for private, nonprofit purchases of lands for conservation.

It is difficult to determine how much of the land protected by land trusts exists as forest land or how well protected that forest may be. Conservation easements can protect traditional agricultural landscapes (ranches and farms) as well as natural ones. Land trusts can use their properties to preserve and encourage historically significant uses as well as functioning biological communities. Indirect evidence suggests the amount of forest conserved is large and the protections significant. In its 2003 National Land Trust Census, the LTA asked land trusts to identify the "primary purpose" of their land protection. The largest number indicated "habitat for plants and wildlife." A significant number identified the preservation of "working forests" as a primary purpose. Of the land conserved by state and local land trusts, 52 percent is in the Northeast, Southeast, and Mid-Atlantic states, which are naturally forested areas; another 44 percent is in the West, including the heavily forested Pacific Northwest.

In 2003, researchers at Virginia Tech surveyed both public and private conservation organizations. The survey identified more than 355 conservation organizations and 16 state agencies holding at least 3,598 forest land conservation easements.[34] Most contained specific limitations on timber management practices. However, the limitations differed from organization to organization and easement to easement.

In 2003, Congress passed the Healthy Forest Restoration Act.[35] Enacted in the wake of the catastrophic fire seasons of 2000 and 2002, the Act was intended primarily to reduce public land wildfire risk, but it also included a "healthy forest reserves" program "to promote the recovery of threatened and endangered species . . . to improve biodiversity; and . . . to enhance carbon sequestration."[36] Under the terms of the law, the Secretaries of the Interior and Agriculture "shall describe and define forest ecosystems that are eligible for enrollment in the healthy forests reserve program." Eligible lands include "private land the enrollment of which will restore, enhance, or otherwise measurably increase the likelihood of recovery of a species listed as endangered or threatened," and "private land the enrollment of which will restore, enhance, or otherwise measurably improve the well-being of species that are candidates for such listing, State-listed species, or special concern species."[37] Additional considerations include the protection of lands to "improve biological diversity" and "increase carbon sequestration."[38] Clearly, the drafters of this legislation were aware of the Montreal Process criteria. The statute provides that private landowners must be willing, and the total acreage of the reserve is limited to 2 million acres.[39] The stated values are preserved through term easements not to exceed 99 years.[40] Initially, Congress authorized $25 million to support the reserve program.[41] The program is administered by the Natural Resources Conservation Service in the Department of the Interior.[42]

As part of the Healthy Forests Restoration Act, Congress also established the Watershed Forestry Assistance Program to assist state foresters to expand their capacity to address watershed protection issues on private forest land.[43] Among the program's findings is that "there has been a dramatic shift in public attitudes and perceptions about forest management, particularly in the understanding and practice of sustainable forest management."[44] The Act authorizes $15 million for the program for each fiscal year from 2004 to 2008.[45]

Other federal incentives for sustainable management of private forests arise out of the Endangered Species Act (ESA) of 1973. Among other things, the ESA makes it illegal for "any person" within the jurisdiction of the United States to "take" any member of any endangered species of fish or wildlife.[46] The United States Fish and Wildlife Service (FWS) has extended similar protections to threatened species by regulation.[47] Endangered plants are protected under a more complicated and less effective provision.[48]

The ESA defines the word "take" to include "harm" to species members. The FWS 1981 regulatory definition of "harm" includes "significant habitat modification or degradation where it actually kills or injures wildlife by significantly impairing essential behavioral patterns, including breeding, feeding or sheltering."[49] Accordingly, a private landowner who destroys essential habitat for an endangered or threatened species has generally violated federal law. Since 1982, the FWS has operated a series of programs designed to mitigate the effect of the take prohibition on private landowners.

Private parties who wish to take protected species on private land may apply for an incidental take permit. To obtain such a permit they must submit what is generally known as a "habitat conservation plan" to the FWS. The agency will issue the incidental take permit if "the taking will be incidental" (in other words, not the purpose of the action); "the applicant will, to the maximum extent practicable, minimize and mitigate the impacts of such taking"; "the applicant will ensure that adequate funding for the plan will be provided"; and "the taking will not appreciably reduce the likelihood of the survival and recovery of the species in the wild."

Habitat conservation plans have been prepared for a variety of forest species, encouraging, indirectly, sustainable forestry practices.[50] In order to promote habitat stewardship on private land, the FWS has developed its system of Safe Harbor Agreements (SHAs) and Candidate Conservation Agreements with Assurances (CCAAs) to protect landowners who engage in conservation efforts on their property from increased ESA regulation. Generally, both types of agreements attempt to encourage, rather than require, private landowners to conduct activities that benefit the status of listed and potentially listed species. SHAs and CCAAs must be published in the Federal Register, are subject to public notice, and must comply with the National Environmental Policy Act (NEPA) and other federal laws.[51]

An SHA applies to land inhabited (or potentially inhabited) by species that have already been designated as "threatened or endangered" under the ESA. The agreements provide "assurances from the Services that additional conservation measures will not be required and additional land, water, or resource use restrictions will not be imposed should the covered species become more numerous as a result of the property owners' actions."[52] FWS determines an appropriate duration for each agreement after considering "the duration of the planned activities, as well as the positive and negative effects associated with permits of the proposed duration on covered species, including the extent to which the conservation activities included in the Safe Harbor Agreement will enhance the survival and contribute to the recovery of listed species included in the permit."[53]

A CCAA applies to species that may be candidates for protection under the ESA and attempts to encourage private landowners to mitigate "threats to the covered species so as to nullify the need to list them as threatened or endangered under the Act."[54] Owners agree to protect and enhance existing populations and habitats of candidate species; in return, the government agrees not to increase the level of ESA regulation on the property for the duration of the agreement, including circumstances where the species may become listed. As with an SHA, an approved applicant will receive an "enhancement of survival" permit, allowing for incidental takings and habitat modification at levels that are specified in the CCAA.[55]

Forest management certification is a nongovernmental system to encourage sustainable forestry in the United States. As Benjamin Cashore, Graeme Auld, and Deanna Newsom put it in a 2003 journal article:

> These "non-state market driven" governance regimes locate their authority not from the state, but from the domestic and global marketplace. Companies all along a sector's production chain are cajoled, enticed, and encouraged by non-governmental organizations to support and adhere to the rules established by these certification systems.[56]

Forest managers, timber processors, and timber retailers participate in certification processes in the hope of gaining a larger market share and/or premium prices associated with certified goods.

In 1989, the Rainforest Alliance established its SmartWood forest certification program. Originally, forest certification groups focused primarily on tropical deforestation. In 1993, a number of international organizations, notably the World Wide Fund for Nature (WWF), launched the Forest Stewardship Council (FSC), an international forest certification entity. Interestingly, since 1941 the United States has had an independent forest certification entity, the American Tree Farm System (ATFS). However, as both its founding date and name would suggest, the ATFS is more concerned with sustained yield and less with sustainability.

According to Cashore, Auld, and Newsom, the growth of forest certification in the United States has been a struggle between the transnational FSC certification system and a U.S.-based industry sponsored program, the American Forest and Paper Association's Sustainable Forestry Initiative (SFI). FSC emphasizes community relations, workers' rights, and the preservation of old growth, as well as more traditional forestry concepts. SFI, on the other hand, emphasizes organizational procedures and flexible performance guidelines.[57]

As of 2005, FSC claimed to have certified 22 million acres of forest land in the United States.[58] SFI claims to have certified 54 million acres of forest in the United States.[59] Roughly 76 million acres of the 651 million acres of forest use lands in the United States (11 percent) are certified by either FSC or SFI. As of 2006, roughly 5 percent of forest land in the northern Appalachians (3.9 million acres) was certified by the FSC.[60]

As yet, the United States has not developed a significant specialty retail market for certified wood products, as it has for organic food.[61] The demand for certified wood products comes from large corporations "that wish to avoid the risk of damaging their brand image"[62] and for construction that meets the Leadership in Energy and Environmental Design (LEED) standards. The LEED system evaluates new construction on a scale of 69 points; one point is awarded for using FSC certified wood.[63]

As Michael Washburn and Nadine Block have pointed out,[64] it is difficult to equate forest certification with the Montreal Process Criteria and Indicators. Certification criteria are, by their very nature, prescriptive—focusing on what forest managers should do in the future—while Montreal Process criteria and indicators are descriptive—focusing on the state of the forest land.[65]

In December 2005, the Rainforest Alliance endeavored to bring together two of the primary sustainability influences on private forest
land in the United States. In *A Guide to Forest Stewardship Council
Certification for Land Trusts*, the Alliance presents the virtues of FSC
certification for private land trusts holding title to or conservation
easements on working forest land.

State Forest Land

According to the National Association of State Foresters (NASF),
more than 63 million acres of forest land in the United States (8 percent) are owned by states,[66] with Alaska, Florida, Idaho, Michigan,
Minnesota, New York, Pennsylvania, Utah, and Washington each
owning more than a million acres of forest land within their respective
borders. In 1997, the NASF, representing state foresters in all 50
states, adopted a resolution endorsing sustainable forestry and adopting the Montreal Process Criteria and Indicators.[67]

While many state forests are managed primarily for recreation or
timber production, in the past few years a significant amount of state
forest land has been certified by the FSC, the SFI, or both. Sustainable
Forest Certification is swiftly becoming a significant force promoting
better forest practices on state land. At least three state forest systems—the 4.4 million acre Minnesota state-administered forest
lands,[68] the 158,000-acre Tennessee state forests, and the 500,000 acre
Wisconsin state forests—have, through independent audits, obtained
both FSC and SFI certification.[69] Washington State has obtained SFI
certification for its Forested Trust Lands and is seeking FSC certification for some of those lands.[70] The 2.1-million-acre Pennsylvania
state forest system and 3.9-million-acre Michigan state forest system
have obtained FSC certification.[71]

In 2006, the NASF and the Society of American Foresters (SAF)
agreed to establish a task force to evaluate the implications of a national policy or legislation for sustainable forest management. The organizations recognized that there is currently no formal national policy in support of sustainable forests.[72] In a resolution, NASF noted
that a "national policy for sustainable forests" should "clarify and enhance the roles of federal, state, and local governments, promoting regional collaboration and joint planning"; "respect the critical role of
private forest ownership while striving to conserve, in a fair and equitable manner, the public benefits that private forests provide"; "pro-

mote new and creative ways to provide education, research and technical assistance to address trends in forest ownership, management and investment"; "lead to a revision of forest and tax legislation, ensuring keeping forests as forests is both economically competitive with selling land for development, and forest landowners are compensated for the clean water, wildlife habitat and other public values they provide"; and "recognize the global influences that impact U.S. forests."[73]

Federal Forest Land

The national forests include 192 million acres of the roughly 749 million acres of forest land in the United States (roughly 25 percent). Almost every official activity in the national forests is subject to a variety of federal laws. Few of these laws have anything to do with sustainable forest management, and many embody the principle of sustained yield. Still, recent legislation and agency action suggests the National Forest System is incorporating sustainable forest management into its policymaking.

The summer of 2002 was a bad season for wildfires on federal lands: 6.3 million acres burned, 2,100 homes were destroyed, and 21 people died.[74] On December 3, 2003, President Bush signed into law the Healthy Forests Restoration Act of 2003.[75] While the law's primary purpose is to reduce the threat of destructive wildfires, it is also the most extensive piece of forestry legislation passed since the federal government committed itself to sustainable forest management in 1993. The stated purpose of the law is, among other things, "to protect, restore, and enhance forest ecosystem components . . . to promote the recovery of threatened and endangered species; . . . to improve biological diversity; and . . . to enhance productivity and carbon sequestration. . . ."[76]

Of the 192 million acres of forest within our National Forest System, approximately 58.5 million acres are roadless.[77] This distinction has played a major role in the management of our nation's forests ever since the automobile became a staple of American life.[78] The Forest Service had identified and preserved, as primitive areas, roadless stretches within the Forest System long before the passage of the Wilderness Act in 1964. However, the Wilderness Act and subsequent laws require that agencies inventory and protect roadless lands that are eligible for congressional designation as wilderness areas.[79]

Recognizing roadless areas as a unique resource within the National Forest System, in 1999 President Clinton directed the Forest Service to "provide appropriate long-term protection for most or all of these currently inventoried roadless areas."[80] The Forest Service issued the final 2001 Roadless Rule on January 12, 2001, eight days before Clinton was to leave office. The rule established prohibitions on road construction, road reconstruction, and timber harvest in designated roadless areas, while recognizing seven exceptions to an outright ban.[81] In presenting the Roadless Rule, President Clinton emphasized that the forests are a system, facilitating multiple uses, and that preserving roadless areas does not necessarily disrupt the balance of uses. In his remarks, he stated that:

> Ultimately, this is about preserving the land which the American people own for the American people that are not around yet, about safeguarding our magnificent open spaces, because not everyone can travel to the great places of the world, but everyone can enjoy the majesty of our great forests. Today we free the lands so that they will remain unspoiled by bulldozers, undisturbed by chainsaws, and untouched for our children. Preserving roadless areas puts America on the right road for the future, *the responsible path of sustainable development.*[82]

On January 20, 2001, the day of President George W. Bush's inauguration, the White House directed all executive agencies to delay the implementation of last-minute Clinton-era regulations. Citing multiple concerns among the affected states and various legal challenges to the 2001 Roadless Rule, the Forest Service embarked on a new rulemaking process for the management of roadless areas on federal lands.[83] The resulting 2005 Petition Rule allows the "governor of any State or territory that contains National Forest System lands" to "petition the Secretary of Agriculture to promulgate regulations establishing management requirements for all or any portion of National Forest System inventoried roadless areas within that State or territory."[84] The language of the 2005 Petition Rule contains no guidance as to what types of "management requirements" are appropriate for these areas. Although governors may request regulations that promote sustainable forestry and reflect the criteria of the Montreal Process, the ultimate decision of which roadless areas are to be preserved, as well as what protections will be put in place, remains with the Secretary and the Forest Service.

In 2006, U.S. Magistrate Judge Elizabeth Laporte of the Northern District of California invalidated the 2005 Petition Rule on the ground that the Forest Service had violated NEPA in promulgating it.[85] Judge Laporte's ruling enjoined application of the 2005 Petition Rule and reinstated the 2001 Roadless Rule. In April 2007 the U.S. Department of Justice appealed Judge Laporte's ruling.[86]

Recommendations

Based upon the state of forest land in the United States as described in this chapter, four recommendations are offered:

1. State and federal land management agencies in the United States should explicitly subscribe to the Montreal Process criteria as overall goals for sustainable forest management. President Clinton adopted a policy in 1993 to ensure that "our national objectives are that: our nation's forest should be healthy and productive; the growth of our timber should exceed harvest; and our forests should be reservoirs of biological diversity and carbon."[87] More than a decade later, this policy perspective is only beginning to percolate down to the federal and state agencies that actually manage public forests in the United States. Adoption of a uniform policy based on the Montreal Process criteria would both further sustainable forest management and facilitate cooperation among state and federal land management agencies.

2. Public and private partners involved in forestry on both public and private land should work together to promote forest certification as a consumer preference decision, which can have beneficial effects on the world's forests. Already forest certification has proved an important influence in encouraging sustainable forest management on both private and state forest land. The U.S. Forest Service is considering certification for some of its forest lands.[88] Increasing awareness of the significance of forest certification among the consumers of forest products could significantly enhance this influence.

3. State and federal governments should promote sustainable forest management on private lands. This goal can be achieved through a series of more coordinated incentives (particularly tax incentives) and regulations, while simultaneously discouraging landowners from converting forested land to less regulated uses (suburban development, agriculture, industry). While many states have experimented with sustainable forestry incentives, more can be done.

4. State and federal governments should continue to survey and inventory the nation's changing forest mosaic as new threats, use technologies, and management practices develop. The nature of forests in the United States will continue to change rapidly. Today, for example, pine beetle epidemics in the Rocky Mountains are dramatically altering the lodgepole pine community. New recreational activities, new markets for wood products, and new development patterns will continue to shape the forest landscape. To be effective, policies must deal with the forest that exists and will exist in the future, not forests that have existed in the past.

Conclusion

The federal government, state governments, and the National Association of State Foresters have committed themselves to the concept of sustainable forest management. However, the various statutory and administrative schemes surrounding sustainable forest management have created a patchwork of rules, incentives, and policies. The Montreal Process provides a framework for determining what sustainable forest management means. Its seven criteria, however, provide more of an overall goal rather than a roadmap for getting there. Widespread sustainable forest management in the United States can be accomplished with increased education, political will, and the creative use of incentives, certification, and regulation.

ENDNOTES

1. U.S. Dep't of Agric. (USDA), Econ. Research Servs., Major Use of Land in the United States, 2002 (May 2006), *available at* www.ers.usda.gov/publications/EIB14/eib14_reportsummary.pdf.

2. *Id.* at 1.

3. *Id.* at 25.

4. USDA, Forest Serv., National Report on Sustainable Forests—2003, at 8, *available at* www.fs.fed.us/research/sustain.

5. *Id.* at 9-10.

6. Reid Ewing & John Kostyack, *Endangered By Sprawl: How Runaway Development Threatens America's Wildlife* (2005), *available at* www.nwf. org/nwfwebadmin/binaryVault/EndangeredBySprawlFinal.pdf.

7. 16 U.S.C. §528.

8. 16 U.S.C. §531.

9. Report of the World Commission on Environment and Development, U.N. Doc. A/RES/42/187, *available at* www.un.org/documents/ga/res/42/ares42-187.htm.

10. USDA, National Report on Sustainable Forests, *supra* note 4, at 3.

11. 16 U.S.C. §528.

12. Presidential Decision Directive/NSC-16, Environmental Policy on International Desertification, Forest Conservation, and Water Security: Section on Forest Conservation and Sustainable Use, Nov. 1993, *available at* www.fs.fed.us/sustained/pres-decision-11-1993.doc.

13. *Id.*

14. *See* Montreal Process Working Group, What Is the Montreal Process?, *available at* www.rinya.maff.go.jp/mpci/whatis_e.html.

15. USDA, Forest Serv., 2000 RPA Assessment for Forest and Range Lands 11 (2000).

16. Thomas Lundmark, *Methods of Forest Law-Making*, 22 B.C. Envtl. Aff. L. Rev. 783 (1995).

17. Soc'y of Am. Foresters, Public Regulation of Private Forest Practices: A Position of the Society of American Foresters (2002), *available at* www.safnet.org/policyandpress/psst/PubReg.cfm.

18. Lundmark, *supra* note 16, at 793.

19. Big Creek Lumber Co. v. County of Santa Cruz, 136 P.3d 821, 828-29 (Cal. 2006).

20. Alaska Stat. §§41.17.010-.110 (originally enacted in 1978); Cal. Pub. Res. Code §§4511-4621 (the California Z'Berg-Nejedly Forest Practice Act of 1973); Idaho Code §§38-1301; Nev. Rev. Stat. Ann. §§528.010-090; Or. Rev. Stat. §§527.610-.730; Wash. Rev. Code. Ann. §§76.09.010-.950.

21. Alaska Stat. §41.14.010; Cal. Pub. Res. Code §4512; Idaho Code §38-1302; Mass. Gen. Laws ch. 132, §40; Nev. Rev. Stat. Ann.

§528.030; OR. REV. STAT. §527.630; WASH. REV. CODE ANN. §76.09.010.

22. CAL. CODE REGS. tit. 14, §§932, 957.4, 954.6; MASS. REGS. CODE tit. 304, §11.04; NEV. REV. STAT. §§528.053-.057; MASS. GEN. LAWS ANN. ch. 21, §17B; VA. CODE ANN. §10.1-407.

23. CAL. CODE REGS. tit. 14 §923; OREGON DEP'T OF FORESTRY, FOREST PRACTICE WATER PROTECTION RULES §629-24-521; WASHINGTON FOREST PRACTICE BD., WASHINGTON FOREST PRACTICES §222-24-020.

24. CAL. CODE REGS. tit. 14, §§913, 927.9; MASS. REGS. CODE tit. 304, §11.03; NEV. REV. STAT. §528.050.

25. Michael J. Mortimer et al., *When Worlds Collide: Science and Policy at Odds in the Regulation of Virginia's Private Forests*, 17 J. NAT. RES. & ENVTL. L. 1 (2003).

26. OHIO REV. CODE ANN. §1517.05; IOWA CODE ANN. §427c.4; N.D. CENT. CODE §§57-57-02 to -08; DEL. CODE ANN. tit. 7, §3502; R.I. GEN. LAWS §44-3-8 (1988); MO. REV. STAT. §§254.010-.300.

27. Lundmark, *supra* note 16, at 798.

28. MASS. REGS. CODE tit. 304, §11.04(1)(e); IDAHO CODE §38-1302; TENN. CODE ANN. §§11-14-101 et al.

29. Lundmark, *supra* note 16, at 804.

30. LAND TRUST ALLIANCE, 2005 NATIONAL LAND TRUST CENSUS REPORT, *available at* www.lta.org/aboutus/census.shtml.

31. *Id.*

32. I.R.C. §170(h) and regulations; I.R.C. §2031.

33. *See, e.g.*, Colorado and Virginia tax credit systems.

34. Michael J. Mortimer et al., *A Survey of Forestland Conservation Easements in the United States: Implications for Forestland Owners and Managers*, 6 SMALL SCALE FORESTRY 35-47 (2007).

35. 16 U.S.C. §§6501 et seq.

36. 16 U.S.C. §6571(a).

37. 16 U.S.C. §6572(b).

38. 16 U.S.C. §6572(c).

39. 16 U.S.C. §6572(e).

40. 16 U.S.C. §6572(f).

41. 16 U.S.C. §6578; www.lta.org/publicpolicy/hr1904v_summary.htm.

42. *See* Envtl. Defense Fund, Ctr. for Conservation Initiatives, Healthy Forest Reserve Program, *available at* www.edf.org/page.cfm?tagID=21.

43. 16 U.S.C. §6541.

44. 16 U.S.C. §6541(a)(1).

45. *See* 16 U.S.C. §6556; JACQUELINE VAUGHN & HANNA CORTNER, GEORGE W. BUSH'S HEALTHY FORESTS: REFRAMING THE ENVIRONMENTAL DEBATE 172 (2005).

46. 16 U.S.C. §1538(a)(1).

47. 50 C.F.R. §§17.21 & 17.31; 16 U.S.C. §1533(d).

48. 16 U.S.C. §1538(a)(2).

49. 50 C.F.R. §17.3. In 1995, the U.S. Supreme Court upheld that regulation in *Babbitt v. Sweet Home Communities for a Great Oregon*, 515 U.S. 687 (1995).

50. *See* CRAIG HANSEN, U.S. FISH & WILDLIFE SERV., THE NATION'S FIRST MULTI-SPECIES HCP FOR A FORESTED LANDSCAPE, *available at* www.fws.gov/endangered/bulletin/95/murryhcp.html.

51. 50 C.F.R. §17.32(c)(1)(iv); 50 C.F.R. §17.32(d)(1).

52. 64 Fed. Reg. 32717-01.

53. 50 C.F.R. §17.32(c)(8).

54. Announcement of Draft Policy for Candidate Conservation Agreements, 62 Fed. Reg. 32183 (Feb. 18, 1997).

55. U.S. FISH & WILDLIFE SERV., CANDIDATE SPECIES AND CANDIDATE CONSERVATION AGREEMENTS WITH ASSURANCES FOR NON-FEDERAL PROPERTY OWNERS, *available at* http://training.fws.gov/library/Pubs9/cca01.pdf.

56. Benjamin Cashore et al., *The United States' Race to Certify Sustainable Forestry: Non-State Environmental Governance and the Competition for Policy Making Authority*, 5 BUSINESS AND POLITICS 219-20 (Nov. 2003).

57. *Id.* at 222-23.

58. *See* Forest Stewardship Council website, www.fscus.org/images/documents/FSC_prospectus.pdf.

59. *See* Sustainable Forestry Initiative (SFI) Certified Forests Search web page, www.certifiedwoodsearch.org/sfiprogram/searchforests.aspx.

60. Constance L. McDermott, *FSC in the Northern Appalachians, A Regional and Sub-Regional Analysis of Forest Stewardship Council Certification as a Tool for Forest Conservation* (Dec. 2006) (Yale Program on Forest Policy and Governance).

61. E. Hansen et al., *Forest Certification in North America*, Oregon State Extension Service, at 9 (Feb. 2006).

62. *Id.*

63. *Id.*

64. Michael Washburn & Nadine Block, *Comparing Forest Management Certification Systems and Montreal Process Criteria and Indicators* (Oct. 2001) (unpublished paper).

65. Interestingly, the Canadian Standards Association Sustainable Forest Management Standard offers a forest management certification scheme that directly builds on Montreal Process Criteria and Indicators, *available at* www.certificationcanada.org.

66. Statistics from National Association of State Foresters (NASF), *available at* www.stateforesters.org/statistics/FY04_Statistics/FY2004Statistics.pdf.

67. *See* NASF website, www.stateforesters.org/positions/1997.C&I.pdf.

68. *See* Minnesota's forestry certification website, www.dnr.state.mn.us/forestry/certification/index.html.

69. Program available at SFI website, www.sfiprogram.org/miscPDFs/TN.pdf.

70. *See* Washington state government news releases web page, www.dnr.wa.gov/htdocs/adm/comm/2007_news_releases/nr07_023.html.

71. *See* Pennsylvania forestry certification website, www.dcnr.state.pa.us/forestry/certification.aspx; Michigan state government agreements web page, www.michigan.gov/documents/Treatiesagreements-FSC-CAR1_165073_7.pdf.

72. NASF resolution *available at* www.stateforesters.org/resolutions/res_06.html#NASF_Resolution_No._2006-4.

73. *Id.*

74. Victoria Sutton, *The George W. Bush Administration and the Environment*, 25 W. New Eng. L. Rev. 221, 233-34 (2003).

75. 16 U.S.C. §6501; 16 U.S.C. §§6511-6516.

76. 16 U.S.C. §6501(6).

77. USDA, Forest Service, Roadless Area Conservation, *available at* http://roadless.fs.fed.us (last visited Nov. 18, 2007).

78. *See generally* Paul S. Sutter, Driven Wild: How the Fight Against Automobiles Launched the Modern Wilderness Movement (2002).

79. Wilderness Act, 16 U.S.C. §1132(b); National Forest Management Act, 16 U.S.C. §1604(e); Federal Land Management Policy Act, 43 U.S.C. §1782(b).

80. President William J. Clinton, Memorandum for the Secretary of Agriculture, Protection of Forest "Roadless" Areas, Oct. 13, 1999.

81. USDA Forest Service, Final Rule: Special Areas; Roadless Area Conservation, 66 Fed. Reg. 2244 (Jan. 12, 2001).

82. President William J. Clinton, Remarks on Action to Preserve America's Forests, Jan. 12, 2001 (emphasis added). Transcript available through the Government Printing Office at www.gpo.gov.

83. USDA, Forest Service, National Forest System Land and Resource Management Planning; Special Areas; Roadless Area Conservation, 66 Fed. Reg. 35918 (July 16, 2004).

84. 36 C.F.R. §294.12.

85. California ex rel. Lockyer v. U.S. Dep't of Agric., 459 F. Supp. 2d 874 (N.D. Cal. 2006).

86. Information on the government's appeal *available at* www.ens-newswire.com/ens/apr2007/2007-04-09-09.asp#anchor1.

87. *Id.*

88. World Bus. Council for Sustainable Dev., U.S. Weighs Sustainability Seal for National Forests, Nov. 26, 2007, *available at* www.wbcsd.org/includes/getTarget.asp?MenuId=MTY2&ClickMenu=&doOpen=1&type=DocDet&id=MjcONjc; *see also* www.fs.fed.us/news/2005/releases/08/factsheets.pdf.

V. Waste and Toxic Chemicals

Chapter 20

Toxic Chemicals and Pesticides: Not Yet Preventing Pollution

Lynn R. Goldman

This chapter considers the progress made since 2002 in the sustainable environmental management of chemicals and pesticides in the United States. The issue is also of global importance because the United States is the largest manufacturer of chemicals and pesticides, as well as the largest consumer of chemicals and products containing them. As evidenced by the recent episodes of lead-contaminated toys imported from China, the United States is interested in assuring the safe management of chemicals globally. Global impacts also have resulted from releases of harmful chemicals—for example, the chlorofluorocarbons that have caused thinning of Earth's ozone layer.

The general principles of sustainable development provide the framework for the chapter's analysis of progress on industrial chemicals, pesticides, right-to-know, and persistent organic pollutants (POPs). The challenge of developing a regulatory framework for emerging nanotechnology is also addressed, as well as U.S. participation in global efforts to ensure sound management of chemicals. The chapter concludes with recommendations for action in the next decade.

The report card since 2002 is mixed. The least progress has been in the management of toxic chemicals. Further, a completely new set of nanomaterials likely to have novel toxicities has emerged with unknown impacts on ecological and human health. The U.S. Environmental Protection Agency (EPA) has not provided clear guidance to industry as to how nanomaterials used as chemicals, pesticides, drugs, and medical devices should receive safety evaluations. This new challenge illustrates Lewis Carroll's maxim that "you have to run as fast as you can just to stay where you are. If you want to get anywhere, you'll have to run much faster." EPA has not been running as fast as it can, and is losing ground on the sustainable management of chemicals.

For pesticides, the United States has clearly made progress toward sustainability in terms of exercising appropriate caution, assuring intergenerational equity, and removing the most hazardous pesticides and pesticide uses from commerce. There is still a long way to go, however, and EPA no longer provides up-to-date information about pesticide sales and usage.

Right-to-know, a core sustainability principle, has suffered a major setback with the new Toxic Release Inventory (TRI) "burden reduction" rule promulgated by the EPA. It remains to be seen whether the rule will withstand congressional challenge and, if not, what the rule's impact will be on access to information.

On the international front, the United States has continued to shrink from joining major chemical agreements, including the Stockholm Convention on Persistent Organic Pollutants, adopted in 2001, and the Rotterdam Convention on hazardous chemicals, which went into force in 2004. Both were signed by the U.S. government, but have not been ratified. The promise of the Strategic Approach to International Chemicals Management (SAICM), a global system for managing chemicals in commerce adopted in 2006, is immense given the lack of technical capacity in most countries for assessing the hazards of all chemicals. It remains to be seen whether the United States will be part of such a system.

Sustainability for Chemicals

The management of chemicals is at the very heart of sustainable development because chemicals are used to manufacture materials for fabricating the built environment, producing consumer goods, and producing and distributing energy. Four principles of sustainable development adopted in 1992 at the Rio Environmental Summit are particularly relevant to chemicals:

- *The precautionary principle.* This is the willingness to take action in the face of uncertainty to avert irreversible and serious threats to health and the environment.
- *Intergenerational equity.* This acknowledges the importance of protecting health and avoiding the imposition of large costs for future generations.
- *Control of the trade of hazardous chemicals in commerce.* Developing countries especially have supported the establishment of international agreements to control trade in very hazardous chemicals.

- *Access to information and integrated decisionmaking.* At the core of sustainable development is the principle that decisions for economic development be fully informed by consideration of environmental impacts, not only by decisionmakers but also by civil society.

There is an increasing recognition that it is better to prevent the entry of hazardous chemical substances into the environment than to address their known and unknown consequences at a later date. "Green chemistry" is the development of new chemicals that, by design, are more sustainable—of lower toxicity, less wasteful in manufacture, and harmless to the environment across their entire life cycle.

"Chemicals" are defined as substances that are manufactured, processed, or used in commerce, other than those marketed as pesticides, pharmaceuticals, or food additives. "Pesticides" are substances that are marketed for their ability to kill or repel pests, such as insecticides, fungicides (which kill molds and fungi), herbicides (weed killers), and rodenticides (rat killers). The basic structure of U.S. law for these two categories was established first in 1972 for pesticides in the Federal Insecticide, Fungicide and Rodenticide Act (FIFRA) and then in 1976 for industrial chemicals in the Toxic Substances Control Act (TSCA). FIFRA requires the registration of pesticides that are marketed in the United States; TSCA gives EPA authority over testing of chemicals and pesticides, review of new introductions, and assessment and management of risks of existing chemicals. The Federal Food, Drug and Cosmetic Act (FFDCA) authorizes EPA to regulate food uses of pesticides. In 1986, Congress enacted the Emergency Preparedness and Community Right to Know Act (EPCRA), thereby establishing the TRI for tracking the releases and transfers of chemicals from industry; the Pollution Prevention Act (PPA) of 1990 authorized such activities and expanded TRI reporting.

Regulatory Systems for Sustainability of Chemical Production and Use

Industrial Chemicals: TSCA

While there has been little progress on chemical management in the United States, fundamental changes are occurring in the European Union and Canada, and they offer a standard for assessing current and future developments in the United States. The European Union, after a long effort, has adopted a new set of regulatory standards called

REACH (Registration, Evaluation, and Authorization of Chemicals).[1] At present, REACH has been adopted, but it is uncertain precisely how it will be implemented. There is no doubt, however, that this new regulatory approach will force industry to generate much more information about hazards of existing as well as new chemicals in the international marketplace, and will change chemical use patterns across Europe.

Canada has made significant progress in advancing its chemicals legislation, beginning with the Canada Environmental Protection Act (CEPA), enacted in 1999. A recent review by the Canadian House of Commons identified a number of areas for further legislative reform that also are potentially relevant to the circumstances in the United States.[2] In recognition of the regulatory sweep of REACH, the review specifically recommended "[t]hat, should REACH come into effect, the government immediately initiate negotiations toward an agreement to gain access to test data submitted under REACH that has been deemed confidential business information. In addition CEPA 1999 should be amended to require that information submitted to REACH on substances imported into Canada be submitted to Canadian authorities."

In the light of this progress in Europe and Canada, it is disappointing that there has been very little movement toward amending TSCA in recent years. It is widely thought that TSCA, a 30-year-old statute, needs reauthorization to address several issues:

- mandating premarket as well as premanufacture approvals of new chemicals, including minimal standards for review and registration of such chemicals prior to entering the market;
- establishing an evaluation and approval process for uses of existing chemicals on the market to promote green chemistry;
- creating a health-based safety standard;
- shifting the burden to industry to prove safety of chemical uses and providing EPA with authority to call in data;
- informing chemical use and consumer choices; and
- strengthening the coordination of chemicals safety with media specific (air, water, waste) and other (consumer protection, food safety, occupational health and safety) statutes.[3]

In 2005, the U.S. Government Accountability Office (GAO) recommended that Congress give EPA additional authority to require
generation of information about chemicals, to manage risks, and to
share data with states. It also recommended that EPA use the authority
that it has under TSCA more aggressively.[4] Shortly after the GAO report, Senator James Jeffords introduced the Child, Worker, and Con-
sumer-Safe Chemicals Act of 2005, known as the Kid Safe Chemicals
Act (KSCA), to "fundamentally overhaul the nation's chemical management framework." The bill proposed major amendments to TSCA,
including a new public health standard for chemical safety, new mandates on industry to demonstrate that chemicals meet such a standard,
new requirements for reporting and monitoring chemical exposures in
the population, and increased sharing of certain information that is
now considered confidential.[5] The bill had several cosponsors but did
not receive a hearing.

At the same time, there were a number of notable efforts at the state
level. Brominated flame retardants, polybrominated diphenyl ethers
(PBDEs), have emerged as a major issue in chemicals regulation. As
of July 2007, 11 states had taken action to ban two forms of PBDEs,
penta- and octaBDE, and two states had banned decaBDE. Similar
bills were introduced in other state legislatures as well.[6] This is not an
isolated example; increasingly states are taking the initiative to regulate specific chemicals.

Gathering of new information about existing chemicals under
TSCA also has been judged unproductive.[7] The point of such information gathering is to identify and manage new risks, given that under
TSCA the EPA must make a finding of "unreasonable risk" to justify
taking action. EPA has had a set of overlapping initiatives to generate
new information about (1) chemicals produced in large volume,
so-called "high production volume chemicals" (HPVs); (2) chemicals
that have the potential to disrupt or modulate endocrine (hormone)
systems (endocrine disruptors); and (3) chemicals of potential risk
to children.[8]

Little progress can be reported with regard to endocrine-disruptor
and child health-related assessments. EPA's endocrine disruptor
screening program, required by the 1996 Safe Drinking Water Act and
the 1996 Food Quality Protection Act (FQPA) amendments to FIFRA
and FFDCA, has narrowed its focus only to high production chemicals (of which there are 2,708), which are also inert ingredients in pes-

ticides. (There are 2,775 chemical inerts, of which 643 are also HPV chemicals.) After establishing a priority for chemicals that have at least three routes of exposure and/or are found present in humans, EPA has proposed for screening nine industrial chemicals that are used to formulate pesticides: acetone, butyl benzyl phthalate, dibutyl phthalate, diethyl phthalate, dimethyl phthalate, di-sec-octyl phthalate, isophorone, methyl ethyl ketone, and toluene. EPA issued this list for 90-day comment in June 2007.[9] In December 2007 EPA identified an additional 73 industrial chemicals for which it wants to collect basic information.[10] Also, it published a draft set of policies and procedures for comment.[11] No schedule for these actions has been published. Likewise, EPA's Voluntary Children's Chemical Evaluation Program (VCCEP) pilot,[12] which was supposed to assess chemicals that are used around children, continues to move at a snail's pace, and the agency is still waiting for industry submission of most of the pilot data.[13]

While EPA's HPV Challenge Program has been more productive, it has been criticized for being both behind schedule and incomplete. According to the Environmental Defense Fund, one-fifth of 1,900 HPV chemicals that chemical companies agreed to test still lack initial data submissions, and one-third with initial submissions are still incomplete.[14] Also, as noted by the GAO in 2005, "The chemical industry has not agreed to provide testing for 300 chemicals originally identified in the HPV Challenge Program, and EPA believes that some of the chemicals produced in lesser quantities might potentially warrant testing." Furthermore, even with the test data provided under the HPV Challenge Program, EPA would need to demonstrate that chemicals pose unreasonable risks in order to control their production or use under TSCA. While TSCA does not define what risk is unreasonable, according to EPA officials, the standard has been difficult to meet. In order to withstand judicial scrutiny, a TSCA rule must be supported by substantial evidence in the rulemaking record.[15]

Pesticides

In contrast to chemicals, there has been continued progress over the last few years in making pesticide use more sustainable and less hazardous for children. Much of this progress can be attributed to a strong statutory framework with firm deadlines and expectations.

For pesticides on the market, EPA for some time now has needed to: (1) complete reregistration of older pesticides and aggressively address risks to workers, groundwater, and ecosystems as required under the 1988 FIFRA amendments; (2) complete reassessments of tolerances (regulations for allowable pesticide residues on food) as required under the Food Quality Protection Act of 1996 (FQPA); (3) provide stronger direction to the federal integrated pest management (IPM) effort; (4) strengthen pesticide enforcement, including the need for citizen suits; (5) provide agricultural workers with notice of specific pesticide hazards; (6) provide more information about pesticide usage patterns; and (7) implement the registration fee provision that was established in the 1996 FQPA.[16]

Nothing has been done to strengthen EPA's enforcement capacity under FIFRA, nor has EPA moved to increase hazard notification for pesticide applicators and farm workers. EPA has not updated its *Pesticide Industry Sales and Usage Report* since the 2000 and 2001 market estimates were published in 2004, thus making it difficult to track national trends since then. As for registration fees, additional legislation was passed and EPA has promulgated a registration fee schedule.[17]

The FQPA gave EPA a 10-year schedule to reassess all 9,721 tolerances on the books at the time of its enactment. This is a large effort that has required review not only of the toxicity of the pesticides, but also of all exposure routes and reasonable combinations of exposures with similar pesticides. In August 2006 EPA announced the completion of all of the reassessments. EPA's Office of Inspector General (OIG) reviewed progress.[18] The OIG analysis showed that the total dietary risk to children of pesticides in food had declined by nearly 50 percent by 2004, and that 98 percent of the reduction of risk of domestic food pesticide residues involved cancellation of uses of organophosphate pesticides, most significantly chlorpyrifos and parathions.[19]

As of October 2006, EPA had nearly completed the review and reregistration of old pesticides, with 559 completed (of which 229 were taken off the market by EPA or the manufacturers) and 54 scheduled for completion in the next two years.[20] In addition, EPA published a final set of procedural regulations for registration review, required under the FQPA to assure that all pesticides have a comprehensive review every 15 years to assure that they meet registration standards under the law.[21]

Right-to-Know

Community right-to-know is a powerful driving force for reducing pollution. It was first introduced at a national level in the United States with the passage of the 1986 Emergency Preparedness and Community Right-to-Know Act (EPCRA) and establishment of the Toxic Release Inventory (TRI), which require manufacturers to report releases of certain toxic chemicals to the public. Recent changes in EPA regulations for TRI reporting have significantly reduced the amount of information that is available via the TRI and make it more difficult to track trends.

The TRI has been a major success, both in providing information and in motivating reductions of toxic releases in the United States. However, the 4.34 billion pounds reported in 2005 reflected an increase of 3 percent from 2004, driven mainly by the metal mining, electric utilities, and primary metals sectors. Also, the 2005 data show an increase in persistent bioaccumulative toxins (PBTs), chemicals that persist in the environment and accumulate in tissues, and carcinogens. In December 2006, despite much opposition from the environmental community, EPA issued the Toxic Release Inventory Burden Reduction Final Rule, which raised the threshold for detailed reporting for most of the 650 TRI chemicals from 500 pounds to 5,000 pounds (up to 2,000 pounds of which can be released directly to the environment). This rule also allows facilities to withhold details on low-level waste generation of PBTs such as mercury and lead.[22] The 2006 TRI data have been released but are difficult to interpret. On the one hand, total releases seem to have gone down 2 percent. On the other hand, there was a 13 percent increase in short forms filed (for a total of 12,365), so it is likely that at least some percentage of this reduction is actually due to lack of reporting below the new higher threshold. On February 19, 2007, Senator Frank Lautenberg introduced the Toxic Right-to-Know Protection Act, which proposes to reverse the "burden reduction" rule. The same bill has been introduced in the House of Representatives by Congresspersons Frank Pallone and Hilda Solis.

Persistent Organic Pollutants

The United States has made progress on persistent organic pollutants (POPs); however, it has failed to take a seat at the table for the Stockholm Convention. POPs are toxic chemicals and pesticides that travel long distances and accumulate in food chains. In other words, they are cumulative and they cross national boundaries, requiring that international measures be taken to control environmental releases. In recent years EPA's focus related to POPs has been on efforts to curtail emissions of mercury to the environment, to identify safe methods for disposal of high-level mercury wastes, and for ratification of the Stockholm Convention on Persistent Organic Pollutants (POPs) to control transnational movement of POPs.[23]

Progress has been achieved on some POPs. While TRI reporting has suffered in other areas, EPA issued a rule that is likely to increase available information on dioxins.[24] Dioxins are a family of toxic chemicals that occur as contaminants in the manufacture of other chemicals and as byproducts of combustion. Since 2002, little progress has been made on methylmercury reductions, and the EPA has not yet issued regulations for approved disposal practices for mercury. As already noted, brominated flame retardants (PBDEs) have been regulated by a number of states but not by EPA. The only U.S. manufacturer of two PBDE commercial products (pentaBDE and octaBDE) voluntarily agreed to phase out production by the end of 2004. Since 2002, EPA has taken a number of steps to reduce environmental and health impacts from several polyfluorinated compounds, most notably perfluorooctanoic acid (PFOA), which is used to make nonstick coatings and many other industrial products, and perfluorooctyl sulfonate (PFOS), which was once used to make stain repellants.

Most importantly, the Stockholm Convention on Persistent Organic Pollutants entered into force in May 2004 and now includes 147 parties. The United States has not ratified it.

Nanotechnology

In recent years, chemical and pesticide nanomaterials have rapidly entered commerce, despite the shortcomings in our basic knowledge of how these materials move and transform in the environment and what their impact is on biological systems. As was the case for biotechnology 15 years ago, the assessment and indeed even identification of these as unique materials pose significant challenges for safety evaluations. The U.S. government has opted to use only voluntary approaches for managing risks of nanomaterials, and to ignore their unique properties and possible implications for health and the environment.

Nanomaterials occur in nature. Engineered nanomaterials are designed and produced to have structural features with at least one dimension of 100 nanometers or less. Nanoparticles, the basis for such materials, are based on a wide array of chemistries, including fullerenes (C60 or Bucky Balls), carbon nanotubes, metal and metal oxide particles (such as the nanozinc sunscreens and nanosilver antimicrobials), polymers and quantum dots.[25] There are many potential commercial uses of such materials, ranging from industrial coatings to paints, pharmaceutical delivery systems, energy production, and even sunscreens and cosmetics. The same properties that make such materials commercially desirable or provide a potential for medical uses may also lead to altered biological activity. Just as a nanomaterial may have vastly different commercial potential than a bulk material with the same chemical composition, such a material may also have toxicological activity that would not be predictable from the properties of the constituent chemicals.

In March 2007 an internal working group of EPA's Science Policy Council completed a white paper on nanotechnology that recommended more research on environmental applications as well as potential risks of nanomaterials. The white paper touts the potential of nanomaterials for environmentally beneficial applications like green energy, green design, green chemistry, and green manufacturing. However, it also identified numerous data gaps in risk assessment, including methods for chemical and physical identification and characterization of these materials; how they move through the environment; environmental detection and analysis; potential releases and human exposures; and human health and ecological effects. It indicated that EPA needs to promote pollution prevention, sustainable resource use, and good product stewardship in the production, use, and end-of-life management of nanomaterials.[26] Areas in which EPA has begun to look at nanomaterials from the regulatory perspective include new chemical submissions, pesticides, and air.

In July 2007, EPA released two draft documents for public review and comment: "TSCA Inventory Status of Nanoscale Substances—General Approach" and "Concept Paper for the Nanoscale Materials Stewardship Program under TSCA." The first document describes how EPA determines whether a nanomaterial is a "new" or "existing" chemical substance under TSCA.[27] It is disappointing that EPA proposes to treat nanoscale materials as if they are no different than their conventional counterparts. After all, their unique properties are the reasons they are entering the market in the first instance. Environmental groups have urged EPA to implement mandatory reporting rules to level the playing field for the nanotechnology industry, but the agency's latest step seems to indicate a lack of commitment to a mandatory system. The second paper describes EPA's approach to a voluntary stewardship program for nanomaterials.[28] EPA proposes no regulatory backstop that would kick in place if the voluntary program is unsuccessful.

International Chemicals Management

By failing to assist developing countries with building capacity for the management of chemicals, the United States risks losing its leadership role in chemicals management internationally. Like the Stockholm Convention on POPs, the Rotterdam Convention on the Prior Informed Consent Procedure for Certain Hazardous Chemicals and Pesticides in International Trade has come into force. Once again, the United States has signed but not ratified an important chemicals convention. Likewise, the United States has remained outside the Biodiversity Convention, which includes the Cartagena Protocol on Biosafety,[29] an international framework for managing the trade of genetically modified organisms and seeds. The United States is unlikely to join the Biodiversity Convention until other issues have been addressed, most notably concerns about intellectual property rights and financing.

The United States plays an active role in the Intergovernmental Forum on Chemical Safety (IFCS), which implements Chapter 19 of Agenda 21. The IFCS plays a number of coordinating roles and recently assisted in the development of the Strategic Approach to International Chemicals Management (SAICM), adopted in February 2006 in Dubai, United Arab Emirates. The SAICM, which goes beyond Agenda 21, provides a framework by which international efforts, which have been piecemeal and incompletely coordinated, can be brought together and strengthened. In both contexts, the United States has in recent years pressed to minimize international efforts to manage chemicals on the grounds, as a general principle, of not wanting to create new international entities.

Recommendations

There are a few areas that are seriously in need of action in the next decade. The following recommendations address those needs.

1. Amend TSCA in favor of a modern approach to chemicals management consistent with emerging regulatory systems in Europe and Canada. TSCA reforms that are needed include stronger national mandates to manage chemical risks, promotion of green chemistry, enhancement of the right-to-know for chemical users and the public; and scientific advances in toxicity testing and exposure assessment. Such reforms would put the United States on a path to more sustainable development, production, and use of greener chemicals. Assessment of chemical risks and exposures could also be improved by: (1) adoption of aggregate and cumulative risk assessment tools; (2) continuation and expansion of efforts to monitor levels of chemicals in people; (3) incorporation of stronger reporting requirements about the use of chemicals; and (4) development and validation of new chemical hazard assessment methods based on advances in genomics, proteomics, and other technologies.

2. Strengthen children's health protections for both chemicals and pesticides.

3. Encourage pollution prevention. Promotion of green chemistry is but one approach that can be taken. Additionally, EPA should make concerted efforts to coordinate regulatory and permitting efforts for its "media" offices (air, water, waste) to identify opportunities for pollution prevention.

4. Ratify the Stockholm Convention on Persistent Organic Pollutants (POPs) as well as the Rotterdam Convention on Prior Informed Consent; provide support (including monetary) for the IFCS and the SAICM. U.S. participation in the POPs convention would be good for the global environment and also for U.S. interests, particularly given our role in the production and consumption of chemicals.

5. Develop a regulatory framework for the assessment and management of risks related to nanotechnology. The current EPA voluntary approach falls well short of this goal in that it does not assure that the government will be provided with sufficient information about these new chemical structures.

Conclusion

Although much progress has been achieved, there is still a long way to go. None of it will be accomplished unless both Congress and the Executive Branch make chemical reform a priority. To date, TSCA has been the Teflon-coated statute, impervious to attempts at reform from all quarters. Perhaps continued state-based initiatives on individual chemicals and on chemicals policies more broadly will help to catalyze federal efforts to adopt a more REACH-like approach to chemicals management in the United States.

ENDNOTES

1. U. Lahl & K.A. Hawxwell, *REACH—The New European Chemicals Law*, Env't., Sci. & Tech. 7115-21 (Dec. 2006).

2. Canada, House of Commons, Standing Comm. on Env't & Sustainable Dev., The Canadian Environmental Protection Act, 1999—Five-Year Review: Closing the Gaps, 39th Parl., 1st Sess.

3. L.R. Goldman, *Preventing Pollution? U.S. Toxic Chemicals and Pesticides Policies and Sustainable Development*, 32 ELR 11018-41 (Sept. 2002).

4. U.S. Gov't Accountability Office (GAO), Chemical Regulation: Options Exist to Improve EPA's Ability to Assess Health Risks and Manage Its Chemical Review Program (2005).

5. Remarks of Senator James Jeffords, 151 Cong. Rec. S177, 8236.

6. Press Release, National Caucus of Environmental Legislators, Maine Joins Washington, Bans PBDEs (June 18, 2007), *available at* www.ncel.net/newsmanager/news_article.cgi?news_id=175 (last visited July 20, 2007).

7. Nat'l Research Council, Comm'n on Life Sciences, Toxicology Testing: Strategies to Determine Needs and Priorities (1984); Congress of the United States, Office of Tech. Assessment, Screening and Testing of Chemicals in Commerce (1995); U.S. EPA, Office of Prevention, Pesticides & Toxic Substances, Chemical Hazard Data Availability Study: What Do We Really Know About the Safety of High Production Volume Chemicals? EPA's 1998 Baseline of Hazard Information That Is Readily Available to the Public (1998).

8. Goldman, *supra* note 3.

9. U.S. EPA, Draft List of Initial Pesticide Active Ingredients and Pesticide Inerts to Be Considered for Screening Under the Federal Food, Drug, and Cosmetic Act [EPA-HQ-OPPT-2004-0109; FRL-8129-3], 72 Fed. Reg. 33486-503 (2007).

10. U.S. EPA, Proposed Collection Comment Request; Tier 1 Screening of Certain Chemicals Under the Endocrine Disruptor Screening Program (EDSP); EPA ICR No. 2249.01 [EPA-HQ-OPPT-2007-1081; FRL-8155-8], 72 Fed. Reg. 7083941 (2007).

11. U.S. EPA, Endocrine Disruptor Screening Program (EDSP); Draft Policies and Procedures for Initial Screening; Request for Comment [EPA-HQ-OPPT-2007-1080; FRL-8340-3], 72 Fed. Reg. 70842-62 (2007).

12. U.S. EPA, Voluntary Children's Chemical Evaluation Program, 65 Fed. Reg. 81700-18 (2000).

13. U.S. GAO, Chemical Regulation, *supra* note 4.

14. Richard A. Denison, Envtl. Defense Fund, High Hopes, Low Marks. A Final Report Card on the High Production Volume Chemical Challenge (2007).

15. U.S. GAO, Chemical Regulation: Options Exist to Improve EPA's Ability to Assess Health Risks and Manage Its Chemical Review Program (2005).

16. Goldman, *supra* note 3.

17. U.S. EPA, Pesticides; Fees and Decision Times for Registration Applications, 69 Fed. Reg. 12771-80 (2004).

18. U.S. EPA, OFFICE OF THE INSPECTOR GENERAL (OIG), MEASURING THE IMPACT OF THE FOOD QUALITY PROTECTION ACT: CHALLENGES AND OPPORTUNITIES (2006).

19. U.S. EPA, OIG, SUPPLEMENTAL REPORT: DETAILS ON DIETARY RISK DATA IN SUPPORT OF REPORT NO. 2006-P-00028, MEASURING THE IMPACT OF THE FOOD QUALITY PROTECTION ACT: CHALLENGES AND OPPORTUNITIES (2006).

20. U.S. EPA, NATIONAL PESTICIDE PROGRAM FY 2006 ANNUAL REPORT: CAPPING A SUCCESSFUL DECADE (2006).

21. U.S. EPA, Pesticides; Procedural Regulations for Registration Review, 71 Fed. Reg. 45719-34 (2006).

22. U.S. EPA, Toxics Release Inventory Burden Reduction Final Rule, 71 Fed. Reg. 7693244 (2006).

23. Goldman, *supra* note 3.

24. U.S. EPA, Dioxin and Dioxin-Like Compounds; Toxic Equivalency Information; Community Right-to-Know Toxic Chemical Release Reporting Final Rule, 72 Fed. Reg. 26544-54 (2007).

25. G. Oberdorster et al., *Nanotoxicology: An Emerging Discipline Evolving From Studies of Ultrafine Particles*, 113 ENVTL. HEALTH PERSPECTIVES 823-39 (2005).

26. U.S. EPA, SCI. POL'Y COUNCIL, NANOTECHNOLOGY WHITE PAPER (2007).

27. U.S. EPA, OFFICE OF POLLUTION PREVENTION & TOXICS, TSCA INVENTORY STATUS OF NANOSCALE SUBSTANCES—GENERAL APPROACH (July 12, 2007).

28. U.S. EPA, OFFICE OF POLLUTION PREVENTION & TOXICS, CONCEPT PAPER FOR THE NANOSCALE MATERIALS STEWARDSHIP PROGRAM UNDER TSCA (July 12, 2007).

29. U.N. Environment Programme, Secretariat of the Convention on Biological Diversity, Cartegena Protocol on Biosafety (2001).

Chapter 21

Hazardous Waste and Superfund: Few Changes and Little Progress

Joel A. Mintz

The disposal and release of hazardous wastes and other toxic chemicals into the natural environment remains an immense problem in the United States and throughout the world. According to the U.S. Environmental Protection Agency (EPA), in 2004 (the last year for which current data is available) roughly 81.5 million pounds of persistent bioaccumulative toxic compounds—which EPA has identified as "priority chemicals"—were released to the environment in the form of hazardous wastes.[1] This staggering rate of discharge represents a substantial increase over the preceding year,[2] and these released hazardous wastes pose a particular threat to human health and the natural environment. As EPA has noted:

> Existing releases of these chemicals often linger in some form for decades, repeatedly cycling among land, water, and air, being carried airborne across state and national borders, depositing on soils and water bodies, settling in sediments, and being consumed by and stored in fat reserves of living organisms. Continued use of these chemicals increases these unwelcome global reservoirs.[3]

With particular attention to the years since 2002, this chapter assays the ways in which U.S. domestic laws pertaining to hazardous waste have or have not conformed to norms of sustainable development. After defining sustainability as it pertains to hazardous waste, and exploring some critical features of current U.S. law and policy respecting its remediation and management, the chapter argues that, notwithstanding past progress, significant legal changes are needed to move the country toward sustainable development in this crucial area. These reforms must include new legislation to mandate specific, phased decreases in the volume of hazardous waste generated at industrial facilities. The reforms must also encompass replenishment of the Superfund trust fund through renewal of the Superfund petroleum tax and modification of the statute's secured creditor exemption. Ratification of the Basel Convention on the Control of Transboundary Movement of Hazardous Wastes is also needed, as are amendments to the Resource Conservation and Recovery Act to clarify its definition of hazardous waste and to expand its regulatory coverage to include hazardous-waste-bearing domestic sewage and irrigation return flows.

Sustainable Development in the Context of Hazardous Waste

Sustainable development connotes the use of resources, and the conduct of economic activities, so as to meet present human needs without compromising the ability of future generations to meet their needs. In regard to the management and remediation of hazardous waste, the need for a sustainable approach is particularly urgent. Such wastes include a wide variety of substances that are toxic, ignitable, explosive, and/or corrosive, ranging from pesticides and cleaning fluids to the byproducts of many manufacturing processes. Human exposure to them may result in any number of serious, chronic diseases (from cancer to nerve damage), harm to fetuses, fires, explosions, and other dire consequences. The improper release of wastes can also pose grave threats to wildlife, agriculture, and water supplies.

A sustainable hazardous waste regime poses significant challenges. It requires, whenever possible, that the use of toxic chemicals that produce hazardous wastes be eliminated entirely. Where that is not possible, the use of such chemicals must be minimized, and a cycle of use and reuse of hazardous chemicals must be created, to minimize or eliminate their release. In addition, hazardous wastes that were improperly disposed of in the past must be remediated in order to remove the dangers they may pose to human health, water resources, land and wildlife.

At the same time, sustainable hazardous waste management creates genuine opportunities for industries and their managers. Sustainable approaches to managing hazardous waste may reduce the costs of purchasing raw materials, decrease workplace risks and accidents, minimize industrial liability, improve community relations, and ease the burdens of waste management paperwork and record keeping.

At the international level, sustainable development with respect to hazardous wastes has been appropriately defined by two international agreements: Agenda 21,[4] the action plan that came out of the 1992 Rio Earth Summit, and the Basel Convention on the Control of Transboundary Movements of Hazardous Wastes.[5] Agenda 21 includes the "overall objective" of preventing and minimizing the generation of hazardous wastes, as well as managing those wastes "in such a way that they do not cause harm to health and the environment."[6] Moreover, one of the stated "overall targets" of Agenda 21 is "preventing or minimizing the generation of hazardous wastes as part of an overall integrated cleaner production approach."[7] It would have governments intensify their research and development activities regarding "cost-effective alternatives for processes and substances that currently result in the generation of hazardous wastes that pose particular problems for environmentally sound disposal or treatment."[8] Moreover, Agenda 21 calls upon governments to work with industry, "on sector-by-sector cleaner production and hazardous waste minimization campaigns."[9]

Another significant focus of Agenda 21 is facilitating "international cooperation in the environmentally sound management of hazardous wastes, including control and monitoring of the transboundary movements of such wastes."[10] The agreement calls for a prohibition on "the export of hazardous wastes to countries that do not have the capacity to deal with those wastes in any environmentally sound way"[11] and the development of "control procedures for the transboundary movement of hazardous wastes destined for recovery operations."[12] It expressly "urges" governments to ratify the Basel Convention;[13] and it declares that governments should (1) adopt and implement national legislation to prevent their illegal import and export of hazardous wastes, and (2) develop appropriate national enforcement programs to monitor compliance with such legislation.[14]

One way that certain countries have found to dispose of their wastes is to ship them to other, usually impoverished, nations. While cost-effective for the exporters, this "solution" may have devastating environmental and public-health consequences for the residents of the countries where the wastes end up.

The Basel Convention that Agenda 21 refers to is an international effort to craft a new set of rules for transboundary shipment of hazardous waste. Some of the Convention's provisions require written notification (to importing states) of the nature of transboundary hazardous waste shipments and advance consent by importing states that such shipments may take place.[15] Additionally, the Basel Convention requires that each party refrain from allowing hazardous wastes to be exported to a state "if it has reason to believe that the wastes in question will not be managed in an environmentally sound manner."[16]

Each party must require that hazardous wastes to be exported are managed in an environmentally sound manner "in the state of import or elsewhere."[17] Each party must also ensure that transboundary movements of hazardous wastes will not occur unless the exporting state lacks the technical capacity and the necessary facilities, capacity or suitable disposal sites to dispose of those wastes in an environmentally sound and efficient manner.[18]

Clearly, implementation of the Basel Convention would contribute significantly to sustainable development with regard to hazardous wastes. The export of such wastes to countries that lack the adequate disposal facilities to manage them in an environmentally sound fashion has obvious short-term economic advantages for exporting states, which no longer need to spend the time and money required to treat their own wastes properly. Nonetheless, hazard waste exports can result in devastating consequences for human health and the environment in the (usually underdeveloped) countries that receive these wastes. International cooperation would curb transboundary movements of hazardous waste and help to assure that present and future generations around the globe will enjoy lives free of the crushing burdens of disease and environmental ruin.

The Superfund Statute and Hazardous Waste Sustainability

United States domestic law respecting hazardous waste consists primarily of two pieces of voluminous and comprehensive legislation, as amended: the Comprehensive Environmental Response Compensation and Liability Act (CERCLA), also known as the Superfund statute; and the Resource Conservation and Recovery Act (RCRA).[19]

CERCLA creates a multifaceted scheme for eliminating dangerous conditions resulting from hazardous waste spills and past misdisposal of hazardous waste. It was intended by Congress to address those hazardous waste spill and disposal sites around the United States that pose the greatest risk to human health and the environment. CERCLA imposes a liability regime with the goal of holding those who generated, transported, or misdisposed hazardous wastes financially accountable for their remediation. This liability scheme casts a broad net of strict, joint, and several liability over potentially responsible parties (PRPs) at inactive hazardous waste sites. Joint and several liability means that each party responsible for polluting a specific area may be held responsible for paying the entire cleanup cost; the government need not find each and every responsible party to ensure that the site is fully cleaned up. Notwithstanding this progressive, sensible feature, however, the Superfund programs fall well short of achieving sustainable development in some respects.

CERCLA contains a secured creditor exemption that excludes from liability any person who own a hazardous waste facility primarily to protect his security interest "without participating in the management" of the facility. The act was amended to resolve conflicting decisions as to the extent to which that exemption affords protection to lenders who foreclose on contaminated properties. Under the Asset Conservation, Lender Liability, and Deposit Insurance Protection Act of 1996,[20] it is clear that lenders may undertake a variety of activities relating to the facility without incurring liability as PRPs. After foreclosure, a lender may maintain business at a contaminated facility where that lender divests itself of the property "at the earliest practicable, commercially reasonable time, on commercially reasonable terms."[21]

Unfortunately, the 1996 extension of the Superfund secured creditor exemption was a step away from the achievement of sustainable development. By affording banks (and other lending institutions) more potential opportunities to avoid CERCLA liability, this change in the law appears to have removed a significant source of private institutional pressure on hazardous waste site operators/debtors to manage their facilities in an environmentally sound manner. The absence of such benevolent pressure has persisted since 2002.

Throughout the years since 2002, the efficacy of the Superfund program has been compromised by a shortage of resources. When it was enacted in 1980, CERCLA included taxes on crude oil and certain chemical substances that were to be used for a trust fund to finance the response to and cleanup of various substances. Since then, Congress has failed to reinstate the taxes specifically intended to support the CERCLA trust fund. Thus, by the end of 2003, general revenues financed all appropriations to EPA for Superfund implementation. In addition to undermining the statute's "polluter pays" approach, this recent financial arrangement has contributed to a decline in overall appropriations for the CERCLA program, together with a marked decline in the rate at which sites have been remediated.[22]

In 1996, for example, EPA deleted some 34 hazardous waste sites from its Superfund National Priorities List (NPL), a national listing of highly contaminated sites that the agency has targeted for top priority remedial action. By contrast, in 2006 only seven such sites were deleted because they no longer pose significant hazards.[23] Similarly, in 1997 EPA reported that it had "completed construction" of cleanup projects at 88 contaminated hazardous waste facilities.[24] From 2003 to 2006, the number of construction completions had fallen to only 40 per year, and in 2007 remedial construction work was completed at a paltry seven U.S. hazardous waste sites.[25]

Since 2002, the Superfund program has been affected by two major decisions of the U.S. Supreme Court. In *Cooper Industries, Inc. v. Aviall Services, Inc.,*[26] the Court interpreted CERCLA, which previously had been construed as allowing PRPs to seek contribution under the statute, in a way that limited the legal ability of those parties to seek contribution in voluntary cleanup cases. When many parties are responsible for the contamination of a site, contribution allows one of the responsible parties to bring a lawsuit seeking reimbursement for cleanup costs from other responsible parties. The Court ruled that a private party could seek contribution under the Superfund statute only after having been sued by the government. This ruling significantly undercut voluntary cleanups by responsible parties. For several years, those entities seemed only able to seek contribution from other parties after they had been sued by EPA in a CERCLA lawsuit. That widely held perception discouraged many unilateral private remedial actions because private parties were understandably reluctant to clean up disposal sites that other PRPs had contributed to if they would ultimately have to bear the entire cost of that activity on their own.

Fortunately, a 2007 decision by the Court appears to have remedied the confusion and difficulties created by the *Aviall* case. In *United States v. Atlantic Research Corp.,*[27] the Court interpreted CERCLA to find an alternative means for private parties to recover their response costs. It ruled that the statute allows PRPs to obtain cost recovery from other PRPs, whether or not those plaintiffs had previously been made defendants in an action by the government pursuant to CERCLA. Although arguably tardy, this decision effectively restored private party contribution rights to the Superfund scheme.

One other aspect of the current Superfund program also bears mentioning: Neither the Superfund statute nor CERCLA's extensive implementing regulations and guidance require hazardous waste generators to reduce the volume of their waste generation. As noted above, the recent trend in this country has been toward an increase in industrial creation of hazardous waste, and at this writing there seems little reason to predict an imminent reversal in that disquieting trend.

RCRA: An Engine for Hazardous Waste Sustainability

In contrast to CERCLA, the Resource Conservation and Recovery Act (RCRA)[28] is focused on cradle-to-grave regulation of ongoing hazardous waste generation, transportation, and disposal. This progressive legislation has indeed moved the United States a long way toward sustainability. Nonetheless, RCRA's hazardous waste program requirements do not yet fully comport with principles of sustainable development.

One set of problems arises from the statute's convoluted and archaic definitional scheme. As Professor William H. Rodgers Jr., has observed:

> The legal search for hazardous wastes must proceed through an impenetrable jungle of rules and requirements.... Wastes can be "hazardous" for purposes of one section of RCRA but not for another. Wastes can be functionally "hazardous" but legally exempt under various exclusions from the law. Wastes can slip in and out of the "hazardous" category as a result of initiatives by state authorities, or by individual parties making use of the listing or delisting process.[29]

This definitional morass has led to regulatory uncertainties, disputes, and delays that have blunted or diverted RCRA's thrust.

Another continuing problem with respect to sustainable development has resulted from RCRA's self-imposed limitations on regulatory coverage. Two statutory exclusions are particularly troubling in this respect. In its definition of solid waste (of which hazardous waste is a subset, for statutory purposes), RCRA excludes "solid or dissolved material in domestic sewage" and "solid or dissolved materials in irrigation return flows."[30] These two seemingly innocuous exceptions are illogical and environmentally unsound.

Although domestic sewage is nominally regulated under the Clean Water Act, there is evidence that significant environmental harm has been caused by hazardous materials discharged to publicly owned treatment works and inadequately treated there. As Rodgers has aptly noted:

Obviously, toxics that ride along with the sewage are subject not
only to the caprice of the chosen host—wet weather overflows, er-
ratic diversions, improper treatment—they also can pass through
the treatment plant, or remain there to corrupt, poison, and disable
the system. Putting the stuff into the sewers is not a guarantee that it
will be treated.[31]

Similarly, RCRA's express exclusion of irrigation return flows (i.e.,
water that has been used for irrigation and then flows back to a river)
has provided comfortable legal shelter for concentrated accumula-
tions of toxic wastes in the dry beds of evaporated lakes and reservoirs. These toxic deposits have proven both attractive to and deadly
for many species of water fowl.[32] Thus, like the domestic sewage exclusion, the continued exemption of irrigation return flow wastes remains an environmentally detrimental loophole in the statute's
scheme of hazardous management.

Ratification and implementation of the Basel Convention will fill
other gaps in RCRA's regulatory coverage. In particular, adoption of
Basel's standards would prohibit hazardous waste generators from
adopting the "quick and dirty," yet presently lawful, approach of ship-
ping hazardous wastes to impoverished lands where those substances
threaten vulnerable nations and individuals with environmental harm
and chronic disease. By thus limiting generators' options, this change
will create incentives for more U.S. industrial managers to reduce, reuse, and recycle their hazardous wastes in a sustainable manner.

From the standpoint of sustainable development, however, the most
glaring shortcoming of RCRA appears to be the fact that, like the
Superfund statute, RCRA lacks any enforceable regulatory provisions
directly intended to decrease or eliminate the generation of hazardous
wastes. The legislation continues to place no limitations on the volume of hazardous wastes that may be generated in the United States.

Voluntary Waste Minimization Programs

RCRA states that hazardous waste generators must "reduce the volume or quantity and toxicity of [hazardous] waste to the degree determined by the generator to be economically practicable."[33] This language, however, hardly creates a binding requirement.

One interesting programmatic development with respect to hazardous waste sustainability since 2002 has been EPA's creation and promotion of a wholly voluntary waste minimization program. Accord-

ing to the agency, its voluntary program is designed to promote the use of "advanced production and management tools" that foster a "sustainable manufacturing culture."[34] EPA has identified 31 toxic, persistent, and bioaccumulative "priority chemicals" as the focus of this effort. Through its National Partnership for Environmental Priorities,[35] the agency has elicited industrial participation in toxic waste minimization. Thus far, EPA has touted a number of specific industrial success stories,[36] and the program is ongoing.

Despite some anecdotal successes, however, this voluntary program seems anything but an adequate substitute for an effective mandatory program to minimize hazardous waste generation. Although the 31 chemicals chosen by EPA for priority treatment may well be a logical starting point for waste minimization, they are well short of a comprehensive inventory of the toxins that threaten public health and the environment. Moreover, it appears most doubtful that a fully voluntary program will result in the volume of toxic waste reduction that a truly sustainable approach requires. While some firms will certainly volunteer to participate, many will not do so. Clearly, the greater the number of nonparticipants and the more wastes they generate, the less likely it will be that sustainable management of hazardous wastes will result.

Indeed, EPA's own reported hazardous waste trend data provides little basis for optimism as to the efficacy of its voluntary toxic waste minimization efforts thus far. In 2005, the agency reported that more than 38 million tons of hazardous waste were created in the United States.[37] Notwithstanding the institution of EPA's voluntary minimization program, this figure reflects a sharp *increase* over the slightly more than 30 million tons of hazardous waste reportedly generated in 2004.[38] Thus, at least to date, voluntary hazardous waste reduction programs have not resulted in the significant cutbacks in hazardous waste generation that sustainable development requires.

What Is Needed? Recommendations for Making U.S. Hazardous Waste Laws More Sustainable

Additional measures are required in order to move the United States closer to attaining the goal of sustainable development and to fulfilling its international commitments respecting hazardous wastes.

1. The United States can achieve a cleaner integrated production approach by amending CERCLA, RCRA, and other federal envi-

ronmental legislation to require industrial facilities to decrease their generation of hazardous wastes, in phased increments, by fixed dates. Such requirements (which might include waste generation cap-and-trade programs in their early phases, in order to promote economic efficiency) would be roughly parallel to the technology-forcing provisions of the Clean Air Act and Clean Water Act, which required industrial emitters and dischargers to invent new pollution-control technologies to meet mandated standards by specified deadlines. The requirements I propose would set numerical goals as to hazardous waste generation without mandating specific techniques (such as changes in raw materials, modification of production methods, etc.) to be employed by industrial firms to meet those goals. The firms can use their ingenuity to design and implement tailored approaches to their (often unique) manufacturing processes that will result in compliance with the established goals.

Unquestionably, methods of production vary from plant to plant and industry to industry, and hazardous wastes differ from one another in their nature, concentration, and toxicity. These facts, however, should not create insurmountable barriers to mandatory reductions in hazardous waste generation. The establishment of strict yet carefully phased-in numerical goals for waste reduction can allow those who manage industrial plants sufficient time to design and implement operational changes tailored to the specific circumstances of their own facilities. Moreover, cap-and-trade programs can be crafted to categorize hazardous wastes in ways that take account of the varying strengths and toxicities of those materials, and assure that only like-to-like trading of waste reduction credits will occur.

2. CERCLA should be amended to deny secured creditor exemption status to lending institutions that have the capacity to influence hazardous waste management practices at borrower facilities in which they hold a security interest. Congress should also reinstate Superfund's taxes on certain industries to replenish the CERCLA trust fund and restore, in full, the salutary "polluter pays" principle.

3. RCRA must also be amended. Its current, flawed definition of hazardous waste should be replaced with a consistent, straightforward, and comprehensive definition; and toxic-containing domestic sewage and irrigation return flow deposits must be made subject to regulatory coverage.

4. The United States should ratify the Basel Convention. Once the Convention is ratified, Congress will also need to alter those provisions of RCRA that would hinder our full compliance with that sensible international agreement.

The adoption and implementation of these suggestions will make a considerable difference. If faithfully implemented, mandated decreases in the generation of hazardous wastes will shrink the vast and growing volume of such wastes that are released annually in the United States. Such an approach will lower the disease burden for current and future generations by diminishing the bioaccumulation of toxic materials in the human food chain, and it would decrease the incidence of human exposure to these dangerous chemicals. At the same time, full funding of the Superfund program, and elimination of continuing gaps in the coverage of both RCRA and Superfund, will help those progressive yet limited statutes achieve their full potential as tools for the protection of the natural resources that future generations will have available. And U.S. ratification of the Basel Convention will at long last join our country in a cooperative international effort to prevent the irresponsible export of hazardous wastes that threaten health and the environment in impoverished nations.

Conclusion

After a bold and impressive start in the 1970s and 1980s, the United States has largely failed to follow up its initial hazardous waste legislation with the steps necessary to bring it into compliance with norms of sustainable development. In this regard, the years since 2002 have been regrettably consistent with the inaction that occurred in the decade immediately following the solemn promises and high hopes of the 1992 Rio Summit. The enactment and full implementation of the measures suggested above remains much needed. They are long overdue.

ENDNOTES

1. U.S. EPA, MEASURING PROGRESS 2000-2004: THE NATIONAL PRIORITY CHEMICALS TRENDS REPORT, *available at* www.epa.gov/epaoswer/ hazwaste/minimize/trends.html.

2. *Id.*

3. *See* U.S. EPA, WASTE MINIMIZATION: BASIC INFORMATION, *available at* www.epa.gov/epaoswer/hazwaste/minimize/about.htm.

4. U.N. Conference on Environment and Development, Agenda 21, U.N. Doc. A/CONF. 151.26 (1992) [hereinafter Agenda 21].

5. Basel Convention on the Control of Transboundary Movements of Hazardous Wastes and Their Disposal, Mar. 22, 1989, U.N. Doc. UNEP/WG 190/4 (1989) [hereinafter Basel Convention].

6. Agenda 21, *supra* note 4, ¶ 20.6.

7. *Id.* ¶ 20.7(a).

8. *Id.* ¶ 20.13(c).

9. *Id.* ¶ 20.19(c).

10. *Id.* ¶ 20.33(a).

11. *Id.* ¶ 20.33(b).

12. *Id.* ¶ 20.33(c).

13. *Id.* ¶ 20.35.

14. *Id.* ¶ 20.42(a), (b).

15. *See* Basel Convention, *supra* note 5, art. 6.

16. *Id.* art. 4(2)(e).

17. *Id.* art. 4(8).

18. *Id.* art. 4(9).

19. *See* the Comprehensive Environmental Response, Compensation, and Liability Act (CERCLA or the Superfund Act), 42 U.S.C. §§9601-9675; and the Resource Conservation and Recovery Act (RCRA), 42 U.S.C. §§6901-6992. For summaries of the key provisions of these statutes, see SUSAN M. COOKE, THE LAW OF HAZARDOUS WASTE (2005), vols. 1-3.

20. *See* Subtitle E, The Omnibus Consolidated Appropriations Bill for Fiscal Year 1997, Pub. L. No. 104-208 (Sept. 30, 1996). CERCLA's initial secured creditor exemption appears at 42 U.S.C. §9601(20)(A).

21. *Id.* For a cogent analysis of this set of amendments, see William Buzbee, *CERCLA's New Safe Harbors for Banks, Lenders, and Financial Institutions*, 25 ELR 10652 (Dec. 1996).

22. Rena Steinzor & Margaret Clune Giblin, *Reforming the Comprehensive Environmental Response, Compensation, and Liability Act, in* CPR FOR THE ENVIRONMENT: BREATHING NEW LIFE INTO THE NATION'S MAJOR ENVIRONMENTAL STATUTES (2007).

23. U.S. EPA, Number of NPL Site Actions and Milestones by Fiscal Year, *available at* www.epa.gov/superfund/sites/query/queryhtm/nplay.htm.

24. *Id.*

25. *Id.*

26. Cooper Indus., Inc. v. Aviall Servs., Inc., 543 U.S. 157 (2004).

27. United States v. Atlantic Research Corp., __U.S.__, 127 S. Ct. 2331 (2007).

28. RCRA, *supra* note 19.

29. WILLIAM H. RODGERS JR., ENVIRONMENTAL LAW 569-70 (2d. ed. 1994).

30. 42 U.S.C. §6903(27), RCRA §1004(27).

31. RODGERS, *supra* note 29, at 578.

32. *See* MARC REISNER, CADILLAC DESERT: THE AMERICAN WEST AND ITS DISAPPEARING WATER (1986).

33. 42 U.S.C. §6922(b)(1).

34. U.S. EPA, Waste Minimization: Basic Information, *supra* note 3.

35. This program is described on EPA's website at www.epa.gov/epaoswer/ hazwaste/minimize/partnership.html.

36. *See* U.S. EPA, NPEP Success Stories, *available at* www.epa.gov/epaoswer/ hazwaste/minimize/success.html.

37. U.S. EPA, National Analysis: The National Biennial RCRA Hazardous Waste Report (Based on 2005 Data) at 1-1.

38. *Id.*

Chapter 22

Municipal Solid Waste: Building Stronger Connections to Jobs and the Economy

Marian Chertow

The most obvious and tangible result of consumption in the United States is the amount and variety of the trash we generate. Agenda 21, the action plan resulting from the 1992 U.N. Conference on Environment and Development, states that "unsustainable patterns of production and consumption are increasing the quantities and variety of environmentally persistent wastes at unprecedented rates."[1] Since 2002, these patterns have intensified in the United States: larger homes, more possessions, and increasing levels of construction and demolition wastes. The question of how to measure this growth is compounded by ongoing confusion over how to count and classify what is discarded.

This chapter begins with a discussion of standards for progress in sustainability in waste management. It then examines recent trends in the management of municipal solid waste (MSW)—everyday trash from homes and businesses—including its generation, recovery, and disposal. Better data analysis since 2002 has enabled us to have a clearer picture of the problems of MSW management. There are wide variations in recycling and composting levels among states. "Pay-as-you-throw" programs, in which disposal fees are based on the amount of waste generated, now reach one-fourth of the country's population, and studies indicate they can be successful in reducing residential waste generation. The chapter concludes with several recommendations for the next decade, including the need to make greater efforts to create opportunities for economic development and job creation in preventing, reusing, recycling, and remanufacturing MSW.

Can Waste Management Be More Sustainable?

To define sustainability for U.S. solid waste management with future generations in mind, we must separate total *waste generation*—the sum of discards that are reused, recovered, and disposed—from *waste disposal* alone, which includes landfilling of

waste with all of the attendant land use and environmental problems
that can last for generations. While it is best not to create waste in the
first place, once we have discarded material, in most instances the
most desirable path is reuse and recovery.

There are four broad indicators by which to measure progress toward sustainability in waste management:

- *Substantially decreasing dependence on landfilling for disposal.* Even if more waste is generated, larger percentages
  should go to recycling and composting as a means of reducing the hundreds of millions of tons of solid waste that today is landfilled. In addition to the many problems of
  landfilling, there is now evidence to suggest that we have
  underestimated the greenhouse gas impacts of the methane
  emitted by landfills.

- *Achieving steady state or decreasing levels of overall
  waste generation.* At the simplest level, a system heading
  toward sustainability should plateau in absolute terms and
  should generate less waste over time. Because increasing
  generation strongly correlates with increasing population,
  per capita generation is an essential metric to control as the
  population grows.

  A technical means of defining sustainability for solid
  waste would be to ask at what level of solid waste generation acceptable levels of damage would occur; or even to
  ask at what level, on a lifecycle basis, the impact from solid
  waste would be sustainable. Critics have often argued that
  because the United States is land-rich, solid waste can be
  isolated in a few areas at little expense to environmental
  health. This view is short-sighted. It misses, for one thing,
  the opportunities to preserve embedded energy and materials over time and to restore them to the productive economy. Further, it does not consider the potential of reduced
  production and consumption at all. A middle ground seeks
  steady state or declining generation of waste over time
  but, if generation does rise, to achieve a level of composting and recycling that keeps decreasing the amount of
  waste that is disposed.

- *Decoupling increases in waste generation from increases
  in GDP.* There is a clear statistical relationship between
  waste generation and wealth as measured by GDP per capita: the stronger the economy, the more trash generated.

Because, to a large extent, waste generation is a function of consumption, decoupling waste from wealth would imply that Americans could increase their income but still consume less material in the process.

- *Devising a reliable measurement system at both state and federal levels.* Without establishing some standard definitions and practices to enable accountability for waste, it is impossible to discern if the United States is even pointed in the direction of decreasing generation and disposal.

To be able to move in a more sustainable direction with waste management, it is necessary to understand the prevailing regulatory authority. Some of the challenges to achieving sustainability lie in the structure of U.S. environmental law. For example, both hazardous and nonhazardous wastes are regulated by the federal Resource Conservation and Recovery Act (RCRA).[2] Under RCRA there are strict federal management regimes for hazardous wastes. But there is little federal authority over nonhazardous materials, where most of the regulatory authority is left to state and local governments. Consequently, behavior and practices across the country vary from state to state and region to region.

Physically, the waste streams, too, vary a great deal from place to place based on differences in climate, concentration of population, level of economic growth and mix of industries, availability of recovery sectors, and many other variables. Different conditions require different responses. EPA has provided, and almost all states have adopted in some form depending on local conditions, a four-pronged hierarchy of integrated waste management options. These four options are intended to complement each other, with the most preferable options near the top of the list. As stated in EPA's waste program description in October 2006, these options are:

1. Source reduction (or waste prevention), including reuse of products and on-site (or backyard) composting of yard trimmings;
2. Recycling, including off-site (or community) composting;
3. Combustion with energy recovery;
4. Disposal through landfilling or combustion without energy recovery.[3]

The tiers of the hierarchy comport with sustainability choices. Underlying the order of presentation are relative estimates of environmental impact and cost. Each successive tier involves more materials use and loss, and therefore less economic value and more environmental impact than the previous level.

Trends and Progress Toward Sustainability Since 2002

A review of solid waste management since 2002 reveals four major trends:

1. Landfills continue to receive most of the waste generated, according to both EPA and the journal *BioCycle*. There is, however, great regional variation in the amount of waste landfilled; for example 36 percent is landfilled in New England, where waste-to-energy and recycling are popular, compared to 77 percent in the Midwest and 85 percent in the Rocky Mountain states.[4]

2. Recycling and composting continue to make some gains, but with dramatic variations among the states. As reported by *BioCycle*, some states recover less than 5 percent of waste generated (Mississippi, Oklahoma, and South Dakota), while others recover over 40 percent (Minnesota, New York, Oregon, Tennessee, and Washington).[5]

3. Shifts in consumption patterns have caused particular items in the waste stream to draw attention, such as the 30 billion plastic water bottles consumed in the United States in 2005.[6] With a change in taste toward water, juice, wine, and iced tea, several state legislatures are now debating whether to initiate or update container deposit laws passed in the 1970s and 1980s, which focused primarily on beer and soda containers.

4. International regulatory regimes have affected U.S. companies. Notably, European Union regulations concerning waste electronics (WEEE) and restrictions on hazardous substances in products (RoHS) have made companies much more conscious of what is in waste and how it must be handled to maintain sales in European markets.

Because of methodological differences among EPA, *Biocycle*, and others, it is not possible to draw a conclusion on whether overall waste generation is increasing or decreasing at the national level. Still, some state officials have been conducting research to try to explain why *their* waste is increasing. A 2006 report released in North Carolina notes that disposal rates for construction and demolition waste since 2002 have increased three times faster than for MSW.[7] Recognition in Oregon of a 70 percent rise in waste generation from 1993 to 2005 (including construction and demolition waste) led to a study that produced the 2007 report "Solid Waste Generation in Oregon: Composition and Causes of Change."[8] The study tested 16 hypotheses to try to account for increases in waste in Oregon. It found that although part of the increase can be attributed to methodological factors, some 50-80 percent is real growth in waste-generating activities such as construction and demolition, purchases of household furnishings, and shorter-lasting durable goods.

One effective approach to more sustainable solid waste management is pay-as-you-throw programs, which have been shown both to reduce waste generated and to increase the incentives to recycle. In such a program, the more waste one discards, the more one owes. That is, if one resident generates more waste than another, it is still her right to do so, but she must pay an increased price for her waste services. In these schemes there is no comparable charge for recycling or composting, which provides an incentive to divert materials to these less expensive options. Pay-as-you-throw programs began in the mid-1980s. A 2006 report from EPA shows that the total number of programs grew from 5,200 in 2001 to 7,100 programs in 2006. Nearly 25 percent of the U.S. population is now covered by pay-as-you-throw programs.[9]

Data Issues: The Thorny Problem of Accounting for Waste

What is most baffling on the sustainability front is how difficult it is to reliably measure and account for trash. Attempts to do so are thwarted by problems in both defining *what* is considered to be municipal solid waste and deciding *how*, methodologically, that waste is to be counted. In fact, measuring waste has been highly inconsistent—especially in regard to what is generated, what is recovered, and how to analyze what used to be counted but now is not based on "waste prevention" programs. The numbers are more reliable for materials sent to carefully controlled waste-to-energy facilities and for some recyclables such as cans and bottles. Still, inconsistencies in counting recycling abound, centering on issues such as what types of scrap and which dealers are to be included, what is composted in backyards versus organized collection of yard waste, and where the divide is between commercial and industrial recovery.

The biggest problem concerning *what* is counted is that MSW is often co-managed with additional waste streams including sludge, non-hazardous industrial wastes, ash from waste-to-energy plants, and other commercial wastes such as construction and demolition (C&D) debris. Counting even some of these other wastes drives up both the quantity of tons landfilled and the quantity recycled, for some parts of the co-managed wastes can also be recovered.

The heart of the problem of *how* to count is that EPA uses a theoretical model to measure what ought to be in the waste based on what is produced, imported, and exported in the country. Because this materials flow approach relies on a system of estimates based on national production data, it also does not differentiate waste by states or regions. The states and large private waste facility operators do not rely on theory; their methodology is to count actual tons brought to various waste or recovery facilities, and these numbers tell a different tale from those of EPA, as discussed below.

The discrepancies created by problems of what and how to count are enormous. EPA reported that in 1999 there were 132 million tons of solid waste landfilled and 64 million tons recycled (see Figure 1). For the same year, *BioCycle* reported 226 million tons landfilled with 126 million tons recycled, and private-sector haulers through the Environmental Research and Education Foundation (EREF) found 370 million tons landfilled with 146 million tons recycled.[10] Clearly, these are substantially different conclusions about the trends in waste management. According to EPA's October 2006 report *Municipal Solid Waste in the United States: 2005 Facts and Figures*, from 2000 to 2004 generation was almost steady state, and even declined slightly when population increase is factored out. In contrast, the *BioCycle* figures in its "State of Garbage in America" survey for 2000-2004 show a 24 percent increase in overall waste generation (compared to EPA's small, 3 percent total rise). It seems that EPA's theoretical system is a consistent snapshot, but not of the waste stream public and private managers must deal with every day.[11]

Figure 1
Comparing Data Sources: Municipal Solid Waste
in the United States

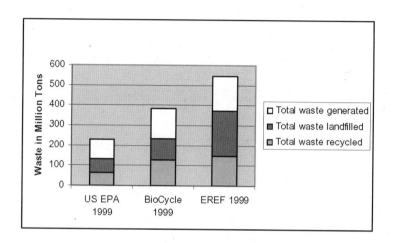

Source: EPA, *Biocycle*, and private-sector data from a study sponsored by the
Environmental Research and Education Fund (EREF).

Some progress has been made in our understanding of the waste
stream. Researchers from Columbia University's Earth Engineering
Center joined with the *BioCycle* staff to improve statistical methods
concerning what and how to count discarded material from states.
This improvement has allowed *BioCycle* to begin to separate out some
of the co-managed wastes from what is more strictly defined as MSW.
Even though this has reduced the generation as reported by the states
by over 100 million tons, the *BioCycle* numbers are still more than 100
million tons greater than the amount that EPA's model projects (see
Table 1).

Table 1
The Counting Gap in Amount of MSW Generated as
Reported by EPA and *BioCycle* for 2004

Total reported MSW generation in tons/year for 2004 (*BioCycle*)	509 million tons
Total tons adjusted by removing non-MSW categories (*BioCycle*)	<u>388 million tons</u>
Adjustment to total MSW generation for 2004	121 million tons
Total MSW tons generation as reported by US EPA for 2004	247 million tons
Discrepancy between EPA and adjusted *BioCycle* figure	141 million tons

Recommendations

1. Address the counting basics. Good data is essential for measuring and moving toward sustainability. *BioCycle* and the Environmental Research and Education Fund (EREF) (Figure 1) offer empirically collected data sources, while EPA's are based on modeling. The EPA methodology is useful as a starting point for tracking specific products and materials with respect to generation and recovery, but it does not deal effectively with the problem of disposal. EPA should take a more open source approach and make its existing datasets more transparent for interested public, private, and NGO user groups who could help to monitor and measure disposal more accurately. At a policy level, efforts to continue to standardize MSW statistics across the states, as *BioCycle* has begun to do, should continue through organized meetings of interested federal, state, and local officials.

2. Intensify the focus on industrial and construction/demolition waste. Given the enormity of non-MSW streams, especially construction and demolition (C&D) waste and nonhazardous industrial waste, more attention must be paid to monitoring and policy setting in these areas even if they are outside the immediate arena of public attention. These two streams most often muddy the data on municipal solid waste, confounding our ability to understand trends.

In July 2006, Massachusetts launched a new approach based on a decision to ban items from the C&D stream from disposal, specifically asphalt pavement, brick, concrete, metal, and wood. As explained by the Massachusetts Department of Environmental Protection, "increasing recycling and other diversion of C&D materials helps support development of in-state processing businesses and preserves valuable, limited disposal capacity in the Commonwealth."[12] If the Massachusetts model is successful, many states could replicate it.

With respect to nonhazardous industrial waste, a comprehensive study of generation and disposal quantities of these materials has not been undertaken since the 1980s. At that time, the data showed this stream to be 20-30 times larger than the MSW stream. Quantities have likely decreased, given the increased costs of water and energy, but this has not been verified. EPA should work with states to count and categorize nonhazardous industrial wastes, note where progress has been made, highlight where the largest problems remain, and make appropriate recommendations to public and private actors.

3. Expand pay-as-you-throw programs. State and local governments, with support from EPA, should expand the pay-as-you-throw programs. Statistical analysis from more than one thousand communities shows that pay-as-you-throw programs reduce residential disposal by 17 percent. About 5-6 percent of that total comes from growth in recycling, another 4-5 percent from increases in yard waste programs, and about 6 percent apparently from source reduction.[13] These encouraging results show that not only does pay-as-you-throw provide appropriate economic incentives to increase recovery, but that buying decisions of customers could also be affected by the presence of these programs.

4. Connect waste management with job creation. This idea has taken various forms since the 1970s, but many today believe that, as Thomas Friedman has written, "Green technology is emerging as the most important industry of the 21st century."[14] Not only has interest in recycling and composting created many jobs, but as resources become more constrained, we can expect new opportunities in key environmental industry sectors, such as resource recovery, for parts of the country that are ready with both investment and training for job growth. Although job creation does not, on its own, reduce MSW generation, it does reduce disposal as materials are diverted to an economic second life.

The National Research Council should examine the potential opportunities for reuse of industrial byproducts to catalyze economic activity by entrepreneurs, community developers, and military personnel. Beyond MSW, large opportunities are available in numerous industrial sectors that could help to align economy and environment. Conferences such as the Byproduct Summit jointly sponsored by EPA and *Waste News* bring together the parties who want to reuse their discards beneficially in environmentally and economically successful ways.

Conclusion

This chapter has reviewed trends in solid waste management in the last few years to assess whether practices are leading to sustainable results. Numerous studies reveal that many states are quite aware of the growing waste problems but do not know how to curb them effectively, given the multiple actors and practices involved well beyond the domain of waste and recycling managers. There are clearly successful programs to emulate, such as pay-as-you-throw, which continues to grow, and new experiments such as the program in Massachusetts to ban some construction materials from landfill and assist with reuse opportunities. Most important, solid waste management must be understood as the end of the production system when most opportunities have already passed by. The greatest hope for sustainability is to connect the end of the system with earlier stages through reuse, remanufacturing, and the broadest possible view of the connections possible between waste, people, and the economy.

ENDNOTES

1. U.N. Conference on Environment and Development (UNCED), Agenda 21, Chapter 21, *available at* www.un.org/esa/sustdev/agenda21chapter21. htm.

2. 42 U.S.C. §§6901-6992k.

3. U.S. EPA, MUNICIPAL & INDUSTRIAL SOLID WASTE DIVISION, MUNICIPAL SOLID WASTE IN THE UNITED STATES: 2005 FACTS AND FIGURES, Executive Summary, Oct. 18, 2006.

4. Phil Simmons et al., *The State of Garbage in America*, BIOCYCLE, April 2006.

5. *Id.*

6. Beverage Marketing Corporation data, 2006.

7. N.C. DEP'T OF ENV'T & NATURAL RES., NORTH CAROLINA SOLID WASTE MANAGEMENT ANNUAL REPORT, JULY 1, 2005-JUNE 30, 2006, *available at* www.wastenotnc.org/SWHOME/AR05-06.pdf.

8. DAVID ALLAWAY, OREGON DEP'T OF ENVTL. QUALITY, *Solid Waste in Oregon: Composition and Causes of Change* (Feb. 6, 2007).

9. Lisa Skumatz & David Freeman, *Pay As You Throw in the US: 2006 Update and Analyses—Final Report.* Cosponsored by U.S. EPA Office of Solid Waste and Skumatz Economic Research Associates, Inc.

10. For a more complete rendering of the numbers, see Marian Chertow, *Pursuing Sustainable Solid Waste Management*, 32 ELR 10812 (July 2002).

11. Simmons et al., *supra* note 4; U.S. EPA, *supra* note 3; Chertow, *supra* note 10. *See also* ENVTL. RESEARCH & EDUC. FOUND. (EREF), SIZE OF THE U.S. SOLID WASTE INDUSTRY 1, app. A (2001).

12. *See* MASSACHUSETTS DEP'T OF ENVTL. PROT. (MASSDEP), FAQs about the Massachusetts Construction and Demolition Materials Waste Bans, *available at* www.mass.gov/dep/recycle/solid/cdbanfaq.pdf.

13. Lisa Skumatz & John Green, *Variable Rates Offer Constant Progress*, RESOURCE RECYCLING, June 2001.

14. Thomas L. Friedman, *China's Little Green Book*, N.Y. TIMES, Nov. 2, 2005, *available at* http://query.nytimes.com/gst/fullpage.html?res= 9E0CE1DD163EF931A35752C1A9639C8B63&sec=&spon=&page wanted=1.

VI. Land Use and Transportation

Land Use: Blending Smart Growth With Social Equity and Climate Change Mitigation

Patricia Salkin

Land, and how we use it, is at the heart of our ability to achieve the sustainability goals outlined in Agenda 21. Decisions about what can be built, and where, have an impact on the natural environment, public health and safety, and affordability—all important sustainability concepts. Because land use decisionmaking in the United States is decentralized—meaning that the 50 states each provide their own statutory framework for the tens of thousands of local governments across the country that have broad authority to exercise land use control—sustainability cannot be achieved without reforming the legal structure in which these decisions are made. While a decentralized system of land use control allows local governments to have more flexibility in making tailored land use decisions, it also provides the opportunity for some localities to ignore the need to adopt and implement sustainable land use policies because some goals, such as housing affordability for all and the siting of locally unwanted uses, may not be popular with voting constituents.

This chapter provides a brief background on the evolution of the U.S. system for controlling land use, with a focus on the most recent efforts at modernization to achieve sustainability (the smart growth movement). The chapter identifies and examines current trends that hold promise for sustainability—integration of environmental justice principles with local land use planning, the use of community benefit agreements, and the link between climate change and land use decisionmaking—and which may have enough political power to effect far-reaching reforms in our approach to land use.

Smart Growth

Sustainable land development requires consistent integration of social, environmental, and economic considerations into decisionmaking to produce results that promote a sound, coordinated, and harmonious built environment. The traditional "Euclidian" system of zoning (i.e., separating incompatible land uses), now almost a century old, has proven ineffective when it comes to resource management and sustainable land use. Instead of generating smart growth, it continues to produce sprawling communities that lack efficiencies and economies of scale in housing, transportation, agriculture, energy, and public health. Due in part to this system, land consumption in the United States continues to grow faster than population.

Following a history of unsuccessful attempts to address the inefficiencies of our system of land use control—beginning in the 1960s with an effort to promote regionalism, a movement in the 1970s to shift to a national land use policy, and a desire in the 1980s to promote intergovernmental coordination in land use planning and decision-making—"smart growth" emerged in the 1990s as a concept for creative ways to rethink and redefine our almost century-old land use system. Akin to Agenda 21, smart growth can best be defined as a series of principles that includes, among other things, mixed land uses, preservation of open space, choice in transportation options, and a focus on reenergizing communities for growth and infill. Other principles include creating walkable communities, maintaining or creating distinctive communities with a sense of place, and encouraging community involvement in development decisions. An overriding theme in the smart growth movement is that no single approach works best for every region and community, so each locality must take its own approach to designing and implementing new land use systems that produce more favorable sustainability patterns.

From 1991 to 2001, smart growth legislation was introduced and implemented at all levels of government. During this time, 17 governors issued 19 executive orders on planning and smart growth. In addition, more than 2,000 land use or planning bills were introduced in statehouses across the country, with approximately 20 percent being enacted into law. The movement may have peaked in 2001, when 27 governors initiated planning and smart growth proposals. Some of this activity can be traced to the modernization efforts initiated by the American Planning Association through the publication of its *Growing Smart Legislative Guidebook*.[1] Although a number of governors continue to list smart growth actions among their initiatives, framing sustainable development purely around the principles of smart growth may have proven to be short-lived. Today, at both the federal and state levels, grant programs and new smart growth initiatives have diminished in number and size. Furthermore, while ballot initiatives supporting smart growth were popular in 2000, by 2007 the pendulum seems to have swung in the opposite direction with a series of ballot initiatives designed to promote agendas that are opposed to zoning, land use, and eminent domain.

The good news, however, is that there is strong evidence of continuing nationwide interest and active implementation of smart growth principles and strategies at the local level, although these actions are not always labeled "smart growth." Perhaps this is attributable to the trickle-down effect of policies and programs adopted earlier. Furthermore, issues of social equity are finally being linked to land use planning and land use controls, and there is a growing realization that sustainable land use policies are the key to dealing effectively with many of the challenges presented by climate change,. These two major issues—social equity and climate change—provide an opportunity to also address a missing ingredient to success: cooperation and coordination between and among all levels of government.

Continuing Interest in Smart Growth: The Good News

Five years ago state governments were vigorously promoting sustainable land use within the smart growth context. Recommendations at the time called for, among other things, sustained leadership, the need to address regionalism and home rule, ensuring consistency in land use policies among the states, realigning federal policies and influences to promote smart growth efforts, and making wise investments through targeted spending in support of sustainable policies and practices. What follows is an update on recent initiatives, demonstrating a reduced level of activity but a continuing interest in innovative approaches for sustainability.

Arizona's Governor Janet Napolitano has continued former Governor Janet Hull's commitment to smart growth, asking the Growing Smarter Oversight Council to create a list of guiding principles, which were included in the Council's 2006 Annual Report.[2] In her 2007 State of the State address, Governor Napolitano's ongoing support of smart growth was evident as she focused on Arizona's rapid population growth, and necessary transportation, air, and water-quality solutions.[3] By executive order she created the Growth Cabinet in the state government, composed of representatives from 15 state departments, agencies, and offices.[4] (In 2008, the Council was reconstituted as the Growth Cabinet Advisory Board.)

Governor Bill Ritter of Colorado has pledged to support smart growth policies, and has stated that he will work with local governments to "encourage greater cooperation among jurisdictions and urge a careful balancing of . . . commercial, residential and transportation needs against protecting [our] natural resources."[5] He has also promised to support water conservation, efficiency, and reuse through better policies and planning. In Connecticut, Governor M. Jodi Rell in 2006 created the Office of Responsible Growth,[6] charged with initiating interagency and regional planning dialogues, developing incentives for communities to engage in planning efforts, and updating the state's Green Plan. She also emphasized continued support of these smart growth policies in her 2007 State of the State address.[7]

Delaware's governor, Ruth Ann Minner, among other things, enacted amendments to the state's Land Use Planning Act to improve the decisionmaking process and is continuing to develop the Livable Delaware program to include statewide strategy maps that illustrate areas where state policies favor or disfavor development. The state's Center of Infrastructure and Intergovernmental Relations, coordinated through the Economic Development Office, helps to guide development to appropriate growth areas and to encourage infill and the reuse of sites with existing infrastructure.[8]

Once a leader with Delaware, Maryland's smart growth efforts waned after Governor Parris Glendenning left office in 2003. In 2007, however, newly elected Governor Martin O'Malley directed the Secretary of Planning to reestablish the Office of Smart Growth. He further pledged to support open space preservation, improvements to water and wastewater systems, and sustainable farming efforts.[9]

In Massachusetts, former governor Mitt Romney in 2003 created the Office for Commonwealth Development, which, among other things, oversees and coordinates the Office of Environmental Affairs, the Department of Housing and Community Development, the Office of Transportation, and certain programs within the Division of Energy Resources.[10] This effort is an example of how states can encourage local governments to coordinate their policies and act regionally when the statehouse facilitates its own interagency coordination. The current governor, Deval Patrick, indicated his support of smart growth in both his campaign materials and in his 2007 State of the State Address.[11]

In Pennsylvania, amendments in 2003 to the Municipality Planning Code included provisions relating to intergovernmental cooperative planning, and in 2005, Governor Ed Rendell launched the Growing Greener II program, providing $625 million over a six-year period for environmental protection and restoration, advanced energy projects, and mixed-use housing and redevelopment projects.[12]

Backlash Against Smart Growth: Measure 37 and *Kelo*

While the above developments in state governments have been positive, the past several years have also seen a backlash against policies favoring sustainable property regulations. Just at the time when smart growth was gaining in popularity, a battle in Oregon pitted private property rights activists against government land regulators. A ballot initiative, Measure 37, was passed by the voters in 2004, entitling property owners to compensation for decreases in fair market property values due to land use regulations passed after their acquisition of their property.[13] If the government either cannot pay or chooses not to pay, Measure 37 requires the government to waive the specific land use regulation. As of May 2007, more than $19 billion in claims had been filed in Oregon,[14] slowing the implementation of new land use controls across the state. There has also been a pull-back on the enforcement of existing land use regulations as officials have felt compelled to approve requested waivers absent sufficient funds to pay under the measure. Measure 37 raised a red flag for government regulators across the country that land use regulations are prone to perhaps increased public scrutiny.

In 2005, the U.S. Supreme Court ruled in *Kelo v. City of New London*[15] that economic development is a valid public purpose to satisfy the Fifth Amendment requirement when government condemns private property. In the aftermath of *Kelo*, another backlash in public opinion erupted. Congress and state legislatures quickly introduced a cascade of "reform" legislation—approximately six hundred bills introduced in 43 states. Of this number, legislatures in 23 states passed 35 pieces of legislation that were signed into law.[16] Tied to the backlash from Measure 37 and *Kelo*, a number of initiatives related to takings and eminent domain were on the ballot in 2006.[17] Only one, Arizona's Proposition 207, the Private Property Rights Protection Act, passed;[18] voters defeated similar measures in California, Idaho, and Washington.[19] But the battle of public opinion is not over; these backlashes serve as a harsh reminder that land use decisionmaking often occurs in a highly charged political environment. Advocates for sustainability will need to reframe the land use issue in a manner that supports other current movements that advance the same goals, such as those briefly discussed below.

Reframing the Land Use Issues: 2007-2012

The two efforts that have the greatest promise of continuing to effect sustainability in land use are: (1) the increasing attention to the linkage between environmental justice and land use; and (2) the connection that is now being articulated between land use and climate change policies. Related to both efforts is the use of community benefits agreements between developers and neighborhoods, which provide a new opportunity to promote community sustainability.

Environmental Justice

According to the U.S. Environmental Protection Agency (EPA), environmental justice (EJ) means:

> the fair treatment and meaningful involvement of all people regardless of race, color, national origin, culture, education, or income with respect to the development, implementation, and enforcement of environmental laws, regulations, and policies. *Fair treatment* means that no group of people, including racial, ethnic, or socioeconomic groups, should bear a disproportionate share of negative consequences resulting from industrial, municipal, and commercial operations or the execution of federal, state, local, and tribal environmental programs and policies. *Meaningful involvement* means that: (1) potentially affected community residents have an appropriate opportunity to participate in decisions about a proposed activity that will affect their environment and/or health; (2) the public's contribution can influence the regulatory agency's decision; (3) the concerns of all participants involved will be considered in the decision-making process; and (4) the decision-makers seek out and facilitate the involvement of those potentially affected.[20]

Environmental justice goes to the core of traditional land use decisions, such as choosing sites for harmful locally unwanted land uses (e.g., toxic dumps, bus depots, and other industrial uses) adjacent to residential neighborhoods (geographic equity); formulating procedures for deciding where to site these unwanted land uses, including the location and timing of public hearings (procedural equity); and assessing sociological factors, including which groups hold the political power inherent in land-use decisions (social equity).[21] With greater awareness to these issues following the enactment of the Civil Rights Act of 1964, it was realized that "the property regulation, planning, and zoning policies of many cities around the country had what must be called a negative impact on EJ."[22] It has also been noted that "zoning tends to act as the 'gatekeeper' in terms of where noxious uses can be legally sited within a municipality, but the ramifications of zoning on environmental health and equity have been somewhat hidden."[23] Still, planning and traditional land-use control laws—including coordinated environmental review with these local government actions—can serve as more proactive measures to address environmental justice concerns.[24] One scholar recently noted that "[t]he next frontier for both the movement and the focus of environmental justice scholarship . . . is land use planning."[25]

A 2003 report by the National Academy of Public Administrators (NAPA)[26] focuses on how local governments can use existing land use planning and zoning tools to further EJ principles. For example, comprehensive plans can articulate goals that include, but are not limited to, several aspects of EJ: housing affordability for all in the community; public participation in land use decisionmaking; clean air and safe drinking water for all in the community; and appropriate public infrastructure in a locality. In addition, the report points to the importance of including representatives from all neighborhoods and ethnic, racial, and cultural groups, as well as people who have different economic means, on planning and zoning boards and commissions. The report also demonstrates how zoning and other land use controls can spread unwanted land uses throughout the community so as not to disproportionately site them in minority or low-income neighborhoods. Furthermore, where uses deemed harmful to public health are discovered in these neighborhoods, rather than simply allowing them to continue as nonconforming uses, municipalities can use an amortization method to phase out the noxious uses over a period of time.

Following the 2003 report, NAPA partnered with the Government Law Center of Albany Law School to develop a model training curriculum for members of planning and zoning boards, local legislative bodies, professional planners, and municipal attorneys. The curriculum was piloted in Albany, Chicago, and San Francisco, followed by a workshop in Albuquerque and a day-long program at Howard Law School in the spring of 2007. The American Planning Association (APA) partnered with NAPA on a forthcoming Planners Advisory Service Report on EJ authored by Professor Tony Arnold, as well as a series of national workshops for planners, lawyers, and municipal officials on EJ. These activities document the beginning of a new paradigm for promoting sustainable land use through the articulation and implementation of EJ principles.

Community benefits agreements (CBAs) have recently emerged as another tool for helping to ensure EJ and sustainability in development projects that have extensive impacts on surrounding communities. A CBA is a private contract negotiated between a developer and community representatives that specifies the benefits that the developer will provide to the community in exchange for the community's support of its proposed development. A promise of community support may be especially useful to a developer seeking government subsidies or project approvals,[27] and the promise of amenities and enhancements that might not otherwise be obtainable by the community can help to bring about greater equity in livability and sustainability.

CBAs are generally negotiated between a developer and coalitions of community groups. Many CBA provisions are inspired by social justice issues; common CBA benefits include living-wage provisions, local hiring plans, guarantees that developments will include low-income housing in their plans, and assurances of minority hiring minimums.[28] Because the agreements are negotiated between community coalitions and interested developers, the benefits can be tailored to meet specific community needs, such as the need for parks, day care centers, or job training facilities.[29]

CBAs are considered by their supporters to be powerful tools for assuring that communities' needs will not be neglected by large developers. Many developers also support the negotiating process as a method by which they can obtain community support and thereby avoid government refusal of their projects. CBAs have been negotiated for nearly 50 development projects in cities across the country.[30]

CBAs represent an opportunity to accomplish redevelopment projects in a manner that achieves social equity and engages all community stakeholders in the project with an eye toward designing a process and product that can be win-win for communities. Infusing sustainability concepts into early CBAs will set a standard, as these agreements are likely to be looked to as models for the future. (There are, to be sure, myriad legal issues for all participants in a CBA, but that is a topic beyond the scope of this chapter.)

Climate Change and Land Use

Climate change can only be addressed comprehensively when decisionmakers take notice of, and incorporate, its land use implications. (For a fuller discussion of climate change, see Chapter 17.) Achieving reductions in the levels of greenhouse gases requires addressing a number of issues that are intertwined with land use, including transportation planning; combating sprawl through revitalization and infill of cities and towns; continued implementation of smart growth principles that include promoting mixed use and walkable communities, and reducing dependency on the automobile; proactively inviting and planning for the siting of alternative energy uses such as wind farms; and promoting other energy-efficient green development construction and renovation projects. Whereas 10 years ago governors were emphasizing smart growth in their annual state of the state messages, in 2007 their emphases shifted to issues surrounding climate change.[31]

If the states are going to meet their promises regarding greenhouse gas emissions, they must address the land use connection and appropriately incentivize municipal regulators to adjust to a new paradigm. According to the Natural Resources Defense Council, "if all new communities were designed using smart growth strategies we could slash emissions by about 595 million metric tons after 10 years, or 10 percent of total U.S. emission of global warming pollution."[32] In April 2007, the intersection of climate change and land use issues came to the forefront when the attorney general of California filed a lawsuit against San Bernardino County for failing to combat sprawl and to address greenhouse gas emissions in its 25-year growth plan.[33] One commentator observed that "if the suit is successful, California cities and counties could be forced to take steps to limit sprawl, promote compact development, require builders to design energy-efficient houses that offer solar power, and encourage less driving, more mass transit, and use of alternative fuels."[34] The August 2007 settlement agreement requires the county to plan for greenhouse gas reductions from its discretionary land use decisions and, more generally, to prepare and implement a greenhouse gas reduction plan.[35]

The New York metropolitan region offers an example of how local governments are making progress in melding climate change and land use goals. A recent study revealed that "New Yorkers produce nearly 70% less greenhouse gas per capita than the national average."[36] One scholar credits the New York City zoning laws, citing smaller residences, a mix of residential and commercial uses, and high population density that makes public transportation more plausible—all of which are the effects of zoning choices.[37]

Recommendations

The analysis in this chapter leads to four recommendations:

1. Sustained state and local leadership remains an essential element of the country's ability to effectively integrate sustainable development into the land use system. Little has been accomplished in addressing the decentralized framework for land use planning, which continues to lead to provincialism in decisionmaking. Today, the stakes are not only regionwide and statewide; they are national in scope (e.g., climate change). Many state governments have slowed their efforts to coordinate varied state-level agency activities related to smart growth and sustainability, and the amount of money being invested in smart growth related initiatives is dwindling rather than increasing. However, the ability to integrate the power of land use planning decisionmaking with climate change is the next major national platform from which sustainability with effective land use controls can spring. Effective leadership must take these issues into account in order to promote sustainability.

2. A national report card on smart growth is essential. Land use planning and land use controls are largely decentralized at the local level, and no entity has stepped in to benchmark the success of the varied programs. Therefore, it is hard to claim successes or label failures, and this lack of follow-up may be partially responsible for the decline in state-level activity. The public needs a scorecard that, among other things, indicates the actual number of acres of land preserved through various smart growth strategies, the number of affordable housing units created through smart growth and EJ initiatives, and the number of road trips reduced as a result of implementing smart growth principles. In short, there is a need for measurable goals to benchmark, and illustrative stories to be shared, if there is to be sustained leadership in this movement. Although a few states and EPA have developed some benchmarking for specific programs,[38] these are not held up as national models and they have failed to capture attention and motivate more sustainable behavior.

3. Sustainability advocates need to step up the political pressure for renewed attention to smart growth principles and for the attendant funding. Advocates must promote greater awareness and understanding of the opportunities for achieving social equity through the EJ and land use connection and through the use of community benefit agreements. Reframing land use issues to encompass and complement these more contemporary dialogues is important to maintaining the appeal and prominence of the sustainable growth movement. The political cachet that has been attached to the concerns over climate change provides a current opportunity that should be utilized to advance the critical connection between land use and sustainability.

4. Encouraging collaboration and cooperation among all levels of government is essential to ensuring the success of smart growth initiatives. Municipalities must coordinate their land use planning efforts on a regional scale. Within each state, interagency task forces should be appointed to work on sustainability with a particular focus on coordinating and implementing land use initiatives. Although achieving sustainable land use rests with the individual states and localities, the federal government should provide national goals and offer funding to states and localities for efforts that will collectively move the United States in the direction of greater sustainability.

Conclusion

Municipalities across the United States are vested with the authority and the responsibility to make decisions about how our use of land affects both the built and natural environments. The ability of local governments to design and implement individualized land use plans enables municipalities to do much to achieve sustainability on a micro scale. Still, effective federal and state tools, policies, and incentives must be put in place to encourage the adoption of local smart growth policies, coordination of local land use decision-making with environmental justice principles, and the implementation of local policies and local laws designed to slow climate change so that the country can more quickly and more efficiently accomplish sustainability. There has been some progress toward this goal since the adoption of Agenda 21, but there is more to be done. The actions recommended above will have negligible financial impacts on government resources but will reap substantial, although financially unquantifiable, sustainability rewards in quality of life, better health, and greater equity.

ENDNOTES

1. AM. PLANNING ASS'N, GROWING SMART LEGISLATIVE GUIDEBOOK: MODEL STATUTES FOR PLANNING AND THE MANAGEMENT OF CHANGE (Stuart Meck ed., 2002); *see also* Patricia E. Salkin, *Implementation of the APA Growing Smart Legislative Guidebook: Beginning to Benchmark Success*, 33 REAL ESTATE L.J. 339 (2004).

2. *See* GOVERNOR'S GROWING SMARTER OVERSIGHT COUNCIL, PROPOSED GROWING SMARTER GUIDING PRINCIPLES FOR ARIZONA (2006), *available at* www.azcommerce.com/doclib/commasst/guiding%20principles%20-%20results/final/principles%204.06.06_final%20draft.pdf.

3. *See* State of Arizona, Gov. Janet Napolitano, State of the State Address, Jan. 8, 2007, *available at* http://azgovernor.gov/documents/2007%20SOS%20Address%20Public.pdf.

4. *See* Exec. Order No. 2007-05, Promoting Smarter Growth, *available at* http://azgovernor.gov/dms/upload/EO2007-05.pdf.

5. State of Colorado, Gov. Bill Ritter, The Colorado Promise 30 (2006), *available at* www.colorado.gov/governor/press/pdf/ritter_policy-book.pdf (last visited July 2007).

6. *See* State of Connecticut, M. Jodi Rell, Governor, Exec. Order No. 15, *available at* www.ct.gov/governorrell/cwp/view.asp?A=1719&Q=320908.

7. *See* Patricia E. Salkin, *Squaring the Circles on Sprawl: What More Can We Do? Progress Toward Sustainable Land Use in the States*, 16 WIDENER L.J. 787, 798 (2007).

8. *See* Delaware Office of State Planning website, www.state.de.us/planning/strategies/document_04/08_jobs.pdf (last visited July 2007).

9. State of Maryland, Gov. Martin O'Malley, State of the State Address (Jan. 31, 2007), *available at* www.gov.state.md.us/speeches/070131-StateOtState.html (last visited July 2007).

10. Massachusetts Office for Commonwealth Development, About Us, www.mass.gov/?pageID=ocdhomepage=1&L0=home&sid=Eocd (follow "About Us" hyperlink) (last visited July 2007).

11. *See* Deval Patrick on the Issues, Deval Patrick on Environment, www.ontheissues.org/Governor/Deval_Patrick_Environment.htm (last visited July 2007).

12. *See* Pennsylvania's Growing Greener website, www.growinggreener2.com (last visited July 2007).

13. The initiative passed by a staggering margin of 61 to 39 percent. Patricia E. Salkin & Amy Lavine, *Measure 37 and a Spoonful of Kelo: A Recipe for Property Rights Activists at the Ballot Box*, 38 URB. LAW. 1065 (2006).

14. *See* State of Oregon website, Measure 37 claims summary page, *available at* www.oregon.gov/LCD/MEASURE37/summaries_of_claims.shtml#Measure_37_Database_Project__Portland_State_University.

15. 545 U.S. 469 (2005).

16. Patricia E. Salkin, *Eminent Domain Legislation Post-Kelo: A State of the States*, 36 ELR 10864 (Nov. 2006).

17. Patricia E. Salkin & Amy Lavine, *Measure 37 and a Spoonful of* Kelo, *supra* note 13.

18. Nancy Kubasek, *Measure 37 Clones Fail at the Ballot Box*, 35 REAL EST. L.J. 611 (2007).

19. *Id.*

20. U.S. EPA, OFFICE OF ENVTL. JUSTICE, GUIDANCE TO ASSESSING AND ADDRESSING ALLEGATIONS OF ENVIRONMENTAL INJUSTICE, Working Draft, 7 (Jan. 10, 2001).

21. *See* Patricia E. Salkin, *Land Use, in* STUMBLING TOWARD SUSTAINABILITY 374 (John C. Dernbach ed., 2002).

22. Michael B. Gerrard, *Environmental Justice and Local Land Use Decisionmaking, in* TRENDS IN LAND USE LAW FROM A TO Z: ADULT USES TO ZONING (Patricia E. Salkin ed., 2001).

23. *See* Juliana Maantay, *Zoning Law, Health, and Environmental Justice: What's the Connection?*, 4 J. L., MED. & ETHICS 572 (2002).

24. CLIFFORD RECHTSCHAFFEN & EILEEN GAUNA, ENVIRONMENTAL JUSTICE: LAW, POLICY & REGULATION 297 (2002).

25. Craig Anthony Arnold, *Planning Milagros: Environmental Justice and Land Use Regulation*, 76 DENVER U. L. REV. 1 (1998).

26. *See* National Academy of Public Administrators (NAPA) website, www.napawash.org/Pubs/EJ.pdf (last visited July 2007).

27. JULIAN GROSS, COMMUNITY BENEFITS AGREEMENTS: MAKING DEVELOPMENT PROJECTS ACCOUNTABLE 9-10 (2005), *available at* www.goodjobsfirst.org/pdf/cba2005final.pdf.

28. *Id.* at 10-11.

29. *Id.* In a CBA created for a major expansion project at Los Angeles' LAX airport, for example, the agreement included provisions for the soundproofing of nearby schools and residences.

30. Harold Meyerson, *No Justice, No Growth; How Los Angeles Is Making Big-Time Developers Create Decent Jobs*, THE AMERICAN PROSPECT (Nov. 2006).

31. *See* NAT'L GOVERNORS ASS'N (NGA), THE GOVERNORS SPEAK — 2007: A REPORT ON THE STATE OF THE STATE ADDRESSES OF THE NATION'S AND U.S. TERRITORIES' GOVERNORS (2007), *available at* www.nga.org/Files/pdf/GOVSPEAK0704.PDF (last visited July 2007).

32. NATURAL RES. DEFENSE COUNCIL (NRDC), IF YOU BUILD IT, THEY WILL COME: AMERICANS WANT SMART GROWTH ALTERNATIVES TO CONVENTIONAL TRANSPORTATION, *available at* www.nrdc.org/building green/factsheets/smartgrowth.pdf, *citing* MARY JEAN BÜRER & DAVID B. GOLDSTEIN, NRDC, AND JOHN HOLTZCLAW, SIERRA CLUB, LOCATION EFFICIENCY AS THE MISSING PIECE OF THE ENERGY PUZZLE: HOW SMART GROWTH CAN UNLOCK TRILLION DOLLAR CONSUMER COST SAVINGS, *available at* http://docs.nrdc.org/air/air_06031001a.pdf (last visited July 2007).

33. Lora A. Lucero, *The Lawyers Confront Hot Air*, 30 ZONING & PLANNING L. REP. (July/Aug. 2007).

34. John Ritter, *Calif. Sees Sprawl as Warming Culprit*, USA TODAY, June 6, 2007, *available at* www.usatoday.com/weather/climate/globalwarming/2007-06-05-warming_N.htm?csp=34.

35. California ex rel. Brown v. County of San Bernardino, No. CIVSS 0700329 (Cal. Super. County of San Bernardino), *Order Regarding Settlement* (Aug. 28, 2007), *available at* http://ag.ca.gov/cms_pdfs/press/2007-08-21_San_Bernardino_settlement_agreement.pdf.

36. John R. Nolon & Jessica A. Bacher, *Zoning and Climate Change*, N.Y. L.J. (2007).

37. *Id.*

38. *See* U.S. EPA's Smart Growth website, Municipal Level Scorecards page, www.epa.gov/smartgrowth/scorecards/municipal.htm.

Chapter 24

Transportation: Challenges and Choices

Trip Pollard

Current transportation patterns and policies in the United States are not sustainable. Transportation consumes enormous amounts of fossil fuels and other resources, generates tremendous pollution, and promotes sprawling development. It is a leading contributor to virtually every serious environmental problem—including air and water pollution, global warming, and habitat destruction—and to pressing social, health, national security, and economic problems.

A new transportation paradigm is urgently needed. Positive steps have been taken since 2002 at the federal, state, and local levels to develop more sustainable transportation policies. These steps, however, are just a beginning. A host of policy alternatives are available to promote cleaner modes of transportation, cleaner and more efficient vehicles, more efficient use of the existing transportation network, and land development patterns that can reduce the length and number of vehicle trips.

This chapter opens with an overview of transportation trends, and then examines steps taken in the past five or so years to develop a more sustainable transportation system. The chapter concludes with recommendations for some of the significant changes that are needed, and needed soon, to create a sustainable transportation system.

Current Transportation Patterns

Americans are highly mobile and have built the world's most extensive transportation system. This system underpins the U.S. economy and has brought many benefits, including economic development, jobs, trade, and personal mobility. Overall, however, current transportation patterns are not sustainable.

Americans traveled over 5.4 trillion passenger-miles in 2005,[1]—a daily average of about 15 billion miles, which is roughly equivalent to 166 trips to the sun every day. Vehicle miles traveled rose almost 25 percent between 1995 and 2005, more than twice as fast as population growth during that period.[2]

Record fuel prices led to a decline in vehicle miles traveled and helped spur rising use of public transit in 2007 and the first half of 2008. Yet motor vehicles remain the dominant means of transportation in the United States.[3] Almost 90 percent of personal travel is in motor vehicles (most of the remainder is by air), and the number of vehicles surpasses the number of drivers.[4] Vehicle purchases have shifted, with the market share of sport utility vehicles increasing for many years and an overall increase in vehicle weight and acceleration.[5] In addition, heavy truck usage has also grown in the last decade, and most freight shipments are now made by truck.

Transportation consumes prodigious amounts of energy. As President George W. Bush noted, "America is addicted to oil."[6] The United States has 5 percent of the world's population, yet accounts for one-fourth of global petroleum consumption. Two-thirds of U.S. petroleum use is for transportation, which consumed an average of 13.8 million barrels of oil daily in 2005.[7] America's appetite for petroleum and increasing reliance on imported oil are not sustainable and threaten the nation's economy and security, particularly with growing evidence that global oil production is likely to peak and begin to decline in the near future.[8] Recent record, volatile fuel prices have underscored the pressing need to curb America's oil consumption.

Transportation also is a primary contributor to most environmental problems in the United States.[9] Motor vehicles are a leading source of air pollution, emitting carbon monoxide, particulate matter, smog-causing nitrogen oxides and volatile organic compounds, and air toxins. Heavy motor vehicle use and the infrastructure to serve it (including 8.4 million lane-miles of paved roads) are also a leading cause of polluted stormwater runoff, wetlands loss, habitat destruction and fragmentation, and other environmental problems.

Global warming is our most urgent environmental threat. The Intergovernmental Panel on Climate Change (IPCC) concluded in February 2007 that evidence of global warming is now "unequivocal," that there is at least a 90 percent certainty that human activities have caused warming, and that potentially massive and long-lasting changes will result.[10] As the U.S. Supreme Court recently noted, "[t]he harms associated with climate change are serious and well recognized."[11] The United States generates about a quarter of global emissions of carbon dioxide, the primary greenhouse gas;[12] one-third of these emissions is from transportation. Transportation is the largest end-use sector emitter of CO_2, and transportation emissions increased 25 percent between 1990 and 2005.

Developing a sustainable transportation system is an enormous challenge, and it is growing more difficult. The U.S. population is projected to increase almost 18 percent between 2005 and 2025, rising by over 52 million people,[13] and total travel is projected to increase about 70 percent during that time, to 8.5 trillion miles. Petroleum consumption, carbon dioxide emissions, land development, and other impacts are expected to rise significantly as well.

Progress Toward Sustainable Transportation

Public policies have played a central role in shaping the current, unsustainable transportation patterns.[14] Transportation policies and investments at all levels of government have focused on road building and motor vehicles for at least the past 60 years; transportation and other policies also have encouraged fossil fuel use and sprawling development. The combination of limited transportation options and sprawl has left most people with little choice but to drive, and to drive long distances, to get to work, shop, or conduct other activities.

What are the alternatives to the current unsustainable transportation patterns and policies?

Although "sustainability" has multiple meanings, the most widely cited definition includes "meeting the needs of the present without compromising the ability of future generations to meet their own needs."[15] A sustainable transportation system thus would be one that meets the need to access goods, services, and activities without harming the environment, communities, or human health. Among other things, a sustainable transportation system would entail far greater development and use of cleaner modes of transportation and cleaner, more efficient vehicles in order to reduce substantially—if not ultimately eliminate—fossil fuel consumption and pollution. It would provide for a greater range of transportation choices as well, including equitable access to quality transportation and desired destinations (such as meeting the needs of those who cannot or do not wish to drive). Moreover, a sustainable transportation system would eliminate the emphasis on new and expanded roads and would instead promote revitalization of existing communities and more compact development patterns to foster vibrant, walkable communities, reduce sprawl, and reduce the length and number of vehicle trips.

Today there is increasing recognition of the role public policies play in shaping unsustainable transportation patterns, and some significant policy reforms adopted in the past five or so years offer hints of a new transportation paradigm.[16] Moreover, rising fuel prices have increased public support for policy reform and have begun to impact travel behavior. Transportation, however, is still far from sustainable, as increases in vehicle miles traveled, petroleum consumed, land developed, and CO_2 emitted attest.

Federal Steps

Federal transportation policies have strongly favored motor vehicles and road building. The Federal Aid Highway Act of 1956,[17] which launched an unparalleled effort to build a 41,000-mile interstate highway system, was particularly instrumental in encouraging driving and set the tone for transportation policy for decades. In 2005, Congress adopted the most recent renewal of the federal surface transportation law—the Safe, Accountable, Flexible, Efficient Transportation Equity Act: A Legacy for Users (SAFETEA-LU).[18] It provides a record level of highway spending, and its funding formulas are based on measures such as vehicle miles traveled and lane miles that reward unsustainable transportation practices.

SAFETEA-LU does contain some important provisions that promote more sustainable transportation. It continues a framework Congress first established in the landmark Intermodal Surface Transportation Efficiency Act of 1991 (ISTEA)[19] that recognizes the need for transportation to promote energy conservation, environmental protection, and other goals in addition to mobility. This framework reduced the focus on building new highways, instead placing greater emphasis on repairing existing roads and supporting other travel modes, including giving states greater flexibility to use federal funds previously restricted to highway projects to support other modes. Further, it strengthened planning, public involvement, and environmental requirements for transportation projects. Although some provisions promoting sustainable transportation were trimmed in SAFETEA-LU, others were added, such as the Safe Routes to Schools program, which funds projects to make it easier for children to walk or bike to school. Despite these steps toward a more sustainable approach, federal transportation policy remains oriented toward motor vehicles.

The Clean Air Act has also improved transportation sustainability. Tailpipe emissions per mile have dropped considerably for some pollutants due in large part to emissions limits and fuel requirements adopted pursuant to the Act. However, the increase in miles driven has negated part of these gains, and new provisions addressing additional pollutants or lowering acceptable pollutant levels in light of emerging evidence of harm to public health have been slow in coming. There have been some important new steps, though, such as EPA's ultra-low sulfur diesel fuel regulations and advanced engine emission controls that have recently begun to be phased in and will substantially reduce certain emissions.[20]

Improving vehicle fuel efficiency is another key step toward sustainable transportation. In December 2007, fuel economy standards (known as Corporate Average Fuel Economy or CAFE standards) for passenger vehicles were significantly increased for the first time in 30 years, requiring automakers to meet a fleetwide average of at least 35 miles per gallon by 2020. If fully implemented, this would be an important improvement but would still be significantly below the standards of a number of European and Asian nations. Actual fuel economy has declined due to purchases of SUVs and light trucks, as well as the increasing weight and power of vehicles. The average fuel economy of light-duty vehicles (cars, SUVs, vans, and pickup trucks) in model year 2007 is expected to be 20.2 miles per gallon, almost exactly the same as in 1997, and less than it was 20 years ago.[21]

Prospects for more significant steps at the federal level are improving due to rising and volatile fuel prices, increased concern over American dependence on foreign oil, a more favorable political climate, and businesses calling for measures to address global warming.

State and Local Steps

State and local transportation policies vary widely. Overall, little progress has been made toward sustainability in recent years. Innovative policies have been adopted in some areas, though, and states and localities are increasingly taking the lead in developing new approaches.

Although states and localities typically devote the lion's share of transportation spending to road projects,[22] some have significantly increased funding of alternative travel modes, including transit, rail, bicycling, and walking. There has been a boom in light rail, for example, with new systems in Denver, Houston, Minneapolis, San Diego, and other areas experiencing ridership levels far above projections. Denver is building 119 miles of rail and 70 stations as part of a $4.7 billion regional rail program approved by voters in November 2004.

In addition, some states have set new priorities for their road spending, focusing on improving existing roadways before undertaking new construction projects. Over 40 percent of urban highways in the United States in 2005 were in fair or poor condition, and more than 30 percent of urban bridges were deficient.[23] The adoption of "fix it first" policies increases the efficiency and safety of existing infrastructure, and reduces land consumption and other adverse impacts of new road projects.

Further, states and localities have taken a variety of steps to promote more sustainable development patterns and to better link transportation and land use, recognizing that it is not possible to reduce the need for driving without reducing sprawl. Localities in the Charlotte-Mecklenberg area of North Carolina, for example, have begun implementing a long-range plan that calls for investing in transit projects in five corridors, local land use changes to guide growth to designated corridors and centers, and incentives for transit-oriented development.

Progress is also evident in state steps to limit vehicle emissions. In 2002, for example, California adopted the first law calling for reductions in greenhouse gas emissions from motor vehicles; in 2004, implementing regulations were adopted that would reduce emissions beginning with model year 2009 vehicles and become increasingly stringent through 2016.[24] Sixteen other states were poised to adopt these standards by the end of 2007. However, EPA rejected the clean car standards in December 2007, a decision that is the subject of pending legal challenges.

These are just some of the positive, though still rather limited, steps that states and localities have taken since 2002. They are serving as laboratories for policy experimentation and have helped to identify and develop key elements of a sustainable transportation system.

Moving Forward: Recommendations for a Sustainable Transportation Future

Progress toward sustainable transportation has been relatively modest in the United States, particularly in light of the extensive damage caused by current travel patterns. There is an urgent need to move much farther much faster to adopt improved policies and practices.

Abundant opportunities exist to develop and implement more sustainable transportation policies. Outlined below are four key recommendations that include a variety of steps that could be taken in the next decade, although there are many other opportunities for progress.[25]

1. Provide and promote transportation choices. Sustainable transportation is not possible without fundamentally changing the current focus on motor vehicles and road building. All too often, people drive their cars and businesses move freight by trucks because there is no realistic option. Development of less energy-intensive, less-polluting transportation modes is needed to provide meaningful transportation choices. Spending priorities should be reoriented. Federal spending on roads has been roughly five times greater than mass transit spending in recent years and over 100 times more than spending on pedestrian and bicycle projects; states often spend an even larger share of their transportation funds on roads.[26] Far more funds need to be devoted to providing attractive, reliable, affordable travel choices—including freight rail, light rail, high-speed rail, bus rapid transit, bicycling, and walking. Funding at both the federal and state levels should also be increased for projects that improve connectivity within and among various modes in order to expand options to use a particular mode or combination of modes.

Additional steps are needed to make alternatives to driving a meaningful choice. Revising street-design standards that mandate unnecessarily wide, high-speed roads, for example, can increase the safety of bicyclists and pedestrians. Existing streets can be modified with traffic-calming measures like narrowing roads and raising crosswalks to slow vehicles and make streets safer for pedestrians, bicyclists, and motorists.[27] These and other steps can help provide "complete streets" that can accommodate all users safely and effectively.

It is important to provide a greater range of choices for drivers as well. Creating a network of streets by connecting roads expands the routes available to drivers to reach their destinations. Providing more route choices can reduce the amount of driving and congestion that results from a system of cul-de-sacs channeling cars onto a relatively small number of roads.

Providing greater transportation choices requires better analysis of alternatives to road projects and of road impacts. In Virginia, for example, the Federal Highway Administration and state transportation department have been considering a proposal to expand Interstate 81 for 325 miles—a project that could exceed $13 billion. Yet the study of potential corridor improvements slighted or ignored the sprawl, greenhouse gas emissions, and other impacts that would result from this proposal. It failed to consider multi-state improvements to rail lines paralleling I-81 that could shift much of the freight in the corridor from trucks to rail, and it ignored upgrades to local street networks and transit that could reduce local traffic on the highway.[28]

Among the many steps needed to foster better analysis of transportation alternatives is to adopt a context-sensitive solutions (CSS) approach to planning and design. CSS uses a more open, collaborative process with substantial public involvement and seeks to design solutions that can meet transportation needs while minimizing environmental and community damage.[29] Another fundamental change would be a provision similar to a referendum adopted in Maine that requires transportation decisionmakers to "give preference" to alternatives to building new roads.[30]

2. Promote cleaner, more efficient vehicles. Energy efficiency and conservation are America's most significant energy resources.[31] Experience from the 1970s and early 1980s, recent studies, and new technologies show the potential to reduce fuel consumption substantially. A 2002 report by the National Academy of Sciences concluded that a 40 percent increase in fuel economy for light trucks and SUVs could be achieved over 10-15 years with existing technology at a cost less than the value of the resulting fuel savings.[32] Yet fuel economy standards have, as noted above, changed little in decades, the new standards adopted in December 2007 are a step in the right direction but still lag behind the standards of a number of other countries, and the average fuel economy of motor vehicles in the United States was higher 20 years ago than it is today. Higher efficiency standards should be adopted to save millions of barrels of oil each year, reduce emissions, and save consumers billions of dollars.

Energy-efficient vehicles can also be promoted through tax relief for customers purchasing high-efficiency vehicles, government fleet purchases, research and development grants, and other steps. A higher tax on the purchase of vehicles that get low gas mileage and a tax on the carbon content of fuels would also encourage the purchase of more efficient vehicles.

Provisions to require or promote cleaner fuels and vehicles offer additional opportunities. The technologies for alternative fuel vehicles are emerging, and promise to reduce—and ultimately eliminate—oil consumption and harmful emissions. Most of these technologies are not yet commercially viable, however, and they require public policy changes and investment to overcome market barriers and obstacles such as the lack of production, storage, and delivery systems.[33] Potential steps include public funding for research and development, the purchase of cleaner vehicles by governments, tax breaks for purchasers of alternative fuel vehicles, regulations that require cleaner fuels, and tighter emission limits. Measures have been adopted in recent years to boost ethanol production and use, but these fuels can raise serious environmental and economic concerns; corn-based ethanol, for example, may generate more greenhouse gases than gasoline if all emissions of producing the fuel are considered, and it can contribute to higher food prices. Fuels made from switchgrass or other plant materials raise fewer concerns. A "plug-in" hybrid vehicle that runs on electricity combined with a fuel such as biofuels is another promising alternative, depending on the source of power producing the electricity and the type of fuel used. Hydrogen fuel cells are also attractive because hydrogen is renewable and emission-free when consumed, although its overall cleanliness depends on the source of power used to produce hydrogen.

In sum, major policy changes should be adopted to catalyze and harness technological innovation to produce cleaner and more efficient vehicles.

3. Reduce driving subsidies and improve price signals. Current policies provide direct and indirect subsidies that mask the costs of driving and distort travel decisions. Although estimates vary, total governmental subsidies for vehicle use have been pegged as high as several hundred billion dollars a year.[34] Policies should be shifted to send more accurate signals of the true costs of driving in order to reduce travel, increase efficient use of roads, and increase demand for more efficient, cleaner vehicles and modes of transport.

Parking policies offer a prime example. Local zoning regulations often require developers to provide large amounts of free parking, and federal tax law allows employers to deduct the cost of providing employees free or discounted parking. According to one estimate, drivers do not pay for parking for 99 percent of trips in the United States.[35] This encourages people to drive more and use other travel modes less. The preferential tax treatment for parking benefits should be eliminated, requirements that businesses provide a minimum number of parking spaces lowered, employees allowed a greater benefit for commuting using other modes, and employees permitted to receive cash in lieu of parking subsidies without paying taxes on this benefit.[36]

Market signals can also promote more efficient use of the existing transportation system. For example, congestion pricing or variable tolls that are highest when congestion is greatest send a signal that driving at peak travel times costs more—including the economic costs of congestion, environmental costs, and the fact that peak congestion can lead to costly road expansion. Better price signals can reduce congestion and more efficiently use road capacity by getting people to eliminate trips, use other travel modes, or drive at other times.

Another market-based tool to improve transportation sustainability is pay-as-you-drive insurance. Most driving costs are fixed (such as vehicle purchase, maintenance, and insurance) and do not change with the amount of driving. Shifting some costs so that they increase as people drive more would send a more accurate price signal and discourage some driving. For example, at least some insurance costs could be imposed when fuel is purchased, or the cost of policies might be tied more to the number of miles driven, providing an incentive to drive less.

Many additional steps would send better price signals and reduce current market distortions, including reducing subsidies such as billions of dollars of tax breaks for oil companies and raising and expanding the gas-guzzler tax on inefficient vehicles.

4. Link transportation and land use, and promote smarter growth. Sustainable transportation is inextricably linked to sustainable land development, and one cannot be achieved without the other. Transportation shapes the prospects for sustainable land use patterns because it influences the pace, location, and form of development. Land use and community design affect the amount, length, and mode of travel. The low density, sprawling development that has dominated most growth in the United States in the past 60 years typically makes driving the only realistic choice for most travel needs.

Development patterns, like transportation patterns, are shaped by public policies. As a result, there are plentiful opportunities to promote sustainable transportation by linking transportation and land use and by promoting more compact, traditional forms of cities and neighborhoods, where residences are close to jobs, shopping, and other activities. These patterns require fewer and shorter vehicle trips, use less land and energy, and produce less pollution.[37]

A range of regulatory hurdles must be addressed to promote smarter growth patterns. Provisions such as single-use zoning, which requires homes and jobs to be geographically separated, large minimum lot sizes, and side and front yard setback requirements can effectively mandate sprawling development and driving; they should be altered or eliminated. Building code provisions that make it much more costly to rehabilitate existing structures should be revised.

A variety of incentives for walkable and transit-oriented development should be adopted as well, such as providing streamlined approval, density bonuses, and tax credits for infill development and development near a transit station; incentives to encourage rehabilitation and reuse of properties; and incentives for people to live near their workplace.

Greater efforts to link transportation and land use are needed as well, such as the Charlotte transit and land use plan mentioned above and a Maryland statute that limits infrastructure funding—including highway spending—to existing communities and designated growth areas, rather than providing subsidies to encourage sprawling development.[38] Perhaps no region has done more than the Portland, Oregon, area to coordinate transportation investments and improved land use policies. These efforts have created a range of attractive travel options and more compact, walkable communities oriented to transit, enabling Portland to accommodate a 50 percent population increase in the region in recent decades with just a 2 percent increase in land base, and 30,000 new jobs downtown with no significant increase in vehicle trips.[39]

Conclusion

Abundant opportunities are available to promote more sustainable transportation policies and practices, and there is growing public support for addressing the pressing challenges presented by current transportation patterns. We urgently need cleaner modes of transportation, cleaner and more efficient vehicles, and smarter development patterns that can reduce the number and length of vehicle trips. Cumulatively, these changes promise a transportation revolution that provides greater travel choices while substantially reducing pollution, helping to address global warming, eliminating our oil dependence, strengthening our economy, and promoting healthier communities. Although considerable hurdles remain,[40] it is imperative that a new transportation paradigm be adopted soon. Our future depends on acting now.

ENDNOTES

1. BUREAU OF TRANSP. STATISTICS, U.S. DEP'T OF TRANSP., NATIONAL TRANSPORTATION STATISTICS 2007 [hereinafter TRANSPORTATION STATISTICS 2007], tbl. 1-37, *available at* www.bts.gov/publications/national_transportation_statistics (updated Apr. 12, 2007).

2. *Id.*, tbl. 1-32; U.S. CENSUS BUREAU, STATISTICAL ABSTRACT OF THE UNITED STATES: 2007.

3. Thus, this chapter will focus primarily on surface transportation and, more narrowly, on cars and trucks because they are responsible for the bulk of transportation activities and impacts in the United States.

4. In 2005, the United States had 201 million licensed drivers and 241 million vehicles. OFFICE OF HIGHWAY POL'Y INFO., FED. HIGHWAY ADMIN., HIGHWAY STATISTICS 2005, chart *available at* www.fhwa.dot.gov/policy/ohim/hs05/xls/dlchrt.xls.

5. *See* OFFICE OF TRANSP. & AIR QUALITY, U.S. EPA, LIGHT-DUTY AUTOMOTIVE TECHNOLOGY AND FUEL ECONOMY TRENDS: 1975 THROUGH 2007 (Sept. 2007) [hereinafter AUTOMOTIVE TECHNOLOGY]. Again, record fuel prices have begun to alter this trend.

6. President George W. Bush, 2006 State of the Union Address.

7. TRANSPORTATION STATISTICS 2007, *supra* note 1, at tbl. 4-1.

8. *See, e.g.*, ROBERT L. HIRSCH ET AL., U.S. DEP'T. OF ENERGY, PEAKING OF WORLD OIL PRODUCTION: IMPACTS, MITIGATION, AND RISK MANAGEMENT (Feb. 2005).

9. For further discussion of these impacts, see Oliver A. Pollard III, *Smart Growth and Sustainable Transportation: Can We Get There From Here?*, 29 FORDHAM URB. L.J. 1529, 1536-8 (2002), and sources cited therein.

10. INTERGOVERNMENTAL PANEL ON CLIMATE CHANGE, WORKING GROUP I FOURTH ASSESSMENT REPORT, CLIMATE CHANGE 2007: THE PHYSICAL SCIENCE BASIS, SUMMARY FOR POLICYMAKERS (Feb. 2007), *available at* www.ipcc.ch/pdf/assessment-report/ar4/wg1/ar4-wg1-spm.pdf.

11. Massachusetts v. EPA, 549 U.S. 497 (2007).

12. ENERGY INFO. ADMIN., U.S. DEP'T OF ENERGY, EMISSIONS OF GREENHOUSE GASES IN THE UNITED STATES 2005, ch. 2 (Nov. 2006). The rest of the data in this paragraph is from this source. Transportation-related emissions are even higher if emissions from every stage of production and consumption related to transportation are considered.

13. U.S. CENSUS BUREAU, STATISTICAL ABSTRACT OF THE UNITED STATES 2007, §1, tbls. 2, 3.

14. *See* Pollard, *supra* note 9; Trip Pollard, *Follow the Money: Transportation Investments for Smarter Growth*, 22 TEMPLE ENVTL. L. & TECH. J. 155 (2004); and Trip Pollard, *Driving Change: Public Policies, Individual Choices, and Environmental Damage*, 35 ELR 10791 (Nov. 2005) for further discussion.

15. WORLD COMM'N ON ENV'T & DEV. (BRUNDTLAND COMM'N), OUR COMMON FUTURE 43 (1987).

16. See F. Kaid Benfield & Michael Replogle, *Transportation, in* STUMBLING TOWARD SUSTAINABILITY (John C. Dernbach ed., 2002) for an assessment of progress toward sustainability in transportation in the first 10 years since the 1992 U.N. Earth Summit in Rio.

17. 23 U.S.C. §§101-118.

18. Pub. L. No. 109-59, 119 Stat. 1144 (2005).

19. Pub. L. No. 102-240, 105 Stat. 1914 (1991). This framework was continued in the Transportation Equity Act for the 21st Century (TEA-21), Pub. L. No. 105-178, 112 Stat. 107 (1998), and now in SAFETEA-LU.

20. *See* U.S. EPA, Heavy-Duty Highway Diesel Program, www.epa.gov/otaq/highway-diesel/index.htm; U.S. EPA, Tier 2 Vehicle and Gasoline Sulfur Program, www.epa.gov/tier2/index.htm.

21. Automotive Technology, *supra* note 5, at ii (average fuel economy reached a peak of 22 miles per gallon in 1987).

22. *See* SURFACE TRANSP. POL'Y PROJECT, THE $300 BILLION QUESTION: ARE WE BUYING A BETTER TRANSPORTATION SYSTEM? (Jan. 2003).

23. TRANSPORTATION STATISTICS 2007, *supra* note 1, tbls. 1-26, 1-27.

24. More broadly, California's Global Warming Solutions Act of 2006 calls for a phased-in cap on state greenhouse gas emissions and requires a 25 percent cut in emissions by 2020 to 1990 levels and an 80 percent cut below 1990 levels by 2050—which would require deep cuts in vehicle emissions.

25. Among other things, this section will not explore many of the opportunities for increasing the performance of existing roads and reducing the impacts of roads, including adopting a "fix it first" approach that places a priority on maintenance and repair, improving access management, employing intelligent transportation system (ITS) measures, improving stormwater measures to reduce polluted runoff, and using recycled construction materials.

26. SURFACE TRANSP. POL'Y PROJECT, TEN YEARS OF PROGRESS: BUILDING BETTER COMMUNITIES THROUGH TRANSPORTATION 7, 10 (2001).

27. CONSERVATION LAW FOUND., TAKE BACK YOUR STREETS: HOW TO PROTECT COMMUNITIES FROM ASPHALT AND TRAFFIC (1998).

28. *See* SOUTHERN ENVTL. L. CTR., COMMENTS ON THE TIER 1 DRAFT AND FINAL ENVIRONMENTAL IMPACT STATEMENT FOR THE I-81 CORRIDOR IMPROVEMENT STUDY, *available at* www.southernenvironment.org/cases/I-81/index.htm.

29. *See, e.g.,* TRANSP. RESEARCH BD., NCHP REPORT 480, A GUIDE TO BEST PRACTICES FOR ACHIEVING CONTEXT SENSITIVE SOLUTIONS (2002).

30. ME. REV. STAT. ANN. tit. 23, §73(B).

31. *See* John C. Dernbach and the Widener University Law School Seminar on Energy Efficiency, *Stabilizing and Then Reducing U.S. Energy Consumption: Legal and Policy Tools for Efficiency and Conservation*, 37 ELR 10003 (Jan. 2007), for further discussion of transportation energy efficiency.

32. COMM. ON THE EFFECTIVENESS & IMPACT OF CAFE STANDARDS, NAT'L RESEARCH COUNCIL, EFFECTIVENESS AND IMPACT OF CORPORATE AVERAGE FUEL ECONOMY (CAFE) STANDARDS (2002). This estimate is con-

servative as it does not include advances in hybrid gas-electric vehicles. Other studies conclude that far greater savings are achievable. *See, e.g.,* AMORY B. LOVINS ET AL., WINNING THE OIL ENDGAME: INNOVATION FOR PROFITS, JOBS, AND SECURITY (2004).

33. *See, e.g.,* CTR. FOR ENERGY & CLIMATE SOLUTIONS, THE CAR AND FUEL OF THE FUTURE: A TECHNOLOGY AND POLICY OVERVIEW (2004), *available at* http://www.energyandclimate.org/ewebeditpro/items/O79F7833. pdf.

34. *See* Pollard, *supra* note 14, at 10795 and sources cited therein.

35. DONALD C. SHOUP, THE HIGH COST OF FREE PARKING 1 (2005).

36. A California statute requiring such a parking "cash out" significantly cut driving and increased commuting by other travel modes. Donald Shoup, *Evaluating the Effects of Cashing Out Employer-Paid Parking: Eight Case Studies,* 4 TRANSP. POL'Y 201 (1997).

37. An EPA study of alternative development scenarios in three metropolitan areas, for example, found that compact development patterns could cut the number of miles traveled by about 50 percent or more. U.S. EPA, OUR BUILT AND NATURAL ENVIRONMENTS: A TECHNICAL REVIEW OF THE INTERACTIONS BETWEEN LAND USE, TRANSPORTATION, AND ENVIRONMENTAL QUALITY (2001).

38. MD. CODE ANN., STATE FIN. & PROC., §§5-7B-01 to 5-7B-10.

39. *See* F. KAID BENFIELD ET AL., ONCE THERE WERE GREENFIELDS: HOW URBAN SPRAWL IS UNDERMINING AMERICA'S ENVIRONMENT, ECONOMY, AND SOCIAL FABRIC 152-53 (1999).

40. *See* Oliver A. Pollard III, *Smart Growth: The Promise, Politics, and Potential Pitfalls of Emerging Growth Management Strategies,* 19 VA. ENVTL. L.J. 247 (2000) for discussion of many of these hurdles.

VII. International Trade, Finance, and Development Assistance

Chapter 25

International Trade: Sustainability as a Multilateral, Bilateral, and Regional Effort

Kevin C. Kennedy

Achieving the goal of sustainable development requires multilateral and regional approaches and solutions. Making sustainable development an integral part of international trade thus must be more than a bilateral or unilateral endeavor. The work of intergovernmental organizations, especially the World Trade Organization (WTO), is crucial to the smooth functioning of the complex interrelationship among trade, investment, environment, and sustainable development. In order to ensure mutual supportiveness between the international trade legal regime administered by the WTO, on the one hand, and the network of multilateral environmental agreements (MEAs), on the other hand, proper policy coordination, cooperation, and information exchange at the national and international level is essential. While some modest steps have been taken in this regard, such as giving the secretariats of various MEAs observer status at the WTO, unquestionably more needs to be done. However, the lack of any serious discussion about the interface of trade, environment, and sustainable development over the past six years at the WTO may mean that no WTO ministerial decision will be issued on this vitally important subject.

Trade and the Environment: The Johannesburg Summit

In recognition of the multilateral scope of sustainable development, the 2002 World Summit on Sustainable Development in Johannesburg (WSSD) identified three goals in its Plan of Implementation on the relationship among trade, environment, and sustainable development:

1. "Promote mutual supportiveness between the *multilateral trading system and the multilateral environmental agreements*, consistent with sustainable development goals, in support of the work programme agreed through WTO, while recognizing the importance of maintaining the integrity of both sets of instruments";[1] (emphasis added);

2. "[E]encourage efforts to promote cooperation on trade, environment and sustainable development . . . between the secretariats of WTO [the World Trade Organization, the leading intergovernmental organization responsible for regulating international trade], UNCTAD [the United Nations Conference on Trade and Development, which assists developing and least-developed countries with integrating into the WTO multilateral trading system], UNDP [the United Nations Development Program, which assists developing countries with issues of governance and poverty reduction], UNEP [the United Nations Environment Program, which assesses global environmental conditions, develops multilateral environmental agreements, and integrates economic development and environmental protection] and other relevant international environmental and development and regional organizations;"[2]

3. "[S]trengthen cooperation among UNEP and other United Nations bodies and specialized agencies, the Bretton Woods institutions and WTO, within their mandates."[3]

The principle of mutual supportiveness, identified in paragraph 98 of the Plan, is based on the assumption that the overall objective of environmental and trade legal regimes is the same, namely, the improvement of the human condition by protecting human, animal, and plant life and health.

As the largest trading nation in the world, the United States is uniquely placed to influence the WTO trade and sustainable development agenda in a positive way. The United States is, for example, a leading advocate for prohibiting harmful fisheries subsidies. It is also committed to safeguarding the integrity of both sets of international obligations at issue—those in the WTO and those in the multilateral environmental agreements (MEAs) to which the United States is a party.[4]

Trade and the Environment: The WTO

In anticipation of the World Summit on Sustainable Development at Johannesburg, in 2001 the WTO launched the Doha Development Agenda, popularly known as the Doha Round, and at its biennial ministerial conference issued the following declaration regarding sustainable development:

> We strongly reaffirm our commitment to the objective of sustainable development . . . . We are convinced that the aims of upholding and safeguarding an open and non-discriminatory multilateral trading system, and acting for the protection of the environment and the promotion of sustainable development can and must be mutually supportive. . . . We welcome the WTO's continued cooperation with UNEP and other inter-governmental environmental organizations. We encourage efforts to promote cooperation between the WTO and relevant international environmental and developmental organizations, especially in the lead-up to the World Summit on Sustainable Development to be held in Johannesburg, South Africa, in September 2002.[5]

In three respects, this declaration broke new ground for multilateral cooperation for sustainability.

First, under paragraph 31 of the Doha ministerial declaration the WTO members agreed to negotiations on a set of three interrelated items: (1) the relationship between existing WTO rules and specific trade obligations set out in multilateral environmental agreements (MEAs); (2) procedures for regular information exchange between MEA secretariats and the relevant WTO committees, and the criteria for the granting of observer status; and (3) the reduction or, as appropriate, elimination of tariff and nontariff barriers to environmental goods and services.[6]

Second, paragraph 51 of the declaration directs two WTO bodies—the Committee on Trade and Development and the Committee on Trade and Environment—"to identify and debate developmental and environmental aspects of the negotiations, in order to help achieve the objective of having sustainable development appropriately reflected."[7] Together, paragraphs 31 and 51 of the Doha Ministerial Declaration represent what might be called the environmental package of the Doha Round negotiations.

Third, one sector-specific item on the Doha Round agenda with a clear sustainable development dimension is found in paragraph 28 of the declaration, namely, the reduction of fisheries subsidies that have encouraged over-fishing and depletion of the world's fish stocks.

For the first time in its 55-year history, the GATT/WTO international trade legal regime agreed to undertake negotiations to enhance the mutual supportiveness of trade and environment policies. The work of the WTO Committee on Trade and Environment (CTE) is now instrumental in achieving this goal.

Progress at the WTO Since Johannesburg

In the way of concrete results, little has been achieved to date at the WTO on the mandates articulated in the Doha declaration. The explanation for the lack of significant progress is that the topic of trade, environment, and sustainable development has taken a back seat at the WTO to negotiations on agricultural trade, with the United States, the European Union, India, and Brazil locked in a battle over farm subsidies. The lack of any serious discussion about the interface of trade, environment, and sustainable development over the past six years will likely mean that no WTO ministerial-level decision will soon be issued on this vitally important subject. The implication for the United States is that bilateral and regional free trade agreements will have to carry more of the load on this score.

Within the WTO, however, the CTE has nevertheless forged ahead by attempting to develop an understanding among the WTO members on what its negotiating mandate is exactly. For example, various terms contained in the WTO ministerial mandate, such as "specific trade obligation" and "multilateral environmental agreement" are not defined. The leadership role at the CTE has been assumed largely by the European Union, with the United States playing a comparatively minor part. At the same time, the United States has not openly opposed developments at the CTE; to the contrary, the United States is on record as being committed to maintaining the integrity of both the WTO agreements and multilateral environmental agreements.[8]

Trade and the Environment: Multilateral Environmental Agreements

There is no international consensus on a definition of "multilateral environmental agreement" (MEA). (Definitional issues such as this one are part of the underbrush that the WTO Committee on Trade and Environment has to clear before it can tackle the substantive issues that it has been assigned.) On the meaning of the term "multilateral environmental agreement," China offered the following definition in a submission to the CTE: "MEAs are international treaties designed to protect and improve environment, and properly exploit natural resources."[9] In China's view, MEAs should have five elements:

- *Authoritativeness.* MEAs should have been negotiated under the auspices of the United Nations system.

- *Universality.* An MEA should have a substantial number of contracting parties that account for a majority of WTO members.

- *Openness.* The agreement should be open for accession by relevant parties.

- *Impact on trade.* MEAs should contain explicit trade measures, the implementation of which should have a substantial impact on trade.

- *Effectiveness.* An MEA should be in force and open for accession.[10]

Consistent with the WSSD Plan of Implementation, WTO members have made the following proposals in the CTE relating to governance principles that are aimed at ensuring mutual supportiveness of WTO and MEA legal regimes:

- *No hierarchy.* MEAs and the WTO legal regime are bodies of international law of equal standing.[11] Thus, there is no hierarchy between the WTO and MEA legal regimes. WTO rules should be interpreted in a manner that does not conflict with MEA rules, and vice versa.[12]

- *Deference.* MEAs and the WTO have distinct competencies within a multilateral governance framework.[13] A corollary is that when a WTO dispute settlement panel examines issues with an environmental content relating to a particular MEA, the panel should defer to the expertise of the MEA in question.[14]

- *Mutual supportiveness.* The principle of mutual supportiveness is based on the assumption that the overall objective of both environmental and trade regimes is the same, namely, the improvement of the human condition.[15] Consequently, under WTO rules no country should be prevented from taking measures for the protection of human, animal, or plant life or health, or of the environment, thus ensuring the level of protection it considers appropriate.[16]

Progress in the United States Since Johannesburg: NAFTA and FTAs

In the Trade Act of 2002,[17] Congress identified sustainable development as one of the many goals to be achieved in any bilateral, regional, or multilateral trade agreement to which the United States is a party. How well has the United States done? After a lull of nearly nine

years since the United States became a party to the North American
Free Trade Agreement in 1993, the Bush Administration concluded
bilateral and regional free trade agreements (FTAs) with 14 countries.
An additional four FTAs were concluded in 2007—with Colombia,
Korea, Panama, and Peru—although all but the Peru FTA still awaited
congressional approval when this chapter went to press.

All of the Bush Administration FTAs contain provisions on trade
and environment that are modeled after the North American Agreement on Environmental Cooperation (NAAEC), NAFTA's environmental side agreement (further explained below). Second, all Bush
Administration FTAs have been subject to environmental reviews.
Third, the four FTAs that were negotiated in 2007 contain enhanced
environmental and sustainable development provisions mandated by
the Bipartisan Agreement on Trade Policy (explained below).

NAFTA's Environmental Provisions

NAFTA's core provisions on trade and environment, on which
these more recent agreements are based, are found in Articles 104 and
1114. Article 104 provides that in the event of any inconsistency between NAFTA and three MEAs—the Convention on International
Trade in Endangered Species of Wild Fauna and Flora (CITES), the
Montreal Protocol on Substances that Deplete the Ozone Layer (Montreal Protocol), and the Basel Convention on the Control of
Transboundary Movements of Hazardous Wastes and Their Disposal
(Basel Convention)—the obligations of the MEAs prevail.

Article 1114 of NAFTA is an environmental sword and shield. The
sword, Article 1114.1, provides that nothing in NAFTA is to be construed to prevent a party from adopting, maintaining, or enforcing any
measure governing investment that it considers appropriate to ensure
that investment activity in its territory is undertaken in an environmentally sensitive manner. The shield, Article 1114.2, exhorts the parties not to relax, waive, or derogate from health, safety, or environmental measures in order to encourage foreign investment from another party.

As originally negotiated, NAFTA had no single chapter dedicated
exclusively to environmental issues, contrary to all post-NAFTA
FTAs. The North American Agreement on Environmental Cooperation (NAAEC), mentioned above, closed this gap in 1994.[18] Briefly
stated, NAAEC augments the environmental provisions of NAFTA

and its commitment to sustainable development and the environment. NAAEC specifically commits the NAFTA parties to effective enforcement of their environmental laws, and establishes the Commission for Environmental Cooperation (CEC), whose competence covers any environmental or natural resource issue that may arise among the NAFTA parties.

NAAEC establishes a citizen submission process under which the NAAEC secretariat may consider a submission from any private person who asserts that a NAFTA party is failing to effectively enforce its environmental laws.[19] The secretariat's function under Article 14 is inquisitorial, not accusatorial. For the petitioning private person, the Article 14 petition process ends with the transmittal of the final factual record to the Council. NAAEC does not provide private remedies and does not create any private right of action against a NAFTA party.[20]

In addition to the dispute settlement mechanisms available to private persons, NAAEC establishes a mechanism for party-to-party dispute resolution in cases where there has been "a persistent pattern of failure by [a] Party to effectively enforce its environmental law."[21] NAAEC Article 45 defines the three key terms "persistent pattern," "effectively enforce," and "environmental law." The term "persistent pattern" is defined as "a sustained or recurring course of action or inaction after the date of entry into force of this Agreement."[22] Rather than state when a party has failed to "effectively enforce its environmental law," Article 45.1 instead states when a party has *not* failed to "effectively enforce its environmental law":

> [W]here the action or inaction in question by agencies or officials of that Party: (a) reflects a reasonable exercise of their discretion in respect of investigatory, prosecutorial, regulatory or compliance matters; or (b) results from bona fide decisions to allocate resources to enforcement in respect of other environmental matters determined to have higher priorities . . . .

Article 45.2 defines "environmental law" as any statute or regulation whose primary purpose is the protection of the environment, or the prevention of danger to human life or health, through (1) the prevention, abatement, or control of the release, discharge, or emission of pollutants or environmental contaminants, (2) the control of environmentally hazardous or toxic chemicals, substances, materials, and wastes, or (3) the protection of wild flora or fauna, their habitat, and specially protected natural areas within a party's territory.

NAAEC establishes an arbitration procedure for resolving party-to-party disputes that is only available where the alleged persistent pattern of failure by the responding party to effectively enforce its environmental law relates to a situation involving "workplaces, firms, companies or sectors that produce goods or provide services: (a) traded between the territories of the Parties; or (b) that compete, in the territory of the Party complained against, with goods or services produced or provided by persons of another Party."[23] To date, there have been no requests to initiate the NAAEC Article 23 dispute settlement process.

Environmental Review of Free Trade Agreements

In the 1990s, U.S. environmental groups pressured the Clinton Administration to subject all proposed FTAs to some type of environmental impact assessment. In 1999, the Clinton Administration obliged by instituting environmental reviews of all free trade agreements.[24] President Clinton's Executive Order 13141 states that "[t]rade agreements should contribute to the broader goal of sustainable development," and that "[e]nvironmental reviews are an important tool to help identify potential environmental effects of trade agreements, both positive and negative, and to help facilitate consideration of appropriate responses to those effects whether in the course of negotiations, through other means, or both."[25]

In 2001, the Bush Administration announced that it would continue the Clinton Administration's policy of conducting environmental reviews of trade agreements pursuant to the latter's executive order and implementing guidelines.[26] The main focus of FTA environmental reviews is the potential environmental impacts of FTAs on the United States. However, reviews include consideration of global and transboundary effects as well.[27]

Bipartisan Agreement on Trade Policy

In May 2007, Congress and the Bush Administration reached a compromise understanding called the Bipartisan Agreement on Trade Policy (Bipartisan Agreement).[28] The Bipartisan Agreement calls for enhanced provisions in all future U.S. bilateral and regional free trade agreements on several topics, including environmental protection and sustainable development.

Under the environmental provisions of the Bipartisan Agreement, the parties to all future FTAs (including those already negotiated with Colombia, Korea, Panama, and Peru) must enact laws to comply with the following seven MEAs: (1) CITES, (2) the Montreal Protocol, (3) the Convention on Marine Pollution, (4) the Inter-American Tropical Tuna Convention, (5) the Ramsar Convention on Wetlands, (6) the International Whaling Convention, and (7) the Convention on Conservation of Antarctic Marine Living Resources.[29] As bold as this requirement may seem, however, it contains three significant qualifications that substantially narrow its application. First, in order to establish a violation of this commitment, the complaining party must show that the responding party's failure to fulfill an obligation under one of the covered MEAs has been "through a sustained or recurring course of action or inaction"—language that echoes NAAEC's "persistent pattern of failure" precondition to bringing an environmental complaint. Second, the sustained or recurring course of action or inaction must be "in a manner affecting trade or investment between the Parties."[30] Third, an escape clause has been added that excuses nonenforcement in the *bona fide* exercise of prosecutorial discretion. For example, Article 18.3(1)(b)(i) of the U.S.-Peru Trade Promotion Agreement provides that "where a course of action or inaction reflects a reasonable, articulable, *bona fide* exercise of such discretion, or results from a reasonable, articulable, *bona fide* decision regarding the allocation of such resources," a party's failure to enforce its environmental laws and the covered MEAs is excused.

Next, in the investment context the Bipartisan Agreement departs from NAFTA, which provides that the parties "should not derogate from" environmental laws to attract investment,[31] and from the Dominican Republic-Central America Free Trade Agreement (DR-CAFTA), which provides that "each Party shall strive to ensure that it does not waive or otherwise derogate from" environmental laws to attract investment.[32] The Bipartisan Agreement amends the nonderogation obligation for environmental laws and the covered MEAs so that NAFTA's "should not" and DR-CAFTA's "shall strive to" now provides "shall not" in the new FTAs, with an allowance for waivers permitted under law, provided they do not violate the covered MEAs.[33]

Third, in a departure from DR-CAFTA where MEAs are not given primacy over the terms of the FTA in the event of a conflict between the two,[34] the four pending FTAs include a provision that roughly parallels NAFTA Article 104, thus creating a legal hierarchy of MEAs above the FTA in the event of a conflict.[35]

The final change introduced by the Bipartisan Agreement deals with the resolution of environmental disputes. The environment chapters of the Colombia, Korea, Panama, and Peru FTAs are largely imitative of the NAAEC. However, in a departure from NAAEC, disputes that cannot be resolved by the NAAEC Council are referred to dispute settlement under the general government-to-government dispute settlement panel mechanism that is overseen by the agreement's Free Trade Commission (composed of the trade ministers of the contracting states). However, if the NAFTA experience is any guide, this change as a practical matter probably signifies nothing. An environmental dispute settlement panel has never been convened under NAAEC, and there have been only three NAFTA government-to-government trade dispute panels convened during the 15 years that NAFTA has been in force. The likelihood of a dispute settlement panel being convened to resolve an environmental dispute under the most recent FTAs seems remote.

One other noteworthy development that is not part of the Bipartisan Agreement itself is the first-ever biodiversity article in a U.S. FTA. The Trade Promotion Agreements with Colombia and Peru exhort the parties to promote biodiversity and sustainable development, and provide that "the Parties remain committed to promoting and encouraging the conservation and sustainable use of biological diversity and all its components and levels, including plants, animals, and habitat . . . ."[36] Although these provisions are obviously hortatory, they nevertheless represent an intriguing innovation in U.S. FTAs.

Finally, the four pending FTAs contain the following clarifying provision in their respective investment chapters: "Except in rare circumstances, nondiscriminatory regulatory actions by a Party that are designed and applied to protect legitimate public welfare objectives, such as public health, safety, and the environment, do not constitute indirect expropriations."[37] This provision was first added to the U.S.-Chile FTA[38] in response to a concern that arbitral tribunals that were resolving NAFTA investment disputes were undermining the ability of host countries to enact and enforce rigorous and nondiscriminatory environmental laws. It has now been carried forward.

In sum, with only the U.S.-Peru FTA having been approved by Congress to date, and with three others pending congressional approval, only time will tell if the modest changes introduced by the Bipartisan Agreement to those four FTAs will in fact promote sustainable development. For the time being, the Bipartisan Agreement appears to be more of a political statement than a legal document.

Next Steps

So what should the next steps be?

1. Successful completion of the WTO Doha Round multilateral trade negotiations could have beneficial effects for the environment and sustainable development. Specifically, in the area of agricultural subsidies, domestic and export subsidies by developed countries—in particular, by the United States and the European Union—have encouraged overproduction of field crops (e.g., corn, cotton, wheat, and soybeans), which in turn has put pressure on natural resources, including water and arable land.[39] If the Doha Round is able to secure meaningful reductions in farm subsidies, important gains for sustainable development in the agriculture sector could be achieved. Moreover, a successful Doha Round could result in duty-free treatment for environmental goods and market openings for environmental services suppliers, two areas where the United States enjoys a comparative advantage. The United States needs to take a leadership role in bringing the Doha Round to successful completion.

2. As the United States pursues its two-track approach of negotiating multilateral and bilateral trade agreements, it needs to make sustainable development a high priority. All free trade agreements negotiated by the United States should ensure that their interpretation and application take account of, and are mutually supportive of, provisions of multilateral agreements on environment and sustainable development. In short, efforts within the United States to safeguard the nondiscriminatory multilateral trading system must go hand-in-hand with the commitment to sustainable development. The most recent FTAs negotiated by the United States reflect such a commitment.

Further, adequate financial resources need to be committed in order to make the legal texts a reality. The best way to effectuate the hortatory goals described in Article 18.11 of the Peru and Colombia Trade Promotion Agreements on promoting sustainable development and protecting biological diversity is to build incentives that reward higher standards. There are many ways to structure such incentives—for example, accelerate tariff reductions for countries that meet certain goals or make funds available based on performance. A creative package of incentives for continually raising environmental and sustainable development standards needs to be developed.

3. A mechanism is needed to measure the progress countries are making toward sustainable development. Future FTAs with developing countries, especially those with fragile ecosystems and rich biodiversity, should contain provisions for sustainable development action plans with periodic benchmarks to measure their progress, together with fully funded budgets to support such plans. A long-range, integrated package of technical assistance, trade capacity building, and environmental cooperation needs to be initiated by the United States, and the United States needs to be prepared to financially support this package over the 10-15 year implementation period of an FTA. If they are implemented with this kind of forward thinking, the pending U.S. FTAs with Colombia and Panama and the approved FTA with Peru will benefit these three developing countries by boosting their economic growth and reducing their crushing poverty but in an environmentally sustainable way.

Conclusion

A necessary but not sufficient condition for the principles of sustainable development to find their way into the WTO legal regime is the success of the Doha Round. The ambition with which those negotiations were launched in late 2001 has waned considerably over the past seven years. Even if the Doha Round negotiations do yield some modest results—which with the negotiations on the brink of collapse seems doubtful—the absence of any serious discussion about the interface of trade, environment, and sustainable development may mean that no ministerial-level decision at the WTO will be issued. If the Doha Round fails, there will be more than enough blame to spread among all of the WTO members, both developed and developing country members.

The implications for the United States are that bilateral and regional free trade agreements will have to carry more of the trade/sustainable development load. The environment chapters of the four pending FTAs signal a departure from the environment chapters of post-NAFTA free trade agreements. Consistent with NAFTA, the pending agreements again give primacy to seven MEAs in the event of an inconsistency between them and the free trade agreement. This return to NAFTA Article 104's hierarchy of MEAs over free trade agreement provisions could prove to be a useful tool to reinforce commitments made under the covered MEAs.

In a departure from NAFTA and its progeny, the Bipartisan Agreement bars FTA partners from derogating from their environmental laws and the covered MEAs in order to attract foreign investment. As a result of the Bipartisan Agreement, a nominally more robust dispute settlement process than the one that exists under NAFTA and other U.S. FTAs has been added. The reality, however, is that with the qualifiers that have been placed on the obligations to enforce environmental laws and observe the terms of the covered MEAs, it seems highly improbable that the improved dispute settlement mechanism mandated by the Bipartisan Agreement will ever be invoked. Finally, and for the first time, the U.S. FTAs with Colombia and Peru contain specific articles on biodiversity and sustainable development, a provision that was not mandated by the Bipartisan Agreement.

ENDNOTES

1. U.N. WORLD SUMMIT ON SUSTAINABLE DEVELOPMENT, PLAN OF IMPLE-MENTATION (2002), ¶ 98, *available at* www.un.org/jsummit/html/documents/undocs.html [hereinafter WSSD PLAN OF IMPLEMENTATION].

2. *Id.* ¶ 91(c).

3. *Id.* ¶ 136.

4. *See* OFFICE OF THE U.S. TRADE REP., DOHA DEVELOPMENT AGENDA POLICY BRIEF (Dec. 2005), *available at* www.ustr.gov/assets/Document_Library/Fact_Sheets/2005/asset_upload_file937_8545.pdf.

5. WTO Ministerial Conference, Ministerial Declaration adopted November 14, 2001, ¶ 6, WT/MIN(01)/DEC/1 (Nov. 20, 2001).

6. *Id.* ¶ 31.

7. *Id.* ¶ 51.

8. *See* OFFICE OF THE U.S. TRADE REP., *supra* note 4.

9. Committee on Trade and Environment, Identification of Multilateral Environmental Agreements (MEAs) and Specific Trade Obligations (STOs), Submission of China, TN/TE/W/35/Rev.1, ¶ 3 (July 3, 2003). No WTO member has formally challenged China's definition.

10. *See* Committee on Trade and Environment, Identification of Multilateral Environmental Agreements (MEAs) and Specific Trade Obligations (STOs), Submission of China, TN/TE/W/35/Rev.1, ¶ 3 (July 3, 2003). Malaysia echoed China's views on the elements of an MEA, expressly noting that regional MEAs are not within the scope of the term. *See* Committee on Trade and Environment, Paragraph 31(i) of the Doha Ministerial Declaration, Submission of Malaysia, TN/TE/W/29, ¶¶ 8-9 (Apr. 30, 2003).

11. *See* Committee on Trade and Environment, Proposal for a Decision of the Ministerial Conference on Trade and Environment, Submission by the European Communities, TN/TE/W/68 (June 30, 2006); Committee on Trade and Environment, The Relationship Between WTO Rules and MEAs, Submission by Switzerland, TN/TE/W/61, ¶ 3 (Oct. 10, 2005).

12. *See* Committee on Trade and Environment, The Relationship Between WTO Rules and MEAs, Submission by Switzerland, TN/TE/W/61, ¶ 4 (Oct. 10, 2005).

13. *See* Committee on Trade and Environment, Proposal for a Decision of the Ministerial Conference on Trade and Environment, Submission by the European Communities, TN/TE/W/68 (June 30, 2006).

14. *Id.*

15. *See* Committee on Trade and Environment, The Relationship Between Existing WTO Rules and Specific Trade Obligations (STOs) Set Out in Multilateral Environmental Agreements (MEAs): A Swiss Perspective on National Experiences and Criteria Used in the Negotiation and Implementation of MEAs, Submission of Switzerland, TN/TE/W/58, ¶ 17(b) (July 6, 2005).

16. *See* Committee on Trade and Environment, Proposal for a Decision of the Ministerial Conference on Trade and Environment, Submission by the European Communities, TN/TE/W/68 (June 30, 2006).

17. Trade Act of 2002, Pub. L. No. 107-210, 107th Cong., 2d Sess., 116 Stat. 933, §2102 (2002).

18. North American Agreement on Environmental Cooperation, Dec. 17, 1993, U.S.-Can.-Mex., *reprinted in* 32 INT'L LEGAL MATERIALS 1480 (1993) [hereinafter NAAEC].

19. *Id.* art. 14.1.

20. *Id.* art. 38. The Secretariat maintains a Registry of Submissions on Enforcement Matters that is available at the CEC website, www.cec.org.

21. *Id.* art. 22.1.

22. *Id.* art. 45.1.

23. *Id.* art. 24.1.

24. *See* Exec. Order No. 13141, Environmental Review of Trade Agreements, Nov. 16, 1999, 64 Fed. Reg. 63169 (1999). The implementing guidelines are published at 65 Fed. Reg. 79442 (1999). The Executive Order and Guidelines are available at www.ustr.gov/environment/environmental.shtml.

25. *See* Exec. Order No. 13141, *supra* note 24.

26. *See* Exec. Order No. 13277, 67 Fed. Reg. 70305 (2001).

27. All environmental reviews are available at www.ustr.gov.

28. *See* Office of the U.S. Trade Rep., Fact Sheet, Bipartisan Agreement on Trade Policy, *available at* www.ustr.gov.

29. *See, e.g.*, United States-Peru Trade Promotion Agreement [hereinafter U.S.-Peru TPA], art. 18.2, signed April 2006, not yet in force. The text of the Agreement is available at www.ustr.gov. The environmental chapters of the FTAs with Colombia, Korea, and Panama that are pending congressional approval track the environmental chapter of the U.S.-Peru TPA almost verbatim.

30. U.S.-Peru TPA, art. 18.2 n.1, art. 18.3.

31. NAFTA art. 1114.2.

32. Dominican Republic-Central America Free Trade Agreement [hereinafter DR-CAFTA], art. 17.2(2).

33. *See, e.g.*, U.S.-Peru TPA, art. 18.3(2) ("a Party shall not waive or otherwise derogate from, or offer to waive or otherwise derogate from, such laws in a manner that weakens or reduces the protections afforded in those laws in a manner affecting trade or investment between the Parties").

34. *See* DR-CAFTA, art. 17.12.

35. *See, e.g.*, U.S.-Peru TPA, art. 18.13(4) (emphasis added).

36. *Id.* art. 18.11; United States-Colombia Trade Promotion Agreement, art. 18.11.

37. U.S.-Peru TPA, Annex 10-B, ¶ 3(b).

38. *See* United States-Chile Free Trade Agreement, Annex 10-D, ¶ 4(b) ("Except in rare circumstances, nondiscriminatory regulatory actions by a Party that are designed and applied to protect legitimate public welfare objectives, such as public health, safety, and the environment, do not constitute indirect expropriations.").

39. *See, e.g.,* Committees on Trade and Environment and Trade and Development, Sustainability Impact Assessments, Communications From the European Communities, Annex III, *Sustainability Impact Assessment of the WTO Negotiations in the Major Food Crops Sector,* WT/COMTD/W/99, WT/CTE/W/208, TN/TE/W/3 (June 3, 2002).

Chapter 26

Official Development Assistance: Toward Funding for Sustainability

Royal C. Gardner and Ezequiel Lugo

Nations act only in their perceived self-interest. As is the case with other countries, U.S. international assistance typically promotes U.S. strategic and national security objectives; assistance is rarely given for the sole purpose of promoting sustainable development. While legal and moral rationales might provide reasons for the United States to provide foreign assistance that encourages sustainable development, a strategic rationale consistent with the national security interests of the United States is the most compelling justification.

Since the 2002 World Summit on Sustainable Development at Johannesburg, the link between sustainable development and national security has become increasingly acknowledged. In April 2007, a group of 12 retired U.S. generals and admirals issued a report characterizing projected climate change as a "serious threat to America's national security interests."[1] The report recommended that the United States assume more of a leadership role in combating greenhouse gas emissions and "commit to global partnerships" to assist developing countries in managing the impacts of climate change.[2] In other words, national security and sustainable development assistance can be mutually reinforcing.

This chapter examines the level of U.S. international assistance since Johannesburg, and explores the link between sustainable development and the war on terrorism. From the perspective of sustainable development, however, the current rubric for measuring a state's foreign assistance efforts, known as Official Development Assistance (ODA), is elusive because it is both overinclusive and underinclusive. ODA figures do not distinguish between the funding of sustainable and unsustainable projects; they also do not capture the full extent of a country's contributions to fostering sustainable development abroad. While cognizant of those limitations on capturing the extent of ODA, the chapter then examines the record of U.S. ODA following Johannesburg, which has increased both in total dollars and as a percentage of gross national income. Much of that ODA increase is related to the Iraq War (debt forgiveness and reconstruction aid), and its effectiveness in accomplishing strategic and sustainable development objectives is in doubt. The chapter next examines recent U.S. contributions to the Montreal Protocol Multilateral Fund and the Global Environment Facility.

The chapter concludes with several observations and recommendations for how international assistance ought to be measured if one wants to align ODA more closely with the goals of sustainable development. First, the definition of ODA should incorporate and promote the concept of sustainable development by requiring that ODA be consistent with Strategic Environmental Assessments (SEAs). Second, the definition of ODA should include assistance necessary to foster the conditions required for sustainable development, contributions that are not currently recognized in a formal manner. The United States must also remain current with respect to its commitments to fund multilateral ODA efforts (such as the Montreal Protocol Multilateral Fund and the Global Environment Facility).

Rationales for International Assistance

There are several overlapping justifications for why the United States should provide assistance to encourage sustainable development abroad: legal, humanitarian, and strategic. To the surprise of some, the last may be the most compelling.

On the legal side, some commentators point to Agenda 21 of the 1992 Rio Earth Summit, which reaffirms the obligation of developed countries to provide 0.7 percent of their GNP to ODA.[3] The United States has expressly declined to accept this obligation. In fact, at Johannesburg the U.S. Department of State declared that "[t]he United States reaffirms that it does not accept international aid targets based on percentages of donor gross national product."[4] Thus, from a legal perspective, the obligation to provide assistance is viewed by the U.S. government as at most a "soft law" obligation.

Another reason for providing sustainable development aid is humanitarian in nature: it is the morally correct action to take. The United States (like many countries) has a long history of offering disaster relief. The U.S. Navy was one of the first responders to assist Indonesia after the 2005 tsunami.[5] Such aid is frequently offered even to adversaries—for example, U.S. assistance to Iran after earthquakes there in 2006.[6]

Yet there is a strategic component to these humanitarian efforts. The provision of charity can also be in the U.S. self-interest. Proponents of increased international assistance would do well to emphasize that such aid can be consistent with and further U.S. national security interests. Not surprisingly, other countries similarly use foreign aid "to further their own national interests, [or to] advance an ideological agenda[.]"[7] For instance, China has recently been using foreign aid in Africa and Indonesia to ensure it has access to natural resources.[8] Venezuela has been using foreign aid throughout Latin America to spread the political ideology of Chavismo.[9] Japan has been providing foreign aid for years to landlocked countries such as Mongolia and Mali to secure sufficient votes in the International Whaling Commission to lift the commercial whaling moratorium.[10] Such uses of international assistance are not necessarily consistent with the principle of sustainable development.

The national-interest or national-security rationale might be the most compelling justification for international assistance, especially when linked with sustainable development. Clearly, it is consistent with the national security interests of the United States to provide aid to prevent the disintegration of states, which is why the U.S. Department of Defense has spent millions of dollars on HIV/AIDS prevention efforts in Uganda and other African countries.[11] We know that weak and failed states can have repercussions far beyond one country's borders.

Measuring International Assistance

The current methodology used by the Organization for Economic Co-operation and Development (OECD) for evaluating a state's foreign assistance effort—that is, measuring a state's foreign assistance efforts through ODA, which consists of financial resources flowing to developing countries and multilateral institutions—is inaccurate. At best, it is a blunt tool that can be both overinclusive and underinclusive. A loan or a grant can qualify as ODA if (1) its primary objective is to further the economic development and welfare of developing countries, and (2) it is concessional in nature, with a grant element of at least 25 percent.[12] An ODA transaction is concessional in nature if it reflects a difference of at least 25 percent between the interest charged and either (1) the market rate of interest that the borrower would otherwise have had to pay or (2) the return that the lender could have expected from the next most profitable means of investing the capital.[13] While ODA is a good starting point for analyzing a country's commitment to promoting sustainable development abroad, it has significant limitations.

First, ODA is overinclusive because ODA funds encourage development that does not necessarily translate into sustainable projects. Sometimes the money is diverted through corruption and bureaucratic inefficiencies in the recipient country. The rampant corruption in the Uzbek government, for example, led the World Bank to suspend loans to Uzbekistan in 2006.[14] Indeed, corruption and waste are often cited as reasons why the United States should not increase its international assistance.

ODA funds can also be used for environmentally damaging projects. In the case of Indonesia, a series of multilateral ODA programs and associated Dutch projects turned out to have unintended and environmentally harmful results. From the 1960s to the 1980s, the World Bank financed projects to promote Indonesia's increased palm oil output.[15] The International Monetary Fund's financial support package for Indonesia after the Asian Financial Crisis in the late 1990s was conditioned on Indonesia's removal of all barriers to foreign investment in palm oil production.[16] As a result, foreign investors applied for permits to convert forested areas into palm oil plantations, and Dutch banks invested at least $1.9 billion in palm oil plantations.[17] After the European Union adopted its Biofuels Directive in 2003, which required all member states to aim to have 5.75 percent of all vehicles running on biofuel by 2010, the Netherlands provided subsidies for energy companies using palm oil.[18] And the Netherlands quickly became the leading importer of palm oil in Europe. While Indonesia's palm oil industry has been a beneficiary of these policies, the global carbon emissions caused by draining and burning Indonesian forests and peatland are now equivalent to 8 percent of global fossil fuel emissions.[19]

Second, while ODA is overinclusive from a sustainable development perspective, it is also underinclusive to the extent that it does not capture the full extent of contributions by the United States (and other countries) to furthering sustainable development abroad. Although peace and security are prerequisites for sustainable development, the incremental costs of U.S. peacekeeping efforts are not factored into ODA totals.[20] Education is also necessary for sustainable development, and private and public U.S. universities offer millions of dollars annually in scholarships and financial assistance to students from developing countries. The United States does not include these educational subsidies from public institutions in its ODA totals, but it should.[21] Nor does the United States include federal money channeled to nongovernmental organizations (NGOs), such as the $97.3 million the State Department provided in 2005 to over 40 NGOs providing protection and humanitarian aid to refugees and victims of conflict.[22]

In addition, the United States does not include in its ODA totals the tax subsidies provided to individuals and corporations that promote sustainable development abroad.[23] Bill and Melinda Gates and Oprah Winfrey are among the highest profile donors. In 2004, the Bill and Melinda Gates Foundation donated $1.2 billion to international health initiatives and, as of 2006, had provided over $1 billion for HIV/AIDS prevention and drug research programs, as well as $1.9 billion to vaccinate millions of children against infectious diseases like malaria and tuberculosis.[24] Oprah Winfrey established the Oprah Winfrey Leadership Academy for Girls in South Africa at a cost of $40 million.[25] A recent estimate indicates that between $1 billion and $2.5 billion of such tax subsidies could qualify annually as ODA.[26]

Finally, focusing exclusively on ODA overlooks what Alan S. Miller has called one of "the most important economic developments of the twentieth century."[27] As Chapter 27 discusses, private financial flows such as foreign direct investment "now dwarf" ODA, noting that "in 2005 total development assistance was worth $106.5 billion, whereas net private flows were $491 billion."[28] Obviously, the volume of private financial flows can have a greater impact on sustainable development efforts than ODA.

Progress Since 2002: U.S. ODA Post-Johannesburg

The United States has significantly increased its ODA and is now the largest net donor, reclaiming that position from Japan.[29] In 2001, U.S. ODA was $12.177 billion (at 2004 prices and exchange rates). By 2005, it had reached $26.888 billion (also at 2004 prices and exchange rates). As a percentage of gross national income, U.S. ODA doubled from 0.11 percent in 2001 to 0.22 percent in 2005 (although the United

States still ranks only 20th among the 22 countries that are members of the OECD Development Assistance Committee).[30]

Figure 1

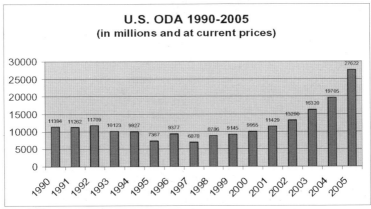

Source: OECD

Figure 2

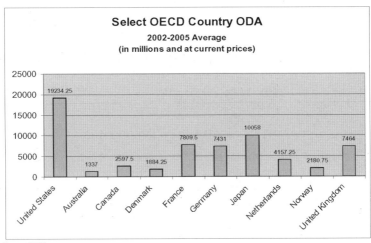

Source: OECD

Figure 3

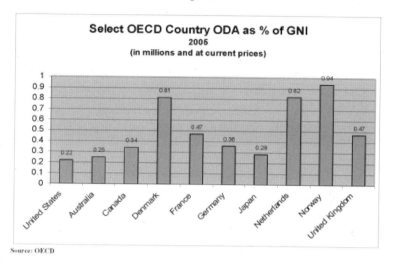

Select OECD Country ODA as % of GNI
2005
(in millions and at current prices)

Source: OECD

On its face, this increase would appear to be excellent progress, although not entirely surprising. A rise in foreign assistance was expected to follow the beginning of the war on terrorism.[31] Indeed, the increase in U.S. ODA since 2002 is largely related to the Iraq War, and its effectiveness in accomplishing strategic and sustainable development objectives is questionable.

The assumptions at the beginning of the war on terrorism were that U.S. ODA would be linked to larger strategic objectives (although not necessarily sustainable development), and that it would grow as a function of rewarding countries that assisted with the war on terrorism. Thus, the United States has focused on sub-Saharan Africa ($4.2 billion in 2005), in part for strategic reasons.[32] Improving the living conditions of people in this region should decrease the pool of the disaffected from which terrorists draw. U.S. reconstruction efforts in Afghanistan ($1.3 billion in 2005) also seek to prevent it from reverting back to a launching ground for terrorists.[33] But much of the increase in 2005 in U.S. ODA is attributable to the Iraq War: $3.9 billion in Iraq debt forgiveness and $6.9 billion in reconstruction aid.[34] Many reports have called into question whether these funds have been spent effectively.[35] On paper, there is an increase in ODA; on the ground, however, increased funding does not necessarily translate into sustainable projects.

U.S. Contributions to the Montreal Protocol Multilateral Fund and the Global Environment Facility: The Link to National Security

One form of ODA that is directly linked to sustainable development is contributions to certain multilateral environmental organizations. Two in particular are worth mentioning here:

- **Montreal Protocol Multilateral Fund (MPMF).** The MPMF was created to implement the Vienna Convention on Substances That Deplete the Ozone Layer (and the subsequent Montreal Protocol, which entered into force on January 1, 1989). The MPMF was established specifically to aid developing countries to meet the environmental standards of the Protocol.

- **Global Environment Facility (GEF).** The GEF is an independent organization that provides financial support to developing countries for projects that support sustainability, including climate change, biodiversity, and the ozone layer.

The OECD Development Assistance Committee (DAC) recognizes 100 percent of contributions to MPMF and 77 percent of contributions to GEF as ODA.[36] The DAC decided to count 77 percent of GEF contributions as ODA and the remaining 23 percent as official aid (OA),[37] presumably because some GEF contributions are disbursed to countries that are not considered "developing."

With respect to the MPMF, the United States made timely payments until 1995. By 1996, the United States owed approximately $27 million in outstanding contributions.[38] It soon made up the shortfall and had no outstanding contributions until 2005 ($11.7 million), 2006 ($29.4 million), and 2007 ($29.4 million).[39] As of June 2008, the United States still had more than $59 million in outstanding contributions to the MPMF.[40]

The United States is similarly in arrears with respect to its commitments to the GEF, with outstanding contributions of $140.7 million (GEF-2), $28.1 million (GEF-3), and $0.8 million (GEF-4).[41] The United States withheld payments, in part, because it wanted the GEF to undertake certain reforms.[42] The GEF and the U.S. Treasury Department negotiated an agreement in which the GEF agreed to the reforms, including enhanced fiduciary standards and provisions to improve institutional effectiveness.[43] In return, the United States has pledged to pay $80 million per year for the next four years.[44]

While contributions to environmental efforts may seem far removed from the strategic objective of fighting terrorism, there is an important, if indirect, link: if the United States wishes to rely on other nations in the war on terrorism, it should abide by its commitments in other international contexts.

Recommendations

Our recommendations fall into two categories. The first focuses on setting improved standards for what constitutes ODA and its relationship to sustainable development. The second relates to the level of U.S. international assistance and U.S. leadership.

1. The definition of ODA should be modified to incorporate and better promote the concept of sustainable development. The DAC, as the OECD body in charge of defining and monitoring ODA, should modify the definition of ODA to include a requirement that its funded projects be sustainable, or at least not environmentally destructive. This recommendation simply recognizes reality: what good is assistance in the long run if it promotes unsustainable or environmentally damaging outcomes?

An initial step in this direction would be to require that foreign assistance be guided by an Environmental Impact Assessment (EIA) or Strategic Environmental Assessment (SEA) in order to qualify as ODA. While EIAs focus on specific projects, the broader SEAs are "analytical and participatory approaches that aim to integrate environmental considerations into policies, plans and programs and evaluate the inter linkages with economic and social considerations."[45] The DAC has already recognized that an SEA is the best way to help decisionmakers avoid turning development successes into environmental nightmares.[46] Developing countries could incorporate SEAs into their national development strategies, and developed countries could include SEAs as part of their assistance plans.[47] In fact, the European Union and the U.N. Economic Commission for Europe already require the application of SEAs in certain contexts,[48] and many developed and developing countries have statutory or administrative provisions requiring SEAs.[49] Under this proposed framework, the DAC would monitor and report which foreign-assistance projects incorporate SEAs and EIAs.

The DAC should also expand the definition of ODA to include assistance related to fostering conditions necessary for sustainable development, such as peacekeeping expenses and tax subsidies that result in the flow of charitable dollars to developing countries. This new definition (which is both more restrictive and broader than the current ODA definition) would better recognize a country's efforts to promote sustainable development abroad. But it is important to note that such efforts do not always result in sustainable projects. Ultimately, of course, the results will matter more than the input.

2. The United States should continue to increase its ODA, but only to the extent that it is effective in both achieving sustainable development goals and furthering U.S. strategic goals. Along these lines, the United States should fully satisfy its MPMF and GEF obligations. This recommendation recognizes that the United States will act in accordance with its perceived self-interests, but emphasizes the importance of following through on its commitments.

Conclusion

While the level of U.S. ODA has increased since 2001, the current yardstick for international assistance does not accurately measure the extent to which U.S. international assistance promotes sustainable development. On the one hand, the definition of ODA does not capture all spending that is related to sustainable development. On the other hand, some expenditures counted as ODA (such as reconstruction projects in Iraq) do not necessarily translate into sustainable projects. Regardless of how ODA is defined, however, national security and sustainable development assistance can be mutually reinforcing, and global partnerships (through ODA or otherwise) that support sustainable development are in the U.S. national interest.

ENDNOTES

1. CNA CORP., NATIONAL SECURITY AND THE THREAT OF CLIMATE CHANGE 44 (2007).

2. *Id.* at 7, 47.

3. U.N. Conference on Environment and Development (UNCED), Agenda 21, ¶ 33, U.N. Doc. A/CONF.151.26 (1992) [hereinafter UNCED, Agenda 21].

4. U.S. Interpretive Statement on World Summit on Sustainable Development Declaration, *available at* www.state.gov/s/l/38717.htm (last visited Apr. 26, 2007); *see also* interview by EMERGING MARKETS with Alan Larson, Under Secretary for Economic, Business, and Agricultural Affairs, U.S. Department of State, Oct. 1, 2004, *available at* www.state.gov/e/rls/rm/2004/38232.htm (answering questions regarding the 0.7 percent target by saying that "[i]t may be a target set by the U.N. but it was never a target that the U.S. government ever subscribed to. . . . It's not a target my country has adopted").

5. *See* Nick Cumming-Bruce, *Relief Teams Push Into Devastated Indonesia as Aid Gains Steam, Asia Aims for Warning System*, INT'L HERALD TRIB., Jan. 4, 2005, at 1, *available at* 2005 WLNR 89270 (stating that U.S. Navy helicopters were first to provide relief supplies to communities in Sumatra); Alan Sipress & Ellen Nakashima, *Towns Found Flattened in Sumatra; Deaths Hit 117,000*, WASH. POST, Dec. 21, 2004, *available at* 2004 WLNR 18274032 (explaining that the U.S. Navy raced to Sumatra shortly after the tsunami).

6. *See, e.g., Iran Turns Down Offer of U.S. Earthquake Aid*, ASIAN POL. NEWS, Apr. 10, 2006, *available at* 2006 WLNR 6511959 (stating that the United States offered aid to Iran in 2006 after a 6.0 earthquake, but Iran declined the offer); Nasser Karimi, *Survivors Look for Relatives Amid Rubble in Iran Death Toll Rises to at Least 549 After Quake*, S. FLA. SUN-SENTINEL, Feb. 25, 2005, at 27A, *available at* 2005 WLNR 23645026 (mentioning that the United States also offered humanitarian assistance to Iran after a 6.4 earthquake in 2005); Ilene R. Prusher, *For the Moment, U.S., Iran Set Hostility Aside American Planes Deliver Emergency Assistance to Victims of Earthquake*, SEATTLE TIMES, Dec. 29, 2003, at A7 (describing United States assistance to Iran after two earthquakes in 1990 and 2003).

7. Moisés Naím, *Rogue Aid*, FOREIGN POLICY (Mar./Apr. 2007), at 96.

8. *Id.*

9. *Id.*

10. Ashley Thompson, *NZ Joins Charge to Try to Ward Off the "Real Danger" of Pro-Whaling Tokyo Running IWC*, NEW ZEALAND HERALD, Apr. 18, 2006, at A1, *available at* 2006 WLNR 6404701.

11. *See* NICOLAS COOK, AIDS IN AFRICA 22 (Congressional Research Service 2006) (explaining that Congress appropriated $5.5 million for the Department of Defense HIV/AIDS Prevention Program in 2006); Stephan Faris, *Containment Strategy*, ATL. MONTHLY, Dec. 2006, at 34-35 (describing the Department of Defense HIV/AIDS Prevention Program).

12. ORGANISATION FOR ECON. CO-OPERATION & DEV. (OECD), GEOGRAPH-ICAL DISTRIBUTION OF FINANCIAL FLOWS TO AID RECIPIENTS 2001-2005, at 267 (2007).

13. *Id.*

14. Paul Blustein, *World Bank Strategy Targets Corruption*, WASH. POST, Apr. 12, 2006, at D5. *But see* David E. Sanger, *Between Bush and the World*, N.Y. TIMES, Apr. 14, 2007, at A1 (indicating that aid to Uzbekistan was suspended after Uzbekistan "denied landing rights to American military aircraft").

15. ANNE CASSON, CTR. FOR INT'L FORESTRY RESEARCH, THE HESITANT BOOM: INDONESIA'S OIL PALM SUB-SECTOR IN AN ERA OF ECONOMIC CRISIS AND POLITICAL CHANGE 12-13 (1999); JAN WILLEM VAN GELDER, WWF INT'L, DUTCH BANKS AND PALM OIL AND PULP AND PAPER IN IN-DONESIA 16 (2001).

16. Enrique R. Carrasco, Commentary, *Tough Sanctions: The Asian Crisis and New Colonialism*, CHI. TRIB., Feb. 3, 1998, at 11.

17. ERIC WAKKER, FUNDING FOREST DESTRUCTION: THE INVOLVEMENT OF DUTCH BANKS IN THE FINANCING OF OIL PALM PLANTATIONS IN INDO-NESIA 14 (Greenpeace Netherlands 2000); *see* VAN GELDER, *supra* note 15, at 113-45 (describing the amount invested by individual Dutch banks between 1994 and 2000).

18. Elizabeth Rosenthal, *Once a Dream Fuel, Palm Oil May Be an Eco-Night-mare*, N.Y. TIMES, Jan. 31, 2007, at C1.

19. *Id.*

20. OECD, DAC STATISTICAL REPORTING DIRECTIVES 22 (2007) [hereinafter DAC, REPORTING DIRECTIVES].

21. Royal C. Gardner, *Official Development Assistance*, *in* STUMBLING TO-WARD SUSTAINABILITY 151 (John C. Dernbach ed., 2002).

22. OECD, DAC PEER REVIEW OF THE UNITED STATES 31 (2006) [hereinafter OECD, U.S. PEER REVIEW].

23. David E. Pozen, Comment, *Tax Expenditures as Foreign Aid*, 116 YALE L.J. 869, 875-77 (2007).

24. John Hechinger & Daniel Golden, *The Great Giveaway—Like Warren Buffett, A New Wave of Philanthropists Are Rushing to Spend Their Money Before They Die*, WALL ST. J., July 8, 2006, at A1.

25. Allison Samuels, *Oprah Goes to School*, NEWSWEEK, Jan. 8, 2007, at 46.

26. Pozen, *supra* note 23, at 875.

27. Alan S. Miller, *Environmental Policy in the New World Economy*, 3 WID-ENER L. SYMP. J. 287, 291 (1998).

28. *See* Smita Nakhooda et al., "Financing Sustainable Development," *infra* Chapter 27.

29. OECD, FINAL ODA DATA FOR 2005, at 3 (2006), *available at* http://www.oecd.org/dataoecd/52/18/37790990.pdf.

30. *Id.* at 7-8.

31. Gardner, *supra* note 21, at 149.

32. *See* U.S. Dep't of State, Congressional Budget Justification Foreign Operations Fiscal Year 2007, at 40 (2006) (justifying appropriations for programs in sub-Saharan Africa partly to "combat terrorism and other forces that undermine prosperity and stability in the region").

33. *See* James P. Rubin, *What Is America's Commitment to Iraq?*, N.Y. Times, Aug. 23, 2002, at A17 (stating that "reconstruction assistance and humanitarian aid was intended to . . . prevent Afghanistan from ever again becoming a terrorist base").

34. OECD, U.S. Peer Review, *supra* note 22, at 25.

35. *See, e.g.*, U.S. Gov't Accountability Office, Securing, Stabilizing, and Rebuilding Iraq, GAO-07-1195 (Sept. 2007) (finding that "a large portion of Iraq's $10 billion capital projects and reconstruction budget in fiscal year 2007 will likely go unspent"); James Glanz, *As U.S. Rebuilds, Iraq Minister Won't Take Over Finished Work*, N.Y. Times, July 28, 2007 (reporting that reconstruction projects are being turned over to "local Iraqis, who often lack the proper training and resources to keep the projects running"). *See also* Rory Stewart, Prince of the Marshes (2007) (recounting challenges in Iraq reconstruction efforts).

36. DAC, Reporting Directives, *supra* note 20, at 25.

37. Dep't for Int'l Dev. (U.K.), Statistics on International Development 2006, at 153 (2006), *available at* http://www.dfid.gov.uk/pubs/files/sid2006/sid06-full.pdf.

38. Royal C. Gardner, *Exporting American Values: Tenth Amendment Principles and International Environmental Assistance*, 22 Harv. Envtl. L. Rev. 1, 40 (1998).

39. United Nations Environment Program (UNEP), Executive Committee of the Multilateral Fund for the Implementation of the Montreal Protocol, *Status of Contributions and Disbursements*, at 7-8, 10, U.N. Doc. UNEP/OzL. Pro/ExCom/51/3 (Feb. 16, 2007) [hereinafter UNEP, *Contributions*]; Gardner, *supra* note 38, at 40.

40. United Nations Environment Program (UNEP), Executive Committee of the Multilateral Fund for the Implementation of the Montreal Protocol, *Status of Contributions and Disbursements*, at 6, U.N. Doc. UNEP/OzL.Pro/ExCom/55/3 (June 13, 2008).

41. Global Environment Facility (GEF), *Trustee Report*, ¶¶ 5, 7, 11, Doc. GEF/C.33/Inf.3 (Apr. 22-25, 2008).

42. 152 Cong. Rec. H3518, H3530-H3531 (daily ed. June 8, 2006) (statements of Reps. Kolbe and Thornberry).

43. *Id.*

44. *Id.*

45. DAC, Applying Strategic Environmental Assessment: Good Practice Guidance for Development Co-Operation 30 (2006) [hereinafter DAC, SEA]. *See generally id.* at 29-39, 49-61, 65-115 (describing the specifics of SEA).

46. *Id.* at 14.

47. *Id.* at 18-19.

48. *See* Protocol on Strategic Environmental Assessment to the Convention on Environmental Impact Assessment in a Transboundary Context, *opened for signature* May 21, 2003, *available at* http://untreaty.un.org/English/notpubl/ 27_4bE.pdf; Council Directive 2001/42/EC, 2001 O.J. (L 197) 30.

49. DAC, SEA, *supra* note 45, at 25.

Chapter 27

Financing Sustainable Development

Smita Nakhooda, Frances Seymour, and Sabina Ahmed

It has been 26 years since the Brundtland Commission presented the world with the concept of sustainable development, recognizing that environmental and social well-being contribute directly to poverty alleviation and are essential to the economic development and welfare of current and future generations. At the United Nations Conference on Environment and Development at Rio in 1992, known as the Rio Summit, governments of the world formally charted out a map to sustainability in the form of Agenda 21, concluding that its achievement would require an annual investment of $600 billion primarily in the form of public overseas development assistance (ODA).[1] At the World Summit on Sustainable Development in Johannesburg in 2002, the international community explicitly recognized for the first time that nongovernmental actors, particularly business and the private sector, would have to work together with public and multilateral institutions to realize these goals. In 2003, governments adopted the Millennium Development Goals to address extreme poverty and hunger by 2015, with a relatively modest price tag of $100 billion per year in ODA to achieve these minimum standards.[2] Nevertheless, commitments have fallen far short of this requirement.

Private financial flows to developing countries now dwarf development assistance: In 2005, total development assistance was $106.5 billion, whereas net private flows were $491 billion (see Figure 1).[3] But only limited progress has been made in aligning either public or private capital flows with either Agenda 21 or the Millennium Development Goals. Private financial flows to developing countries are concentrated in a few emerging economies. Brazil, China, India, Mexico, and Russia receive 80 percent of foreign direct investment (FDI),[4] and it tends to be concentrated in sectors such as oil, gas, and telecommunications, rather than in sectors that have more direct developmental impacts such as health care, sanitation, or education.

Figure 1: Financial Flows to Developing Countries

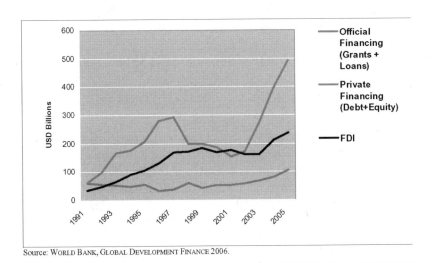

Source: WORLD BANK, GLOBAL DEVELOPMENT FINANCE 2006.

To finance sustainable development, environmental and social considerations need to be integrated into the investment decisions of financial institutions, both public and private. Two types of organizations—export and investment promotion agencies (called export credit agencies or ECAs, and specifically the ECAs of developed countries) and multilateral development banks (MDBs)—are well-situated to lead this process, and should be held accountable for doing so. This chapter focuses on the U.S. role in influencing the policies of ECAs and MDBs in ways that significantly enhance the alignment of private financial flows to developing countries with environmental and social agendas.

Historically, the United States has played an important role in prompting international financial institutions to link environmental and social considerations to their operations and investments.[5] As the majority shareholder in the World Bank group, for example, the United States has exerted its influence to prompt the Bank to adopt environmental and social safeguard policies to ensure that the Bank did not finance efforts that would negatively impact people and the environment. Over the last six years, however, U.S. leadership in these policy arenas has been inconsistent, and in some cases even counterproductive.

Steering International Finance Toward Sustainable Development

Public financial institutions such as ECAs and MDBs are in a position to steer some of the abundant private capital available for investment in the developing world toward countries, projects, and sectors in ways that would serve development objectives. ECAs can provide financial incentives to companies to invest in poor, high-risk countries in sectors that have development benefits. MDBs can set environmental and social standards for their financing and assist governments to construct enabling policy frameworks to make investment in sustainable development more attractive to private-sector actors.

Public financial institutions can help align both private and public financial flows with sustainable development objectives by ensuring that environmental and social standards for lending and investment are in place to provide incentives and frameworks to advance these objectives. Private-sector actors who take their lead from or work in the same countries as these public financial institutions can incorporate these standards into their own policies and practices, thereby supporting the integration of environmental and social concerns into financing decisions. Adoption of such lending standards is an important step toward mainstreaming environmental and social sustainability into development activities.

Export Credit Agencies: Guaranteeing Development

Export credit agencies are public institutions that facilitate financing for home-country exporters and investors doing business overseas, particularly in developing countries and emerging market economies. The U.S. Export-Import Bank (Ex-Im Bank) is the official ECA of the United States; it offers working capital guarantees and export credit insurance to U.S. exporters and offers direct loans and guarantees of commercial loans to foreign buyers of U.S. goods and services. In 2006, the Ex-Im Bank approved US $12.1 billion in loans, guarantees, and export credit insurance, while receiving a US $172.5 million allocation from Congress,[6] which signaled continued political support for the Bank's role in financing export programs that are consistent with broader international U.S. economic and financial policies.

To date, public resources directed via ECAs to support export promotion have contributed very little to sustainable development, and questions are being raised about whether ECAs are needed to fill market gaps supposedly underserved by private banks.[7] Some fiscal conservatives even refer to ECA financing as "corporate welfare" because it supports large corporations in markets where private equity is readily available.[8]

At the same time, ECAs play a significant role in the world's poorest countries, where international private-sector actors have a limited presence. The World Bank has estimated that ECA financing currently represents 80 percent of gross capital-market financing in the 70 poorest countries in the world. Between 1997 and 2002, every commercial bank loan for more than $20 million in these poorest countries was backed by an official guarantee from institutions such as ECAs.[9] It is clear that few private-sector companies are likely to risk investing in these economies without public guarantees.

Within the United States and other OECD countries, ECAs are facing increasing public pressure to address the social and environmental consequences of the large infrastructure projects that they back. As part of its 2006 reauthorization of the Ex-Im Bank, Congress called on the Bank to establish a specialized renewable energy office with staff that has significant renewable energy experience in order to identify opportunities for investment in clean energy.[10] Anticipating that similar demands would be made during its congressional reauthorization, the United States' other major export promotion agency, the Overseas Private Investment Corporation (OPIC), announced its Greenhouse Gas Initiative in June 2007 and set a goal to reduce emissions from its investment portfolio by 20 percent over the next 10 years.[11]

While it is too early to gauge the impact of these new initiatives on the operations of the Ex-Im Bank and OPIC, they represent promising efforts to reform these institutions to do more to support sustainable development, and are prompting a much needed reexamination of portfolio priorities. These initiatives have been prompted by public pressure, including litigation. For example, Friends of the Earth and other environmental groups brought an action in federal court against OPIC and the Ex-Im Bank, claiming that these agencies have provided financial support for coal-fired power plants, oil and gas fields, and pipeline projects around the world without giving legally sufficient consideration to the direct and indirect impacts of those projects on climate change.[12] While initiatives from Congress, advocacy groups, and the agencies themselves have resulted in incremental progress toward a sustainability agenda for U.S. ECAs, progress in raising global sustainability standards for ECAs through multilateral forums has been limited.

In 2003, the ECAs of the OECD countries adopted the Common Approaches on Environment and Officially Supported Export Credits,[13] a policy requiring that all projects comply with the environmental standards of the host country or the World Bank Group, which typically holds projects to higher standards than would national law in many developing countries. The United States played a leadership role in this effort to raise standards for all OECD member ECAs, in part because it recognized that U.S. companies might be disadvantaged by the relative stringency of its own environmental policies.

While the Common Approaches are intended to minimize negative development impacts of ECA-supported projects, they allow significant exemptions. They do not require all pertinent World Bank safeguard policies to apply to all projects. There is limited transparency in the implementation of the Common Approaches; for example, the agreement does not mandate the public release of environmental impact assessments. Nor do the Approaches address the broader human rights impacts of projects supported by ECAs. In 2007, all parties to the Common Approaches reviewed their experiences with the policy and examined their adequacy with respect to the evolving standards at the World Bank Group.[14] Unfortunately, the revisions resulting from the review have not adequately responded to the challenges of ensuring rigor, transparency, and accountability in project assessments. Individual ECAs now have even greater discretion in deciding how to apply environmental and social standards to their investments.

Multilateral Development Banks: Leveraging for a World Free of Poverty

Multilateral development banks play a significant role in influencing the character of investment from developed nations to poorer developing countries. Their missions include global poverty reduction and sustainable growth, and they have committed to helping to achieve the Millennium Development Goals. Thus, they play a major role in affecting the degree to which private financial flows to developing and transition economies are consistent with sustainable development objectives.

World Bank

The World Bank Group[15] has participated in global initiatives such as the Millennium Ecosystem Assessment, which concluded that better ecosystem management is critical to reducing poverty and meeting the MDGs. Recognizing the Bank's potential to help the international community to operationalize this insight, in 2005, the G-8 countries asked the Bank to take the lead in helping its clients address climate change, which poses a particular threat to poor countries and communities.

But many decisions taken by Bank management over the past three years would seem to signal wavering commitment to the sustainable development agenda. In June 2006, World Bank President Paul Wolfowitz reorganized the World Bank Group, merging its infrastructure and environment departments into a new vice presidency for sustainable development.[16] The reorganization created doubt about the extent to which environmental considerations are prioritized as there is no longer a member of the Bank's senior management team responsible solely for environmental and social actions or objectives.

The reorganization began at a sensitive moment, when development professionals seemed less convinced that rigorous environmental and social impact assessments are crucial instruments for avoiding mistakes that could harm fragile ecosystems and vulnerable human communities. Further, there is a perception that the "hassle costs" involved in borrowing from the Bank—including the costs of compliance with environmental safeguard policies—are deterring development, especially as the Bank has seen a decrease in investment in hard-sector infrastructure projects and a concurrent decrease in loans to middle-income countries.[17] The reorganization creates a potential conflict of interest because the same unit tasked with finding environmentally and socially sustainable approaches to development is also tasked with increasing lending to hard-sector infrastructure projects.

There have also, however, been new developments within the Bank that hold significant potential to support the sustainable development agenda. For example, governance and anti-corruption emerged as high-level priorities under President Wolfowitz's leadership. In 2006, the World Bank launched an effort to develop a strategy for, in the words of the report title, *Strengthening World Bank Group Engagement on Governance and Anti-Corruption*. The controversial strategy had the stated purpose of helping member countries create capable, transparent, and accountable government institutions. While the Bank has not explicitly articulated the links between governance and environmental sustainability in its strategy, building strong, accountable states is nevertheless essential to decreasing poverty and realizing sustainable development objectives.

Although environmental and social safeguard standards were initially put in place at the World Bank Group as a result of U.S. pressure, in recent years the United States has made little effort to advance the sustainability agenda within the institution. To the contrary, there are accounts that the United States sometimes used its position on the board of the World Bank to block projects associated with implementation of the Kyoto Protocol.[18] Even as the Bank worked to develop the Clean Energy Investment Framework in response to the G-8's 2005 Gleneagles Plan of Action on Climate Change, President Wolfowitz's deputies with close ties to the Bush Administration reportedly sought to water down references to climate change in the strategy document.[19]

In June 2007, former U.S. Trade Representative Robert Zoellick succeeded Wolfowitz as president of the World Bank. While it is too soon to tell how issues of environmentally sustainable development will be addressed under this new leadership, early signs suggest that President Zoellick sees helping poorer countries benefit from globalization in a more sustainable manner as a priority. A year into his presidency, he has launched a new set of Climate Investment Funds. In January 2008, President Bush announced a contribution of US $2 billion to these funds to support the deployment of clean technologies in developing countries.[20] Serious questions have been raised about whether the Clean Technology Fund will support truly transformational change.[21] Nevertheless these developments may signal the beginnings of a change in attitude from the United States regarding the need for the MDBs to support a global response to climate change.[22]

International Finance Corporation

Recent revisions to the environmental and social standards in place at the International Finance Corporation (IFC)—the arm of the World Bank that lends to the private sector—have raised a new set of challenges. In 2006, the IFC replaced its safeguard policy with a set of performance standards. While the safeguard policy relied on compliance with procedural and substantive requirements, the new standards are outcomes-based and allow investment officers and clients significant discretion in interpreting and conducting environmental and social due diligence, with limited accountability mechanisms to monitor and evaluate the impacts of projects financed. The United States has supported the shift to this new outcomes-based approach.

Any weaknesses in the IFC's performance standards have international ramifications for private financial flows. The IFC's policies also apply to the project finance investments in developing countries by 52 private banks that have signed onto the Equator Principles, a financial industry benchmark for determining, assessing, and managing social and environmental risk in project financing. The banks that have signed onto the Principles are responsible for 80 percent of project financing worldwide.[23] As a result of the adoption of the Equator Principles, the IFC explicitly sets international environmental and social standards for private financing. Yet despite the weaknesses in the IFC's performance standards, the Equator Principles represent a significant step forward within the private banking sector, and a sign of growing awareness and intent to manage environmental and social risks.

Inter-American Development Bank

In 2005, the Inter-American Development Bank (IDB), which has historically had the weakest environmental and social standards of all the MDBs, adopted an Environmental Safeguards Compliance Policy, with U.S. support. In 2006, as part of IDB's contribution to the Gleneagles Plan of Action, it launched the Sustainable Energy and Climate Change Initiative that seeks to scale up IDB support for renewable energy, increase support for biofuels, grow its presence in the carbon markets, and help its member countries adapt to climate change.

However, under the leadership of Luis Alberto Moreno, who took over as president of the IDB in 2005, the Bank has undergone its own internal reorganization bringing its environment and infrastructure departments together, mirroring the World Bank's reorganization. A key challenge will be to ensure that environmental considerations are prioritized in practice under this new operational structure. U.S. members on the IDB Board of Directors have been supportive of the idea that the Bank should promote internal compliance with its safeguard policies through an autonomous unit, and that additional financial and human resources need to be committed to promote environmental mainstreaming as part of the realignment.

Looking Forward

As the world's largest economy, the United States continues to have significant influence over the priorities of multilateral financial institutions. The operations of U.S. ECAs remain significant in global financial markets, particularly in promoting U.S. investments in the world's poorest countries, and give the United States a potentially powerful voice within international forums that set standards for ECA financing. A persistent challenge for financial institutions, and the development community more broadly, is to operationalize the understanding that environmental protection is central to long-term poverty reduction. The United States, for its part, should play a more proactive role in pressuring global financial institutions to facilitate private-sector finance for sustainable development.

1. The operation of U.S. ECAs gives the United States a potentially powerful voice. The United States has led the ECAs of OECD countries to adopt environmental standards under the Common Approaches. But as ECAs based in emerging economies such as Brazil, China, and India become increasingly active in international development finance, the international community confronts new challenges in achieving upward harmonization of environmental standards to include these new actors. Upward harmonization entails a common minimum standard of due diligence so as to prevent any ECA from gaining competitive advantage by lowering its environmental standards. The United States has taken some initiative in raising with China the issue of sustainability standards for projects financed by Chinese ECAs.[24] The United States should seek to ensure that financial institutions in emerging economies adopt robust minimum standards and do not finance projects that have damaging environmental and social impacts. One way to do this would be to demonstrate a commitment to robust standards at institutions over which the United States has direct influence, such as U.S. ECAs and the MDBs.

2. The United States should demonstrate its commitment to robust standards at MDBs. The World Bank Group and other MDBs, in appropriate partnership with others, have the potential to provide leadership on the question of how to balance environmental and social concerns with other factors that influence financing decisions. But the countries that own the MDBs, and their representatives on the respective boards of directors for each institution, must acquiesce to movement in this direction.

Over the past five years, innovations such as the Equator Principles have demonstrated that MDBs can in fact have significant influence over private investors and banks. There is evidence to suggest that private-sector actors increasingly recognize that taking on strong environmental and social standards for their operations can make good business sense, seemingly influenced by the experience of the MDBs. Several private banks such as Goldman Sachs and JP Morgan Chase have gone beyond their commitments under the Equator Principles. Such institutions have now begun to address global environmental sustainability challenges such as tropical deforestation and climate change—for example, by adopting renewable energy targets and greenhouse gas accounting and management practices for their investment portfolios.

Conclusion

While the United States can claim credit for initiating and leading sustainability reforms at the MDBs and ECAs in the 1980s and 1990s, these issues have not been given sufficient priority by the Bush Administration in recent years. There is much that remains to be done to align private investment with sustainable development objectives. The United States has significant influence over the activities and policies of the MDBs, whose goals are to promote sustainable development. Despite some progress over the past six years, however, the agenda of aligning private international flows with sustainable development objectives still remains far from complete.

ENDNOTES

1. U.N. Conference on Environment and Development (UNCED), Agenda 21, the Rio Declaration on Environment and Development, and the Statement of Principles for the Sustainable Management of Forests, *available at* http://www.un.org/esa/sustdev/documents/agenda21/index.htm.

2. U.N. Dev. Programme, Human Development Report 2003, Millennium Development Goals: A Compact Among Nations to End Human Poverty (2003).

3. World Bank, Global Development Finance 2006 (2006).

4. James Harmon et al., Diverging Paths: What Future for Export Credit Agencies in Development Finance? (2005), at 3.

5. Robert Wade, *Greening the Bank: The Struggle Over the Environment 1970-1995, in* The World Bank in Its First Half Century (Lewis et al. eds., 1997).

6. Export-Import Bank of the United States, Annual Report 2006 (2006).

7. Harmon et al., *supra* note 4, at 12-13.

8. *Id.* at 7.

9. World Bank, Global Development Finance 2002: Analysis and Summary Tables (2002).

10. Export-Import Bank Reauthorization Act of 2006, Pub. L. No. 109-438, 120 Stat. 3268 (Dec. 20, 2006), *available at* www.aaainc.org/fileadmin/aaainc/pdf/Key_Legislation/Public_Law_109-438_S._3938_December_20_2006_Export-Import_Reauthorization_Act_of_2006_-_Text.pdf.

11. Jon Sohn, World Res. Inst., OPIC's Greenhouse Gas Initiative, (2007), *available at* www.wri.org/stories/2007/06/opics-greenhouse-gas-initiative.

12. Friends of the Earth v. Mosbacher, 488 F. Supp. 2d 889 (N.D. Cal. 2007) (denying plaintiffs' motion for summary judgment and granting in part defendants' cross-motions for summary judgment).

13. OECD, OECD Adopts Stronger Environmental Common Approaches for Export Credits (2003), *available at* www.oecd.org/document/56/0,2340,en_2649_201185_21688824_1_1_1_1,00.html.

14. Harmon et al., *supra* note 4, at 33.

15. Although multilateral development banks include regional development banks, such as the Asian Development Bank and the African Development Bank, this section focuses on the World Bank Group as the most influential in policy and practice. Recent developments at the Inter-American Development Bank are also discussed.

16. By custom, the president of the World Bank is nominated by the United States. While this custom has become increasingly controversial, for the purposes of this analysis it is reasonable to infer that the policy directions of Presidents Wolfowitz and Zoellick broadly reflect those of the U.S. administration that selected them.

17. Frances Seymour, Sustaining the Environment at the World Bank 6 (2006).

18. Jon Sohn et al., World Res. Inst., Mainstreaming Climate Change Considerations at the MDBs 3 (2005).

19. Krishna Guha, *Deputy's Woes Stir World Bank Turmoil*, Fin. Times, Apr. 25, 2007, *available at* www.ft.com/cms/s/0/e67b4470-f2c8-11dba454-00b5df10621.html?nclick_check=1.

20. As of July 2008, the United Kingdom and Japan have also committed some $3 billion to the Clean Technology Fund of the World Bank-administered Climate Investment Funds.

21. As of July 2008, the World Bank has proposed that a portion of the Clean Technology Fund might be used to finance new coal-fired power plants using more efficient technology such as supercritical or ultra-supercritical coal. The Bush Administration has supported this approach. However, such technologies are already cost-effective, and while marginally more efficient than business as usual, still lock in new infrastructure that will produce significant greenhouse gas emissions for decades to come.

22. Smita Nakhooda, World Res. Inst., Correcting the World's Greatest Market Failure: Climate Change and the Multilateral Development Banks 4 (2008).

23. See the Equator Principles website, www.equator-principles.com.

24. *G-7 to Warn China Over Costly Loans to Poor Countries*, Wall St. J., Sept. 15, 2006.

Chapter 28

Lead Poisoning and Pollution: Opportunities for Internationalized Solutions

K.W. James Rochow

This chapter reviews the status of lead poisoning and pollution[1] and opportunities for expedited reduction and elimination of this long persisting obstacle to sustainable development after the impetus provided by the 2002 World Summit on Sustainable Development at Johannesburg (WSSD).[2] The imminent worldwide phaseout of leaded gasoline, propelled in part by a major partnership formed at the WSSD, provides the momentum for an historic victory over lead poisoning through the systematic control and elimination of its other sources of exposure.

With the elimination of leaded gasoline, the most dispersive source of lead, revised action plans for the prevention of lead poisoning must take into account local and regional variations in priority sources, which could range from industrial emissions, discharges, and waste to community, household, and lifestyle sources such as lead-contaminated soil, lead-based paint, plumbing, housewares, cosmetics, medicine, and children's toys. Controlling the various remaining sources of lead exposure through more localized source priorities will paradoxically require internationalized solutions. Beyond continuing to address the international dimensions of the lead problem in classic definition—the literal crossing of political boundaries through polluting atmospheric emissions, effluent discharges, and products in commerce—such internationalized solutions should also embody a broader understanding of international links to local circumstances. These local circumstances include the retention of unsafe cultural practices (e.g., the use of cosmetics and home remedies containing lead) in diasporic communities and the sharing of best practices for prevention through "interlocal" electronic communications that overcome obstacles of distance and jurisdiction.[3]

The United States is in a particularly strong position to help complete the fight against lead poisoning because of the inherently international dimensions of the lead problem in the country itself, owing to its diversity of populations, growing ethnic communities, concern about toxic product importation, and participation in global trade. The United States needs to apply its own success in controlling and eliminating leaded gasoline and lead-based paint to other priority sources. One principal way of accomplishing that is to fund community needs and resource assessments that include in their problem assessments and program recommendations, analyses of the international dimensions of the lead problem in the community (trade, cultural practices, and so forth). Concomitantly, the United States needs to support interlocal networks that disseminate instructive U.S. experience and to promote the participation in international forums by U.S. community-based organizations (CBOs) and nongovernmental organizations (NGOs).

Lead and Sustainable Development

Lead is a pervasive environmental contaminant, an elemental toxin that, once dispersed, persists and accumulates in the environment unless remediated. Heavily utilized in the centuries since the Industrial Revolution, lead remains the source of an environmental disease that continues to debilitate individuals and communities, especially those in and of the developing world.[4] Systematic and cumulative documentation for over a century has demonstrated that lead poisoning causes and contributes to a host of health problems. Most critically, it impedes the neurological development of children—their readiness to learn, their intellectual potential, their ability to participate in society—and hence compromises society's future, the animating concern of sustainable development. Although no one is immune to lead poisoning by virtue of income and status, the disease disproportionately affects impoverished and minority communities, and its elimination has become a signature environmental justice issue.[5]

As a longstanding, thoroughly understood, and preventable problem, elimination of lead poisoning and pollution has become a litmus test of the world's willingness to address other social ills it faces in a cooperative and concerted manner, and a potential optimism-engendering model for solutions. As Rene Dubos famously prophesied: "The problem [of lead poisoning] is so well-defined, so neatly packaged, with both causes and cures known, that if we don't eliminate this social crime, our society deserves all the disasters that have been forecast for it."[6]

The Basis for U.S. Leadership

The Problem at Home

The United States has made significant, if somewhat fitful, progress in combating lead poisoning and pollution in the past three decades, especially from lead-based paint and leaded gasoline. Public health pioneers such as Drs. Julian Chisolm and Alice Hamilton were among those who cast early warnings about lead hazards from paint and gasoline, and they did so at a time, it must be added, when the U.S. paint and automotive industries were unrestrainedly extolling the virtues of those very products. Although the United States was not in the vanguard of countries that eliminated leaded gasoline (Brazil and Japan were among the first) and its phase-down effort had many twists and turns, the country had essentially phased out leaded gasoline by 1986, a full decade before the congressionally mandated deadline.[7]

The United States banned lead-based paint for residential use in 1978, and after a gap of 15 years Congress mandated a national effort to control and eliminate the large reservoir of lead-based paint hazards that still remained in U.S. housing. The renewed awareness of persisting lead-based paint hazards also catalyzed state and local governments to file public nuisance lawsuits against lead pigment manufacturers.[8]

The twin-pronged focus on lead in paint and gasoline was initiated in the United States by a set of programs run by offices in the U.S. Environmental Protection Agency (EPA) and the U.S. Department of Housing and Urban Development (HUD) rather than by a single, coherent effort based on a national framework for action.[9] Nevertheless, that approach managed to make significant, at times dramatic, steps toward vanquishing lead poisoning. Studies have shown an almost perfect correspondence between the phaseout of leaded gasoline and a subsequent precipitous drop in the levels of lead in children's blood in the United States.[10] Progress in the reduction of lead-based paint hazards is reflected in the continuing decline in both the number of U.S. housing units that contain such hazards and the number of U.S. children who have elevated blood lead levels.[11]

Several features of the relatively successful approach helped overcome persistent barriers and continue to reduce lead poisoning. As noted, the federal government evolved a national program focused on gasoline and paint, the country's two most important sources of lead exposure. The functional, priority-based approach helped overcome the barrier of diffused action posed by the number of exposure sources from both historic and continued uses of lead-containing products and waste.

The emphasis on control and elimination of *sources* of exposure also proved critically important. Programs for lead poisoning prevention have been typically lodged in health departments and too often operated under a medical case management model. This model emphasized secondary prevention, i.e., after-the-fact diagnosis, treatment, and circular tracking of lead poisoned victims, rather than prevention through identification and control of exposure sources in the first instance. Prevention of exposure is the only cure for lead poisoning because its adverse neurological effects are essentially irreversible in children and its symptoms often difficult to detect and discretely identify.

Beginning in 1990, EPA sponsored a pollution prevention project that delineated a Primary Prevention Strategy (PPS) for lead, the first coherent national action plan to combat lead poisoning based on principles of prevention.[12] The subsequent congressional passage of the Lead-Based Paint Hazard Reduction Act of 1992 reflected the emphasis the PPS placed on targeting hazards from lead-based paint at a time when the leaded gasoline phaseout was essentially completed.[13] Title X of the Act set forth a program for prevention based on residential and community lead assessments and inspections, development and application of control and abatement techniques and procedures, mandatory notification of lead hazards in real estate, and a panoply of legal remedies to redress violations.

The Problem Internationalized

Although sources of lead exposure have become more localized as the most dispersive source, leaded gasoline, is nearing worldwide phaseout, and the most common current source in the United States, lead-based paint, is increasingly controlled and abated, significant further progress toward the eventual elimination of lead poisoning now requires an internationalized approach. Lead poisoning and pollution remains a cross-border problem because dispersed lead crosses national boundaries in the form of industrial emissions and discharges, waste streams, and consumer products. In *Trail Smelter*, a formative case in international environmental law, a Canada-

United States arbitration panel found liability for damage caused to crops and resources in Washington State by cross-boundary discharges and emissions from a lead and zinc smelting operation in British Columbia.[14]

As a perverse consequence of increased globalization and the freer flow of trade, the most publicized recent cases of potential lead exposures in the United States have been the wholesale importation of toxic products, especially toys, food products, and gimcracks from China. A barrage of media exposés highlighted the fact that the agency responsible for controlling such unsafe products, the U.S. Consumer Product Safety Commission (CPSC), has weak regulatory powers. The CPSC's reliance on after-the-fact voluntary recalls of offending products ironically echoes the belated responses that characterized lead poisoning "prevention" programs prior to the institution of leaded gasoline phaseout and lead-based paint hazard control and elimination.[15] But international links to the sources and solutions of lead poisoning transcend the most literal definition of "international." Reflecting the country's diversity, ethnic communities in the United States tend to add to the importation of toxics by perpetuating lead-unsafe cultural practices and products (cosmetics, home remedies, food preparation), often "fossilized" ones no longer prevalent in their home countries. Lead poisoning has also been "imported" into the United States by internationally adopted children who have been subsequently diagnosed with lead poisoning contracted in their countries of origin.

The number of children in the United States with elevated blood lead levels has continued to decrease. But there are still significant numbers of affected children concentrated in communities of color and in lower income neighborhoods.[16] This persistent core of lead poisoning serves as a prime exemplar of environmental injustice. The previously noted practice and use of culturally sanctioned unsafe lead products and practices, the inequitable proximity to sources of exposure (e.g., toxic waste sites and residual depositions of leaded gasoline from communities surrounding expressways), and the lead-based paint exposures associated with deteriorated housing are some of the ways that lead poisoning and pollution in U.S. communities mirrors that in the developing world. United States regulatory actions, even those that ostensibly apply only within the United States, can resonate internationally.

EPA's current National Ambient Air Quality Standard (NAAQS) for lead provides an example of an international impact that may not be obvious. The NAAQS for lead is an outdated standard that reflects the long-since superseded state of knowledge in the 1970s concerning lead's effects, but is only now undergoing serious review.[17] Since ambient lead concentrations in the United States had demonstrably dropped over the intervening decades (owing in large part to the phasing out of leaded gasoline), EPA until now never bothered to revise the lead NAAQS to reflect subsequent research that demonstrated lead's pernicious health effects even at very low exposure levels. But because EPA standards are generally regarded as state of the art, a number of developing countries have adopted or are in the process of adopting the NAAQS lead standard on the mistaken assumption that it represents the most protective standard available.[18]

The U.S. Role in International Processes

Lead Poisoning in the International Arena

Beginning with the 1994 meeting of the U.N. Commission on Sustainable Development (CSD), the body established by the Rio Conference to review annually the world's progress toward sustainable development, the extraordinary series of international processes that followed up the 1992 Rio Conference on the Environment and preceded the 2002 World Summit on Sustainable Development cumulatively endorsed the worldwide reduction and elimination of lead poisoning as a consensus priority of the international community, beginning with the global phaseout of leaded gasoline.[19] No doubt in part because the timing was coincident with its national success in completing leaded gasoline phaseout and addressing lead-based paint hazards, the United States played a major role in promoting the priority of lead poisoning prevention in these international processes based on the lessons learned from its own experience.

An important benefit of these international meetings came not from the official deliberations, which often proved laborious exercises in semantic parsing of official texts, but instead from the underlying dynamics of negotiations and the opportunities for accessible side discussions and side events they presented. In particular, these unofficial activities allowed for coordinated internationalized approaches. At the Habitat II conference in 1996,[20] for example, when the government of Australia balked at accepting strong language calling for international action on lead poisoning and pollution, NGOs at the conference called their equivalents in Australia, who in turn successfully exerted pressure on their government's representatives at Habitat II to support a strong resolution on lead poisoning prevention. When the G-77 (the U.N. bloc of developing nations) likewise balked at Habitat II, community representatives from Chicago and other U.S. cities spoke persuasively to G-77 members to highlight the devastating effects of lead poisoning on their communities and the parallels between their situation and the lead poisoning problem in members' countries, which helped catalyze eventual support within the G-77 for making lead poisoning prevention a priority of the Habitat agenda for urban settlements.

WSSD Partnership for Clean Fuels and Vehicles

The reiteration in international and regional processes of the priority need to eliminate lead poisoning and pollution worldwide was not without effect. At a minimum, such repetitive exhortation provided a continuing spotlight on the problem and a collective recognition by governments of the issue; at most, they provided a reinforcing rationale for the launch of focused initiatives such as those of the World Bank and the Summit of the Americas aimed at an accelerated phase-out of leaded gasoline.[21]

These cumulative declarations, however, typically had no coherent framework for follow-up actions to match their rhetorical commitment to lead poisoning prevention. The structure of the international system in which national governments are responsible for enacting and enforcing obligations has an inherent gap between the rhetoric at international meetings and the actual implementation of a program by a government at home. Another aspect of the international system's lack of an implementation focus is the disengagement of community-based organizations from international processes (even those that promote "localism"). A heuristic side event sponsored by the Alliance to End Childhood Lead Poisoning[22] at the 1998 meeting of the CSD, for example, revealed that invited groups working on lead poisoning and toxics pollution in the New York City area had no connection with or information about relevant parts of the Habitat II or other international agendas.

To redress the implementation gaps in the international system and the consequent deficient outcomes of its precedent-setting meetings,

the WSSD fostered the concept of partnerships: voluntary but officially recognized associations of different actors self-chartered to
help solve identified problems of sustainable development.[23]
Carrying out the international consensus on redressing lead poisoning
and pollution, EPA and the United Nations Environment Programme
(UNEP) initiated and have continued to carry out the Partnership for
Clean Fuels and Vehicles (PCFV), a major WSSD partnership to accelerate the global phaseout of leaded gasoline.[24]

The PCFV consists of a loose affiliation of international organizations, businesses, and trade groups (led by the International Petroleum
Industry Environmental Conservation Association (IPIECA) and the
Alliance of Automobile Manufacturers), national governments (including the United States), and NGOs (including U.S. organizations
such as the Natural Resources Defense Council and the Trust for Lead
Poisoning Prevention), all of which have officially registered as partners. The PCFV has been successful in promoting global phaseout, especially in sub-Saharan Africa, through technical reports and outreach efforts that have emphasized persuasion among industry peers
(an especially effective approach in the hidebound petroleum industry). The PCFV has also established a website to serve as an authorita-
tive source of information on the current status of worldwide phaseout
and clean fuels initiatives.[25]

The nearly successful completion of leaded gasoline phaseout
worldwide has rendered the PCFV's future problematic, a victim of its
own success. One role that the PCFV can continue to play is to perfect
worldwide phaseout by facilitating both the environmental cleanup of
facilities that produced the tetraethyl lead additive to leaded gasoline
and the elimination of exceptions to the ban on leaded gasoline that
still prevail (such as exemptions for agricultural uses, motor sports,
vintage cars, and aviation fuel). But the industry-driven aspects of the
PCFV that made it an effective participant in the campaign to expedite
leaded gasoline phaseout do not translate well into the kind of
broad-based community assessments and action necessary to identify
and control the variable sources of lead exposures present in different
regions and localities. The limitations of the PCFV model and the
overhead that would be required to form a new WSSD partnership
preclude using the partnership format to take the next community-
based and interlocal steps necessary to advance lead poisoning prevention systematically.[26]

Recommendations for Internationalized Solutions

1. Disseminate an updated international action plan for prevention. Internationalized solutions should follow a systematic framework for prevention such as that contained in the International Action Plan for Preventing Lead Poisoning, originally produced by the Alliance to End Childhood Lead Poisoning.[27] The complementary roles of the various players at all levels—community, national, regional, and international—and in all sectors should serve as the basis of an integrated, prevention-based approach to lead poisoning. Now that leaded gasoline, the one exposure source that had universal top priority, has been essentially phased out, the action plan should prescribe a protocol to assess lead exposure sources region by region and community by community. Source priority calibration should be conjoined with opportunities for effective intervention and for provision of community benefits (such as training of abatement contractors). That priority- and opportunity-based approach must take into account the phaseout of lead products and substitution and process changes (including strengthened CPSC enforcement authority),[28] as well as abatement of the reservoir of lead from past uses like leaded gasoline. The action plan should be widely disseminated through all relevant networks and serve as an adaptable model for prevention initiatives.

2. Develop networks for interlocal communication. International, regional, and issue networks need to incorporate best practices for lead poisoning prevention and link to community-based programs and to each other. Such a networks-within-networks approach could be anchored by a facilitating global lead network that would help reach out among localities to groups concerned with the full range of sustainable development issues in order to build constituencies of support for lead poisoning prevention, develop a reference set of best practices, and facilitate effective participation in international forums.[29]

3. Start community-based pilot projects to achieve internationalized solutions. Local projects for lead poisoning prevention should build from community diversity to achieve internationalized perspectives on prevention. The identification of cultural practices and perspectives that contribute to lead poisoning and toxics pollution in the community, and tracing them back to countries of origin, which might have subsequently moved to control or eliminate the product or practice, should serve as a starting point. Scrutiny of the varieties of lead-containing products imported into the community should point to a broader understanding of the role of trade and the flow of commerce. Linking to interlocal networks should occasion a working knowledge of the international context of prevention and adaptable policies, programs, and practices from U.S. and foreign counterparts. Prevention programs could adapt the community needs and resource assessment model developed by the U.S. Agency for International Development (USAID) to identify and address sources of lead poisoning, and it may prove useful to comprehend other sources of toxics exposure in the assessment. Use of sister city arrangements between U.S. and developing world cities for coordinated projects to tackle lead poisoning and toxics pollution in their communities offers a special synergistic opportunity.

4. Provide support for internationalized solutions. EPA and HUD, as well as foundations and other funding sources, should cross-fertilize domestic and international programs by enfolding in their lead grant programs funding support for the kind of community-based internationalized initiatives and for the development of interlocal networks discussed in the second and third recommendations above. The United States should include NGO and CBO representatives in its official delegations to international meetings and should report its participation in international processes relevant to lead poisoning and pollution back to interlocal networks in accessible and understandable form. NGO networks in the United States can, in turn, bridge the gap between policy and practice, between international forums and on-the-ground programs, by linking international and policy NGOs in the United States and abroad with local and implementing CBOs.

Conclusion

The successful worldwide phaseout of leaded gasoline (and in the United States the widespread control of lead-based paint hazards) poses the prospect of premature victory declarations and a round of complacency that will perpetuate Dubos' prophetic paradox of social inaction. To counter that disheartening prospect, internationalized approaches such as those recommended here are necessary to address systematically the many other sources of lead poisoning and toxics pollution that still impede sustainable development and to understand the context in which they occur. Furthering internationalized approaches requires the United States to take a leadership role in promoting solutions based on its own instructive experience, an exercise in multilateral cooperation that should at least in part counter the accusations of insularity and unilateralism often levied against it.

ENDNOTES

1. "Lead poisoning and pollution" is used as a singular noun to underscore that environmental pollution is the source of the environmental disease of lead poisoning and that prevention through source control and elimination, not belated after-the-fact treatment, is its only "cure." In addition, "lead poisoning and pollution" alludes to the fact that wildlife also suffers adversely from lead poisoning. Depending on the context, "lead poisoning" is used to refer to the disease itself or to "lead poisoning and pollution" where economy or felicity of expression dictates.

2. This article is a sequel to K.W. James Rochow, Lead, in STUMBLING TOWARD SUSTAINABILITY, 433-41 (John C. Dernbach ed., 2002) (hereinafter STUMBLING, ROCHOW CHAPTER).

3. "Interlocal communications" has become a term of art that refers to the fact that local groups can take advantage of modern technology to communicate directly across boundaries through electronic communications.

4. See, e. g., Jerome O. Nriagu et al., Childhood Lead Poisoning in Africa: A Growing Public Health Problem, 181 SCI. OF THE TOTAL ENV'T 93 (1996).

5. See, e. g., Jerome A. Paulson, Lead Poisoning, at 21, available at www.gwu.edu/~macche/presentations/LEAD_presentation.pdf at 21; NAT'L BLACK ENVTL.. JUSTICE NETWORK, USA, ENVIRONMENTAL AND ECONOMIC JUSTICE FACT SHEET, available at www.ejrc.cau.edu/NBEJNEJFS.html; see also STUMBLING, ROCHOW CHAPTER, supra note 2, at notes 11 and 14.

6. Rene Dubos, Remarks at the First National Conference on Childhood Lead Poisoning (1969), reprinted in Mark W. Oberle, Lead Poisoning: A Preventable Childhood Disease of the Slum, 165 SCIENCE 991, 992 (1969).

7. See Jamie L. Kitman, The Secret History of Lead, 270 THE NATION 11, 38 (2000).

8. E. g., Eric Tucker, Lead Paint Ruling Could Lead to More Lawsuits, Experts Say, Boston.com, Feb. 23, 2006, available at http://www.boston.Com/news/local/rhode_island/articles/2006/02/23/lead_paint_ruling_could_lead_to_more_lawsuits_experts_say/?page=1.

9. The federal government did constitute an interagency task force on lead poisoning prevention, which in practice served as a forum for periodic information exchange, rather than for integrated policy development.

10. NAT'L ACAD. OF SCI./NAT'L RESEARCH COUNCIL, MEASURING LEAD EXPOSURE IN INFANTS, CHILDREN, AND OTHER SENSITIVE POPULATIONS (1993); see also Kitman, supra note 7, at 37 (chart showing correspondence between leaded gasoline phaseout and blood lead level decline in the United States).

11. David E. Jacobs et al., The Prevalence of Lead-Based Paint Hazards in U.S. Housing, 110 ENVTL. HEALTH PERSPECTIVES, A599-A606 (2002); U.S. CTRS. FOR DISEASE CONTROL (CDC), BLOOD LEAD LEVELS: UNITED STATES, 1999-2002, 54(20) MMWR 513-16 (May 27, 2005), available at www.cdc.gov/mmwr/preview/mmwrhtml/mm5420a5.htm.

12. See ALLIANCE TO END CHILDHOOD LEAD POISONING, PRIMARY PREVENTION STRATEGIES HANDBOOK (1993) (3 vols.).

13. Residential Lead-Based Paint Hazard Reduction Act of 1992 (Title X of the Housing and Community Development Act), 42 U.S.C. §§4851 et seq.

14. Trail Smelter Case (U.S. v. Can.), 3 R.I.A.A. (1941). *See also* STUMBLING, ROCHOW CHAPTER, *supra* note 2, at note 1 ("[Although] [l]ead is a heavy metal [a] certain fraction of lead dispersed by human activity scatters more widely [as] [e]vidence[d] by such phenomena as the enhanced levels of lead found in snows in Greenland.")

15. *See, e.g.*, Christian Warren, *The Little Engine That Could Poison*, N.Y. TIMES, Dec. 13, 2007, (op-ed page), *available at* http://query.nytimes.com/ search/query?query=lead+products&n=10&dp=0&sort=closest&daterange= past365days&d=nytdsection%2b&o=e%2b&v=Opinion%2b&c=a%2b.

16. CDC, BLOOD LEAD LEVELS, *supra* note 11.

17. *See* U.S. EPA, Lead (Pb)—National Ambient Air Quality Standards, *available at* www.epa.gov/ttn/naaqs/standards/pb/s_pb_index.html; EPA, Lead (Pb)—Documents From Current Review—Federal Register Notices, *available at* www.epa.gov/ttn/naaqs/standards/pb/s_pb_cr_fr.html.

18. *See* Policy Paper, Trust for Lead Poisoning Prevention (formerly Alliance to End Childhood Lead Poisoning), "Protective" Ambient Standards for Lead?: A Look at the World Health Organization's Ambient Guidelines and the U.S. Environmental Protection Agency's Standard (2000) (on file with author).

19. These international and regional processes included Habitat II, the G-8, the Summit of the Americas, and the United Nations' five-year reviews of the Rio Conference and Habitat II outcomes. *See* STUMBLING, ROCHOW CHAP-TER, *supra* note 2, at 434-35; *see also* TRUST FOR LEAD POISONING PRE-VENTION, LEAD COMMITMENTS IN KEY INTERNATIONAL AGREEMENTS (July 1999), *available at* www.globalleadnet.org/policy_leg/policy/commits. cfm.

20. The Habitat II conference was held in 1996 in Istanbul and was dedicated to following up the first Habitat conference held in 1976 in Vancouver by ad-dressing the relationship between housing and human settlements and sus-tainable development.

21. *See* World Bank, Regional Conference on the Phasing Out of Leaded Gaso-line in Sub-Saharan Africa: Declaration of Dakar (June 28, 2001) *available at* www.worldbank.org/cleanair/caiafrica/africaenglish/learningactivities/ dakar/conclusions/declaration/english.pdf (archived); Press Release, World Bank, World Bank Recommends Global Phase-Out of Leaded Gaso-line: Eliminating Leaded Gas Reduces Health Risks (May 18, 1996), *avail-able at* www.worldbank.org/html/extdr/extme/gaspr.htm (archived); Sum-mit of the Americas, Miami Plan of Action §23 (Dec.11, 1994), *available at* www.summit-americas.org/miamiplan.htm#23; *see also* TRUST FOR LEAD POISONING PREVENTION, PREVENTING LEAD POISONING IN THE AMERI-CAS: HEALTH, ENVIRONMENT, AND SUSTAINABLE DEVELOPMENT, *avail-able at* http://www.globalleadnet.org/publications/alliance_pubs/index. cfm.

22. Succeeded in relevant part by the Trust for Lead Poisoning Protection.

23. INT'L INST. FOR SUSTAINABLE DEV., ANNEX, GUIDING PRINCIPLES FOR SUSTAINABLE DEVELOPMENT ("TYPE 2 OUTCOMES") TO BE ELABORATED BY INTERESTED PARTIES IN THE CONTEXT OF THE WORLD SUMMIT ON SUS-

TAINABLE DEVELOPMENT (WSSD) (June 7, 2002) (vice-chairs' Explanatory Note), *available at* iisd.ca/wssd/download%20files/annex_partnership.pdf.

24. PARTNERSHIP FOR CLEAN FUELS AND VEHICLES (PCFV), OBJECTIVES, *available at* www.unep.org/pcfv/about/objectives.asp. The PCFV's second goal is the reduction and elimination of sulfur in fuels.

25. U.N. Environment Programme, Partnership for Clean Fuels and Vehicles, http://www.unep.org/pcfv.

26. It is especially hard to imagine the PCFV addressing a vanguard issue such as global climate change since the partners run the gamut from those business interests most resistant to special measures for fighting global climate change to those advocacy organizations who believe it constitutes a planetary emergency.

27. TRUST FOR LEAD POISONING PREVENTION, INTERNATIONAL ACTION PLAN FOR PREVENTING LEAD POISONING (3d ed. 2001), *available at* www.globalleadnet.org/policy_leg/policy/intlactionplan.cfm.

28. European Union efforts to regulate lead-containing and other potentially toxic products merit special attention. *See, e. g.*, Brigitta Forsberg, *Getting the Lead Out: European Rules Force Electronic Companies to Clean Up*, S.F. CHRON., Jan. 20, 2005, *available at* www.sfgate.com/cgi-bin/article.cgi?f=/c/a/2005/01/20/BUGCEAT4HC1.DTL.

29. *See* K.W. James Rochow, *Pitfalls and Potentials for Localism: A Model for Internationalized Solutions*, 32 CITNET NEWS, Summer 2005, *available at* http://citnet.org/newsletters/2005-02/rochow1.aspx.

VIII. State and Federal Governance

Chapter 29

State Governance: Leadership on Climate Change

Kirsten H. Engel and Marc L. Miller

Arguably, states and localities are the most plausible governmental entities for substantial progress toward policies that achieve a more sustainable society. State and local governments—not the national government—are the traditional loci of most of the activities that define a more or less sustainable society. States and localities have a much larger voice than the national government on issues such as land use, zoning, taxation and business development, environmental regulations, water policy, transportation policy, public safety, and education. And they feel a much larger impact from failures in those areas.

This chapter begins by briefly surveying current statewide efforts at sustainable development, focusing on a handful of the most promising state "sustainability councils." The record here has been largely disappointing, at least as reflected in state reports, critical literature, and data and other information available on websites.

Only 10 states have governing bodies charged with assessing or enhancing sustainability on a statewide basis. The function of six of the 10 sustainability governing bodies is limited to reducing the energy and environmental impacts of state government operations. Minnesota, New Jersey, Oregon, and Washington each claim, however, to address sustainability from the combined environmental, social, and economic perspective intended by international bodies such as the Brundtland Commission.

The second part of the chapter takes a more specific view of state sustainability efforts, looking at state, local, and regional initiatives on climate change policy—perhaps the most interesting area of state leadership on issues related to sustainability. Climate change may be the quintessential challenge to sustainability. The threat of pervasive and at times rapid change highlights assumptions and ambiguities about what aspects of the environment and culture should or can be sustained.

At first glance climate change would appear to be a quintessentially national, if not multinational and indeed a worldwide problem. We assess the somewhat surprising and counterintuitive efforts on climate policy in some states.[1] One of the classic metaphors celebrating state-level policymaking and authority in the United States is the idea that the states serve as laboratories for social and economic policy.[2] The laboratory metaphor invites more than autonomy; it suggests a spirit of experimentation.

The final section of this chapter suggests ways in which sustainability efforts might help to develop and enhance the elements that would make the laboratory metaphor more meaningful. In particular, we discuss the importance of research, data, and publication to the laboratory or "scientific" model for policy development.

The Importance of State-Level Activities to Sustainability

While policies and developments at the national and international levels are important to sustainable development, today states are at the vanguard of developments that are of great importance for achieving a sustainable society. There is an almost total overlap between the major topics of sustainability discourse and the traditional functions of states in areas such as environmental protection, health, education, public safety, economic development, water policy, the provision or regulation of various natural monopolies, and social and public goods. States also continue to serve as policy innovators in our federal system. The uncertainties and variation involved in seeking a sustainable society (and even our conceptions of sustainability) counsel in favor of variation and experimentation. It is in the states where experimentation takes place—in, for example, environment, education, and health care.

Environment

Despite the dominance of the federal government in establishing minimum standards for air, water, solid waste, and pesticide use, many vexing environmental problems lie disproportionately in areas that federal law leaves to state control, or for which the federal government is taking a passive stance and at least some states are taking an aggressive stance.

Climate change is Exhibit A for state leadership, as many states and localities move forward aggressively to reduce greenhouse gas emissions while the federal government has been largely unresponsive to the problem. But state leadership abounds in just about every area of environmental concern. In the area of water quality, for example, serious problems stem from nonpoint source pollution,[3] yet the federal Clean Water Act largely leaves nonpoint source pollution to state and local control.[4] Key to addressing nonpoint source pollution is the development and enforcement of total maximum daily loads (TMDLs) of pollution to meet state water-quality standards.[5] Again, this is a task delegated by federal law to states, though legal handles exist by which the U.S. Environmental Protection Agency can be compelled to develop TMDLs for the states.[6]

With respect to toxic waste, contaminated urban sites that may be suitable for development have become a focus of environmental policy, a problem largely addressed by state brownfield programs.[7] More generally, land use planning and water quality issues, with all of their implications for the management of economic growth and preservation of healthy ecosystems, continue to be primarily the responsibility of state and local government.

Health Care

Health care is an area of traditional state authority, and provides a very different illustration of how states are forging ahead of the federal government, even in areas where there is significant federal policy and regulation. States either provide or dictate policies with respect to the vast majority of health care-related issues: child welfare and protective services; reporting of child or elder abuse; drug rehabilitation; licensure for medical professionals, hospitals and nursing homes; and patient privacy laws.

States are increasingly going out ahead of the federal government with respect to access to health care and its affordability. Sometimes these state policies fill coverage gaps that exist under the federal Medicare and Medicaid programs. In 2006, for example, Illinois commenced a program to provide health insurance to all children in the state, including those in working class and middle-income families too wealthy to obtain insurance under Medicaid.[8] To expand health care coverage to the uninsured as well as the underinsured,[9] states are experimenting with a variety of strategies to create or take advantage of reinsurance, high-risk pools, limited benefit plans, group purchasing arrangements, and methods of covering young adults.[10]

Education

Education continues to be a basic function of state and local government. Although the influence of the federal government has increased in recent years, that role is still dwarfed by the states' role. While the federal influence over primary education increased dramatically with the enactment of the No Child Left Behind Act in 2001, it is states that are left to implement the law, and it is states that are now seeking reform of the law.[11] In 2004-2005, state and local governments contributed 83 percent of the funding for K-12 education. Just 8.3 percent was contributed by the federal government, with the balance being made up for by private sources.[12]

State-Level Sustainability Initiatives

As in much of modern politics, actors at the state level are incorporating the language of sustainability in their public discourse. But it is not rhetoric that gives meaning to state initiatives; it is action and impact on the ground.[13] To discover whether there is any substance to this rhetoric in state government, the authors of this chapter surveyed state sustainability programs. Our objective was to identify trends with regard to explicit sustainability initiatives and evidence of potential impact on public and private behavior in the states. To the extent that sustainability has been an explicit programmatic goal, we wanted to know whether such programs took a common form, specified common or disparate goals, and whether the programs provided any measures of progress.

We found only 10 states that have instituted a statewide governing body responsible for furthering sustainability: California, Colorado, Illinois, Maine, Massachusetts, Minnesota, New Jersey, Oregon, Pennsylvania, and Washington. Four of them—Minnesota, New Jersey, Oregon, and to a lesser extent Washington State—address sustainability from a combined environmental, social, and economic perspective.[14] These four states are the frontrunners in having state sustainability programs. The other six states—California, Colorado, Illinois, Maine, Massachusetts, and Pennsylvania—have yet to tackle sustainability in a holistic fashion along the lines of the Brundtland Commission report.

Oregon's experience dates from 1988, when Oregon Shines, a statewide strategic planning initiative, was begun. Oregon Shines illustrates both the linkage of economic and environmental issues typical of state sustainability programs and their evolution from a mechanism to jumpstart a state's economy to a more comprehensive program to improve the quality of life in an environmentally responsible manner. Following a serious recession, Oregon Shines began as a statewide economic-planning initiative that articulated three broad goals: building a superior workforce, maintaining an attractive quality of life based upon the state's natural resources and uncongested living areas, and developing an international frame of mind that will distinguish Oregonians as adept at global commerce.[15] In 1989 the state legislature established Oregon Benchmarks, a system of indicators making it possible to gauge the attainment of the goals set forth in Oregon Shines. The two together, Oregon Shines and the Oregon Benchmarks, now function as a comprehensive strategic planning vehicle complete with a monitoring mechanism. The initiative is both steered and overseen by the Oregon Progress Board, a legislatively created body made up of a majority of citizen leaders.

Oregon Shines II was the most recent report issued by the Oregon Progress Board, in 1997. (Oregon Shines III is in the works.) The Board utilized a bottom-up approach to assessing the state's progress in reaching the overall state sustainability goals through the lens of 92 streamlined benchmarks (pared down from 259 benchmarks in the original Oregon Shines) and influenced by meetings with civic leaders across the state.[16] The state had a mixed record of success in achieving its goals (overall economic prosperity that was spread unevenly among the state's residents and hid varied progress in education and other quality-of-life goals). As a result, the state revamped its approach to its upcoming Oregon Shines III report by utilizing expert panels, which have advocated a focus upon the key drivers of the various systems at issue (i.e., economic and environmental) so as to prevent unintended consequences of policy approaches, more and better collaboration among key individuals and groups, and a better understanding of the relationships among the various benchmarks.[17]

Minnesota's experience is similar to Oregon's, except that there is no evidence to date of the type of reevaluation of the goals/benchmarks approach that we are now witnessing in Oregon. In 1991, Minnesota commenced Minnesota Milestones, a stakeholder-driven process that identified 19 statewide goals grouped in four broad areas: people, community and democracy, economy, and environment. The state developed 70 indicators that are designed to provide insight into the progress in achieving the Minnesota Milestones goals.[18]

Minnesota's most recent evaluation of its progress in achieving the Milestone goals occurred in 2002.[19] In general, Minnesota's 2002 report indicated that the state either held steady or made progress statewide toward the goals of a healthy, safe, educated, and prosperous society with a clean environment. However, the report also noted that statewide statistics masked continuing disparities based upon racial and socioeconomic status.[20] Additionally, the report described progress statewide in reducing pollution emissions and increasing the level of recycling efforts, while at the same time recognizing increased pressures on the environment from population growth, energy consumption, and land development.[21]

In a manner somewhat similar to Minnesota and Oregon, New Jersey launched a stakeholder-based process in the mid-1990s for defining and measuring sustainable development in the state. This process culminated in a 1999 report, *Living with the Future in Mind*, which contained 11 goals for an efficient and vibrant economy, a healthy environment, and a just society.[22] Later, the state developed 41 indicators to track progress on the goals.

New Jersey's reports on the state's progress in achieving the goals were issued in 2000 and again in 2004.[23] Responsibility for tracking and reporting on indicators has changed hands over the years. The state's first report was published by New Jersey Future, a public interest advocacy organization that brought stakeholder groups together and spearheaded the state's initial efforts to define sustainability goals and indicators. The second report was published by the New Jersey Department of Environmental Protection.

The state's sustainability project is now run by an independent policy organization, New Jersey Sustainability State Institute, jointly affiliated with Rutgers University and the New Jersey Institute of Technology. According to the 2004 report, turning over the reins of the state's sustainability initiative to the Institute came at the behest of the governor's office, which sought to buffer the process from the advocacy orientation of New Jersey Future and the possible political pressures of state government.[24]

New Jersey established 13 specific targets for the achievement of its 11 economic, environmental, and social goals. For example, it set forth the target of preserving 1.004 million acres of open space by 2002, a target it has achieved, and 1.354 million acres by 2010.[25]

The 2004 report demonstrates that New Jersey, like much of the United States, sustained an economic downturn in the early 2000s, including rising unemployment, and attributed that downturn to the 9/11 terror attacks. The report also presents a mixed picture with respect to environmental progress. Although shellfish habitats and beaches have improved, residents of New Jersey are driving more miles, producing more solid waste, and using more energy than previously.[26] Social indicators of life expectancy, health, education, and housing improved, but voter turnout decreased, as did awareness of public affairs.[27]

Rather than approach sustainability as a mandate to ensure progress on multiple fronts, the other states with statewide initiatives view sustainability more narrowly as a mandate to address the environmental and energy impact of state government operations. The glaring omission from such an approach is any assessment of the social, economic, and environmental health of the state as a whole.

California, Colorado, Illinois, Maine, Massachusetts, and Pennsylvania have developed specific sustainability goals for the purchase of goods and services, resource consumption (including energy use), facility construction, operation and maintenance (green building issues), vehicle use, and climate change. The prioritization of green building goals by some states is consistent with the push for federal and state standards for energy-efficient buildings.[28] Other states place a decided emphasis upon energy issues. Purchasing mandates direct state agencies to take certain steps, such as replacing gasoline-powered vehicles with hybrid vehicles and buying recycled paper and other products.[29]

In seven of the 10 states with statewide sustainability councils—the exceptions being Minnesota, New Jersey, and Oregon—sustainability objectives apply solely within the public sector. Mandates concerning reductions in use of energy, materials, and resources apply to the state's own consumption, not to consumption by the commercial, business, or residential sectors. Similarly, green building mandates apply only to new or renovated public buildings as opposed to private buildings. The public-sector focus of most state sustainability initiatives is not surprising given that these initiatives are primarily a creature of governors' executive orders rather than legislation, and, as a result, focus upon the internal workings of the executive branch.

Our survey also revealed that several state universities have instituted interdisciplinary programs devoted to sustainability research. The model for the public-sector graduate schools appears to be programs instituted earlier at private schools such as Columbia University's Earth Institute.[30] University-based sustainability programs vary considerably in focus. For example, the New Jersey Sustainable State Initiative at the Edward J. Bloustein School of Planning and Public Policy of Rutgers University focuses on public policy. The Center for Sustainability and the Global Environment at the University of Wisconsin, on the other hand, is oriented to environmental science research. Arizona State University's School and Global Institute of Sustainability focuses on urban planning and environmental engineering, while Penn State University's Center for Sustainability is oriented toward the study and development of green business.

State Initiatives on Climate Change

Mitigation of climate change is by far the most unexpected and intense area of state governance addressed to issues of long-term sustainability. Climate change has emerged as the quintessential issue of environmental sustainability, and, in the view of some, as an issue of societal sustainability. Driven in large part by the use of fossil fuels for energy, climate change—even more than land use and the consumption of resources—represents the major environmental peril produced directly by our current path of economic development.

In the absence of strong federal leadership on this issue, states have been filling the void in climate policy with a variety of programs, including energy conservation, the creation of greenhouse gas emissions registries, the promotion of renewable energy, and greenhouse gas emissions limits for vehicles and power plants. Today these programs exist at all levels of development, with some in preliminary stages and others in advanced stages.

Only in 2007 did hope emerge that there would be a federal climate regulatory program in the near future, at least with respect to vehicle emissions. In April 2007 the U.S. Supreme Court ruled that the Clean Air Act applies to climate change.[31] The Court ordered the EPA to determine whether emissions of greenhouse gases from motor vehicles "may reasonably endanger public health or welfare" under Section 202 of the Act. Such a determination would mandate the promulgation of vehicle greenhouse gas emission standards.[32]

The Energy Independence and Security Act of 2007 requires passenger automobiles and light trucks to achieve a combined fuel efficiency standard for model year 2020 of at least 35 miles per gallon for
the total fleet manufactured for sale in the United States.[33] Also in
2007, members of Congress began generating a slew of climate regulation bills, each of which is winding through the legislative process.[34]

The prospect of a federal regulatory program poses the question of
whether state greenhouse gas programs should be preempted to make
way for a more uniform federal program and, if so, to what degree.[35]
Given the dramatic leadership of state and local entities in climate policy, this is far from a minor academic question. In this area, as in many
others of environmental policy, California and many northeastern
states have taken a strong leading role.[36] Further, the development of
regional collaborations on climate change has played an important
role and may play an even larger role in the future. Such initiatives include the following:

- *California Global Warming Solutions Act of 2006.* Under
  this law, California has committed to a 25 percent cut in
  state greenhouse gas emissions by 2020 (lowering the
  state's emissions to 1990 levels), and an 80 percent cut below 1990 levels by 2050.[37]

- *California Greenhouse Gas Vehicle Emission Standards.*
  California has also promulgated the first-in-the-nation vehicle emission standards for greenhouse gases.[38] The California standards must still overcome several legal hurdles
  before becoming law. First, the state must win its effort to
  obtain a judicial reversal of EPA's denial of a waiver of
  federal preemption under the federal Clean Air Act.[39] In
  addition, California must survive a legal challenge filed
  by the automobile industry claiming that the state's standards are preempted by federal fuel efficiency laws.[40]
  California must also counter arguments by the U.S. Department of Transportation that California's standards are
  preempted by a federal fuel economy law.[41] Nevertheless,
  Vermont's law adopting the California vehicle standards
  recently withstood a vigorous attack on federal preemption grounds.[42]

- *Electric Power Generator Standards.* Several states are
  implementing emission standards related to electric power
  plants. In both Massachusetts and New Hampshire, exist-

ing power plants are required to cap and subsequently reduce carbon dioxide emissions.[43] Oregon and Washington
have each passed laws requiring new power plants to reduce their carbon dioxide emissions or purchase offset-
ting reductions.[44]

- *Renewable Portfolio Standards (RPS).* Twenty-eight states
  and Washington, D.C., now require that electric utilities
  generate a certain percentage of their electricity from qualifying renewable technology.[45]

- *Greenhouse Gas Planning Efforts.* Many states have completed or are engaged in the process of planning for greenhouse gas emissions reductions.[46]

- *State-Based Greenhouse Gas Registries.* Related to the
  state climate action planning process are the many programs now being implemented or developed on the state
  level to inventory and register state greenhouse gas emissions and emissions reductions on a facility-by-facility and
  sector-by-sector basis. Climate registries help states to implement their climate mitigation plans by tracking progress
  toward reaching their targets, encouraging emissions reductions, and providing baseline protection for industries
  from future mandatory emission reductions.

- *Regional Mitigation Programs.* One of the most promising developments is the collaboration between states on
  regional programs to mitigate climate change. The most
  advanced effort is the Regional Greenhouse Gas Initiative (RGGI), a project of northeastern states to establish a
  carbon dioxide cap-and-trade program applicable to their
  electric power generation sector. The nine RGGI
  states—Connecticut, Delaware, Maine, Maryland, Massachusetts, New Hampshire, New Jersey, New York, and Vermont—have adopted a model rule that will ensure that
  greenhouse gas emissions from the electric power sector
  are capped at levels present in 2009 (the start date for the
  program) and reduced by 10 percent by 2019.[47]

  Perhaps the most important up-and-coming regional
  collaboration, the Western Climate Initiative, is now being
  developed by the governors of Arizona, California, New
  Mexico, Oregon, and Washington, and the premier of the
  Canadian province of British Columbia.

- *Multi-State Litigation to Reduce Greenhouse Gases.* The states have taken an active litigation posture with respect to compelling reductions in greenhouse gases. The litigation can be divided into two types: (1) litigation against the federal government, specifically the EPA, to compel the federal regulation of greenhouse gas emissions; and (2) common-law actions against individual sources of greenhouse gases seeking emissions reductions.

  The litigation against the federal government includes *Massachusetts v. EPA*,[48] filed by Massachusetts and other states and environmental groups against EPA for failure to regulate greenhouse gas emissions from motor vehicles. This is the lawsuit that resulted in the Supreme Court ruling that the Clean Air Act does, indeed, apply to climate change and, thus, that EPA is compelled to determine whether the conditions that mandate regulation—reasonable anticipation of endangerment—were triggered with respect to vehicle greenhouse gas emissions. In *Coke Oven Environmental Task Force v. EPA*,[49] states and other petitioners are challenging EPA's failure to include greenhouse gases among the pollutants controlled under the agency's new source performance standards (NSPS) for steam-generating units operated by electric utilities and other industrial and commercial facilities.

  Common-law actions include those filed by state attorneys general alleging individual sources of greenhouse gas emissions are contributing to a public nuisance under state and federal law. In the first such case, nine states and the city of New York sued five electric power-generating companies, alleging that these companies, the largest emitters of carbon dioxide in the United States (and among the largest in the world) are substantial contributors to elevated levels of carbon dioxide and global warming. In a second case, California sued six major automobile manufacturers, alleging that the emissions of carbon dioxide and other greenhouse gases produced through the combustion of fossil fuels in passenger vehicles and trucks create and contribute to the public nuisance of global warming. Neither case fared well at the trial court level,[50] but both are currently pending on appeal.

Recommendations for Future Action

We make three recommendations for further action:

1. State policymakers should pay closer attention to the structural and conceptual foundations for effective policy analysis and change. Policymakers should be far more attentive to the idea of states as laboratories within the federal system, a metaphor framed by Justice Louis Brandeis in a dissenting opinion in 1932.[51] Justice Brandeis' opinion in *New State Ice v. Liebmann* reflected more than a faith in our federal system and a desire to allow states to "try novel social and economic experiments." His dissent reflected a theory about knowledge, especially with regard to solving complex social problems. His skepticism about knowledge and policy are very much in keeping with efforts to define and seek a goal as illusive, complex, and shifting as sustainable development.

It is instructive to remember the context in which Brandeis framed the laboratory metaphor. In *New State Ice* the Court rejected as a violation of substantive due process an Oklahoma law establishing a licensing scheme for ice manufacturers and distributors. In his dissent, Justice Brandeis described the history, structure, and regulation of the ice industry, and explained its economic and social importance.

The profound and new challenges of the Great Depression led to a variety of proposals for recovery—some involved more government, some less. Brandeis did not dissent because he believed Oklahoma had the right policy answer on the question of how and whether the ice industry ought to be regulated. Instead, he dissented because he *did not know* the answer, and he was skeptical that others (including those who would limit regulation in the name of substantive due process) had truth more firmly in their hands.[52]

We believe that policymakers could learn by revisiting the explicit assumptions beyond Justice Brandeis' desire to defer to state experimentation, and by exploring the implications of taking the metaphor seriously in ways that Justice Brandeis did not articulate. It is encouraging to see the emergence of sustainability initiatives in some states. A review of lower-level state initiatives within particular executive branch agencies would no doubt have found evidence of sustainability efforts in far more states. But whether the initiatives are systematic or focused, if they are to live up to the laboratory metaphor they will need to be conducted in a manner that will make it easier to learn, compare, and contrast such efforts.[53] Policy efforts that produce standards or goals but no theory about how either government or private actors will get to the desired ends do not satisfy a minimal conception of states as laboratories. It is not sufficient that states retain power merely to take (or not to take) action on various societal challenges.

If the collective benefits of local experimentation are to be realized, executive agents and state councils should be more conscious about what their experiments seek to prove. After articulating the specific goals and assumptions behind different policy experiments, policy actors should identify measures, report with detailed data on an ongoing basis the success *or failure* of their efforts, and share their conclusions in ways that actors in other jurisdictions can access and understand.

2. Encourage more states to follow the lead of Minnesota, New Jersey, and Oregon, and develop comprehensive goals for a sustainable society and specific indicators for progress. We believe that the use of goals and indicators is the only approach that does justice to the integrated objectives of sustainability, permitting review and assessment of human societal development, and the impact of that development upon the natural environment. While concern with the environmental impacts of state government operations is commendable, certainly this does not live up to the broader sustainability goals articulated by such sources as the Brundtland Commission.

3. Preserve state policy innovation by avoiding federal preemption of state climate initiatives except where a direct conflict with federal law exists. State actions have brought much-needed policy focus and public and media attention to climate change and its local effects. State and local climate initiatives prompt critical technological, social, and economic changes essential to mitigating climate change. The strong state efforts on climate change reinforce the vitality of the idea of states as laboratories, even on issues that operate on much larger scales.

These climate change policies have also served as illustrations that state and local initiatives can provide feedback to policy debates at the national level and help to frame national policy. The traditional view has promoted federal preemption as a policy matter and as a legal presumption for various environmental issues. Perhaps the lessons of state sustainability efforts include a more skeptical approach as both a policy and legal matter to federal preemption of state efforts across a wide range of issues related to the many dimensions of the challenge of creating a sustainable society.[54]

ENDNOTES

1. *See* Kirsten H. Engel, *State and Local Climate Change Initiatives: What Is Motivating State and Local Governments to Address a Global Problem and What Does This Say About Federalism and Environmental Law?*, 38 URB. LAW. 1015 (2006); Kirsten H. Engel, *Harnessing the Benefits of Dynamic Federalism in Environmental Law*, 56 EMORY L.J. 159 (2006).

2. New State Ice v. Liebmann, 285 U.S. 262 (1932) (Brandeis, J., dissenting).

3. *See* CONG. RESEARCH SERV., WATER QUALITY: IMPLEMENTING THE CLEAN WATER ACT 6 (2006) *available at* www.ncseonline.org/NLE/CRS reports/06Jun/RL33466.pdf.

4. 33 U.S.C. §§1288, 1329.

5. 33 U.S.C. §1313.

6. *See e.g.*, Alaska Ctr. for the Env't v. Reilly, 762 F. Supp. 1422 (W.D. Wash. 1991), *aff'd* 20 F.3d. 981 (9th Cir. 1994).

7. *See e.g.*, U.S. EPA, STATE BROWNFIELDS AND VOLUNTARY RESPONSE PROGRAMS (Aug. 2006), *available at* http://www.epa.gov/brownfields/ pubs/st_res_prog_report.htm.

8. *See* Monica Davey, *Illinois Law Offers Coverage for Uninsured Children*, N.Y. TIMES, Nov. 16, 2005, *available at* www.nytimes.com/2005/11/16/ national/16children.html?_r=1&oref=slogin.

9. In 2006, 47 million people in the United States (15.8 percent of the population) were without health insurance for at least part of the year. Of children under 18 years, 11.7 percent were without health insurance in 2006.

10. *See* ROBERT WOOD JOHNSON FOUND., STATE COVERAGE INITIATIVES, *available at* http://statecoverage.net/matrix/index.htm.

11. For a summary of state activities to reform the No Child Left Behind Act, see Communities for Quality Education, *available at* www.qualityednow. org/summaries/.

12. U.S. DEP'T OF EDUC., 10 FACTS ABOUT K-12 EDUCATION FUNDING, *available at* www.ed.gov/about/overview/fed/10facts/index.html.

13. *Cf.* Oliver A. Houck, *On the Law of Biodiversity and Ecosystem Management*, 81 MINN. L. REV. 869 (1997) (devastating critique of the meaninglessness of "ecosystem management" in federal forest administration and law).

14. Minnesota has developed specific numeric indicators of sustainability that encompass economic, social, and environmental factors. *See* MINN. PLANNING & ENVTL. QUALITY BD., SMART SIGNALS: AN ASSESSMENT OF PROGRESS INDICATORS (Mar. 2000), *available at* www.gda.state.mn.us/ pdf/2000/eqb/measure.pdf. Washington State's Sustainable Washington Advisory Panel has developed a plan that encompasses environmental stewardship, social development, and economic security. *See* GOVERNOR'S SUSTAINABLE WASHINGTON ADVISORY PANEL, A NEW PATH FORWARD: ACTION PLAN FOR A SUSTAINABLE WASHINGTON (Feb. 2003), *available at* www.sustainableseattle.org/sustpanel/ANewPathFowardActionPlan.pdf. Oregon's Sustainability Board has made similar efforts. *See* www.sustainable oregon.net/oregon.

15. OREGON PROGRESS BD., OREGON SHINES, I-1-2 (1989), *available at* www.oregon.gov/DAS/OPB/os.shtml. In 1997, as part of the Oregon Shines II process, these goals were updated as: "1) quality jobs for all Oregonians, 2) engaged, caring, and safe communities, and 3) healthy, sustainable surroundings." *See* OREGON PROGRESS BD. & GOVERNOR'S OREGON SHINES TASK FORCE, OREGON SHINES II (1997), *available at* www.oregon. gov/DAS/OPB/docs/osII.pdf.

16. *See* OREGON PROGRESS BD., BREAKTHROUGH RESULTS FOR OREGON: REVAMPING OREGON'S APPROACH TO A SUSTAINABLE FUTURE 1 (2007), *available at* www.oregon.gov/DAS/OPB/docs/OSIII/OSIII_Concept.doc.

17. *Id.* at 2-4.

18. *See* MINN. PLANNING DEP'T., MINN. MILESTONES: MEASURES THAT MATTER (2002), *available at* www.mnplan.state.mn.us/mm/index.html.

19. *Id.*

20. *Id.* at 4 (positive statewide trends in health and education mask significant disparities between whites and people of all other racial/ethnic backgrounds).

21. *Id.* at 7.

22. *See* N.J. SUSTAINABLE STATE INST., GOALS AND INDICATORS: OVERVIEW, *available at* http://www.njssi.org/goals.asp?Level2ItemID=9.

23. *See* N.J. SUSTAINABLE STATE INST., LIVING WITH THE FUTURE IN MIND (3d ed. 2004), *available at* www.njssi.org/uploaded_documents/njssi_report.pdf.

24. *Id.* at 1.

25. *Id.* at 4-5. In addition to open space, New Jersey has specific numeric targets for reductions in infant mortality; increases in life expectancy; reductions in cases of infectious diseases, asthma, and occupational-related lead poisonings; infrastructure repairs; traffic fatalities; increases in wetlands acreage; reductions in greenhouse gas emissions, solid waste generation, and air pollution; and an increase in the number of public water systems meeting safe drinking water standards.

26. *Id.* at 108, 76 & 94.

27. *Id.* at 5-6.

28. Green building is a priority of the sustainability efforts of the states of California, Illinois, Maine, Massachusetts, New Mexico, and Washington.

29. *See* California, Illinois, and Washington.

30. Diane Cole, *Greening the World,* U.S. NEWS & WORLD REPORT, *available at* www.usnews.com/usnews/edu/grad/articles/brief/gbarts_brief_2.php.

31. Massachusetts v. EPA, 549 U.S. 497 (2007).

32. 42 U.S.C. §7521(a)(1) (2000).

33. Energy Independence and Security Act of 2007, Pub. L. No. 110-140, 121 Stat. 1492, §102 (2007).

34. For a summary of federal climate bills, see PEW CENTER, GLOBAL CLIMATE CHANGE, *available at* www.pewclimate.org/what_s_being_done/in_the_congress/109th.cfm (summarizing the 106 resolutions and amend-

ments introduced during the 109th Congress that specifically mention climate change).

35. This was the topic of a conference on Feb. 4, 2008, at the University of Arizona James E. Rogers College of Law. Proceedings from the conference, tentatively titled *Federalism and Climate Change: The Role of the States in a Future Federal Regime*, were published in the *Arizona Law Review* in 2008.

36. There are many excellent up-to-date resources for information about state climate change initiatives. The most comprehensive on-line resources are the databases maintained by the Pew Center on Global Climate Change at www.pewcenter.org. For state legislation on climate change specifically, see the National Caucus of Environmental Legislators at www.ncel.net/newsmanager/news_article.cgi?news_id=172.

37. Global Warming Solutions Act of 2006, Cal. Assembly Bill 32. *See* Juliet Eilperin, *California Tightens Rules on Emissions*, WASH. POST, Sept. 1, 2006, at A1, *available at* www.washingtonpost.com/wp-dyn/content/article/2006/08/31/AR2006083100146.html.

38. Cal. Assembly Bill 1493 (Pavley), Cal. Health & Safety Code §43018.5. Under the legislation, the Air Resources Board is charged with adopting standards that will achieve "the maximum feasible and cost-effective reduction of greenhouse gas emissions from motor vehicles," taking into account environmental, social, technological, and economic factors. Regulations by the Air Resources Board implementing the California legislation became effective on Jan.1, 2006, and can be found at Title 13 §1961.1(g).

39. *See* U.S. EPA, California State Motor Vehicle Pollution Control Standards; Notice of Decision Denying a Waiver of Clean Air Act Preemption for California's 2009 and Subsequent Model Year Greenhouse Gas Emission Standards for New Motor Vehicles, 73 Fed. Reg. 12156 (2008). California, joined by several other states, has sued EPA over the denial of the waiver. Felicity Barringer, *California Sues E.P.A. Over Denial of Waiver*, N.Y. TIMES, Jan. 2, 2008, *available at* www.nytimes.com/2008/01/03/us/03suit.html.

40. *See* Central Valley Chrysler-Jeep, Inc. v. Witherspoon, 2007 WL 135688 (E.D. Cal. 2007) (unpublished), 456 F. Supp. 2d 1160 (E.D. Cal. 2006).

41. U.S. Department of Transportation, National Highway Safety Transportation Safety Administration, Average Fuel Economy Standards for Light Trucks Model Years 2008-2011, Final Rule, 71 Fed. Reg. 17566, 17654 (Apr. 6, 2006) (state regulation of motor vehicle tailpipe emissions of carbon dioxide is expressly and impliedly preempted by the Energy Policy and Conservation Act, 49 U.S.C. §32919(a)).

42. Green Mountain Plymouth Dodge Jeep v. Crombie et al., 508 F. Supp. 2d 295 (D. Vt. 2007).

43. CONG. RESEARCH SERV., *supra* note 3, at 15-16.

44. *Id.* at 16.

45. PEW CENTER ON GLOBAL CLIMATE CHANGE, RENEWABLE PORTFOLIO STANDARDS, *available at* www.pewclimate.org/what_s_being_done/in_the_states/rps.cfm.

46. *See* U.S. EPA, GLOBAL WARMING, ACTIONS, STATE, *available at* http://yosemite.epa.gov/OAR/globalwarming.nsf/content/ActionsState. html.

47. *See* Regional Greenhouse Gas Initiative, www.rggi.org.

48. 549 U.S. 497 (2007).

49. No. 06-1322 (D.C. Cir. filed Apr. 27, 2006).

50. *See* Connecticut v. Am. Elec. Power Co., 406 F. Supp. 2d 265 (S.D.N.Y. 2005) (No. 04-5669) (dismissing suit against electric utilities as presenting a nonjusticiable political question incapable of resolution by the courts at this time); California v. General Motors, __ F. Supp. 2d __ (N.D. Cal. 2007), 2007 WL 2726871 (same with respect to lawsuit filed by California against motor vehicle manufacturers).

51. *New State Ice, supra* note 2, 285 U.S. at 280 (Brandeis, J., dissenting). Justice Brandeis' beautiful metaphor has shown strong legs, and continues to appear in case law and academic discussions of federalism after 75 years. But surprisingly there has been almost no examination of the implications, if any, of treating the laboratory metaphor seriously. *See* Marc L. Miller, *Wise Masters*, 51 STAN. L. REV. 1751, 1811-13 (1999); Marc L. Miller, *A Map of Sentencing and a Compass for Judges: Sentencing Information Systems, Transparency, and the Next Generation of Reform*, 105 COLUM. L. REV. 1351 (2005).

52. *New State Ice, supra* note 2, 285 U.S. at 310.

53. *See* Marc Miller, *A Map of Sentencing, supra* note 51, at 1393-94; Marc Miller & Ronald Wright, *"The Wisdom We Have Lost"—Sentencing Information and Its Uses*, 58 STAN. L. REV. 361, 374-78 (2005).

54. For a more elaborate treatment of this point, see David E. Adelman and Kirsten H. Engel, *Adaptive Federalism: Lessons From the Study of Complex Adaptive Systems*, __ MINN. L. REV. __ (2008).

Chapter 30

Public Access to Information, Participation, and Justice: Forward and Backward Steps Toward an Informed and Engaged Citizenry

Carl Bruch, Frances Irwin, and Gary D. Bass

Transparency, participation, and accountability are central to effective environmental management, as well as to democratic governance.[1] Nevertheless, since 2002 the U.S. government has undermined the principle that the public has a "right to know" by quietly but increasingly shifting to policies and practices based on the public's "need to know," a standard that leaves the government in charge of determining who needs to know and what they need to know.

Since 2002, the executive branch in particular has fostered this culture of government secrecy, with a resulting adverse impact on efforts to achieve sustainable development. Starting in 2001, the Bush Administration began to assert executive privilege to curtail legislative and regulatory measures that sought to ensure effective environmental management and government administration through transparency, participation, and accountability. The terrorist attacks of 9/11 provoked—and provided further justification for—additional restrictions on public access.[2] While the threat of terrorism is real, in numerous documented instances the Administration's invocation of concerns regarding terrorism and national security appears to overreach. In response to a general movement by the federal government to restrict access, states have also had an uneven response regarding transparency.

The most dramatic measures to improve public access to information and public participation have occurred outside the political arena. Increased use of cell phones and access to the Internet provide new tools for informing and mobilizing the public. The ability to obtain, combine, link, and share data on the environment has been revolutionized with tools such as Google Earth, YouTube, and Wikipedia. And environmental and political activists have used the Internet to inform and mobilize constituents, as well as to raise funds.

Newer environmental challenges—particularly those relating to climate change, ecosystem services, nanotechnology, and endocrine disruptors—should further shape the evolution of public access in the years to come. This chapter briefly examines the importance of access to sustainable development in the United States, and then analyzes measures affecting access since 2002. It concludes with recommendations for strengthening public access, participation, and justice, particularly at the federal level.

Public Access and Sustainable Development

The transition that the United States must make to achieve sustainability entails numerous reforms in how people live, work, and relate to one another. Transparent and participatory processes are essential if we are to engage the public in this reform process, build support for the reforms, and leverage the necessary resources. The American people need information to fully understand the environmental challenges the country faces, to motivate the commitment of resources necessary to address those challenges, and to track progress toward meeting the goals of sustainable development. Similarly, public participation in decisionmaking provides opportunities to educate potentially affected people about the impacts and options they face (e.g., through an environmental impact assessment or notice-and-comment rulemaking). It also allows different sectors of the public to have their voices heard and bring additional information to the attention of the decisionmakers, and ultimately to improve the quality of decisions and their implementation. Access to the judicial system is also key to ensuring that people's procedural and environmental rights are respected.

As Congress reaffirmed in 2007 when it adopted the OPEN Government Act, broad public access is central to good governance. Indeed, limiting access reduces opportunities for oversight and accountability, providing a context in which unsustainable decisions and actions are more difficult to detect, prevent, or remedy.

Recent Developments in Public Access

Developments in public access since 2002 have been characterized by divergent trends. Even as technological developments generated significant new opportunities for the public to use and share data, the federal government sought to reduce public access in the name of executive privilege, national security, and economic development through regulatory changes and institutional practice. The actions by the federal executive were countered by a few legislative initiatives to enhance public access. Denials of access generated numerous legal challenges; in most cases, the courts upheld the right of those seeking access.

Access to Information

Changes in access to information include those resulting from revisions to federal law (and sometimes state law), modifications in institutional and administrative practices, and technological developments and initiatives outside the governmental sphere.

Legal and Regulatory Frameworks

Recent developments in the legal framework governing access to information have generally related to policies and practices that increase governmental secrecy. This trend includes developments with respect to the Freedom of Information Act, the Presidential Records Act, and the Toxics Release Inventory. The rare exceptions were the 2007 OPEN Government Act and proposed measures to develop publicly accessible greenhouse gas inventories.

Growing Governmental Secrecy. A 2007 report by OpenThe-Government.org, an independent coalition of journalists, consumer advocates, and good government groups, described widespread increases in government secrecy.[3] Classification of documents in 2006 was significantly higher (approximately 47 percent) than in 2001. Indeed, for every dollar spent in 2006 to declassify documents, $185 was spent by the government to keep information secret. The report also noted the dramatic increase in presidential use of the "state secrets" privilege, by which the president can almost unilaterally withhold documents from Congress, courts, and the public. Between 1953 and 1976, during the height of the Cold War, the privilege was invoked only six times; since 2001 President Bush used it 39 times that are known.

There have also been dramatic increases in withholding information that is not classified. Since the terror attacks of 9/11, the federal government has created categories that provide new rationales for withholding information from the public: thus, information is neither classified nor available to the public. The largest of these pseudo-classification categories is SBU (Sensitive But Unclassified), which now will be subsumed under Controlled Unclassified Information.[4]

While recent governmental initiatives to limit public access often invoked national security and occasionally other established exemptions such as confidential business information (albeit historically more narrowly construed), numerous scholars view the efforts as part of a broader push by the Bush Administration to assert and exert executive privilege and authority.

Freedom of Information Act (FOIA). A 2002 memorandum to federal agencies by then-Attorney General John Ashcroft provided guidance on FOIA implementation.[5] The memo assured agencies that the Department of Justice would defend them in the withholding of information as long as there was a "sound legal basis," whereas the previous attorney general memorandum had instructed agencies to withhold information only when the release would cause "foreseeable harm."[6] This change of institutional philosophy—from encouraging disclosure to encouraging withholding whenever possible—was widely criticized as violating the spirit of FOIA.

Agencies' FOIA processes have not been keeping up with demand. In 2006, the government received 21.4 million FOIA requests, an increase of approximately 7 percent from the previous year. However, agency backlogs in responding to FOIA requests continue to grow even faster, with the oldest pending request now more than 20 years old.[7]

In 2007, Congress enacted the OPEN Government Act to strengthen FOIA.[8] This law makes a number of modest changes to FOIA, including provisions that are intended to speed up the FOIA process, reduce fees for a broader segment of journalists, expand the reach of FOIA to certain government contractors, create an ombudsman-type office to handle complaints, establish a publicly available tracking system of requests, and make it easier to recover attorney's fees. The OPEN Government Act, however, neither reversed the 2002 Ashcroft directive nor reinstated a presumption of disclosure.

Toxic Chemicals. At the end of 2006, the U.S. Environmental Protection Agency (EPA) changed the Toxics Release Inventory (TRI), the nation's premier right-to-know program, by relaxing reporting requirements for the companies and other facilities that emit toxic chemicals.[9] EPA estimated that the new reporting thresholds would

eliminate reporting on only 16 chemicals, while OMB Watch estimated that it would eliminate reporting on 39 chemicals and reduce
the reporting on 28 more by at least one-half. More than 122,000 public comments were received when EPA's plans were announced, with
virtually all of them (more than 99.9 percent) opposing the plan.[10]
State legislatures and Congress have attempted to reverse the effects
of this rule.[11] Officials from the Government Accountability Office
(GAO) testified at an October 2007 congressional hearing that "EPA
did not follow guidelines to ensure that scientific, economic, and policy issues are addressed at appropriate stages of rule development."[12]
Within two months of GAO's testimony, 12 states sued EPA to challenge the 2006 regulation.[13]

Shortly after the 9/11 terrorist attacks, EPA removed from its website all risk management plans (RMPs), documents describing risks
around chemical plants that the Clean Air Act requires companies to
prepare and EPA to post.[14] EPA replaced the RMPs with a message explaining that in light of the terrorist attacks the database had been
"temporarily removed." The message also stated that the agency
hoped to make the information available online again "as soon as possible." In 2004, EPA revised RMP reporting requirements to ensure
that sensitive data would not be put in the executive summary. Yet, as
of this writing, EPA has not replaced any of the data on its website, including the executive summaries.

Since 9/11, one of the most pressing issues has been chemical plant
security and vulnerabilities. Despite initial discussions by EPA and
the new U.S. Department of Homeland Security (DHS), there was no
action on this topic until late in 2006 when Congress required DHS to
issue regulations within six months.[15] On April 9, 2007, DHS released
its interim final rule that imposes federal security regulations for
high-risk chemical facilities.[16] The rule established risk-based performance standards for many chemical facilities and required them to
prepare security vulnerability assessments, select security measures
to satisfy risk-based performance standards, and develop and implement site security plans.

In the process leading to the 2007 rule, DHS stated in a December
2006 proposal that any state or local provisions that frustrate the
"carefully balanced regulatory relationship" that "preserve[s] chemical facilities' flexibility to choose security measures to reach the appropriate security outcome" would be preempted. This created a fire-

storm of protest from states, emergency responders, and environmental advocates. DHS used less emphatic language in the final regulations but reaffirmed that state rules that conflict or interfere with federal provisions would be preempted. DHS said it knew of no state rules that would be preempted, and that it would allow a facility, state, or locality to submit a provision for review and receive an opinion from DHS regarding whether the provision is preempted.[17]

DHS would not speculate as to whether stricter state rules, such as requiring companies to use inherently safer technologies, would be preempted. This prompted some states, such as New Jersey, to strongly protest the new federal rules. Frustrated by DHS, Congress took stronger action. In the FY 2008 appropriations bill for DHS, Congress added language explicitly preserving the states' right to write stronger chemical security provisions than the federal rules.[18] Congress has also been wrestling with legislation to make chemical security regulations permanent, but none of the bills supports public access to the vulnerability assessments or addresses how the issue should be resolved.

Administrative Practice

In addition to legal and regulatory reforms, administrative actions and practices over the past five or so years have significantly affected public access. These developments include changes in how scientific information is used and disseminated (reducing public access), development of indicators and a report on environment (some movement toward increasing access), implementation of the Information Quality Act (reducing), and closing of EPA libraries (reducing).

The same time period has seen a dramatic increase in the politicization of scientific information, leading one author to characterize it as "a war on science."[19] This trend has been particularly evident with respect to climate change,[20] but also in establishing health-based regulations for air pollutants and in determining the listing status for threatened and endangered species. The extent of scientific manipulation is so extensive that the Union of Concerned Scientists (UCS) prepared the *A to Z Guide to Political Interference in Science*, and more than 12,000 scientists signed a statement denouncing the trend.[21] In 2007, the UCS received survey responses from 1,586 EPA scientists, with 60 percent saying there was some degree of political meddling, ranging from unnecessary delays to forced resignations over the past five years.[22] In response, Congress held numerous hearings on the integrity of science in various committees and several bills were introduced to address some of the problems.

The government has not adopted integrated economic, social, and environmental indicators to track sustainable development. In 1995, Congress decided that many reports, including the annual State of the Environment published under the National Environmental Policy Act starting in 1970, were no longer required unless explicitly requested by Congress. EPA has focused on developing environmental indicators, and introduced these indicators in a 2003 draft report. The *Report on the Environment* issued in May 2008 refines indicators on the condition of air, water, land, and related changes in human health in the United States. Regular revisions are slated to feed into EPA's planning process.[23]

A little-noticed legislative amendment to a 2000 spending bill, known as the Information Quality Act (sometimes called the Data Quality Act, or DQA), has drawn increased attention. The DQA required the Office of Management and Budget (OMB) to issue guidelines to federal agencies "for ensuring and maximizing the quality, objectivity, utility, and integrity of information (including statistical information) disseminated by Federal agencies."[24] OMB then issued guidelines to implement the law.[25] By 2004 the Congressional Research Service (CRS) concluded the DQA can have "a significant impact on federal agencies and their information dissemination activities."[26]

While ostensibly directed at improving the data used by federal agencies, the DQA has had adverse effects. An example is how the DQA has been used to thwart the use and dissemination of research addressing the harmful effects of endocrine disruptors such as atrazine, a leading weed killer. Existing research showed that atrazine had developmental effects on frogs at low-dose exposures and was expected to also impact humans.[27] As EPA was compiling research about atrazine's carcinogenicity, it was also preparing a review on whether to stop the market use of the chemical, as had been done in Europe. The manufacturer, Syngenta, funded its own research that did not replicate the findings of damaging health effects. This allowed groups such as the Center for Regulatory Effectiveness, the Kansas Corn Growers Association, and the Triazine Network to file a DQA challenge to EPA's use of research showing a link between atrazine and cancer. EPA largely dismissed the challenge, but concluded that hormone disruption cannot be considered a "legitimate regulatory end-point at this time"—that is, it is not an acceptable reason to restrict a chemical's use—because the government had not settled on an officially accepted test for measuring such disruption. EPA added "that based on the existing data uncertainties, the chemical should be subject to more definitive testing once the appropriate testing protocols have been established."[28] This illustrates how the DQA has become a means for slowing regulation, such as that of atrazine, because of scientific uncertainty—and since uncertainty always exists it will be difficult to regulate.

Since the initial challenge on atrazine, DQA challenges are frequently filed with agencies regarding proposed actions.[29] There are many other examples, such as the challenges filed on the National Toxicology Program's *Report on Carcinogens* (ROC), which is used by local, state, and federal authorities to set environmental policies, explore regulations on dangerous substances, and provide for preventative health measures. The latest ROC has been delayed for over a year. This may be why the CRS added in its 2004 annual report to Congress on implementation of the DQA that there were "numerous examples of agencies changing their policies and publications in response to administrative requests for correction from affected parties." In addition, DQA challenges can be used to delay reports: according to the National Academy of Sciences, compliance with the law has resulted in serious delays in the U.S. Climate Change Science Program's release of 19 of the 21 planned reports on climate change.[30] Congress held its first hearing on the DQA in July 2005 with three agencies—EPA, the Department of Health and Human Services, and the Fish and Wildlife Service—acknowledging that they had diverted resources to respond to DQA challenges.

Anticipating a proposed FY 2007 budget cut from $2.5 million to $500,000 for its network of 26 libraries, EPA closed some of its regional libraries. The agency presented the closings as part of an effort to keep pace with the changing way that people access information and to make research more efficient. Over 10,000 EPA scientists and researchers—more than one-half of the agency's total workforce—signed a letter saying that the cuts would put thousands of scientific studies out of reach and hinder emergency preparedness, anti-pollution enforcement, and long-term research.[31] EPA postponed any further closings pending review by Congress and until a better plan could be developed.[32] Congress approved $3 million in the FY

2008 spending bill to enable EPA to reopen the closed libraries and to report to Congress within months of this writing on steps that it has taken.

The Internet

In contrast to the generally growing constraints imposed by the Bush Administration on access to information, the private sector has enhanced access in many ways. The Internet has continued to revolutionize public access to information in the United States and around the world. For example, using Google Earth and other sources people can combine geospatial data to make their own maps. Websites continue to be an essential means for nongovernmental organizations (NGOs), as well as government agencies, to disseminate environmental information and engage the public. There has been a dramatic increase in YouTube and other file-sharing websites, which are becoming an important means for disseminating information on environmental issues.[33] By early January 2008, an average of 825,000 new videos were posted each day on YouTube alone, with approximately 70,000 environmental videos, including 11,000 relating specifically to climate change.

Internet-based news institutions supplement blogs and Web pages as a significant means for educating the public on environmental issues. In addition to advocacy organizations and the government, environmental and independent news organizations such as Grist and Indymedia.org have become popular e-news sites.

Public Participation

Developments in public participation since 2002 are also characterized by increasing governmental restrictions (particularly with respect to public participation in environmental impact assessment) and nongovernmental opportunities.

Since 2002, the Bush Administration has changed, largely through regulations, the procedural requirements for environmental impact assessment under the National Environmental Policy Act (NEPA). Many environmentalists assert that these changes significantly restrict public involvement in governmental decisions regarding public resources, undermine governmental accountability, and ultimately enable "environmentally damaging projects."[34]

In 2003, the White House's Council on Environmental Quality recommended that federal agencies scale back the analyses contained in their environmental assessments and expand use of categorical exclusions, which allows projects that do not have an effect on the environment to skip assessment and public review altogether.[35] The Bush Administration has used categorical exclusions particularly for forest management, for example through President Bush's "Healthy Forests Initiative,"[36] and changes in rules implementing the National Forest Management Act. Environmental groups have challenged the categorical exclusions in court, and at least one federal court has held that they violate NEPA.[37]

The Internet has facilitated environmental activism. For example, in January 2007 a small group of climate change activists launched stepitup2007.org to help link groups and individuals working on climate change in the United States through an "open source, web-based day of action." Using the Internet, Step It Up engaged thousands of people in raising awareness about climate change and in building political support to respond to climate change.[38] In 2007, Step It Up organized about 2,000 demonstrations in all 50 states, helping to shift the debate on Capitol Hill.

Online social network services such as MySpace, Facebook, and Second Life have enabled like-minded people to find one another and come together, sometimes for social good. Telecommunications technologies—particularly the use of cell phones and text messaging—have also changed how environmental activists undertake campaigns.[39] Taken together, these Internet-based resources provide enhanced opportunities to inform, engage, and coordinate.

Access to Justice

The last five or so years have seen generally favorable judicial decisions regarding standing of citizens, NGOs, and states to sue to protect the environment and to compel compliance with environmental laws. The most dramatic ruling was in *Massachusetts v. EPA*, in which the U.S. Supreme Court recognized the standing of states, cities, and environmental NGOs to compel EPA to promulgate regulations for greenhouse gas emissions from motor vehicles, perhaps peeling back some of the hurdles to standing that had been created over the past 20 years.[40]

There has also been a series of important federal circuit court cases on environmental standing over the past few years.[41] Many of the recent cases adopt an expansive approach to NEPA standing.[42] Even with an expansive approach to procedural standing, though, environmental plaintiffs sometimes are unable to satisfy the standing requirements.[43] One of the primary challenges is proving increased risk of harm (for example, from cancer) associated with an agency action and whether that comprises constitutionally cognizable injury-in-fact. The D.C. Circuit, which hears most challenges to environmental regulations, established a "substantial probability" test for determining standing in such cases, which has made it more difficult to prove standing.[44] This new test is not likely to settle the issue of standing, as questions remain regarding the scope and application of the test.[45]

With many courts requiring rigorous evidence to support standing, plaintiffs are facing increased burdens, costs, and risks. Plaintiffs with sufficient resources are undertaking increasingly sophisticated analyses to prove standing; others who cannot afford to undertake such analyses must hope that the court does not reject their claims due to a failure to meet the heightened requirements for proof of injury. Since the 1990s, recovery of attorney's fees has become less reliable, as defendants drag out litigation and generally reduce the certainty that public interest environmental plaintiffs will be able to recover their fees.[46]

The favorable developments in standing case law are not secure. There is a solid block of four justices on the U.S. Supreme Court who have indicated in strongly worded dissents that they would reduce standing.[47] The retirement or death of one Supreme Court justice could convert this minority into a majority opposing a broad view of standing. Moreover, the Bush Administration has pushed hard to place conservative judges on federal courts, including about 300 on district and circuit courts in the first seven years, resulting in a solid majority for Republican appointees.[48] A statistical survey of 325 NEPA cases decided between 2001 and 2004 showed that there can be significant differences in how judges approach environmental cases, with judges appointed by a Democratic president ruling in favor of environmental plaintiffs more than twice as often as judges appointed by a Republican president, and about four times as often as judges appointed by President George W. Bush.[49] Anecdotal evidence also suggests similar distinctions with respect to judicial perspective on standing in environmental cases.[50]

Trade Agreements

Since the incorporation of environmental and public participation considerations in the North American Agreement on Environmental Cooperation (NAAEC), an increasing number of bilateral and multilateral trade agreements and accompanying environmental instruments negotiated by the United States have incorporated provisions to promote access to information, public participation, and access to justice. These agreements include those with Central America (CAFTA-DR), Australia, Bahrain, Chile, Israel (on agriculture), Jordan, Morocco, Oman, and Singapore. These agreements have continued to promote public access, albeit not to the same extent as the NAAEC.

Recommendations

A 2002 assessment of public access in the United States recommended measures to improve public access for sustainable development.[51] These recommendations included, inter alia, measures to adopt a new generation of access principles, organize and deliver data (including the development and use of indicators), engage citizens in decisionmaking, and provide international leadership. However, there has been little progress toward these recommendations. In most instances, the government has become less transparent, participatory, and accountable; most measures to improve the organization and delivery of data for sustainable development have come from nongovernmental sources.

The 2002 recommendations remain relevant today. Indeed, in light of governmental actions and inaction since that time, they are as necessary as ever. Recent events provide an additional context and guidance for future directions. Accordingly, we propose two broad recommendations with differing dimensions. Many of the dimensions were alluded to in the 2002 assessment, and recent scholarship and sociopolitical developments further inform these recommendations.

1. Focus access particularly in areas such as climate change, ecosystem services, and newer environmental and health risks. Since 2002, there has been dramatic growth in our understanding of environmental challenges and the measures necessary to move to a more sustainable nation and world. These developments particularly include understanding of climate change, ecosystem services, nanotechnology, and endocrine disruptors. The political momentum in addressing these areas provides a window for enhancing public access, and improving access in these areas provides an architecture of good governance for tackling these challenges.

It is important to *devise and use indicators based on the relationship of humans and ecosystems.* For example, clean drinking water and climate regulation (including carbon sequestration) are benefits of nature—ecosystem services—that require new ways of collecting, synthesizing, and providing clear information to the public. In order to protect our shared resources, we need to provide better information to the public and more effectively engage the public in sustainable development. With new information technologies, access to information can also serve as a feedback mechanism to understand how the United States as well as organizations, corporations, and local governments are using natural resources.

Particular attention should be paid to *improving access to information, participation, and justice related to climate change.* These improvements include collecting, organizing, sharing, and disseminating data on the potential effects of climate change, the effectiveness of adaptation measures, and information on mitigation measures. Climate change will also raise issues of public participation and use of the information to reduce our human footprint. With real-time information synthesized in ways that the public can understand, it is possible that right-to-know principles can lead to behavioral changes. However, many of the people who will be the most affected by climate change and by the responses to climate change will likely be those least able to cope. In order to ensure climate justice, effective participation of poor and marginalized communities will require particular attention. With numerous lawsuits seeking to compel action on climate change—and it is foreseeable that in the near future there will also be lawsuits resisting measures to respond to climate change—access to justice is likely to remain an issue, particularly in light of the shared nature of the injury. The efforts to adapt to climate change will also likely require new information, new ways of using the information, and means for engaging stakeholders in the management process.

Moreover, it should be a high priority to *collect and disseminate information related to new types of health and environmental risks, including those from nanotechnology and endocrine disruptors.* For nanotechnology, "existing science is clearly inadequate to manage the potential adverse effects of the technology. We do not know much about what adverse effect to look for, and there is no consensus on the type of data necessary to determine adverse effects."[52] These considerations also apply to endocrine disruptors, and to a certain extent to the effects of climate change.

2. Propose and adopt a new generation of access principles. As set forth in the 2002 assessment, a new generation of access principles is essential. This is particularly true in light of the threat of terrorism and the overreaching response to limit access since that time. *Government must embrace the principle that secrecy does not always make us safer.* The Bush Administration has promoted a paradigm that is framed as national security versus public access, but that is a false choice. Making information available to the public can enable and empower citizens to take actions to make communities less vulnerable.

Specifically, *Congress and the next president should institute new national right-to-know standards.* Federal agencies should have an affirmative responsibility to disseminate information, making FOIA the vehicle of last resort. With the default assumption that disclosure is preferable, agencies would need to justify any action to withhold information.

Congress and the next president need to review and revise the classification and declassification systems. Too many documents are unnecessarily being classified, and not enough information that was classified is being declassified. Moreover, Congress and the next president should take actions that stop the proliferation of pseudo-classification.

Congress needs to address unchecked and unbalanced presidential powers. One step to addressing the unbalanced growth in presidential powers can be to strengthen the opportunities for citizens and NGOs to challenge executive branch actions that violate the law, including enhanced standing and expedited opportunities for obtaining attorney's fees.

Congress and the next president should adopt policies that make public accessibility of online content and resources a priority. As a part of this effort, government databases need to be made searchable by indexers (such as Google) and by the public, and agencies should make application programming interfaces available to Web developers.

The next president should strengthen the infrastructure for agency dissemination practices and provide adequate resources. The quality of information should be timely and accurate. Common identifiers should be developed for facilities and parent companies so that information in different databases can be linked through mashups (Web applications that combine data from multiple sources) and other means. And agencies should have adequate resources to provide timely information to the public, including the capacity to meet FOIA demands and reduce backloads.

Congress and the next president should identify ways of providing incentives within the civil service system for strengthening the public's right to know. Rewards should be provided for innovative and efficient dissemination approaches, including free online translation tools. Protections for whistleblowers should be strengthened to reduce potential secrecy and threats to the integrity of science.

There also remains a profound need for leadership on international environmental matters and for advancing public access globally. This is an area where the *United States could provide significant international leadership.*

Conclusions

From a regulatory and administrative perspective, public access has generally stalled or declined since 2002. Executive privilege and national security (particularly in the wake of 9/11) have been frequently invoked to deny public access to information. There have been some modest positive measures to improve access from the Bush Administration, Congress, and federal courts, mostly since 2007. The most dramatic measures to improve public access to information and public participation have occurred outside of the political arena as the ongoing technological revolution, coupled with broadening access to the Internet and other telecommunications technologies, has increased the ability to obtain, combine, link, and share data.

Most important in the coming decade will be adopting and implementing a new generation of principles of transparency, participation, and accountability. Achieving sustainable development depends on the public having easy access to accurate, timely information, the opportunity to participate in making decisions, and the ability to hold government accountable. As technologies continue to evolve, it is difficult to foresee specifically what the next five or 10 years will bring.

These technologies present many opportunities, though, and governmental bodies need to work with the public to use these new and emerging technologies to advance sustainable development.

ENDNOTES

1. *See* Frances Irwin & Carl Bruch, *Public Access to Information, Participation, and Justice, in* STUMBLING TOWARD SUSTAINABILITY 511, 514-15 (John C. Dernbach ed., 2002).

2. *See, e.g.*, TED GUP, NATION OF SECRETS: THE THREAT TO DEMOCRACY AND THE AMERICAN WAY OF LIFE (2007).

3. PATRICE MCDERMOTT & EMILY FELDMAN, SECRECY REPORT CARD 2007: INDICATORS OF SECRECY IN THE FEDERAL GOVERNMENT (2007), *available at* www.openthegovernment.org/otg/SRC2007.pdf.

4. News Release, Pres. George W. Bush, Memorandum for the Heads of Executive Departments and Agencies, Designation and Sharing of Controlled Unclassified Information (CUI), May 9, 2008, *available at* www. whitehouse.gov/news/releases/2008/05/20080509-6.html.

5. Ashcroft Memo, *available at* www.usdoj.gov/oip/foiapost/2001foiapost 19.htm.

6. *Id.*

7. MCDERMOTT & FELDMAN, *supra* note 3.

8. Openness Promotes Effectiveness in Our National Government Act of 2007, cited as the OPEN Government Act, Pub. L. No.110-175, 121 Stat. 2524 (Dec. 21, 2007), *available at* www.washingtonwatch.com/bills/show/110_PL_110-175.html.

9. Toxics Release Inventory Burden Reduction Final Rule, 40 C.F.R. Part 372, 71 Fed. Reg. 76932 (Dec. 22, 2006).

10. OMB WATCH, AGAINST THE PUBLIC WILL (Dec. 2006), *available at* www.ombwatch.org/info/TRICommentsReport.pdf.

11. *See, e.g.*, California A.B. 833, *available at* www.leginfo.ca.gov/pub/07-08/bill/asm/ab_0801-0850/ab_833_bill_20070601_amended_asm_v97.pdf.

12. Testimony of John B. Stephenson Before the House Energy and Commerce Committee, Environmental Right to Know: EPA's Recent Rule Could Reduce Availability of Toxic Chemical Information Used to Assess Environmental Justice, Government Accountability Office: GAO-08-115T (Oct. 4, 2007), *available at* energycommerce.house.gov/cmte_mtgs/110-ehm-hrg.100407.Stephenson-Testimony.pdf.

13. New York v. Johnson, No. 07-CV-10632 (S.D.N.Y. filed Nov. 28, 2007), *available at* www.oag.state.ny.us/press/2007/nov/07-11-28%20TRI%20 Complaint.pdf.

14. OMB WATCH, OMB WATCH WINS IN COURT FOR ACCESS TO RISK MANAGEMENT DATA (2005), *available at* www.ombwatch.org/article/articleview/2915/1/242?TopicID=1. Risk Management Plans are required under Section 112(r) of the Clean Air Act.

15. The provision was attached to the FY 2007 Department of Homeland Security Appropriations Act, Pub. L. No. 109-295, signed into law Oct. 4, 2006, *available at* www.iaem.com/committees/governmentaffairs/documents/PL109-295DHSAppropFY07andFEMAReform.pdf.

16. Chemical Facility Anti-Terrorism Standards (CFATS), 6 C.F.R. Part 27. The April version of the CFATS regulation only had a preliminary list of the

chemicals covered by the regulation (i.e., Appendix A to the regulation). The regulation was not to come into effect until the final Appendix A was published. It was published November 20, 2007, and included a list of approximately 300 chemicals and "associated screening threshold quantities" in Appendix A.

17. 6 C.F.R. §27.405.

18. New Jersey's Sen. Frank Lautenberg added the language to the appropriations bill, *available at* http://lautenberg.senate.gov/newsroom/record.cfm? id=290166&.

19. Chris C. Mooney, The Republican War on Science (2005).

20. Andrew Revkin, *Report by E.P.A. Leaves Out Data on Climate Change*, N.Y. Times, June 19, 2003, *available at* www.nytimes.com/2003/06/ 19/politics/19CLIM.html?ex=1371441600&en=95b0a43f25f8e0c8&ei= 5007; Andrew Revkin, *Ex-Bush Aide Who Edited Climate Reports to Join ExxonMobil*, N.Y. Times, June 15, 2005, *available at* www.nytimes. com/2005/06/15/science/14cnd-climate.html.

21. Union of Concerned Scientists, A to Z Guide to Political Interference in Science, *available at* www.ucsusa.org/scientific_integrity/ interference/a-to-z-guide-to-political.html, updated May 28, 2008).

22. Scientific Integrity Program, Union of Concerned Scientists, Interference at the EPA: Science and Politics at the U.S. Environmental Protection Agency, April 2008, *available at* www.ucsusa.org/ news/press_release/hundreds-of-epa-scientists-0112.html.

23. *See* U.S. EPA, EPA's 2008 Report on the Environment, *available at* www.epa.gov/roe.

24. Treasury and General Government Appropriations Act for Fiscal Year 2001, Pub. L. No. 106-554, 114 Stat. 2763 (Dec. 21, 2000).

25. Office of Mgmt. & Budget, Information Quality: A Report to Congress, FY2003, *available at* www.whitehouse.gov/omb/inforeg/ fy03_info_quality_rpt.pdf.

26. Curtis W. Copeland, Cong. Research Serv., The Information Quality Act: OMB's Guidance and Initial Implementation (updated Sept. 17, 2004), *available at* www.ombwatch.org/info/dataquality/ RL32532_CRS_DQA.pdf.

27. The research was conducted by Tyrone Hayes, a professor in the department of integrative biology at the University of California, Berkeley. Ironically, the initial research was funded by atrazine manufacturer Syngenta, which in 1998 hired EcoRisk, a small Seattle-based environmental and toxicology consulting firm, to test and analyze possible health effects associated with the herbicide. Hayes later received additional funds and replicated the initial research.

28. EPA response to DQA challenge, Mar. 26, 2003, at 18, *available at* www. Epa.gov/QUALITY/informationguidelines/documents/2807Response_ 03_27_03.pdf.

29. *See, e.g.*, two challenges at HHS, *available at* http://aspe.hhs.gov/info quality/request&response/18a.shtml; http://aspe.hhs.gov/infoquality/ request&response/25a.shtml; and two challenges at EPA, *available at* http://epa.gov/quality/informationguidelines/documents/05001.pdf and

www.epa.gov/quality/informationguidelines/documents/2807.pdf. All are
industry-led challenges.

30. NAT'L RESEARCH COUNCIL OF THE NAT'L ACADEMIES, EVALUATING
PROGRESS OF THE U.S. CLIMATE CHANGE SCIENCE PROGRAM: METHODS
AND PRELIMINARY RESULTS (2007), *available at* www.nap.edu/catalog/
11934.html.

31. *See* www.libraryjournal.com/index.asp?layout=articlePrint&articleID-
CA6349087.

32. DAVID M. BEARDEN & ROBERT ESWORTHY, RESTRUCTURING EPA'S LI-
BRARIES: BACKGROUND AND ISSUES FOR CONGRESS (updated June 15,
2007).

33. Nielsen/Net Ratings reported that YouTube had 51 million users in June
2007, more than MySpace, AOL, and Yahoo combined. Miguel Helft,
Google Aims to Make YouTube Profitable With Ads, N.Y. TIMES, Aug. 21,
2007, at C1, C7.

34. *See* Natural Resources Defense Council report, *available at* www.nrdc.
org/legislation/rollbacks/rr2004.pdf.

35. MODERNIZING NEPA IMPLEMENTATION, THE NEPA TASK FORCE RE-
PORT TO THE COUNCIL ON ENVIRONMENTAL QUALITY (2003), *available at*
www.nepa.gov/ntf/report/finalreport.pdf.

36. Information on Bush Administration's "Healthy Forests" *available at*
www.whitehouse.gov/infocus/healthyforests/; www.fs.fed.us/news/2004/
releases/12/planning-rule.shtml; www.eenews.net/eenewspm/2007/03/30/
archive/1.

37. *See* www.eenews.net/features/documents/2007/03/30/document_pm_01.
pdf (subscription required).

38. *See* Step It Up website, http://april.stepitup2007.org.

39. *See* Mobile Active website, http://mobileactive.org; *Connecting to Earth*,
WORLD CONSERVATION 21 (May 2008), *available at* http://cmsdata.iucn.
org/downloads/00_w_c_2008_02_connect.pdf. More broadly, cell phones
are transforming environmental governance in remote corners of the world.
Indigenous people in the Pizarro Reserve in northwest Argentina have used
mobile phones to monitor environmental conditions and call for help when
state government threatened to auction their land. J. Oberman, SMS Mobi-
lizes to Demobilize Rainforest Destruction (2005), *available at* www.
personaldemocracy.com/node/756.

40. 549 U.S. 497 (2007).

41. Natural Res. Defense Council (NRDC) v. EPA I, 440 F.3d 476 (D.C. Cir.
2006); NRDC v. EPA II, 464 F.3d 1 (D.C. Cir. 2006); Util. Air Reg. Group
(UARG) v. EPA, 471 F.3d 1333 (D.C. Cir. 2006). *See also* Friends of the
Earth v. Mosbacher, No. C-02-04106-JSW, 2005 WL 2035596 (N.D. Cal.
Aug. 23, 2005).

42. *See, e.g.*, Citizens for Better Forestry v. U.S. Dep't of Agric., 341 F.3d 961
(9th Cir. 2003); Nulankeyutmonen Nkihtaqmikon v. Impson, 503 F.3d 18
(1st Cir. 2007); Ouachita Watch League v. Jacobs, 463 F.3d 1163 (11th Cir.
2006). *See also* Ctr. for Biological Diversity v. Brennan, 2007 WL 2408901
(N.D. Cal. 2007).

43. *E.g.*, Nuclear Info. & Resource Serv. v. Nuclear Reg. Comm'n, 457 F.3d 941 (9th Cir. 2006); Ctr. for Biological Diversity v. Lueckel, 417 F.3d 532 (6th Cir. 2006).

44. *See* ELI, Recent Cases: DC Circuit Cases Involving "Increased Risk of Harm" From Agency Action, *available at* www.endangeredlaws.org/case_DC.htm.

45. NRDC v. EPA, 489 F.3d 1364 (D.C. Cir. 2007); Public Citizen v. Nat'l Highway Traffic Safety Admin. (NHTSA), 489 F.3d 1279 (D.C. Cir. 2007).

46. *See* William W. Buzbee, *The Story of Laidlaw, Standing and Citizen Enforcement, in* ENVIRONMENTAL LAW STORIES (Richard Lazarus & Oliver Houck eds., 2005), *available at* http://papers.ssrn.com/abstract=721643.

47. *See, e.g.*, Chief Justice Roberts' dissent in *Massachusetts v. EPA, supra* note 40 (Roberts, C.J., dissenting).

48. David G. Savage, *Conservative Courts Likely to Be Bush Legacy*, L.A. TIMES, Jan. 2, 2008, *available at* www.latimes.com/news/nationworld/nation/la-na-judges2jan02,1,7304700.story.

49. JAY E. AUSTIN ET AL., JUDGING NEPA: A "HARD LOOK" AT JUDICIAL DECISION MAKING UNDER THE NATIONAL ENVIRONMENTAL POLICY ACT (2004), *available at* www.endangeredlaws.org/pdf/JudgingNEPA.pdf.

50. Savage, *supra* note 48.

51. Irwin & Bruch, *supra* note 1.

52. J. CLARENCE DAVIES, PROJECT ON EMERGING NANOTECH., EPA AND NANOTECHNOLOGY: OVERSIGHT FOR THE 21ST CENTURY (2007), at 17.

Chapter 31

National Governance: Still Stumbling Toward Sustainability

John C. Dernbach

Much of what is required for national governance for sustainable development is also required for good governance in general: effective governmental institutions and national laws, a favorable investment climate, public access to information, informed and science-based decisionmaking, public participation in governmental decisionmaking, and access to justice. National governance for sustainability, however, also requires at least three more elements, which are the topics of this chapter:

- a legally grounded national-level strategic process;
- sustainable development indicators to measure progress;
- public engagement and education on sustainability.

Since 2002, U.S. progress on all three fronts has been modest at best.

The United States has made some progress toward greater strategic efforts and interagency coordination concerning the environment since 2002, and has developed a more sophisticated system of environmental reporting. But the effort has been overshadowed by the federal government's preoccupation with antiterrorism and the war in Iraq, ideological and partisan divisions in our national political life, and the government's inability or unwillingness to address climate change—perhaps the most urgent and obvious of all sustainability issues. The national government was stumbling toward sustainability in 2002 (borrowing from the title of this book's predecessor volume), and it is still stumbling. To move ahead, the federal government must formally integrate sustainable development into its existing strategic efforts, develop a set of sustainable development indicators, and support and encourage efforts by the private sector and the public on behalf of sustainability.

National Strategic Process

At the World Summit on Sustainable Development in Johannesburg in 2002, the United States and other countries agreed that nations should take "immediate steps to make progress in the formulation and elaboration of national strategies for sustainable development and begin their implementation by 2005."[1] The United States has made some progress toward strategic thinking since 2002. But the federal government still has no overall national strategy for sustainable development, and is a long way from employing the strategic analysis and decisionmaking required for sustainable development. Nor is there an effective legal framework for ensuring agency adherence to sustainability principles.

A sustainability strategy is a "navigation tool for identifying priority sustainability issues, prioritizing objectives, and coordinating the development and use of a mix of policy initiatives to meet national goals."[2] It is directed at the achievement of specified goals or objectives; it is a process, not merely a document; it reflects the priorities and circumstances of the country that produces it; and it requires a governmental coordinating or implementing body to make sure it is properly carried out.[3]

Some progress toward strategic thinking has occurred under the Government Performance and Results Act of 1993 (GPRA), which obligates federal agencies to develop and implement multiyear strategic plans. These plans are to include a mission statement, goals and objectives for major agency activities, a description of how those goals and objectives will be achieved, and an evaluation method that measures achievement of those goals and objectives.[4] The GPRA also requires each agency, as part of its annual budget submission, to prepare and submit to the Office of Management and Budget a performance plan that is consistent with its strategic plan.[5] In addition, the act requires agencies to publish a report after each fiscal year comparing the agency's performance goals for that fiscal year with what was actually achieved, evaluating successes in achieving goals, and, where performance goals were not met, explaining why.[6]

According to a 2004 evaluation of GPRA by the Government Accountability Office (GAO), the act has "established a solid foundation of results-oriented performance planning, measurement, and reporting" for the federal government.[7] The GAO also concluded that GPRA has created a closer connection between agency objectives and the budget process, and provided a basis for reviewing agency objectives, activities, and results.[8] Environmental and sustainable development goals are contained in some but not all agency strategic plans.

The strategic goals of 15 federal agencies (the 14 cabinet departments and the U.S. Environmental Protection Agency), as reflected in their current GPRA strategic plans, are set out in Table 1. Six agencies (EPA plus the Departments of Agriculture, Commerce, Energy, Interior, and Transportation) identify environmental or natural resources protection, environmental stewardship, or environmental responsibility as a strategic goal, and one plan (the joint strategy of the Department of State and the U.S. Agency for International Development) expressly identifies the advancement of sustainable development as a strategic goal. These are ahead of the other nine agencies, but even they have a long way to go. Although many agencies have points of contact for sustainability, considerable variation exists in the extent to which environmental matters are integrated into economic and investment decisions.[9] For example, there continue to be significant and environmentally damaging subsidies for highways, fossil fuels, agriculture, and marine fishing.[10] On balance, interagency coordination concerning the environment is uneven at best.[11]

The Office of Federal Environmental Executive (OFEE), which was created to promote "sustainable environmental stewardship throughout the federal government,"[12] is improving agency coordination on some issues. Its primary responsibility is to implement an executive order, "Strengthening Federal Environmental, Energy, and Transportation Management," issued by President George W. Bush in January 2007.[13] The executive order requires, among other things, that federal agencies reduce their energy intensity (energy consumption per dollar expended) by 30 percent by fiscal year 2015, ensure that new buildings and major renovations of existing buildings conform to federal guidelines for high-performance green buildings, and acquire goods and services that are energy-efficient, water-efficient, and, in the case of office paper, contain 30 percent post-consumer recycled content. The order also requires agencies to use environmental management systems and to set up procedures for reporting and review on its implementation.[14] This coordination, however, is limited to these issues; it does not begin to approach the integrated analysis and decisionmaking across social, economic, environmental, and security spheres that are required for sustainable development.

Some interagency strategies have been prepared and adopted on specific issues that are relevant to sustainable development, although each has been done more or less independently of the others. These include:

- A 2001 national energy policy, prepared by a group of federal officials headed by Vice President Richard B. Cheney, which asserts that the energy crisis is caused by a "fundamental imbalance between supply and demand."[15]
- A 2003 climate change research strategy,[16] which focuses on research "conducted, sponsored, or applied" by 13 U.S. government agencies over the next 10 years, and which was peer-reviewed in both draft and final form by the National Research Council.[17]
- A national security strategy issued in 2002 in which President Bush identifies "a single sustainable model for national success: freedom, democracy, and free enterprise."[18] The strategy was revised and reissued in 2006.[19] The revised strategy, like the 2002 strategy, is primarily directed at national defense and the war against terrorism, but it places greater emphasis on fostering economic growth, democracy, and development in other countries.

Such strategies are important, but they do not appear to reflect the kind of integrated understanding or analysis that is necessary to sustain the country's well-being. The revised national security strategy, for instance, recites the government's position on climate change but does not contain or reflect any analysis of the likely effect of climate change on American security. By contrast, the Military Advisory Board, composed of 11 retired admirals and generals, concluded in April 2007 that "climate change poses a serious threat to America's national security" by exacerbating threats and tensions around the world.[20] Nor is climate change the only probable serious environmentally related threat to American well-being and security. A variety of other threats exist, including loss of biodiversity and the dramatic breakdowns in regional ecosystems due to multiple stresses, leading to resource scarcity and violent conflicts. There does not appear to be any current systematic inventory, ranking, or analysis of these threats.[21]

Sustainable Development Indicators

The federal government has moved toward adopting environmental indicators since 2002, but not sustainable development indicators. Indicators, which quantitatively measure various human activities and natural events, have "enhanced collaboration to address public issues, provided tools to encourage progress, helped inform decisionmaking and improve research, and increased public knowledge about key economic, environmental, and social and cultural issues."[22] Sustainable development indicators also shed light on the relationships among various trends, enable decisions to be based on integrated data, and provide a data platform for moving toward sustainability.[23]

In 2003, the EPA published for comment its Draft Report on the Environment, which it described as "its first-ever national picture of the U.S. environment."[24] (The 2003 report was not finalized.) EPA has now finalized its 2007 Report on the Environment. The report includes a public document that is intended to communicate information and trends in an understandable way,[25] a technical document that provides scientific and technical background, and an interactive website.[26] Like its 2003 predecessor, the 2007 report describes environmental and human health trends and identifies major knowledge gaps. It states, for example, that the amount of developed land in the United States increased at twice the rate of population growth between 1982 and 2002, but it is difficult to track more specific trends because of the differences among agencies in how land use data is collected.[27] Unlike the 2003 draft, the 2007 report addresses climate change, including U.S. greenhouse gas emissions, warming trends, and carbon storage in forests.[28]

An interactive, Web-based set of key social, economic, and environmental indicators is being developed by State of the USA (SUSA), a nonprofit organization advised by the National Academy of Sciences, which itself has published several major reports on environmental indicators.[29] SUSA's "mission" is "to deepen our knowledge and understanding of the country's most pressing issues" by providing Americans with "a new tool to help them assess where our nation is moving forward and where it has stalled."[30] SUSA will not set national goals or assess progress in meeting them; rather, it aspires to "provide shared, reliable and usable facts to fuel more focused public debate."[31]

Comparative assessments based on common indicators do not put the United States in a position of global leadership on sustainability. A 2008 assessment of environmental performance, published by the Yale Center for Environmental Law and Policy and the Center for International Earth Science Information Network at Columbia University, ranked the United States 39th of 149 countries.[32] Switzerland, Sweden, and Norway were the top ranking countries, and the United States was bracketed by Argentina (no. 38) and Taiwan (no. 40).[33] The index focuses on two objectives: "reducing environmental stresses to human health" and "promoting ecosystem vitality and sound natural resource management."[34] While the United States ranked very high on environmental health, it received a very low ranking on ecosystem vitality because of its climate change and air pollution policies.[35] And according to the Organisation for Economic Co-operation and Development (OECD), the "pollution, energy, water and material intensities" of the U.S. economy continue to be high compared to other developed countries.[36]

Public Engagement and Education

While there has been a serious effort to engage the public on behalf of the nation's antiterrorism effort, there has been no comparable effort to engage the public to address the variety of other sustainability threats we face. According to the Rio Declaration, nations are to "facilitate and encourage public awareness and participation" in sustainable development efforts "by making information widely available."[37] Public participation provides the basis for the development of a consensus on key issues, introduces new perspectives and information to the decision-making process, and provides the basis for public and stakeholder "ownership" of a strategy that will enable it to succeed.[38] Public education is important not only to build a greater sense of personal responsibility but also to achieve the kind of public understanding of, and debate about, sustainable development that is necessary in a democratic society.

The Bush Administration has downplayed the risks of problems other than terrorism, especially climate change (until recently). In 2001, for instance, President Bush asked the National Academy of Sciences for an assessment of climate change science. The request was consistent with the Academy's historic role; it was chartered by Congress in 1863 to advise the federal government on science and technology matters.[39] The report described current and projected warming trends, linked warming to increasing greenhouse gas emissions, and described serious risks to the United States, but included appropriate qualifications on issues where the science is less certain. Instead of reading the report for what it said, the federal government used the report ideologically. For instance, EPA used the report as authority for the proposition that scientific uncertainties were too great to justify regulation of greenhouse gases from motor vehicles.[40] In its 2007 decision in *Massachusetts v. EPA*, the Supreme Court remanded that ruling back to EPA, citing the 2001 report for the serious risks that it actually described.[41]

The national strategies created in recent years were developed with different degrees of public or peer review. The Bush Administration's energy policy was developed behind closed doors, while the climate change research strategy was publicly peer reviewed. The lack of public review for the energy policy has damaged its credibility and effectiveness. The President's Council on Sustainable Development, formed during the Clinton Administration, can be criticized for generating little public interest and little governmental follow-up on its recommendations.[42] But it did represent *some* effort to reach out to the public.

Another approach to public engagement and education occurs when government fosters or engages in collaborative relationships with market and community actors.[43] Such approaches are consistent with the view reflected in Agenda 21 that it is important to engage all relevant public and private stakeholders in the work of sustainable development. At the World Summit on Sustainable Development in 2002, the United States played a major role in encouraging the use of partnerships between government and private-sector actors to help meet sustainable development objectives.[44] A number of such partnerships have grown in importance in recent years, including Energy Star®, a government-industry partnership for energy efficiency involving more than 12,000 public and private entities, that is "designed to promote energy-efficient products to reduce greenhouse gas emissions."[45] Energy Star is a voluntary labeling program for more than 50 product categories; products that meet specified efficiency criteria are allowed to publicly display the Energy Star label. On the other hand, the Bush Administration has more or less abandoned the practice of working collaboratively with states on environmental matters, including (but not limited to) climate change.[46] Nor has the federal government engaged in any large-scale effort to collaboratively engage the business community or state or local governments on sustainable development in general.

Recommendations for the Next Decade

1. Congress should amend GPRA to require each agency's strategic plan, and the annual reports on its implementation, to be explicitly directed toward achieving sustainable development, and to di-

rect each agency to cooperate with others toward that end. Canada provides a useful model from which to learn. The Canadian Auditor General Act authorizes the auditor general not only to audit the books of government agencies and report what is found, but also to report when "satisfactory procedures have not been established to measure and report the effectiveness of programs, where such procedures could appropriately and reasonably be implemented."[47]

Under 1995 amendments to the act, each major department in the Canadian government is required to prepare a sustainable development strategy and update the strategy every three years. The Commissioner of the Environment and Sustainable Development, a newly created office that reports directly to the auditor general, is to monitor and report on departmental progress toward sustainable development.[48] To be sure, Canada is experiencing challenges implementing this act; in October 2007 the commissioner issued a report strongly criticizing the national government's implementation of the act.[49] Still, the legal obligation to work toward sustainable development, coupled with a public accountability mechanism like that provided by the commissioner (in the United States, perhaps the GAO), would raise the profile of sustainability in agencies' GPRA planning and budgeting.

More broadly, and perhaps in the longer term, the federal government should consider a single strategic plan that both synthesizes various agency plans and identifies key sustainability issues and challenges. The United States needs to conduct, on an ongoing basis, an analysis of actual or potential threats (including environmental threats) to its interests and prioritize them accordingly.[50] That analysis also needs to be integrated into agency strategies under GPRA as well as multiagency strategies. As the Military Advisory Board recommended, the "national security consequences of climate change should be fully integrated into national security and national defense strategies."[51] This single strategic plan would need to be developed in a way that considered the views of all stakeholders, including Congress and the public, and then implemented in a way that integrates those strategies into the actual decisions of the federal government.[52] In recommending changes to improve GPRA in 2004, GAO stated:

> If fully developed, a government wide strategic plan can potentially provide a cohesive perspective on the long-term goals of the federal government and provide a much needed basis for fully integrating, rather than merely coordinating, a wide array of federal activities. Successful strategic planning requires the involvement of key

stakeholders. Thus, it could serve as a mechanism for building consensus. Further, it could provide a vehicle for the President to articulate long-term goals and a road map for achieving them.[53]

This effort would need to be managed by an appropriate government entity. One option is an entity within the executive branch, under the control of the president, that would, among other things, consider the various reports agencies issue under GPRA. The OFEE's authority is too limited for that job, although the Council on Environmental Quality (CEQ) might be able to perform it. The CEQ is located in the executive office of the president; it has statutory responsibility "to develop and recommend to the President national policies to foster and promote the improvement of environmental quality to meet the conservation, social, economic, health, and other requirements and goals of the Nation."[54] Although the statute was adopted in 1969, the language is much in keeping with sustainable development. A second option is for Congress to create an independent commission, governed by a board appointed over staggered terms so that it would have some independence from any president. Such a commission would ostensibly be more objective in its assessments, and could be a useful counterweight to political partisanship on environmental matters.

2. The federal government should develop a set of sustainable development indicators that cover the environmental, social, economic, and security aspects of national life. While the SUSA project would be an important supplement to this work, federal national indicators could more readily be tied to national and agency strategic plans and goals. In 2004, GAO recommended consideration of a comprehensive set of national indicators:

> They would add a key dimension to how we inform ourselves. We now have many diverse and extensive bodies of information on issues of limited focus (e.g., health care). But we could use comprehensive key indicator systems on a broader array of critical issues to help generate a broader perspective, clarify problems and opportunities, identify gaps in what we know, set priorities, test effective solutions, and track progress towards achieving results.[55]

3. Congress should establish an Office of Sustainability Assessment to advise it on matters relating to sustainable development. Such an office would be staffed with professionals from a variety of disciplines, which would increase the capacity of Congress to under-

stand and address the great variety of sustainability challenges and opportunities that the country faces (including but not limited to environmental sustainability).

*4. To fully integrate environmental objectives with social, eco-
nomic, and security objectives, the United States needs to make
greater use of legal and policy tools that send appropriate economic
signals.* The federal government should, for example, make greater
use of environmentally related taxes in a variety of contexts. The
government should also reduce or eliminate environmentally damaging subsidies.[56]

*5. The national government should lead, support, and encourage,
in a variety of contexts, sustainable development efforts by individuals, nongovernmental organizations, and corporations, and reestablish and reinvigorate its collaborative relationship with state and
local governments.* Too much work is needed on too many fronts for
the federal government to do it alone. Growing public interest in and
awareness of sustainable development provide reason to believe that
substantial segments of the public and affected interests would respond positively.

*6. The United States needs to consider the possibility that signifi-
cant changes in governance are needed to put the country on a sustainable course.* The prior recommendations, and those contained in
the rest of this volume, may (or may not) be enough to put the United
States on a direct and rapid course toward sustainability. We are faced
with a variety of challenges to sustainability—climate change, the
budget deficit, health care, and Social Security—that often seem politically intractable. A major obstacle, though certainly not the only
one, is the challenge that two-, four-, and six-year election cycles pose
to solving problems that will take decades to solve.[57] In response, the
John Brademas Center for the Study of Congress at New York University, and other organizations, including the Brookings Institution and
the RAND Corporation, have initiated a project examining the ability
of Congress to address long-term problems such as climate change,
with the aim of developing strategies to make Congress more responsive.[58] Similarly, the president or Congress should consider establishing a National Commission for a Sustainable America to evaluate and
make recommendations on changes in national governance, including
both Congress and the executive branch, that may be needed to address these issues.

Conclusion

In *The March of Folly: From Troy to Vietnam*, Barbara Tuchman recounts the many times in history when governments pursued policies that were contrary to their own interests.[59] "Mental standstill or stagnation—the maintenance intact by rulers and policy-makers of the ideas they started with—is fertile ground for folly," she writes.[60] Sustainable development recasts the role of the environment in human affairs—from something that can be degraded in the pursuit of achieving security, economic, and social goals to something that must be protected and restored to achieve those goals. Sustainable development is profoundly in the national interest, and will better equip us to address the dangers and challenges of coming decades. And if these dangers and challenges are great, so are the opportunities.

Table 1: Federal Agency Strategic Goals in Current GPRA Plans

Department of State and U.S. Agency for International Development	1) Achieve peace and security; 2) Advance sustainable development and global interests; 3) Promote international understanding; 4) Strengthen diplomatic and program capabilities.[61]
Environmental Protection Agency	1) Clean air and global climate change; 2) Clean and safe water; 3) Land preservation and restoration; 4) Healthy communities and ecosystems; 5) Compliance and environmental stewardship.[62]
Department of the Interior	1) Resource protection; 2) Resource use; 3) Recreation; 4) Serving communities.[63]
Department of Commerce	1) Maximize U.S. competitiveness and enable economic growth for American industries, workers, and consumers; 2) Promote U.S. innovation and industrial competitiveness; 3) Promote environmental stewardship.[64]
Department of Transportation	1) Safety; 2) Mobility; 3) Global connectivity; 4) Environmental stewardship; 5) Security; 6) Organizational excellence.[65]
Department of Homeland Security	1) Awareness; 2) Prevention; 3) Protection; 4) Response; 5) Recovery; 6) Service; 7) Organizational excellence.[66]
Department of Education	1) Create a culture of achievement; 2) Improve student achievement; 3) Develop safe schools and strong character; 4) Transform education into an evidence-based field; 5) Enhance the quality of and access to postsecondary and adult education; 6) Establish management excellence.[67]
Department of Health and Human Services	1) Reduce the major threats to the health and well-being of Americans; 2) Enhance the ability of the nation's health care system to effectively respond to bioterrorism and other public health challenges; 3) Increase the percentage of the nation's children and adults who have access to health care services, and expand consumer choices; 4) Enhance the capacity and productivity of the nation's health science research enterprise; 5) Improve the quality of health care services; 6) Improve the economic and social well-being of individuals, families, and communities, especially those most in need; 7) Improve the stability and healthy development of our nation's children and youth; 8) Achieve excellence in management practices.[68]
Department of the Treasury	1) Promote prosperous U.S. and world economies; 2) Promote stable U.S. and world economies; 3) Preserve the integrity of financial systems; 4) Manage the U.S. government's finances effectively; 5) Ensure professionalism, excellence, integrity, and accountability in the management and conduct of the Department of the Treasury.[69]

Table 1 (cont.)

Department of Justice	1) Prevent terrorism and promote the nation's security; 2) Prevent crime, enforce federal laws, and represent the rights and interests of the people; 3) Ensure the fair and efficient administration of justice.[70]
Department of Agriculture	1) Enhance international competitiveness of American agriculture; 2) Enhance the competitiveness and sustainability of rural and farm economies; 3) Support increased economic opportunities and improved quality of life in rural America; 4) Enhance protection and safety of the nation's agriculture and food supply; 5) Improve the nation's nutrition and health; 6) Protect and enhance the nation's natural resource base and environment.[71]
Department of Defense	1) Fighting the long war; 2) Operationalizing the national defense strategy; 3) Reorienting capabilities and forces; 4) Reshaping the defense enterprise; 5) Developing a 21st century total force; 6) Achieving unity of effort.[72]
Department of Energy	1) Energy security; 2) Nuclear security; 3) Scientific discovery and innovation; 4) Environmental responsibility; 5) Management excellence.[73]
Department of Housing and Urban Development	1) Increase homeownership opportunities; 2) Promote decent affordable housing; 3) Strengthen communities; 4) Ensure equal opportunity in housing; 5) Embrace high standards of ethics, management, and accountability; 6) Promote participation of faith-based and community organizations.[74]
Department of Veterans Affairs	1) Restore capability of veterans with disabilities; 2) Ensure a smooth transition from active service; 3) Honor and serve veterans; 4) Contribute to the public health, emergency management, and socioeconomic well-being.[75]

ENDNOTES

1. World Summit on Sustainable Development, Plan of Implementation, U.N.Doc. A/CONF.199/20 & A/CONF.199/20/Corr.1, ¶ 162(b) (2002).

2. INT'L INST. FOR SUSTAINABLE DEV. ET AL., NATIONAL STRATEGIES FOR SUSTAINABLE DEVELOPMENT: CHALLENGES, APPROACHES, AND INNOVATIONS IN STRATEGIC AND CO-ORDINATED ACTION 41 (2004), *available at* http://www.iisd.org/pdf/2004/measure_nat_strategies_sd.pdf [hereinafter NATIONAL STRATEGIES FOR SUSTAINABLE DEVELOPMENT].

3. John C. Dernbach, *National Governance*, in STUMBLING TOWARD SUSTAINABILITY 723, 724-27 (John C. Dernbach ed., 2002).

4. 5 U.S.C. §306(a).

5. 5 U.S.C. §306(c).

6. 31 U.S.C. §1116.

7. U.S. GOV'T ACCOUNTABILITY OFFICE (GAO), RESULTS-ORIENTED GOVERNMENT: GPRA HAS ESTABLISHED A SOLID FOUNDATION FOR GREATER RESULTS 6-7 (2004).

8. *Id.* at 100.

9. ORGANISATION FOR ECON. CO-OPERATION & DEV. (OECD), ENVIRONMENTAL PERFORMANCE REVIEWS: UNITED STATES 25, 130 (2005).

10. *Id.* at 132-35.

11. *Id.* at 147.

12. Office of the Federal Environmental Executive, http://ofee.gov/sustain/sustainability.asp (last modified Oct. 23, 2007).

13. *Id.*

14. Exec. Order No. 13423, Strengthening Federal Environmental, Energy, and Transportation Management, 72 Fed. Reg. 3919 (Jan. 26, 2007).

15. NAT'L ENERGY POL'Y DEV. GROUP, NATIONAL ENERGY POLICY viii (2001), *available at* http://www.whitehouse.gov/energy/National-Energy-Policy.pdf. The United States has described this policy as a "long-term, comprehensive strategy that provides reliable and affordable energy, while accelerating the protection and improvement of the environment." *See also* United States of America, Country Profile 11 (2002), *available at* www.un.org/esa/agenda21/natlinfo/wssd/usa.pdf (prepared for World Summit on Sustainable Development).

16. CLIMATE CHANGE SCIENCE PROGRAM AND THE SUBCOMMITTEE ON GLOBAL CHANGE RESEARCH, STRATEGIC PLAN FOR THE U.S. CLIMATE CHANGE SCIENCE PROGRAM (2003), http://www.climatescience.gov/Library/stratplan2003/final/ccspstratplan2003-all.pdf.

17. *Id.* at 1; NAT'L RESEARCH COUNCIL, PLANNING CLIMATE AND GLOBAL CHANGE RESEARCH: A REVIEW OF THE DRAFT U.S. CLIMATE CHANGE PROGRAM STRATEGIC PLAN (2003); NAT'L RESEARCH COUNCIL, PLANNING CLIMATE AND GLOBAL CHANGE RESEARCH: A REVIEW OF THE FINAL U.S. CLIMATE CHANGE PROGRAM STRATEGIC PLAN (2004).

18. GEORGE W. BUSH, THE NATIONAL SECURITY STRATEGY OF THE UNITED STATES (2002), http://www.whitehouse.gov/nsc/nss.pdf (introductory message by President George W. Bush).

19. THE NATIONAL SECURITY STRATEGY OF THE UNITED STATES (2006), http://www.whitehouse.gov/nsc/nss/2006/nss2006.pdf.

20. MILITARY ADVISORY BD., NATIONAL SECURITY AND THE THREAT OF CLIMATE CHANGE 6-7 (2007), *available at* http://securityandclimate.cna. Org/report/National%20Security%20and%20the%20Threat%20of%20 Climate%20Change.pdf.

21. William C. Clark, *America's National Interests in Promoting a Transition Toward Sustainability, in* U.S. POLICY AND THE GLOBAL ENVIRONMENT: MEMOS TO THE PRESIDENT 183, 189-96 (2000).

22. U.S. GAO, INFORMING OUR NATION: IMPROVING HOW TO UNDERSTAND AND ASSESS THE USA'S POSITION AND PROGRESS 14 (2004), *available at* http://www.gao.gov/new.items/d051.pdf.

23. BOARD ON SUSTAINABLE DEV., NAT'L RESEARCH COUNCIL, OUR COMMON JOURNEY: A TRANSITION TOWARD SUSTAINABILITY 258-65 (1999).

24. U.S. EPA, DRAFT REPORT ON THE ENVIRONMENT 2003, at i (2003) [hereinafter DRAFT REPORT]; U.S. EPA, DRAFT REPORT ON THE ENVIRONMENT 2003, TECHNICAL DOCUMENT (2003) [hereinafter TECHNICAL DOCUMENT].

25. U.S. EPA, 2007 REPORT ON THE ENVIRONMENT: HIGHLIGHTS OF NATIONAL TRENDS (2007), *available at* http://www.epa.gov/indicators/docs/ roe-hd-draft-08-2007.pdf [hereinafter HIGHLIGHTS OF NATIONAL TRENDS].

26. U.S. EPA, REPORT ON THE ENVIRONMENT: SCIENCE REPORT (last visited Aug. 8, 2007).

27. *Id.* at 20.

28. *See, e.g.*, HIGHLIGHTS OF NATIONAL TRENDS, *supra* note 25, at 8, 31-32.

29. STATE OF THE USA, INC., THE STATE OF THE USA, http://www.state oftheusa.org/index.asp (last visited June 3, 2008). The National Academy of Sciences has produced several reports on indicators. *See, e.g.*, NAT'L RESEARCH COUNCIL, ECOLOGICAL INDICATORS FOR THE NATION (2000); NAT'L RESEARCH COUNCIL, NATURE'S NUMBERS: EXPANDING THE NATIONAL ECONOMIC ACCOUNTS TO INCLUDE THE ENVIRONMENT (William D. Nordhaus & Edward C. Kokkelenberg eds., 1999).

30. STATE OF THE USA, *supra* note 29.

31. *Id.* at 2, 4.

32. YALE CTR. FOR ENVTL L. & POL'Y, YALE U. & CTR. FOR INT'L EARTH SCI. INFO. NETWORK, COLUMBIA U., 2008 ENVIRONMENTAL PERFORMANCE INDEX 10 (2008), *available at* www.yale.edu/epi/files/2008EPI_Text.pdf.

33. *Id.*

34. *Id.* at 8.

35. *Id.* at 24 & 31.

36. OECD ENVIRONMENTAL PERFORMANCE REVIEWS: UNITED STATES, *supra* note 9, at 26.

37. U.N. Conference on Environment and Development, Rio Declaration on Environment and Development, Principle 10, U.N. Doc. A/CONF.151/5/Rev.1, 31 I.L.M. 874 (1992), *available at* http://www.unep.org/Documents. Multilingual/Default.asp?DocumentID=78&ArticleID=1163.

38. OECD, STRATEGIES FOR SUSTAINABLE DEVELOPMENT: PRACTICAL GUIDANCE FOR DEVELOPMENT CO-OPERATION 29-35 (2001).

39. NAT'L RESEARCH COUNCIL, CLIMATE CHANGE SCIENCE: AN ANALYSIS OF SOME KEY QUESTIONS PREFACE (2001).

40. *See, e.g.*, 68 Fed. Reg. 52922, 52931 (Sept. 8, 2003) (2001 National Research Council report shows scientific uncertainties too great to justify regulation of greenhouse gases from motor vehicles).

41. 549 U.S. 497 (2007).

42. The first and best known of these reports is PRESIDENT'S COUNCIL ON SUSTAINABLE DEV., SUSTAINABLE AMERICA: A NEW CONSENSUS FOR PROSPERITY, OPPORTUNITY, AND A HEALTHY ENVIRONMENT FOR THE FUTURE (1996), *available at* http://clinton2.nara.gov/PCSD/Publications/TF_ Reports/amer-top.html. For criticisms of the President's Council on Sustainable Development, see OECD ENVIRONMENTAL PERFORMANCE REVIEWS: UNITED STATES, *supra* note 9, at 241; Dernbach, *supra* note 3, at 730-39.

43. Maria Carmen Lemos & Arun Agrawal, *Environmental Governance*, 31 ANN. REV. ENV'T & RES. 297, 309-12 (2006).

44. *See* Iana B. Andova & Marc A. Levy, *Franchising Global Governance: Making Sense of the Johannesburg Type II Partnerships*, *in* YEARBOOK OF INTERNATIONAL CO-OPERATION ON ENVIRONMENT AND DEVELOPMENT 19 (Olav Schram Stokke & Øystein B. Thommessen eds., 2003/2004).

45. U.S. EPA, ENERGY STAR, HISTORY OF ENERGY STAR, *available at* http://www.energystar.gov/index.cfm?c=about.ab_history (last visited June 3, 2008).

46. Barry Rabe, *Environmental Policy and the Bush Era: The Collision Between the Administrative Presidency and State Experimentation*, 37 PUBLIUS 413 (2007).

47. Auditor General Act, R.S.C., ch. A-17 (1985) (Can.).

48. Amendments to the Auditor General Act, 1995 S.C., ch. 43 (Can.).

49. Report of the Commissioner of the Environment and Sustainable Development—October 2007, Ch. 1—Sustainable Development Strategies (2007), *available at* http://www.oag-bvg.gc.ca/domino/reports.nsf/html/ c20071001c_e.html/$file/c20071001c_e.pdf.

50. Clark, *supra* note 21, at 196.

51. MILITARY ADVISORY BD., *supra* note 20, at 7.

52. Alfred Ho, *GPRA After a Decade: Lessons From the Government Performance and Results Act and Related Federal Reforms*, 30 PUB. PERFORMANCE & MGMT. REV. 307, 310 (2007).

53. U.S. GAO, RESULTS-ORIENTED GOVERNMENT, *supra* note 7, at 104-05.

54. 42 U.S.C. §4342.

55. U.S. GAO, INFORMING OUR NATION, *supra* note 22, at 2 (letter from David M. Walker, Comptroller General of the United States, to Senator Sam Brownback).

56. OECD ENVIRONMENTAL PERFORMANCE REVIEWS: UNITED STATES, *supra* note 9, at 26.

57. "It's hard to convince an elected official to alienate existing constituencies in order to make the world better in 15 years." John M. Broder, *Sweeping Energy Bill Will Get Its Day in House*, N.Y. TIMES, Aug. 3, 2007, at A17 (quoting Jason S. Grumet, executive director of the National Commission on Energy Policy).

58. *See, e.g.*, Barry Rabe, Can Congress Govern the Climate? (2007), *available at* www.brookings.edu/~/media/Files/rc/papers/2007/0423climate change_rabe.pdf.

59. BARBARA W. TUCHMAN, THE MARCH OF FOLLY: FROM TROY TO VIETNAM (1984).

60. *Id.* at 383.

61. U.S. DEP'T OF STATE & U.S. AGENCY FOR INT'L DEV., STRATEGIC PLAN FISCAL YEARS 2004-2009: ALIGNING DIPLOMACY AND DEVELOPMENT ASSISTANCE 18-29 (2003), *available at* www.state.gov/documents/organization/24299.pdf.

62. U.S. EPA, 2003-2008 STRATEGIC PLAN: DIRECTION FOR THE FUTURE (2003), *available at* www.epa.gov/ocfo/plan/2003sp.pdf.

63. U.S. DEP'T OF THE INTERIOR, GPRA STRATEGIC PLAN 2007-2012 at 12 (2006), *available at* http://www.doi.gov/ppp/Strategic%20Plan%20FY07-12/strat_plan_fy2007_2012.pdfc%20Plan%20FY07-12/strat_plan_fy2007_2012.pdf.

64. U.S. DEP'T OF COMMERCE, STRATEGIC PLAN: FY 2007-FY 2012 (2006), *available at* www.osec.doc.gov/bmi/budget/07strplan/DOC07strplan.pdf.

65. U.S. DEP'T OF TRANSP., STRATEGIC PLAN 2003-2008 (2003), *available at* www.dot.gov/stratplan2008/strategic_plan.htm.

66. U.S. DEP'T OF HOMELAND SEC., SECURING OUR HOMELAND: U.S. DEPARTMENT OF HOMELAND SECURITY STRATEGIC PLAN (2004), *available at* www.dhs.gov/xlibrary/assets/DHS_StratPlan_FINAL_spread.pdf.

67. U.S. DEP'T OF EDUC., STRATEGIC PLAN 2002-2007 (2002), *available at* www.ed.gov/about/reports/strat/plan2002-07/plan.pdf.

68. U.S. DEP'T OF HEALTH & HUMAN SERVS., STRATEGIC PLAN FY 2004-2009 (2004), *available at* http://aspe.hhs.gov/HHSPlan/2004/hhsplan2004.pdf.

69. U.S. DEP'T OF THE TREASURY, TREASURY STRATEGIC PLAN FOR FISCAL YEARS 2003-2008 (2003), *available at* www.treas.gov/offices/management/budget/planningdocs/treasury-strategic-plan.pdf.

70. U.S. DEP'T OF JUSTICE, STEWARDS OF THE AMERICAN DREAM: THE DEPARTMENT OF JUSTICE STRATEGIC PLAN FY 2007-2012 (2006), *available at* www.usdoj.gov/jmd/mps/strategic2007-2012/strategic_plan20072012.pdf.

71. U.S. DEP'T OF AGRIC., STRATEGIC PLAN FOR FY 2005-2010 (2006), *available at* www.ocfo.usda.gov/usdasp/sp2005/sp2005.pdf.

72. U.S. DEP'T OF DEFENSE, QUADRENNIAL DEFENSE REVIEW REPORT
    (2006), *available at* www.defenselink.mil/qdr/report/Report20060203.
    pdf. *See* OFFICE OF INSPECTOR GEN., U.S. DEP'T OF DEFENSE, DOD
    COMPLIANCE WITH THE GOVERNMENT PERFORMANCE AND RESULTS
    ACT OF 1993, at 6-7 (2005), *available at* www.dodig.mil/Audit/reports/
    FY06/06-038.pdf (stating that quadrennial defense review could be used to
    satisfy GPRA if prepared in accordance with GPRA requirements).

73. U.S. DEP'T OF ENERGY, DEPARTMENT OF ENERGY STRATEGIC PLAN
    (2006), *available at* www.energy.gov/media/2006_DOE_Strategic_Plan.
    pdf.

74. U.S. DEP'T OF HOUSING & URBAN DEV., HUD STRATEGIC PLAN FY
    2006-FY 2011 (2006), *available at* www.hud.gov/offices/cfo/reports/hud_
    strat_plan_2006-2011.pdf.

75. DEP'T OF VETERANS AFFAIRS, STRATEGIC PLAN FY 2006-2011 (2006),
    available at www1.va.gov/op3/docs/VA_2006_2011_Strategic_Plan.pdf.

Index

A

abortion, 19, 171, 175-176, 178, 180, 184-185

access to justice, 8, 470-471, 479

acid rain, 150, 241, 243-44

Agenda 21, 4, 7-9, 11, 13, 43, 45, 54, 60, 76, 82, 130, 179, 221-222, 233, 239-240, 247, 251, 315, 322-323, 332, 335, 345, 349-350, 359, 400, 409, 413, 423, 485

air pollutants, 240-241, 247, 464

air pollution, 20, 29, 35, 49, 81, 96, 149, 239-241, 243-244, 247, 366, 455, 484

air quality, 59, 145-146, 149, 239, 241-242, 247

alternative fuel vehicles, 373

American Planning Association, 350, 355

aquatic ecosystems, 19, 205-206, 211, 213, 215-216, 270

areawide brownfields initiatives, 30, 62

Auditor General Act, Canada, 494

automobiles, 19, 28, 51, 154, 156, 187, 260, 449

B

Basel Convention on the Control of Transboundary Movement of Hazardous Waste, 322

Berry, Thomas, 12, 14

best management practices, 211

bioaccumulation, 331

biodiversity, 15-16, 20-21, 35, 37-38, 94, 130, 134, 171-172, 181, 213, 221, 231, 253, 269-280, 282, 284, 290, 392, 394-395, 406, 482

biodiversity assessment, 270

biodiversity conservation, 21, 37-38, 269-273, 275-280, 282

Bipartisan Agreement on Trade Policy, 388, 390, 397

brownfields, 57-62, 65, 67-69, 454

Brownfields Development Area, 62, 68

Brundtland Commission, 7, 130, 145, 270, 286, 413, 441, 444, 453

Bush Administration, 20-21, 23, 25, 71, 178, 180-181, 200, 227-228, 234-235, 252, 254, 256-258, 260, 263, 269, 272-273, 275, 282, 302, 388, 390, 419, 422, 424, 459, 462, 467-469, 472-473, 477, 484-485